The Ethics of Obscene Speech in
Early Christianity and Its Environment

Supplements
to
Novum Testamentum

VOLUME 128

The Ethics of Obscene Speech in Early Christianity and Its Environment

by

Jeremy F. Hultin

BRILL

LEIDEN • BOSTON
2008

This book is printed on acid-free paper.

Library of Congress Cataloging-in-Publication Data

Hultin, Jeremy F.
    The ethics of obscene speech in early Christianity and its environment
by / Jeremy F. Hultin.
        p. cm. — (Supplements to Novum Testamentum, ISSN 0167-9732 ; v. 128)
    Includes bibliographical references.
    ISBN 978-90-04-16803-9 (hardback : alk. paper) 1. Clean speech. 2. Oral
communication—Religious aspects—Christianity. I. Title. II. Series.
    BV4597.53.C64H85 2008
    241'.69509015—dc22

                                                                        2008009751

ISSN 0167-9732
ISBN 978 90 04 16803 9

Copyright 2008 by Koninklijke Brill NV, Leiden, The Netherlands.
Koninklijke Brill NV incorporates the imprints Brill, Hotei Publishing,
IDC Publishers, Martinus Nijhoff Publishers and VSP.

PRINTED IN THE NETHERLANDS

For my parents

CONTENTS

ACKNOWLEDGMENTS

This book began as my doctoral dissertation in the Religious Studies Department at Yale University. It is a pleasure to thank some of the people who have contributed to it at its various stages. I owe special gratitude to my dissertation advisors, Dale B. Martin and Harold W. Attridge, and to Adela Yarbro Collins, Wayne A. Meeks, and Diana Swancutt, who served on the dissertation committee. The members of Yale's New Testament/Ancient Christianity Dissertation Colloquium discussed my research on several occasions, and I thank Bentley Layton and David Bartlett, in particular, for their advice and support.

This project could never have been completed were it not for the friendship (and philological advice!) of many colleagues at Yale, including Ward Blanton, Kevin Wilkinson, Emma Wasserman, John Vonder Bruegge, Marcus Elder, Shane Berg, and George Parsenios. Matt Everard provided the book's initial impetus and offered much help along the way. I have also had the support of outstanding research assistants: Nicholas Lauer, Robert Leacock, Jessica Misener, Michael Stoops, and Jonathan Meyer. Amber R. Kohl helped edit an earlier version of chapter 1. My mother, Jill F. Hultin, read the entire manuscript and offered many helpful suggestions.

I am grateful to Margaret M. Mitchell and David P. Moessner for accepting this book for publication in the *Novum Testamentum Supplement Series*, and for their guidance, encouragement, and patience as the manuscript was prepared. I also thank Ivo Romein and Anita Roodnat of Brill.

Above all, I would like to thank my family. My brother has kept my spirits high with his capacity to exploit the humorous potential of αἰσχρολογία. And I can think of nobody who has offered more support in more ways than my parents, to whom this book is gratefully dedicated.

LIST OF FIGURES

LIST OF ABBREVIATIONS

AB	Anchor Bible
ABD	*Anchor Bible Dictionary*. Edited by D. N. Freedman. 6 vols. New York, 1992
ANF	*Ante-Nicene Fathers*
ANRW	*Aufstieg und Niedergang der römischen Welt: Geschichte und Kultur Roms im Spiegel der neueren Forschung.* Edited by H. Temporini and W. Haase. Berlin, 1972–
ANTC	Abingdon New Testament Commentaries
BDB	Brown, F., S. R. Driver, and C. A. Briggs. *A Hebrew and English Lexicon of the Old Testament.* Oxford, 1907.
BDAG	Danker, F. W., W. Bauer, W. F. Arndt, and F. W. Gingrich. *Greek-English Lexicon of the New Testament and Other Early Christian Literature.* 3d ed. Chicago, 2000.
BETL	Bibliotheca ephemeridum theologicarum lovaniensium
BJS	Brown Judaic Studies
BSac	*Bibliotheca Sacra*
BNTC	Black's New Testament Commentary
BS	The Biblical Seminar
BSOAS	*Bulletin of the School of Oriental and African Studies*
BZ	*Biblische Zeitschrift*
BZNW	Beihefte zur Zeitschrift für die neutestamentliche Wissenschaft
CIL	*Corpus Inscriptionum Latinarum*
CNT	Commentaire du Nouveau Testament
ConBNT	Coniectanea Biblica: New Testament Series
CSCO	Corpus scriptorum christianorum orientalium. Edited by I. B. Chabot et al. Paris, 1903–
CSS	Cursus scripturae sacrae
CRINT	Compendia Rerum Iudaicarum ad Novum Testamentum
DNP	*Der neue Pauly: Enzyklopädie der Antike.* Edited by H. Cancik and H. Schneider. Stuttgart, 1996–2003.
Ebib	Études bibliques
EDNT	*Exegetical Dictionary of the New Testament.* Edited by H. Balz, G. Schneider. ET. Grand Rapids, 1990–1993

HALOT	Koehler, L., W. Baumgartner, and J. J. Stamm, *The Hebrew and Aramaic Lexicon of the Old Testament*. Translated and edited under the supervision of M. E. J. Richardson. 4 vols. Leiden, 1994–1999.
HAR	*Hebrew Annual Review*
HB	Herders Bibelkommentar. Die Heilige Schrift für das Leben erklärt
HNT	Handbuch zum Neuen Testament
HTKNT	Herders theologischer Kommentar zum Neuen Testament
HTR	*Harvard Theological Review*
ICC	International Critical Commentary
JAAR	*Journal of the American Academy of Religion*
JBL	*Journal of Biblical Literature*
JSNT	*Journal for the Study of the New Testament*
JSNTSup	Journal for the Study of the New Testament: Supplement Series
JRS	*Journal of Roman Studies*
KEK	Kritisch-exegetischer Kommentar über das Neue Testament (Meyer-Kommentar)
KLPauly	Der kleine Pauly
KNT	Kommentar zum Neuen Testament
LASBF	*Liber annuus Studii biblici franciscani*
LCL	Loeb Classical Library
LCM	*Liverpool Classical Monthly*
LSJ	Liddell, H. G., R. Scott, H. S. Jones, *A Greek-English Lexicon*.
MM	Moulton, J. H., and G. Milligan. *The Vocabulary of the Greek Testament*. London, 1930. Reprint, Peabody, Mass., 1997
NIGTC	New International Greek Testament Commentary
NovT	*Novum Testamentum*
NovTSup	Supplements to Novum Testamentum
NTS	*New Testament Studies*
OBC	Orientalia Biblica et Christiana
OBS	Oxford Bible Series
OCD	*Oxford Classical Dictionary*. Edited by S. Hornblower and A. Spawforth. 3d ed. Oxford, 1996
OLD	*Oxford Latin Dictionary*. Edited by P. G. W. Glare. Oxford, 1982
OTP	*Old Testament Pseudepigrapha*. Edited by J. H. Charlesworth. 2 vols. New York, 1983, 1985
PG	Patrologia graeca. Edited by J.-P. Migne. 162 vols. Paris, 1857–1886

PL	Patrologia latina. Edited by J.-P. Migne. 217 vols. Paris, 1844–1864
PGL	*Patristic Greek Lexicon.* Edited by G. W. H. Lampe. Oxford, 1968
PGM	*Papyri graecae magicae: Die griechischen zauberpapyri.* Edited by K. Preisendanz. Berlin, 1928
PFES	Publications of the Finnish Exegetical Society
RAC	*Reallexikon für Antike und Christentum.* Edited by T. Kluser et al. Stuttgart, 1950–
SBLMS	Society of Biblical Literature Monograph Series
SBLSCS	Society of Biblical Literature Septuagint and Cognate Studies Series
SGRR	Studies in Greek and Roman Religion
Str-B	Strack, H. L., and P. Billerbeck. *Kommentar zum Neuen Testament aus Talmud und Midrasch.* 6 vols. Munich, 1922–1961
SVF	*Stoicorum veterum fragmenta.* H. von Arnim. 4 vols. Leipzig, 1903–1924
SVTP	Studia in veteris testamenti pseudepigrapha
TAPA	*Transactions of the American Philological Association*
TDNT	*Theological Dictionary of the New Testament.* Edited by G. Kittel and G. Friedrich. Translated by G. W. Bromiley. 10 vols. Grand Rapids, 1964–1976
TLNT	*Theological Lexicon of the New Testament.* C. Spicq. Translated and edited by J. D. Ernest. 3 vols. Peabody, Mass., 1994
TWNT	*Theologische Wörterbuch zum neuen Testament.* Edited by G. Kittel and G. Friedrich. Stuttgart, 1932–1979
WBC	Word Biblical Commentary
WGRW	Writings from the Greco-Roman World
WUNT	Wissenschaftliche Untersuchungen zum Neuen Testament
WZWPUR	*Wissenschaftliche Zeitschrift der Wilhelm-Pieck-Universität Rostock*
ZNW	*Zeitschrift für die Neutestamentliche Wissenschaft und die Kunde der älteren Kirche*
ZPE	*Zeitschrift für Papyrologie und Epigraphik*

Translations of ancient authors are typically from the Loeb Classical Library (as indicated throughout); where no translator is named, the translation is my own. Unless otherwise noted, translations of biblical texts are taken from the New Revised Standard Version. Translations from the Mishnah are from H. Danby, *The Mishnah* (Oxford, 1933). Abbreviations of ancient texts follow the standards of *The SBL Handbook of Style.*

PREFACE

Given the great quantity of scholarly literature on most aspects of early Christian morality, it is surprising how little has been written about the early Christian opposition to foul language. This study aims to contextualize early Christian rhetoric about foul language by asking such questions as: Where was foul language encountered? Were there conventional arguments for avoiding (or for using) obscene words? How would the avoidance of such speech have been interpreted by others? I hope to show that looking at the ancient uses of and discourse about foul language can shed light on how various Christians conceived their identity and mission in their own time and culture.

My own interest in these questions began in seminary when a friend asked why I insisted on so regularly "dropping the F-bomb." Unlike most of my fellow seminarians, my introduction to the faith had taken place in a church that, although very conservative in its theology, saw nothing wrong in such "adiaphora" as smoking, drinking, and swearing. In some ways, such activities were not merely tolerated, but were almost a source of pride—an aspect of our group's sense of itself as more discriminating than other evangelical churches when choosing which aspects of the Christian life to emphasize. But as my friend at seminary pointed out, unlike smoking and drinking, the Bible *did* seem to prohibit foul language. I actually asked a pastor in my church what he made of Eph 5:4 and Col 3:8, and he said something about "Paul's cultural situation" being different from ours.[1]

The ancient cultural situation is in fact the starting point for this study, and the first chapter describes various ways obscene language was used and perceived in the ancient world (Chapter 1). After describing some of the challenges of defining foul language, I begin with two of the earliest objections to obscene language, those of Plato and Aristotle. In describing how they would legislate against foul language in an ideal state, Plato and Aristotle indicate the various realms in which such language was actually encountered: religious rites, jocular conversations,

---

[1] Actually, first he said (with a wry smile), "Come on, man, don't be a fucking fundamentalist."

verbal abuse, dramatic performances, iambic poetry. Taking a cue from their treatment, I survey how obscene speech functioned in each of these spheres. Seventh-century iambic poetry and fifth-century Athenian drama are admittedly far removed from early Christianity. But authors contemporary with the first Christians often express their views about foul language in terms of these literary and dramatic genres (many of which were still alive), so to understand first- and second-century Christian speech ethics, it is helpful to have some broader taxonomy of obscenity in the classical world. Assembling evidence for when foul language was and was not used makes it possible to articulate some of the (constantly contested and shifting) rules of linguistic decorum.

In Chapter 2 I consider how a particular stance toward foul language might align with—and contribute to—a sense of cultural identity. In particular, I look at the Cynics and the Stoics, many of whom challenged the norms against foul language. For the Cynics, brash language was part of their assault on polite—and in their view *unnatural*—human conventions. It was of a piece with other acts of shamelessness, meant to alert the world to the fact that "nature" had been buried by conventional opinion. The Stoics shared the Cynics' desire to get beyond culture and back to nature. But for the Stoics, with their earnest investigations into the nature of language, the "life according to nature" took a linguistic turn. Stoics eschewed euphemisms in favor of calling things by their "real names," and denied that there was anything obscene in obscene words; "the wise man," said Zeno, "will speak bluntly."

The relationship between speech ethics and philosophical identity is seen in greater relief when one observes how the Stoics' attitude toward foul language changed over time. The second-century Stoic Panaetius of Rhodes abandoned the older Stoic arguments and taught that nature itself demanded modesty in the choice of words. Panaetius seems to mark a shift in Stoic thinking about linguistic decorum. In the next century Philodemus reports that contemporary Stoics were embarrassed by some of what Zeno had written; and we know from another source that at about this time the Stoic Athenodorus, head of the library at Pergamum, was caught deleting offensive lines from Zeno's *Republic*. This trend is continued in the popular Stoic philosophers such as Musonius Rufus, who enshrined modesty as a chief goal of philosophy, and his disciple Epictetus, who warned explicitly against using or tolerating foul language.

Chapter 3 lays the groundwork for the prohibitions of foul language in Colossians and Ephesians by studying the speech ethics in various

permutations of Second Temple Judaism, including earliest Christianity.
Naturally, biblical passages about speech were influential for Jews and
Christians. Biblical laws about blasphemy, oaths, and false testimony
were applied strenuously by some Jewish groups; similarly, the wisdom tradition's advocacy of silence and warnings against gossip were
frequently reiterated. Yet there was also a seamier side to the biblical
heritage, as the Israelite prophets (and also the historical writers, if we
are to judge by what later scribes felt the need to emend) occasionally
used vulgar language. But these bawdy aspects of the Bible do not seem
to have inspired much imitation. In the Second Temple period there
was no school of Jewish prophets analogous to the Cynics, rebuking
sinners with Ezekiel's coarse imagery. To the contrary, later Jews and
Christians were sometimes uneasy with the language they found in
their own sacred texts.

Jewish wisdom traditions had much to say about prudent speech, but
only two passages directly address obscene language: Sirach 23:12–15
and the *Didache* 3.3; 5.1. Sirach rejects lewd speech as shamefully
"uneducated," and warns that making an indecent comment in the
wrong company would be a social catastrophe. The *Didache* warns
simply that foul langauge leads to adultery.

Finally, before turning to the deutero-Pauline Ephesians and Colossians, I consider briefly instances from Paul's genuine epistles that have
raised questions about the register of his own language, namely, his use
of σκύβαλα (Phil 3:8) and his mordant reference to castration (Gal
5:12). The word σκύβαλα was not the equivalent of the English *shit*;
it was actually as decent a term as one could have used for refuse or
excrement. Paul's wish that his opponents would castrate themselves
would have struck some contemporary moralists as malicious and inappropriate; but it was not lexically indecent.

Chapter 4 analyzes Col 3:8 and Eph 5:3–12. I demonstrate that
Colossians's concern is with saying indecent things about others when
angry. This is a rather different concern from that of the *Didache* or
Sirach. Philosophers and moralists from Plato to Philo to Plutarch worried that in the heat of a dispute people would utter some disgusting
term of reproach and, in so doing, would degrade their own dignity
and inflame hostilities.

Although Ephesians's statements about foul language are, on the
surface, quite similar to those of Colossians, I argue that they suggest
a rather different constellation of concerns. In the first place, Ephesians
is more extreme. It forbids "even naming" the sins committed by the

"sons of disobedience," and prohibits not only "ugly, foolish talk" but even "wittiness" (εὐτραπελία), the word Aristotle used to designate the happy mean between crass and cringing.

In addition to excluding the "wittiness" that most people found pleasant, Ephesians is also striking in how it grounds its prohibitions. It says such speech is "not fitting for holy people." Whereas others had declared foul speech not fitting "for free men" (Aristotle) or "for serious people" (Pliny and Cicero) or "for wise men" (Epictetus and Apuleius) or "for a well-ruled community" (Plato), for Ephesians it was the *holiness* of the congregation that made lewd talk inappropriate. I argue that this was because of the author's sense that the community of believers lived in God's presence, and hence their whole existence was a sanctum where nothing frivolous, let alone disgusting, was appropriate. For Ephesians, the community is "God's household" and "temple"; the believers, who are "seated with Christ in heavenly places" (2:6), are described with cultic terms for holiness (1:4; 5:27). Just as certain texts from Qumran could invoke the biblical rules about God's dwelling places—rules that excluded anything disgusting or unbecoming (e.g. Num 5:1–4; Deut 23:10–15)—I suggest that Ephesians wants to exclude all that is unseemly from the divine presence. One of the Qumran texts (1QS) even contrasts uttering something "foolish" and "disgusting" with expressing "thanksgiving," a contrast remarkably similar to Eph 5:4 ("no obscenity or foolish talk or wittiness, but rather thanksgiving"). Thus I contend that Ephesians is not primarily concerned with the sinful behavior that might follow from obscene speech (contrast the *Didache*) or how it might reflect on Christians; rather, it is concerned above all that Christians speak properly in God's holy presence.

Finally, Ephesians's stern opposition to all humorous talk can be contrasted with Colossians's stance on witty language. I argue that Col 4:6 (literally: "Let your speech be with grace, seasoned with salt") is advocating witty, pungent speech. "Grace" (*charis*) here is not a theological term, but rather means "charm" or "winsomeness"; and "salt" refers to pungent "wit." In both Jewish and secular sources *charis* is used in tandem with another Greek word for delightfully witty speech: *eutrapelia*!

Thus it becomes apparent that Col 3:8 and Eph 5:4 are not simply "parallel" prohibitions of obscene language. Colossians opposes the abusive use of base language, a topic that concerned many Greeks and Roman moralists. Satirists like Lucian give us some idea of how absurd (and funny) it appeared when "high-minded" religious or philo-

sophical people were reduced to flinging filthy accusations. But unlike
Ephesians, Colossians does not concern itself with witty badinage *per se*.
And there is nothing in Ephesians—with its dark view of the outside
world—that corresponds to Colossians's suggestion that believers can
make the most of their contact with outsiders when their speech is
"graciously winsome and seasoned with the salt of wit" (as Col 4:6 has
been paraphrased by Murray J. Harris).

In Chapter 5 I discuss Clement of Alexandria's comments on foul
language. Although Clement also urged Christians to avoid obscene
speech, he states that, since God was the creator both of body parts and
of the words that name them, there was no cause for shame in either.
Here Clement sounds remarkably like the older Stoics who claimed
that whatever was natural was good. But despite the bold claim that
words did not embarrass God, Clement worried a lot about how words
would affect other people. For Clement, an obscene word was a bit like
a patch of uncovered flesh: neither offended the deity, but both had
the power to stir up lust. Furthermore, obscenity appeared vulgar and
uncultured. Clement wanted words—along with all aspects of dress and
deportment—to project an image of dignity and sexual self-mastery.
Thus Clement, even as he imagines himself to be following the "rule"
of Ephesians, has rather different concerns about obscenity, and, in
fact, hoped that Christians' speech would help them find a home in
genteel society.

CHAPTER ONE

A SURVEY OF FOUL LANGUAGE IN
THE ANCIENT WORLD

"Our knowledge of the full variety of swearing in past cultures must necessarily be incomplete." Geoffrey Hughes, *Swearing: A Social History of Foul Language, Oaths and Profanity in English*

WHAT IS FOUL LANGUAGE?

For anyone who has ever been embarrassed by letting an obscene word slip at the wrong time, it might come as a surprise to learn that in some languages such a mistake is impossible. Some languages simply have no obscene vocabulary.[1] The native American Hopi language, for instance, has "no 'proper' versus 'obscene' words. All words are on the same mundane, matter-of-fact level."[2] When Hopi Chief Don Talayesva was introduced into the YMCA, he experienced a new linguistic possibility: "I learned to preach pretty well, and to cuss too. The Hopi language has no curse words in it. At first so much of it made me tired; but when I got into the habit myself it was alright."[3]

But in this aspect, the Greeks and the Romans were like speakers of the majority of the world's languages, having at their disposal a range of more and less polite terms for sexual and scatological topics.[4]

---

[1] David Crystal states that "several peoples, such as the Amerindians, Polynesians, and Japanese, swear very little, or not at all" (*The Cambridge Encyclopedia of Language* [2d ed.; Cambridge: Cambridge University Press, 1997], 61). Other languages without an obscene vocabulary could be added. There is, for instance, only one term for vulva, urinating, and defecating in the African languages Yoruba and Akan (Charles Muscatine, "The Fabliaux, Courtly Culture, and the (Re)Invention of Vulgarity," in *Obscenity: Social Control and Artistic Creation in the European Middle Ages* [ed. Jan M. Ziolkowski; Leiden: Brill, 1998], 283, citing anthropologist D. Michael Warren).

[2] Weston LaBarre, "Obscenity: An Anthropological Appraisal," *Law and Contemporary Problems* 20 (1955): 538.

[3] Cited by Ashley Montagu, *The Anatomy of Swearing* (New York: Macmillan, 1967), 80–81.

[4] For detailed studies of the obscene vocabularies of Greek and Latin, cf. J. N. Adams, *The Latin Sexual Vocabulary* (Baltimore: Johns Hopkins University Press, 1982) (Adams notes that Latin did not have polite *technical* terms for the sexual organs [p. 227],

Roman rhetoricians were in fact so concerned about certain terms that they advised not only against using them, but even against combining words that, when pronounced quickly, might resemble them. So *cum nobis* was to be avoided because it could sound like *cunnus*.[5] Such an anxiety strikes us as more extreme than our own only until we imagine the embarrassment of the philosopher who, discussing the property of some item "X" as its "X-ness," proceeds to discuss the properties of "A" or "P" in like manner.[6]

Among Greeks and Romans we can perceive a range of prohibitive forces against certain words that is not totally unlike our own. Cicero says that there were words "nobody would have tolerated"; words "they dare not utter"; words in which there was something "shocking" or "outrageous" (*flagitium*), or which were simply "not allowed" (*non licet*) or which "you are not able" (*non putes*) to say (*Fam.* 9.22.4).[7] When the medical author Celsus had to discuss the genitalia, he preferred to use Greek rather than Latin words[8] in much the same way a Victorian translation of Aristophanes might render his obscenities in Latin. Greek authors make similar references to certain terms that must be avoided[9] or for which one must apologize.[10] In short, it is clear that both languages

---

but they had non-offensive euphemisms); D. M. Bain, "Six Greek Verbs of Sexual Congress," *Classical Quarterly* 41 (1991): 51–77; Jeffrey Henderson, *The Maculate Muse: Obscene Language in Attic Comedy* (2d ed.; New York: Oxford University Press, 1991); H. D. Jocelyn, "A Greek Indecency and its Students: λαικάζειν," *Proceedings of the Cambridge Philological Society* n.s. 26 (1980): 12–66.

[5] Many other objectionable collocations noted by grammarians can be found in Wilhelm Wendt, "Ciceros Brief an Paetus IX 22" (Ph.D. diss., Gießen 1929), 6–11. Cf. also Fr. Ritter, "Übertriebene Scheu der Römer vor gewissen Ausdrücken und Wortverbindungen," *Rheinisches Museum für Philologie* 3 (1835): 569–80.

[6] An example mentioned by Keith Allan and Kate Burridge, *Euphemism and Dysphemism: Language Used as Shield and Weapon* (New York: Oxford, 1991), 29.

[7] This letter, a *locus classicus* for the topic, is discussed in greater detail below (pp. 89–93).

[8] Celsus says, "Next come subjects relating to privy parts [*partes obscenas*], for which the terms employed by the Greeks are the more tolerable, and are now accepted for use, since they are met with in almost every medical book and discourse. Not even the common use has commended our coarser words [*foediora verba*] for those who would speak with modesty [*verecundius*]. Hence it is more difficult to set forth these matters and at the same time to observe both propriety [*pudorem*] and the precepts of the art" (*De medicina* 6.18.1 [Spencer, LCL]).

[9] Pseudo-Aristotle, *Rhetorica ad Alexandrum* 1441b21: "Guard against describing even his shameful actions with shameful names [φυλάττου δὲ καὶ τὰς αἰσχρὰς πράξεις μὴ αἰσχροῖς ὀνόμασι λέγειν]...but indicate such matters allusively, and make the matter clear by using words for other things."

[10] In Menander's *Phasma* 39–43, a slave says, "The trouble with you is—well, it makes me think of something rather vulgar, I hope you don't mind, but everything's

had primary obscenities. In some cases, the force of these obscenities lasted many centuries: some were still being avoided by scholiasts hundreds of years later,[11] and others have retained their offensive force in modern languages (cf. the Latin *cunnus* and English *cunt*).

Like English words, Greek and Latin words could be placed on a continuum of offensiveness. So, for instance, the pattern of occurrences suggests that χέζω was much milder than λαικάζω, with βινῶ somewhere in between.[12] Cicero describes one word as "shameless" and another as "even more shameless" (*impudenter* and *multo impudentius* [*Fam.* 9.22]). In addition to "nakedly" obscene words,[13] Greeks and Romans also had (and sometimes tried to avoid) the not-so-innocent *double entendre*. Quintilian says that "obscenity should not merely be absent from [an orator's] words, but even from his *meaning*."[14] In Greek or Latin, as in English, words that began as metaphorical expressions could became direct obscenities over the course of time as the metaphor faded (cf. English *cock* or *bitch*). The Greek verb κινῶ, for instance, so often designated sexual intercourse that it became a "quasi-obscenity"[15] when used in sexual contexts. And Cicero reports that the Latin word *penis* was once a decent term for a tail, but had become obscene in his day.[16]

---

so perfect, as they say, you've nowhere to shit" (ἡ νόσος τρυφὴ / ἔσθ᾽ ἣν διῆλθε—φορτικώτερον δέ τι / ἐπέρχεταί μοι, τρόφιμε, συγγνώμην ἔχε, / τὸ δὲ λεγόμενον—οὐκ ἔχει ὅποι χέσῃς). The example and translation are from K. J. Dover, *Greek Popular Morality in the Time of Plato and Aristotle* (Oxford: Basil Blackwell, 1974), 207–8n7 (with further examples of such modesty).

[11] Jocelyn, "A Greek Indecency," 21.

[12] Determining whether certain words were strongly or only mildly obscene—or if they were not *obscene* at all, but were avoided in polite speech for some other reason (such as being too intimate)—is made difficult by the limitations of the sources. The discussions of the word βινῶ (generally agreed to have roughly the force of the English *fuck*) in the pages of the *Liverpool Classical Monthly* illustrate this difficulty. C. Collard, "βινεῖν and Aristophanes, Lysistrata 934," *LCM* 4.10 (December 1979): 213–14; A. H. Sommerstein, "BINEIN," *LCM* 5.2 (February 1980): 47; H. D. Jocelyn, "Attic BINEIN and English F…," *LCM* 5.3 (March 1980): 65–67; Jeffrey Henderson, "Further thoughts on BINEIN," *LCM* 5.10 (December 1980): 243; D. M. Bain, "Two further observations on BINEIN," *LCM* 6.2 (February 1981): 43–44; H. D. Jocelyn, "BINEIN yet again," *LCM* 6.2 (February 1981): 45–46.

[13] Cf. Quintilian, *Inst.* 8.3.38: *obscena nudis nominibus enuntientur.*

[14] *Obscenitas vero non a verbis tantum abesse debet, sed etiam a significatione* (*Inst.* 6.3.29).

[15] Bain, "Six Greek Verbs," 51n2, who discusses the verb in detail (63–67).

[16] *Fam.* 9.22.2.

So Greek and Latin had "bad words," but did either language have a specific *term* for this concept? And was "foul language" recognizable as a category? Before considering Greek and Latin, it is helpful to reflect on the situation in English. We have a recognizable category "obscene language" (although there is disagreement about what locutions should count), but we have no single technical term for it. A typical newspaper article exemplifies the range of terms currently in use for this concept: "dirty words," "cursing," "the line between *foulness* and literature," "obscenity."[17] Even linguists use these terms quite loosely,[18] speaking of "swearing," "foul language," "'four-letter' words," or "obscenity."[19] Although there would be no unanimity as to what sorts of expressions should count as "obscene," we recognize this category as distinct from other forms of improper language (e.g. bad grammar, lying, etc.). Even people who find nothing problematic in "obscene" words or innuendos are aware that such language might be offensive to someone else.

Just as in English, in Greek and Latin there was a variety of terms for "bad language," but the existence of a more or less discrete category can be perceived. The Greek word αἰσχρολογία is virtually a technical term for "foul language, obscenity" or "foul abuse."[20] But in Greek, offensive language could also be described as "corrupt,"[21] "unseemly

---

[17] Michael Wines, "He Celebrates That Word, but He'd Stamp It Out," *New York Times*, 3 June 2002.

[18] Wilhelm von Timroth has pointed out that the lack of agreed upon nomenclature in linguistics is not necessarily to be lamented. He cites Karl Popper: "The view that the precision of science and of scientific language depends upon the precision of its terms is certainly very plausible, but it is none the less, I believe, a mere prejudice. The precision of a language depends, rather, just upon the fact that it takes care not to burden its terms with the task of being precise" (*Russian and Soviet Sociolinguistics and Taboo Varieties of the Russian Language (Argot, Jargon, Slang and "Mat")* (trans. Nortrud Gupta; Slavistische Beiträge 205; Munich: Otto Sagner, 1986), 59, citing K. R. Popper, *The Open Society and Its Enemies* (2 vols.; London: George Routledge & Sons, 1945), 2:18.

[19] *The Cambridge Encyclopedia of Language* treats "profanities or obscenities" as a subset of "cursing and swearing" (*The Cambridge Encyclopedia of Language*, 61). This encyclopedia uses "swear-words," "'four-letter' words," and "expletives," apparently as synonyms for "profanities and obscenities" (ibid.). Similarly, Allan and Burridge gloss "the act of swearing" as "uttering an expletive" (*Euphemism and Dysphemism*, 32). R. L. Trask defines "swearing" as "Using language which is considered vulgar, obscene or blasphemous by the community as a whole" (*A Student's Dictionary of Language and Linguistics* [London: Arnold, 1997], 213).

[20] LSJ, s.v. For further discussion of the uses of αἰσχρολογία, see below pp. 156–67.

[21] Dio Chrysostom complains about the "terrible zeal for filthy language"—literally "spoiled" or "corrupt words" (λόγων διεφθορότων κακοὺς ζήλους) (*2 Regn.* 55).

and intemperate,"[22] "lewd,"[23] "vulgar,"[24] "buffoonish,"[25] or "blunt,"[26] or it could be contrasted with language that was uttered "in good taste"[27] or in a "seemly" manner. One comment even describes a poem's indecency simply as "too iambic."[28] A foul-mouthed person could be called αἰσχρολόγος or αἰσχρορρήμων, or something more creative, like a κυσολέσχης.[29] Similarly, in Latin one finds foul language designated not only by *obscenitas* or *obscena verba*, but also by "naked words,"[30] "lewd abuse,"[31] "foul words,"[32] or simply "ugliness,"[33] as well as by peculiar expressions such as *praetextata verba*.[34]

On the question of whether there was a category for obscene language, the word αἰσχρολογία is a useful starting point. When describing

---

[22] ἀπρεπῶς καὶ ἀκολάστως (Plutarch, *Mor.* 520A–B, of Archilochus's writings). Plutarch uses τὸ ἀκόλαστον to pick out the offensive quality of the language in Old Comedy (*Mor.* 711F; 854A) or Archilochus (in addition to *Mor.* 520A–B, cf. *Cat. Min.* 7.2). Cf. Lucian, *Salt.* 2: ᾄσμασιν ἀκολάστοις.

[23] For the adverb ἀσυρῶς, cf. Athenaeus, *Deipn.* 5.220D–E and 11.507A. For the adjective, cf. Sir 23.12: ἀπαιδευσίαν ἀσυρῆ μὴ συνεθίσῃς τὸ στόμα σου, a passage discussed below, pp. 122–28.

[24] φορτικός (Plutarch, *Mor.* 853D).

[25] βωμολόχος (very often).

[26] εὐθυρρημονεῖν/εὐθυρρημονῶς. These did not in themselves designate *obscene*, but *blunt* language (cf. Clement of Alexandria, *Strom.* 2.120.2); but Cicero says that the motto that justified Zeno's *obscene* language was ὁ σοφὸς εὐθυρρημονήσει ("the wise man will speak bluntly"); cf. Cicero, *Fam.* 12.16.3, and also Pollux, *Onom.* 2.129, where εὐθυρρημοσύνη and αἰσχρορρημοσύνη appear in succession.

[27] ἐμμελῶς.

[28] ἰαμβικώτερο[ν] (*SEG* 15.517 [third century B.C.], column 3, line 38). Since the poem in view is not iambic in meter, this "must refer to the content of the fragment, in all likelihood to its obscenity" (Douglas E. Gerber, *Greek Iambic Poetry* [LCL; Cambridge: Harvard University Press, 1999], 3).

[29] From κυσός=κύσθος (an obscene term for the vagina), and λέσχη, talk (Suetonius, Περὶ βλασφημιῶν 3.16).

[30] *nuda verba* (Pliny the Younger, *Ep.* 4.14).

[31] *probra* (Pliny the Elder, *Nat.* 19.120).

[32] *foediora verba* (Celsus, *De medicina* 6.18.1).

[33] *deformitas* (Quintilian, *Inst.* 8.3.48); *turpitudo* (Cicero, *Fam.* 9.22.3).

[34] From *praetexta*, the toga worn by children. For this use, cf. Macrobius, *Saturn.* 2.1.9 (*impudica et praetextata verba*); Aulus Gellius, *Noct. Att.* 9.10.4 (*non praetextatis sed puris honestisque verbis*); Suetonius, *Ves.* 21.1. Festus (282–84) reports two explanations for why *sermo praetextatus* should mean obscene language. Some said it was because youth (*praetextati*) were not allowed to use obscene words; others thought it had something to do with the fact that at weddings obscene things were shouted by the boys when the *togae praetextae* had been laid down (*Praetextum sermonem quidam putant dici, quod praetextatis nefas sit obsceno verbo uti: alii quod nubentibus depositis praetextis a multitudine puerorum obscena clamentur*). On the license of speech allowed to young men in some Roman ceremonies, see M. Kleijwegt, "*Iuvenes* and Roman Imperial Socieity," *Acta Classica* 37 (1994): 88.

the foul language used at some religious festivals, many writers (e.g.
Aristotle, Diodorus Siculus, and Plutarch) used αἰσχρολογία, but others,
identifying precisely the same phenomenon, used different terms. When
Aristotle discusses the obscenity in Old Comedy, he uses αἰσχρολογία,
but Plutarch talks about the "*coarseness…vulgarity* and *ribaldry.*"[35] The fact
that Aristotle talked about the αἰσχρολογία of Old Comedy, religion,
and casual conversation also suggests that he recognized a specific feature of the language even in very different settings. That this consisted
above all in the use of certain prohibited terms is suggested by the way
he distinguishes between the αἰσχρολογία of Old Comedy and the
seemlier "innuendo" of the comic stage in his day, for it is precisely the
obscene words that tended to disappear from Middle Comedy.

When we look at what sorts of speech were labeled as αἰσχρολογία
or *obscenitas* we consistently find words that were considered ugly,
inappropriate, obscene, offensive. When Cicero responds to his friend
Paetus's use of the word *mentula* ("dick"), he gives many examples of
obscene words (in Latin *and* Greek!).[36] Furthermore, he recognizes that
the Stoics had addressed this same topic centuries earlier. And when
Cicero likens the use of such language to farting or belching (*Fam.*
9.22.4),[37] we can see that he did not perceive such words as primarily
inauspicious or cruel or imprecise (or any of the multitude of other ways
words could be "bad"), but rather as shocking violations of etiquette. It
is true that discussions of obscene words often touch on related vices,
such as abusiveness, excessive jocularity, or lewdness, since obscene
words could be used toward these ends. It is not always clear when
aischrologia or *obscenitas* (and their synonyms) designate primary obscenities and when they are extended to include overly strong innuendo.
Quintilian's comment (*Inst.* 6.3.29, cited above, p. 3) shows that he
could make a conceptual distinction between *obscenitas* of words and of
meaning.[38] His comment also shows that, had he simply spoken about

---

[35] Τὸ φορτικόν, φησίν, ἐν λόγοις καὶ θυμελικὸν καὶ βάναυσον ὥς ἐστιν Ἀριστοφάνει
(Plutarch, *Mor.* 853B [Fowler, LCL]).

[36] Cf. the way *Priapea* 29 recognizes that both *cunnus* and *mentula* belong to the same
group of "obscene and improper words"—words, the poem adds, that one *can* say in
the presence of a god who is displaying his own genitals (*Obscenis, peream, Priape, si non/
uti me pudet improbisque verbis/sed cum tu posito deus pudore/ostendas mihi coleos patentes/cum
cunno mihi mentula est vocanda*).

[37] For the combination of abusive language and farting, cf. Petronius, *Sat.* 117.

[38] A distinction made often. Cf. Cicero, *Fam.* 9.22.1: *totus est sermo verbis tectus, re
impudentior.*

avoiding *obscenitas*, it would not have been entirely clear whether he meant the narrower (obscene words) or the broader (obscene meanings) category.

The ultimate aim of this study is not simply to determine the precise list of words or jokes or types of verbal abuse that Ephesians, Colossians, the *Didache*, or Clement wanted to prohibit, but rather to explore what their rhetoric about such language reveals about their values, their understanding of language, their social location, and their attempt to construct a Christian identity. Therefore, rather than attempting at the outset of the investigation some definition of the essence of obscene language[39]—something that changing mores and the changing register of specific words make impossible—it will be more helpful to begin with a fairly broad definition of "obscenity" as indecent, vulgar, or lewd language.[40] Such a definition will allow the comparison of a variety of ancient discussions of propriety in language.

Naturally, the various discourses about foul language have some reflex in the actual practices of the day, particularly in the occasions when obscene language was characteristically used. That the *Didache* associates αἰσχρολογία with sex, and Colossians associates it with angry abuse, is unsurprising: the obscene vocabulary was used in Greek and Latin humorously, abusively, and lewdly. It was, of course, possible to be humorous, abusive, or lewd without the use of the most obscene vocabulary (a fact nicely illustrated by the Palatine Anthology). But what is clear is that for many ancient authors, foul language is recognizably distinct from other transgressions of speech. Considering a broad range of overlapping discussions of foul language can help put the early Christian advice into some relief. The first two chapters of this study explore the contexts for the use of foul language and the contours of the discussions about it.

Part of the difficulty of defining obscenity in language is that even perfectly familiar realities of obscene language in our own culture are surprisingly puzzling. *Poop*, *crap*, and *shit* are all words with four letters

---

[39] The attempt to define an essence for obscenity has, of course, often been undertaken—usually by those eager to demonstrate that their own (or their favorite) language should not be categorized as *genuinely* obscene. The various attempts to pin down precisely why certain forms of linguistic representation should or should not be considered obscene is surveyed by P. Gorsen, "Obszön," *Historisches Wörterbuch der Philosophie*, 7:1081–89.

[40] The *Oxford English Dictionary* has for *obscenity*, "impurity, indecency, lewdness (esp. of language)," and for the plural, "obscene words or matters."

that refer to excrement, but only the last is a "four-letter word," and only the last two are likely to be used in exclamations of anger or surprise. Linguists will point out that there are taboos on certain sexual and scatological realms, and that words for such topics may likewise fall under the taboo.[41] But this fails to explain why we can say "excrement" and "feces" but not "shit," or "have sex" but not "fuck"—or why words with such different meanings as "shit," "fuck," and "Jesus Christ" work as nearly equivalent expletives. As one linguist put it, "Who ever stubbed his toe in the dark and cried out, 'Oh, faeces!'?"[42]

It has been suggested that obscene and blasphemous (or profane) language involves displacements,[43] so that "the social force of the expressive word is greater the further apart the contexts are from which it was taken and into which it has been inserted. The contexts of biological intimacy and of religious seriousness from which the expressions, which when displaced become the obscene and the blasphemous, are very distant from everyday, public life."[44] Thus the power of bad language "comes from the distance of its displacement from its original contexts of use," and that in this respect, "obscenity and blasphemy are typical metaphors."

This is an intriguing suggestion, but it fails to account for the fact that only some of the words which are displaced have this power. *Poop* and *shit* are both "displaced" when used as expletives; but *poop* has almost no function as an expletive, and this despite the fact that it begins and ends with a plosive, which might have made it ideal for this purpose.[45] Furthermore, the displacement of *Christ* is clear enough (it belongs properly to sacred settings; it is displaced when screamed in traffic); but it will hardly do to say that such strong obscenities as *cunt* or *fuck* are simply *displaced* from their natural, biological, or romantic domain, for these words are just as offensive in the doctor's office or the bedroom as anywhere else. If anything, such words are *more* offensive when used of sex ("he fucked her") than when "displaced" ("he fucked up").

---

[41] "Taboo terms are contaminated by the taboo topics that they denote" (Allan and Burridge, *Euphemism and Dysphemism*, 22).

[42] Robert M. Adams, cited by Allan and Burridge, *Euphemism and Dysphemism*, 11.

[43] Rom Harré, "Obscenity and Blasphemy from the Linguistic Point of View," in *A Matter of Manners? The Limits of Broadcast Language* (ed. Andrea Millwood Hargrave; London: John Libbey, 1991), 85–90.

[44] Ibid., 90.

[45] For observations on the sounds and stress patterns that some obscene expressions have in common, cf. Geoffrey Hughes, *Swearing: A Social History of Foul Language, Oaths and Profanity in English* (2d ed.; London: Penguin, 1998), 21–24.

Which words are obscene clearly has *something* to do with certain realms (private or sacred or disgusting—although that is already a rather odd trio). There are, after all, no obscene words for trees or lamp shades, for hiking or holding hands; and we blurt out "God" or "Jesus Christ" much more often than "Aphrodite." But even in these particular realms—sexual, scatological, and religious—only a few of the words can be used in an offensive way.

In the end we can only say that certain words are themselves often found to be offensive, not because of sound or semantics, but because the language is organized in such a way that they have been put off limits, and to use them in the wrong occasions is to transgress social decorum. The same thing could be said of gestures, such as showing the middle finger: its capacity to offend depends entirely on its place in a system.[46] Few speakers of English find anything offensive in the sound of a word like *puck* or in using the expression "sexual intercourse," but there is a strong prohibition against the word that sounds like the first and means the second. *Shit* is not off limits because it sounds worse or is somehow tied more intrinsically to its referent than *feces*.

If we find it difficult to give an account of why only some words are offensive, we are not the first. Some ancient Stoics, in reflecting on this very question, argued that it was absurd that it was culturally acceptable to call something really horrible, such as patricide, by its real name, when one had to dance around perfectly moral activities (trying to conceive a child) with circumlocutions. A philosopher named Bryson argued that it was in fact *impossible* to use obscene language, since the referent is the same regardless of one's choice of words.[47]

Aristotle was probably right to argue that Bryson's line of reasoning is a bit reductionistic, since there is more to a word than simply its sound and its referent.[48] So while "passing stool," "relieving oneself," and "taking a shit" may all refer to the same bodily function, the activity in question is being perceived and described in different ways.[49] Furthermore, in the eyes of someone like Aristotle (and many since), some words have been tainted because of who has used them most frequently. Here the existence of an obscene vocabulary is inextricably

---

[46] Cf. the observations of Jacques E. Merceron, "Obscenity and Hagiography in Three Anonymous *Sermons Joyeux* and in Jean Molinet's *Saint Billouart*," in Ziolkowski, *Obscenity*, 334–35.

[47] Discussed on pp. 97–99.

[48] Aristotle, *Rhet.* 1405b5–21.

[49] Cf. Henderson, *Maculate Muse*, 35–36.

bound to social distinctions. But given the amount of foul language that was (and is) used by people of even the highest echelons of society, I would argue that it is not so much usage that imbues certain words with their "vulgar" character, but rather the discourse that labels certain language as unrefined. Aristotle disliked the fact that citizens peppered their conversation with "slavish" language, and worried that free-born children would develop a taste for such talk. But this way of putting the problem shows that such language was not exclusively (perhaps not even primarily) the language of slaves! Rather than being empirical, his discussion reinforces the sense that some words are vulgar—and thereby creates another mark by which a citizen with good *paideia* could potentially distinguish himself. Alternatively, this also makes it possible for those of higher status to exhibit a sort of solidarity with those beneath them by using or enjoying their "vulgar" language (one thinks of Augustus at the public entertainments,[50] or university professors in their lectures).

Furthermore, the propriety or impropriety of specific expressions will vary according to circumstances. The same words that were used unselfconsciously among a group of men of the same age and class might not be possible to utter in the presence of someone older or younger, or in the presence of women.[51] But although there is a greater tolerance for obscene words in some contexts than in others, even when such language is acceptable its speakers still recognize that they are using "obscene words."

There is abundant anecdotal evidence that among some social groups (soldiers are often mentioned in the linguistic literature) four-letter words can become virtually the only terms for certain body parts and functions.[52] But even in situations in which such words neither degrade the speaker nor offend the hearers, there remains an awareness that

---

[50] Suetonius, *Aug.* 45.1, and discussion in Nicholas Horsfall, *The Culture of the Roman Plebs* (London: Duckworth, 2003), 68.

[51] Allan and Burridge note that "numerous surveys leave no doubt that in nearly all societies, if not all, males 'swear' more and use more 'obscene' language than females." They also point out that "the use of taboo terms in epithets and expletives is sometimes a display of macho—a sign of masculinity" (*Euphemism and Dysphemism*, 119).

[52] See Edward Sagarin, *The Anatomy of Dirty Words* (New York: L. Stuart, 1962), 47, cited by Muscatine, "(Re)invention of Vulgarity," 284. Robert Graves offers the example of the soldier who had been shot in the buttocks and was asked by a woman where he was wounded. He could only stammer, "I'm so sorry, ma'am, I don't know: I never learned Latin" (Robert Graves, *Lars Porsena; or, the Future of Swearing and Improper Language* [London: Martin Brian & O'Keefe Ltd, 1972 (1927)], 10–11).

these same speech-acts would be offensive in other contexts. They are "offensive words" even when nobody is offended.

It should also be pointed out that, although Greeks and Romans had decent and indecent words, they did not use them on the same occasions as English speakers. Several of the ways that they *did* use foul language will be discussed in this chapter; but it is worth noting at the outset that Greeks and Romans did not generally use obscene words to fill out speech ("that's a fucking good cup of coffee," "abso-fucking-lutely"). The Greeks and Romans also did not use their obscene words in response to a sudden shock. Speech practices in several cultures attest that in moments of anger, fear, or pain, the use of prohibited words releases nervous energy.[53] A friend has related that once her mother, a religious woman who strenuously avoided foul language, hit another car while parking and blurted out an obscene word. After a moment of uncomfortable silence, she attempted the following explanation: "I'm sorry dear. I've tried the other words, but sometimes they don't work." *Work* here is the interesting word, and this episode confirms that "the very fact that a term is taboo may improve its value as autocathartic: the breaking of the taboo is an emotional release."[54] An instructive analogue to this stress-releasing use of a prohibited *obscene* word can be found in a tribe of Australian aborigines who, when they stub a toe or break a tool, call out the name of a dead relative. The tribe in question has both acceptable and prohibited terms for body parts and some other topics, but the obscene terms are used only at certain festivals, never under stress or fear. However, when someone from the tribe dies, his or her name is unmentionable for a period, and "hence a great constellation of inhibited emotion is built up about the names of such deceased relatives."[55]

The Greeks and Romans did not generally use their obscene words in moments of surprise or pain. Theophrastus says of "the grouch," "If he

---

[53] *The Cambridge Encyclopedia of Language*, 61: "[Swearing] is an outlet for frustration or pent-up emotion and a means of releasing nervous energy after a sudden shock"; cf. Montagu, *Anatomy of Swearing*, 67.

[54] Allan and Burridge, *Euphemism and Dysphemism*, 118. When Vice President Dick Cheney was asked if he had actually said "Go fuck yourself!" to Senator Patrick Leahy, he answered in the affirmative: "I said it, *and I felt better afterwards.*"

[55] Montagu, *Anatomy of Swearing*, 16, reporting the findings of Donald F. Thomson, "The Joking Relationship and Organized Obscenity in North Queensland," *American Anthropologist* 37 (1935): 460–90.

stumbles on the street, he is apt to curse the stone"[56]—that is, pronounce a curse over it, not call it a bad name. As Jeffrey Henderson puts it, "A cursing Greek...uses the names of gods and resorts to specific (and usually nonobscene) epithets to insult enemies."[57] Although there were occasional objections to using the gods' names too frequently,[58] crying out "Hercules!" was not viewed by pagans as profane in the way "Jesus Christ!" can be for Christians. (Christians, in fact, continued to blurt out the names of *pagan* gods, which was itself troubling to Tertullian and Jerome,[59] but was not treated as an instance of "bad language.")

I. Plato and Aristotle on Foul Language

As is the case for so many nobler topics in the history of ideas, Plato and Aristotle provide a fine place to begin a survey of ancient views of obscene language. Not only are their comments on the topic among the first from the Greek tradition, but they indicate where foul language might occur and, in their own complaints about foul language, they adumbrate the moral sentiments that would be expressed over the next centuries. For instance, both Plato and Aristotle say that they would ban foul language from an ideal state. Some cities actually did ban lewd forms of literature and drama,[60] and half a millennium after Plato and Aristotle gave their views, Aelius Aristides[61] and Dio Chrysostom made similar arguments.[62]

---

[56] καὶ προσπταίσας ἐν τῇ ὁδῷ δεινὸς [sc. ὁ αὐθάδης] καταράσασθαι τῷ λίθῳ. (Theophrastus, *Char.* 15.8 [Rusten, LCL]). So Encolpius speaks of people cursing (*male dicere*) whatever body parts cause them pain (Petronius, *Sat.* 132).

[57] Henderson, *Maculate Muse*, 40. Cf. Kenneth Dover, "Some Evaluative Terms in Aristophanes," in *The Language of Greek Comedy* (ed. Andreas Willi; Oxford: Oxford University Press, 2002), 94–97.

[58] See Th. Klauser, "Beteuerungsformeln," *RAC* 2.219–24.

[59] Tertullian, *Idol.* 21; Jerome, *Ep.* 21.13.8.

[60] Demosthenes says that the Athenians drove out the authors of mime and of shameful songs (*2 Olynth.* 19); Valerius Maximus has a similar report of the Lacedaemonians: "The Lacedaemonians ordered that the works of Archilochus be removed from their community because they thought them immodest and immoral reading [*parum verecundam ac pudicam lectionem*]. They did not wish their children's minds to be imbued with it, lest it do more harm to their character than good to their intelligence. So they punished with banishment the greatest, or at least the second greatest, of poets because he had lashed a family he hated with obscene insults [*obscenis maledictis*]" (*Facta et dicta memorabilia* 6.3 ext. 1 [Shackleton Bailey, LCL]).

[61] Aelius Aristides, *Or.* 29, urging the inhabitants of Smyrna not to incorporate comedy in their festivals for Dionysus.

[62] Dio Chrysostom, *2 Regn.* 55–56 [Cohoon, LCL]: "However, I do not believe that the king should simply be distinguished in his own person for courage and dignity, but

I.A. *Plato and the Dangers of Mimesis*

Plato expresses his concerns about foul language in the third book of the *Republic*, in the course of pondering whether it would be fitting for the members of his state to compose or to perform tragedies or comedies.[63] Plato insists that the guardians of his state were only to imitate men "who are brave, sober, pious, free, and all things of that kind." If they imitated anything "shameful" or "unbecoming the free man," they would imbibe the reality (3.395C). Imitation, Plato explains, leads to habits and nature in "the body, the speech [φωνάς], and the thought" (3.395D). Hence there must be no role-playing of women or slaves or even of bad men "who are cowards and who do the opposite of the things we just now spoke of [i.e. being brave, sober, pious, free], reviling and lampooning one another, *speaking foul words* when drunk or when sober and in other ways sinning against themselves and others in word and deed after the fashion of such men."[64] This comment clearly has Comedy[65] in mind, for one of the things the characters in Old Comedy do is use taboo terms—not only as part of their "reviling" and "lampooning" (κωμῳδεῖν) each other, but as part of the jocular bawdiness of the whole production. So when Plato considered the dangers inherent in acting Comedy, he noted not only the fact that the actors would have to imitate slaves or women or cowards, but also that they would use obscene language.

It is striking that Plato immediately adds to this that they must not imitate *madmen* (μαινομένοις) in words or in deeds (396A), for speaking foul language is actually regarded as a symptom of madness in

---

that he should pay no heed to other people either when they play the flute or the harp, or sing wanton and voluptuous songs [ἀνειμένα μέλη καὶ τρυφερά]; nor should he tolerate the mischievous craze for filthy language [λόγων διεφθορότων] that has come into vogue for the delight of fools; nay, he should cast out all such things and banish them to the uttermost distance from his own soul, first and foremost, *and then from the capital of his kingdom*—I mean such things as ribald jests and those who compose them, whether in verse or in prose, along with scurrilous gibes [γέλωτάς τε ἀκράτους καὶ τοιούτου γέλωτος ποιητὰς μετὰ σκωμμάτων, ἐμμέρου τε καὶ ἀμέτρου]."

[63] *Resp.* 394d.

[64] κακηγοροῦντάς τε καὶ κωμῳδοῦντας ἀλλήλους καὶ αἰσχρολογοῦντας, μεθύοντας ἢ καὶ νήφοντες, ἢ καὶ ἄλλα ὅσα οἱ τοιοῦτοι καὶ ἐν λόγοις καὶ ἐν ἔργοις ἁμαρτάνουσιν εἰς αὐτούς τε καὶ εἰς ἄλλους (395E [Shorey, LCL, adjusted]).

[65] So Karsten Siems, "Aischrologia: Das Sexuell-Hässliche im antiken Epigramm" (Ph.D. diss., Göttingen, 1974), 9–10. Kenneth J. Reckford sums up Plato's point: "There is absolutely no place for an Aristophanes in the well-ordered state" (*Aristophanes' Old-and-New Comedy* [Chapel Hill: University of North Carolina Press, 1987], 369). Nonetheless, Plato could credit Aristophanes with "charm" (Quadlbauer, "Dichter," 43).

several ancient medical works.⁶⁶ In *Laws* 11 (934C), Plato also connects foul and abusive language to his laws for the "madman" (μαινόμενος, 934E). Plato says that when people fight they "abuse one another slanderously" (κακῶς ἀλλήλους βλασφημοῦντες [934E]), and they cannot resist ridiculing their opponent (935A, D). Plato's law concerning abuse (περὶ κακηγορίας) is quite simply that no one shall abuse anyone (μηδένα κακηγορείτω μηδείς [934E]). Otherwise "hatreds and feuds" will arise from the "shameful words" (δι' αἰσχρῶν ὀνομάτων) used in fights (935A).⁶⁷ These ugly words poison a soul, feeding anger, pampering passion (935C), undoing the humanizing work of παιδεία (935A), turning a person into a beast. Anyone who indulges in such base wrangling, Plato says, sacrifices high-mindedness and fails to achieve a noble disposition (935A).

From these observations about the destructive nature of abusive speech Plato rejects foul language under *any* circumstances: "*No* man, therefore, shall ever in *any* wise utter such words in *any* holy place or at *any* public sacrifice or public games, or in the market or the court or *any* public assembly..." (935B [Shorey, LCL]; μή- words are used eight times in this sentence). Although Plato had been talking strictly about fighting, here he expands the possible sphere of foul language to include "holy places," where, as we shall discuss later, foul language played a role in some religious rites. He also adds that it makes no difference whether abuse is done in anger or in jest: "A composer of a comedy or of any iambic or lyric song shall be strictly forbidden to ridicule any of the citizens either by word or by mimicry" (935E [Shorey, LCL]).⁶⁸

---

⁶⁶ Cf. the Hippocratic diagnosis of people speaking obscenely when unwell and raving: "As night began there were fears, much rambling, depression and slight feverishness. Early in the morning frequent convulsions; whenever these frequent convulsions intermitted, she wandered and uttered obscenities [ᾐσχρομύθει]" (*Epid.* 3.17.11 [Jones, LCL]); "He was delirious on the eighth day, I think, in the irrepressible way: leapt up, fought, used very foul language [αἰσχρομυθεῖν ἰσχυρῶς]. (He wasn't that type.)...Then his madness resumed and he died suddenly on the eleventh day" (*Epid.* 4.15 [Smith, LCL]). Seneca also mentions the *maledicta* of a person with a fever (*Const.* 13.1); cf. Lucian, *Hist.* 1.

⁶⁷ On "light" words having serious consequences, cf. Plato, *Leg.* 4 (717C–D).

⁶⁸ Siems says that Plato modified his strict prohibition of mocking in *Laws* 11, permitting men to joke if it was in fun, without passion, and not directed at a citizen (Siems, "Aischrologia," 9n7, citing *Leg.* 11, 935D). Plato does indeed raise the possibility a loophole, but he then closes it emphatically (Reckford, *Old-and-New Comedy*, 369). Plato objected to Comedy on several other grounds as well: In *Resp.* 10, he says that the vicarious enjoyment of pity and grief lowers the threshold of emotional self-

I.B. *Aristotle and the Bounds of Humor*

Aristotle, like Plato, wanted to ban foul language from an ideal state: "Therefore the lawgiver should banish foul language from the state altogether, as much as anything else (for when saying shameful things is tolerated, doing them is near at hand)."[69] Aristotle worries particularly about the corrosive effects of foul language on the young, who "must not be allowed to be spectators of iambic poetry or comedy" (*Pol.* 1336b20–21). He also takes up the topic of obscenity in religious rites, but whereas Plato banned any such talk from "holy places," Aristotle makes an exception for those gods whose worship customarily involved ritual abuse (*Pol.* 1336b16–17). Still, Aristotle would spare youth and women exposure to this nasty language: he says that men may worship on their behalf (*Pol.* 1336b14–19). The prohibition of women at these cults is striking, since several of the rites that involved ritual aischrology were conducted solely by women[70] (as will be discussed below).

But aside from this difference from Plato in tolerating obscenity in certain cultic settings, the really new thing in Aristotle is an extended discussion of obscene language as it could occur in light-hearted conversation, where the paramount concern is not what foul language might *do* to its user but what it might *say* about the user's character.

Aristotle views playful conversation—along with sleep and drink—as a part of relaxation (ἀνάπαυσις).[71] And although amusement and relaxation are not ends in themselves, they are nevertheless necessary because

---

restraint, so that in laughing at clowns one releases that "clownish" part of oneself that wants indecency and hostility. In the *Philebus* he complains that laughter indulges an element of envy. It is in *Laws* 7 that Plato allows Comedy a small educational role (816D–817A). If a person is to avoid saying or doing something "ludicrous" or "out of place," Plato reasons, he has to know not only what is earnest but also its opposite, the burlesque (816D–E). For this, the artists of "ludicrous burlesque in diction, song, [and] dance" have some function—not in catharsis or mere pleasure, but in moral improvement, by showing what not to do. But even in this limited role, comedies must be performed by slaves or aliens, and the performances must vary lest they leave too strong an impression on the viewers (Reckford, *Old-and-New Comedy*, 368–69).

[69] ὅλως μὲν οὖν αἰσχρολογίαν ἐκ τῆς πόλεως, ὥσπερ ἄλλο τι, δεῖ τὸν νομοθέτην ἐξορίζειν (ἐκ τοῦ γὰρ εὐχερῶς λέγειν ὁτιοῦν τῶν αἰσχρῶν γίνεται καὶ τὸ ποιεῖν σύνεγγυς) (*Pol.* 1336b3–6).

[70] For examples of men worshipping on behalf of their families, cf. Eckart Schütrumpf, *Aristoteles: Politik Buch VII/VIII* (Darmstadt: Wissenschaftliche Buchgesellschaft, 2005), 552.

[71] *Eth. nic.* 1127b33; *Pol.* 1339a17. Plato had Socrates make the same point about jokes (*Phil.* 30E). On the relaxing potential of laughter more generally, see Stephen Halliwell, "The Uses of Laughter in Greek Culture," *Classical Quarterly* 41 (1991): 279–96 (especially 282).

one cannot toil continuously (*Eth. nic.* 1176b27–1177a11). Like having a drink, play relaxes the mind and encourages affection in friendship. People who have the tact to take jokes and to make them in a tasteful manner[72] know how to pass the time pleasantly.[73] Changing the metaphor from drinking to eating, Aristotle says that when it comes to pleasant conversation, one can be fussy and hard to please or one can overindulge by going too far to raise a laugh:

> For just as in the matter of food the squeamish man differs from the omnivorous in that the former takes nothing or little, and that reluctantly, and the latter accepts everything readily, so the boor [ἄγροικος] stands in relation to the vulgar man [φορτικός] or buffoon [βωμολόχος]—the former takes no joke except with difficulty, the latter accepts everything easily and with pleasure. Neither course is right: one should allow some things and not others, and on principle,—that constitutes the witty man [εὐτράπελος]. (*Eth. eud.* 1234a5–11 [Rackham, LCL])

In the *Nichomachean Ethics*, Aristotle argues that even listening to such language can reflect badly on a person:

> Those then who go to excess in raising laughs seem to be vulgar buffoons. They stop at nothing to raise a laugh, and care more about that than about saying what is seemly and avoiding pain to the victims of the joke.
>
> Those who would never say anything themselves to raise a laugh, and even object when other people do it, seem to be boorish and stiff.
>
> Those who joke in appropriate ways are called witty [εὐτράπελοι], or, in other words, agile-witted, since these sorts of jokes seem to be movements of someone's character, and characters are judged, as bodies are, by their movements. Since there are always opportunities at hand for raising a laugh, and most people enjoy amusements and jokes more than they should, buffoons are also called witty because they are thought cultivated; nonetheless, they differ, and differ considerably, from witty people, as our account has made clear.
>
> Dexterity is also proper to the intermediate state. It is proper to the dexterous person to say and listen to what suits the decent and civilized person. For some things are suitable for this sort of person to say and listen to by way of amusement; and the civilized person's amusement differs from the slavish person's, and the educated person's from the uneducated person's.

---

[72] οἱ ἐπιδέξιοι τωθάσαι καὶ ὑπομεῖναι...δυνάμενοί τε σκώπτεσθαι καὶ ἐμμελῶς σκώπτοντες (*Rhet.* 1381a34–36).

[73] Cf. Pseudo-Lucian, *Amor.* 1, where Lycinus says that his friend's wanton erotic tales have slaked his "thirst" for relaxation, and adds that people cannot pursue serious topics without such respite.

This can also be seen from old and new comedies; for what people used to find funny was indecent language [αἰσχρολογία], but what they now find funny instead is innuendo, which is considerably more seemly.

Then should the person who jokes well be defined by his making remarks not unsuitable for a civilized person, or by his avoiding pain and even giving pleasure to the hearer? Perhaps, though, this [avoiding pain and giving pleasure] is indefinable, since different people find different things hateful or pleasant. The remarks he is willing to hear made are of the same sort, since those he is prepared to hear made seem to be those he is prepared to make himself. Hence he will not be indiscriminate in his remarks. For since a joke is a type of abuse, and legislators prohibit some types of abuse, they would presumably be right to prohibit some types of joke too. Hence the cultivated and civilized person, as a sort of law to himself, will take this [discriminating] attitude. This, then, is the character of the intermediate person, whether he is called dexterous or witty.

The buffoon cannot resist raising a laugh, and spares neither himself nor anyone else if he can cause laughter, even by making remarks that the sophisticated person would never make, and some that the sophisticated person would not even be willing to hear made.

The boor is useless for such gatherings.[74] For he contributes nothing himself, and objects to everything, even though relaxation and amusement seem to be a necessary in life. (*Eth. nic.* 1127b34–1128b4)[75]

In the playful conversation that is one part of relaxation, there is a middle state, a right way to speak and to listen to things: εὐτραπελία, a "wittiness" or "urbanity," the praiseworthy "mean between buffoonery and boorishness, concerning humor."[76] Aristotle says that *eutrapelia* is both the ability to make jokes and also to appreciate them—even when one finds oneself the butt (*Eth. eud.* 1234a14–17).

What stands out is that Aristotle does not have any non-circular[77] way to *analyze* these boundaries: *eutrapelia* is that sort of wit that a *eutrapelos*

---

[74] Or, "The boor is useless *for such conversations*" (ὁ δ'ἄγροικος εἰς τὰς τοιαύτας ὁμιλίας ἀχρεῖος).

[75] The translation, except for minor changes, is that of Terence Irwin, *Aristotle: Nichomachean Ethics* (Indianapolis: Hackett Publishing Company, 1985).

[76] εὐτραπελία δ'ἐστὶ μεσότης βωμολοχίας καὶ ἀγροικίας, ἔστιν δ' περὶ τὰ σκώμματα (*Magna moralia* 1193a11–12). *Eudemian Ethics* also defines *eutrapelia* as a middle state (μεσότης): the witty person is between the boorish (ἄγροικος) or stiff (δυστράπελος), on the one hand, and the buffoon (βωμολόχος) on the other (*Eth. eud.* 1234a4–5). Elsewhere Aristotle defines *eutrapelia* as "insolence tempered by education" (ἡ γὰρ εὐτραπελία πεπαιδευμένη ὕβρις ἐστίν [*Rhet.* 1389b10–12; 2.12]).

[77] The circularity is noted by Simon Goldhill in *Foucault's Virginity: Ancient Erotic Fiction and the History of Sexuality* (Cambridge: Cambridge University Press, 1995), 18.

person will make or will find pleasant when made against him.[78] He
assumes that it is "clear" that it is possible to exceed or fall short of
the mean in the matter of playful conversation. The one who exceeds
will appear (to people with "good" judgment) buffoonish, vulgar, and
harsh. Aristotle does say that the buffoon fails to take thought for the
feelings of others; but Aristotle has already admitted that what offends
is not a reliable ethical guide, since some people will take offense at
everything. All of Aristotle's terms depend on his own judgment. He
says that the buffoon will not take adequate care to say "seemly things"
(εὐσχήμονα), and that only a "witty" person will joke "in appropriate
ways" or "in good taste" (ἐμμελῶς). But defining *seemliness* or *appropriate* or *in good taste* is no easy task; after all, Aristotle acknowledges that
many people have the *wrong* estimation of what should be counted as
witty since they are too eager for a laugh. Thus when he insists (*contra*
this widespread craving for laughs) that buffoons and witty people "dif-
fer considerably, as our account has made clear," it is not at all clear
which part of his account was to have had this clarifying effect. It does
not help much when Aristotle explains the concept of *eutrapelia* with
a new term, "tact" or "dexterity" (ἡ ἐπιδεξιότης), and says that the
"dexterous" person says and listens to such things as befit a "decent
and civilized person" (τῷ ἐπιεικεῖ καὶ ἐλευθερίῳ ἁρμόττει). Nor does
it help when he adds that only certain jokes are "fitting for such a
person" (ἔστι γάρ τινα πρέποντα τῷ τοιούτῳ). The difference between
"civilized and slavish" and "educated and uneducated" depends in no
small part on Aristotle's judgment.

The circularity of Aristotle's discussion could leave one without any
way to calibrate what sorts of words or jokes constituted a breach of
decorum in his eyes were it not for his reference to the different kinds
of comedy. Aristotle says that the distinction he is getting at can be seen
in the difference between older and contemporary comedy: the humor
in Old Comedy depended on ἡ αἰσχρολογία, the contemporary comedy
on the more seemly ἡ ὑπόνοια, "innuendo." Aristotle, though he could
praise an Aristophanes for his verbal acuity,[79] considered the sort of
foul language found in his plays beneath the dignity of an educated
gentleman. Even tragedy was not as noble—nor was its audience as

---

[78] Cf. *Eth. eud.* 1234a22–23.
[79] Reckford, *Old-and-New Comedy*, 380.

gentlemanly—as epic.[80] As A. T. Edwards noted, "If tragedy is vulgar in comparison to epic, then comedy is doubtlessly that much worse."[81]

This sense of social lowness of foul language is also evident in Aristotle's comments in the *Politics*, where he suggests that foul language could corrupt patrician taste. In the case of children, their education has not yet rendered them immune to ignoble delights. To ensure that they grow up properly—that is, aristocratically—even their earliest amusements must not be ignoble (ἀνελεύθερος [*Pol.* 1336a29]), and free children should have as little contact as possible with slaves (*Pol.* 1336a41). This is the context—whether playing with slaves is an appropriate pastime—that opens the discussion of foul language in his *Politics*: "Even at such an age they are likely to enjoy illiberality through the things that they hear and see. Therefore the lawgiver should banish foul language from the state altogether, as much as anything else (for when saying shameful things is tolerated, doing them is near at hand)—so especially foul language should be kept from the young, that they neither say nor hear any such thing" (*Pol.* 1336a41–b8). Any adult who violates these rules and says something prohibited is to be punished "for *slavish* behavior" (ἀνδραποδωδίας χάριν [*Pol.* 1336b12]). Since people are attracted by what they hear first (*Pol.* 1336b28–35), the young must not be allowed to hear iambic verse or see comedy before their education and culture have rendered them immune to the damage of such delights (*Pol.* 1336b20–23).

We already noted that in the *Eudemian Ethics* Aristotle described two types of wit, one of enjoying a good joke, the other of making one. But in the *Nicomachean Ethics*, he emphasizes the need for some limits to what someone should be willing to hear. Five times Aristotle links speaking *and listening to* such light talk, since what one listens to reflects on his character as much as what one says: "The remarks he is willing *to hear* made are of the same sort, since those he is prepared to hear made seem to be those he is prepared to make himself." Unlike Epictetus or Clement of Alexandria centuries later, Aristotle offers no specific advice as to how someone is supposed to react when a buffoon makes one of those jokes "a sophisticated person would not even be willing to hear made." Was one to frown? To blush? To complain? Aristotle

---

[80] *Poet.* 1461b26–62a4.
[81] A. T. Edwards, "Historicizing the Popular Grotesque: Bakhtin's *Rabelais* and Attic Old Comedy," in *Theater and Society in the Classical World* (ed. R. Scodel; Ann Arbor: The University of Michigan Press, 1993), 113n32.

does not say. But it is clear that it was not enough, in his view, simply to watch one's *own* mouth. Others were watching what company one kept, what one could stand to hear, and this, as much as what one said, reflected on one's character.

In addition to saying that foul language is not fitting for people of refinement (and mentioning the idea that words are close to deeds), Aristotle also points out that jokes are a sort of abuse (τὸ γὰρ σκῶμμα λοιδόρημά τί ἐστιν [*Eth. nic.* 1128a30]). Since there *are* laws against verbal abuse, Aristotle reasons, perhaps there should also be laws against abusive joking. In lieu of such laws against joking, the "cultivated and civilized person,"[82] as a sort of law to himself, will take this [discriminating] attitude." Here Aristotle argues that there really is something *wrong* with joking, since it is part of a practice, namely abuse, which is forbidden by law.

II. ABUSE

It is not accidental that Plato included laws for public abuse when describing an ideal state, for verbal attacks were a prominent and potent feature of ancient life. Demosthenes said that average people took care to avoid wrongdoing because they feared the courts and the pain of shaming insults.[83] Aelius Aristides cited the same opinion half a millennium later: "people behave with moderation through their fear of being satirized."[84] Seneca says that, unless one can attain an indifference to abuse, one will live in constant fear of "everyone's laughter, everyone's tongue" (*Const.* 19.2).[85] In Rome, public abuse was a pri-

---

[82] In all, Aristotle labels this right sort of person χαρίεις (cultivated, elegant), ἐλευθέριος (free, a gentleman), ἐπιδέξιος (dexterous or tactful), and εὐτράπελος (witty). In *Eth. eud.*, the terms for the stiff extreme are ἄγροικος, ψυχρός, and δυστράπελος; the other extreme is described as φορτικός and βωμολόχος.

[83] τῷ φόβῳ τῷ πρὸς ὑμᾶς καὶ τῷ τοῖς αἰσχροῖς καὶ λόγοις καὶ ὀνείδεσιν ἀλγεῖν εὐλαβουμένους ἐξαμαρτάνειν (1 *Aristog.* 93, cited by K. J. Dover, *Greek Popular Morality*, 228); cf. Laurie O'Higgins, *Women and Humor in Classical Greece* (Cambridge: Cambridge University Press, 2003), 83. Cf. also Sir 9:18: the loud of mouth are *feared* in their city.

[84] *Or.* 29.16 (this was one of the arguments anticipated as he argued *against* comic drama).

[85] In his *De Constantia*, Seneca explains how a wise man can inure himself to the power of insult. The essay offers an almost Searlean analysis of Roman abuse, noting that uttering X (*probra, convicia, maledicta,* etc.) will counts as the act Y (*iniuria* or *contumelia*) only in the context Z. What Seneca is at pains to point out is that, in a great many contexts, utterances that are cheeky or even obscene do *not* count as *iniuria* or

mary means of influencing an election or settling a private grudge.[86] A standard way to get a debt repaid was to surround the debtor and heap him with ridicule.[87] Slaves and clients might be expected to shout out abuse against the opponents of their owners or patrons.[88] Cicero describes the hired gangs of Clodius shouting down Pompey with curses (*maledicta*) and abuse (*convicium*); then when it was Clodius's turn to speak, Pompey's men reciprocated, overwhelming him with obscene chants (*versus obscenissimi*).[89] Seneca mentions the challenge of retaining equanimity while being "hooted through the forum by the vile words of a foul-mouthed crowd."[90] Examples of obscene abuse could be added from Egypt[91] and Palestine.[92]

Not only was verbal abuse a potent means toward various social and political ends, but the abuse itself was clearly relished when it was particularly sharp or witty.[93] This was as true for extempore outbursts

---

contumelia (e.g. when spoken by children, by silly slaves, by someone delirious with a high fever, etc.).

[86] On this phenomenon in Roman culture, see Herman Usener, "Italische Volksjustiz," *Rheinisches Musuem* 56 (1901): 1–28. Treating the broader topic of popular songs in Rome, Nicholas Horsfall demonstrates both the abundance and the potency of songs that expressed abuse and protest (*Culture*, 33–42).

[87] Paul Veyne, "The Roman Empire," in *A History of Private Life: From Pagan Rome to Byzantium* (ed. Paul Veyne; trans. Arthur Goldhammer; vol. 1 of *A History of Private Life*, ed. Philippe Ariès and Georges Duby; Cambridge: Harvard University Press, 1987), 169; cf. also Paul Veyne, "La folklore à Rome et les droits de la conscience publique sur la conduite individuelle," *Latomus* 42 (1983): 3–30. Note the reference in Sir 29:28 to the "insults of the money lender."

[88] Cf. Martial, *Epig.* 3.46. Surely when masters had their slaves trained in the art of witty insults, it was not only for domestic entertainment (Seneca, *Const.* 11.3).

[89] *Quint. fratr.* 2.3.2. Cf. Plutarch, *Cic.* 30.7, of Clodius using "violent and insolent men" to meet Cicero in the streets and "jeer him without restraint" (χλευάζοντες ἀκολάστως).

[90] *si obscenorum vocibus improbis per forum agetur* (*Const.* 15.1 [Basore, LCL]).

[91] Cf. Philo, *Flacc.* 34: the crowds who jeer Agrippa I show their "natural ability in things of shame."

[92] Josephus says the crowds shouted the most shameful abuse at Florus when he withdrew money from the temple (λοιδορίας αἰσχίστους εἰς τὸν Φλῶρον ἐκεκράγεσαν [*Bell.* 2.295]; cf. 2.298: οὕτως ἐλοιδόρησαν αἰσχρῶς). Upon the death of Agrippa I, the inhabitants of Caesarea and Sebaste used terms of reproach that Josephus says he cannot mention (βλασφημίας...ἀπρεπεῖς λέγεσθαι [*A.J.* 19.357]). One can gather a good idea of what the content must have been from the fact that the crowds were also doing obscene things to the statues of his daughters.

[93] Cf. Lucian, *Pisc.* 25, for the masses laughing at public reviling. A talent for verbal abuse has been appreciated in a wide variety of cultures. Geoffrey Hughes describes the traditional verbal dueling of northern Europe as the "equivalent of virtuoso sword-play"; although its language could be "grotesque and astonishingly scatological," it exhibited extraordinarily complex plays on words (Hughes, *Swearing*, 47). On the phenomenon

as it was for carefully crafted comedies, satires, and epigrams. Seneca said that some people trained their slaves in the art of insult so as to entertain guests with playful abuse (*Const.* 11.3), and children's naughty speech could also be the source of amusement (Quintilian, *Inst.* 1.2.7). Theocritus (*Id.* 5.41–44, 116–19) and Virgil (*Ecl.* 3) portray rustics heaping foul abuse on each other; and Plautus includes a good many scenes in which hilarious abuse is traded back and forth (e.g. *Pers.* 406–27 and *Pseud.* 357–70).

Once a battle of words was joined, each person would try to say something that others found funny;[94] victory lay in seeing the other person laughed down.[95] Many *chreiai* about philosophers celebrate the way they could degrade their interlocutors with an amusing and biting riposte. So when a reputed pathic told Arcesilaus that nothing seemed larger than anything else, Arcesilaus asked him if ten inches did not seem to be greater than six (D.L. 4.34; cf. Plutarch, *Mor.* 634A). Similarly, Menedemus of Eretria was said to have terrified others by being "cutting and outspoken."[96] The examples given to illustrate these characteristics exhibit a blunt sexual humor, as when he reminded an adulterer that the one who likes "cabbage" might also enjoy the radish,[97] or, when he silenced the boasting Hierocles by asking why Antigonus was screwing him (ἠρώτησε δὲ εἰς τί αὐτὸν Ἀντίγονος περαίνει [D.L. 2.127]). Among the ways the Emperor Gaius taunted his military tribune Cassius Chaerea was by making him use humiliating passwords.[98] Chaerea was angry simply to receive the words, but worse by far was being *laughed* at by others as he used them (Josephus, *A.J.* 19.31).[99]

---

of verbal dueling more broadly, cf. *The Cambridge Encyclopedia of Language* (Cambridge: Cambridge University Press, 1997), 60.

[94] Plato, *Resp.* 395A, C; Clement, *Paed.* 3.75.1.

[95] On this, see Halliwell, "The Uses of Laughter in Greek Culture," who analyzes the role of laughter both on the street and also in the courtroom.

[96] ἦν γὰρ καὶ ἐπικόπτης καὶ παρρησιαστής (D.L. 2.127; cf. 1.129).

[97] D.L. 2.128. On the insertion of a radish into the anus as punishment for an adulterer, cf. C. Carey, "The return of the radish, or, Just when you thought it was safe to go back into the kitchen," *LCM* 18.4 (1993): 53–55; K. Kapparis, "Humiliating the Adulterer: The Law and the Practice in Classical Athens," *Revue internationale des droits de l'antiquité* 43 (1996): 63–77.

[98] θήλεά τε ἐδίδου τὰ ὀνόματα καὶ ταῦτα αἰσχύνης ἀνάπλεα (Josephus, *Antiquities* 19.29–30). Seneca mentions "Venus" and "Priapus" (*Const.* 18.3) as two of the passwords.

[99] Chaerea was so humiliated, in fact, that he helped to plot Gaius's assassination, and, after Gaius gave him one final mocking password, Chaerea returned the insult and struck the emperor with his sword (Josephus, *A.J.* 19.105; Seneca, *Const.* 18.3–4).

Graffiti attest that abuse could be scrawled on the walls just as well as shouted in the streets.[100] Unlike oral abuse, graffiti could be anonymous[101] and therefore immune to repercussions. Terms of abuse familiar from Comedy, such as καταπύγων,[102] occur also in graffiti (e.g. Ἀνθύλη καταπύγαινα [*SEG* 13.32]).[103] Rarer words are also attested. In Aristophanes's *Clouds*, Strepsiades abuses his son with various terms, culminating in λακκόπρωκτος (*Nub.* 1330), derived from λάκκος ("cistern") and πρωκτός ("ass").[104] The same word shows up also on a fifth-century Athenian vase.[105] Likewise, contempt for those who performed oral sex is expressed with the same words in comedy (e.g. λαικάστρια, Aristophanes, *Ach.* 529, 537) and in graffiti (for instance, on a fourth-century spindle-whorl from the Athenian agora [C 34]).[106] In several instances, graffiti exhibit attempted erasure, confirming that such comments as "Theodosia sucks well"[107] were not appreciated.

The range of time and place for abusive obscenities in graffiti is extraordinary. Mabel Lang remarked that "[o]ne of the very earliest uses to which the art of writing was put, along with alphabetic exercises and marks of ownership, was sexual insult and obscenity."[108] The obscene vocabulary appears in archaic inscriptions in a sanctuary of Apollo on

---

[100] And graffiti could hold the same fear for its victims (cf. Plautus, *Merc.* 409).

[101] Although the authors sometimes identified themselves, e.g. *CIL* 4.7497: [*h*]*omullus amat spuncles fel[at] scribit asciola cum gemino.*

[102] Dover catalogues the range of metaphorical uses of the term in Old Comedy ("Some Evaluative Terms," 94).

[103] Marjorie J. Milne and Dietrich von Bothmer discuss seven graffiti that label someone καταπύγων or, as in the case just cited, καταπύγαινα ("ΚΑΤΑΠΥΓΩΝ, ΚΑΤΑΠΥΓΑΙΝΑ," *Hesperia* 22 [1953]: 215–24); cf. also Eduard Fraenkel, "Neues Griechisch in Graffiti," *Glotta* 34 (1954), 42–45. One example from the Athenian agora (C 5) is particularly humorous if, as Mabel Lang proposed, Titas was an "Olympic victor" only in his capacity as καταπύγων (Mabel Lang, *Graffiti and Dipinti* [vol. 21 of *The Athenian Agora*; Princeton: The American School of Classical Studies at Athens, 1976], 12).

[104] A variant of the more common εὐρύπρωκτος, "'wide-arsed', implying frequent subjection to sodomy" (Dover, "Some Evaluative Terms," 94).

[105] C 23: ἔτλη λακκόπρ[ο]κτος ὁ Συδρόμαχος, "Sydromachus of the gaping anus submitted" (trans. Thomas K. Hubbard, *Homosexuality in Greece and Rome: A Sourcebook of Basic Documents* [Berkeley: University of California Press, 2003], 85).

[106] Jocelyn cites other examples ("Greek Indecency," 15).

[107] Θειοδοσία λαικάδε[ι] εὖ (Inv. P. 6153), from a fourth-century Athenian skyphos (discussed by Jocelyn, "A Greek Indecency," 46n30). For further instances of erasure, see Milne and von Bothmer, "ΚΑΤΑΠΥΓΩΝ, ΚΑΤΑΠΥΓΑΙΝΑ," 220–21.

[108] Mabel Lang, *Graffiti in the Athenian Agora* (Excavations of the Athenian Agora Picture Books 14; Princeton: American School of Classical Studies at Athens, 1974), 4.

the island of Thera,[109] a second-century B.C. graffito from Karnak,[110] and, in terrific abundance, on the walls of Pompeii.[111] Walking around Pompeii, an ancient person would have learned that Laenas was a "cunt-licker" (*CIL* 4.5263), as was Martialis (*CIL* 4.1331), and Amandus (*CIL* 4.1255), and Fronto the slave of Planius (*CIL* 4.2257); the list goes on and on.[112] For some ancient person in Pompeii perhaps this was all a bit much: his or her exasperation is expressed in two words: *Sodoma Gomora* (*CIL* 4.4976).

The sexual activities that were written as insults were also written as threats. The obscene vocabulary appears in graffiti threatening the reader,[113] a passerby,[114] someone who might write on the wall,[115] potential thieves,[116] or acquaintances.[117] Again, the words on the walls represent what people threatened out loud. As Jocelyn notes, "Latin

---

[109] *IG* xii.3.536, 537, 538, 539 all use οἴφω (538 names who did it to whom). Against the view that these inscriptions are related to rites of initiation, Bain argues that they are rather "simply boasts and insults of a kind attested in graffiti containing coarse sexual language found elsewhere in the ancient world" ("Six Greek Verbs," 73).

[110] Πτολεμαῖος βινοῦσιν αὐτὸν ἐν τῇ ῥύμῃ / Πτολεμαῖος Ἀβδαίου ἐπυγίζοσαν αὐτὸν ἐν τῆι αὐτῇ ῥύμῃ, ὁ πυγίσας αὐ / τὸν...(Sammelbuch 6840). Bain notes that the nominative of the name is here a sort of rubric ("Six Greek Verbs," 56): Ptolemy is the one whom "they fucked" and "buggered."

[111] E.g. *Martialis fellas Proculum* ("Martial, you suck Proculus" [*CIL* 4.8844]); *Sabina felas, non belle faces* ("Sabina, you suck, and you don't do it well" [*CIL* 4.4185]). For translations and discussions of such graffiti from Pompeii, see Werner A. Krenkel, "Fellatio and Irrumatio," *WZWPUR* 29 (1980): 85–87; and idem, "Tonguing," *WZWPUR* 30 (1981): 53. For a more general survey of Pompeii's graffiti (with tracings and commentary), see Krenkel's *Pompejanishe Inschriften* (Heidelberg: L. Schneider, 1962).

[112] At Pompeii the same comments that are so abundant in Latin also survive in Greek: ΜΟΥΟΑΙΟΣ ΕΝΘΑΔΕ ΒΙΝΕΙ (*CIL* 4.2216); ΣΥΝΕΡΩΣ ΚΑΛΩΣ ΒΙΝΕΙΣ (*CIL* 4.2253).

[113] So a vase-graffito from fifth-century Gela in Sicily: "The writer will bugger the reader" (ὁ γράψας τὸν ἀννέμο<ν>τα πυγίξει [*SEG* 31.824]). There are several graffiti from Pompeii that indicate the reader will be buggered (e.g. *CIL* 4.2360, 4.4008, 4.1798); see the discussion in Bernhard Forssman, "ANNEMOTA in einer dorischen Gefäßinschrift," *Münchener Studien zur Sprachwissenschaft* 34 (1976): 39–46. One scribe even wrote in a margin ψωλοκοπῶ τὸν ἀναγιγνώσκοντα (P. Lond. 3.604 B column 7, cited by Bain, "Six Greek Verbs," 53n21).

[114] A Hellenistic graffito from Thasus: τὸν παράγοντα πεπύγικα. Bain calls the perfect a "performative": "once you have read this, you will have been buggered" ("Six Greek Verbs," 69).

[115] From Ostia: πυγίζω πάντες τού<τους> οἵ ἐπὶ τοῦ τοίχου γράφουσι (Bain, "Six Greek Verbs," 69; cf. the discussion of the graffito by John Rea, "ΕΠΙΤΟΙΧΟΓΡΑΦΟΣ," *ZPE* 36 [1979]: 309–10).

[116] On a first-century A.D. bowl from Nikopilis in Epirus: ὅς ἂν ἄρηι πυγισθήσεται (*SEG* 27.240). Cf. *Priapea* 13, 22, 74.

[117] So the peculiar graffito from Rome (second or third century A.D.), which ends with Eutyches threatening Gamos with anal and oral penetration (πυγιζέσθω ἢ ληικαζέτω).

speakers of all classes frequently threatened to thrust their penises down the throats of those who had offended them and sometimes actually did so."[118] The Greek syntagm λαικάζειν τῷ δεῖνι λέγω was common enough to be quoted in Latin; like *irrumare*,[119] it could be used metaphorically. Neither cold weather nor greed can literally be subjected to *irrumatio*, but the freedman Seleucus could nevertheless tell the cold to "go suck" (*frigori laecasin dico* [Petronius, *Sat.* 42]), and Martial has a penis say the same thing to greed.[120] For those who did not want to use the word itself, λάβδα σοι λέγω was also apparently available as a variant.[121]

II.A. *Laws Against Slander*

Although public abuse was a fact of life, there were laws that limited what one could say. In Athens there was actually a list of prohibited words that could not be uttered abusively,[122] but it was not the *obscene* words that were banned as "unmentionable." Rather, it was forbidden to call someone a "shield thrower"[123] or a "patricide," or to reproach any citizen with working in the market.[124] Several speeches survive that record one side of a δικὴ κακηγορίας, "a private indictment for slander." This was a private crime, meaning that only the injured party

---

See the discussions by Heikki Solin, "Ergüsse eines Lebemannes," *Glotta* 62 (1984): 167–74, and Bain, "Six Greek Verbs," 69n138.

[118] Jocelyn, "A Greek Indecency," 19.

[119] "In some registers of the language the verb *irrumare* was used so much in statements expressive of annoyance as to become practically synonymous with *contemnere*" (Jocelyn, "A Greek Indecency," 19).

[120] Martial, *Epig.* 11.58.11–12: *at tibi nil faciam, sed lota mentula lana* λαικάζειν *cupidae dicet auaritiae* ("To you, however, I shall do nothing, but with washed wool my cock shall tell your eager avarice to go suck" [Shackleton Bailey, LCL]).

[121] Jocelyn, "A Greek Indecency," 17, citing Varro, *Men.* 48.

[122] S. C. Todd, *The Shape of Athenian Law* (Oxford: Clarendon Press, 1993), 381.

[123] Lysias, 10.9. The force of this prohibition seems to have extended to drama. Only one person is named in Old Comedy as having thrown his shield (Cleonymus at *Nub.* 353; noted by Eric Csapo and William J. Slater, *The Context of Ancient Drama* [Ann Arbor: The University of Michigan Press, 1995], 183). On Comedy's relationship to laws against slander, see Halliwell, "Comic Satire and Freedom of Speech in Classical Athens," *Journal of Hellenic Studies* 111 (1991): 48–70.

[124] Demosthenes, *Eub.* 57.30: "Eubulides has acted, not only contrary to your decree, but also contrary to the laws which declare that anyone who makes business in the market a reproach against any male or female citizen shall be liable to the penalties for evil-speaking [τῇ κακηγορίᾳ]" (Murray, LCL). It was also illegal to insult a public official in his court (Lysias 9.6; 9.9).

could press charges.[125] But it was not possible to take someone to court for just any slanderous expression: they had to have used one of a list of prohibited words.

In a speech written by Lysias,[126] the plaintiff claims that Theomnestos called him a patricide (10.1), and adds that he would not have pressed charges for any of the other "forbidden terms" (τι ἄλλο τῶν ἀπορρήτων), since going to law for slander (κακηγορίας δικάζεσθαι) would normally have been beneath him (10.2).[127] Theomnestos does not deny the charge, but appears to seek refuge in the specificity of the law's list of "unmentionables" (ἀπόρρητα), claiming that to say someone "killed his father" does not actually make use of one of the forbidden words.[128] The law did not cover the phrase Theomnestos used, for only ἀνδροφόνος ("homocide") was explicitly forbidden (10.6). The speaker, however, assumes the jurors will be more concerned with meaning (διανοία) than with specific words (ὀνόματα [10.7]), and points out that "killing" someone and being a "murderer" amount to the same thing. What emerges from this and other cases is that the list of ἀπόρρητα implies "a system in which the words themselves are in issue, irrespective of whether they can reasonably be applied to the plaintiff."[129] But, to reiterate, there were no *laws* against obscene abuse.

Roman law had no such list of ἀπόρρητα, but the Twelve Tables forbade exposing someone to *infamia* by raising a demonstration against them in public (*occentare*) or composing a song to that end.[130] After a

---

[125] Isocrates, *Loch.* 2–3, treats *hybris* as a public crime, which means that people other than the one wronged could bring charges: "They thought it so terrible a thing that one citizen strike another that they even established a law that requires any *who say something forbidden* [to another citizen] to pay a fine of five hundred drachmas. And so how great must the retribution be on behalf of those who have actively suffered ill, when you appear so angry on behalf of those who have only verbally heard ill" (Van Hook, LCL).

[126] *Against Theomnestos* (Lysias 10).

[127] On enduring verbal abuse bravely, cf. Antisthenes in D.L. 6.3, 7; Seneca, *Const.* 15.1.

[128] ἐτόλμα λέγειν καὶ πρὸς τὸν διαιτητήν, ὡς οὐκ ἔστι τῶν ἀπορρήτων, ἐάν τις εἴπῃ τὸν πατέρα ἀπεκτονέναι (10.6).

[129] Todd, *Athenian Law*, 260. For more on slander, cf. Stephen Halliwell, "The Uses of Laughter in Greek Culture," and Jeffrey Henderson, "The *Demos* and Comic Competition," in *Nothing to do with Dionysos?* (ed. J. J. Winkler and F. I. Zeitlin; Princeton: Princeton University Press, 1990), 300.

[130] Cicero, *Rep.* 4.10.12: *si quis occentavisset sive carmen condidisset quod infamiam faceret flagitiumve alteri*. Horace proposes that the law came about to cope with the taunts of the Fescennina: "Through this custom came into use the Fescennine licence, which in alternate verse poured forth rustic taunts; and the freedom, welcomed each returning year, was innocently gay, till jest, now growing cruel, turned to open frenzy, and stalked

senatusconsultum, perhaps dating from the reign of Augustus,[131] defamation was treated as a form of *iniuria*,[132] and hence could be "proceeded against either for civil damages or before the jury courts."[133] According to the jurists, verbal abuse was not to violate good mores;[134] and according to Paulus, "Abuse is considered to be contrary to good mores if somebody should have attacked with an obscene word or with the lower part of his body bare."[135] Someone who used base language (*qui turpibus verbis utitur*) with a woman was liable for insult (*Digest*, 47.10.15.21).

The details of Roman law make it clear that what verbal offenses "injured" was a person's reputation. Hence public abuse was more serious than private. When a wife or an engaged woman was insulted, the husband or fiancé could sue, for it was *his* honor that suffered (*Digest*, 47.10.11.7; 47.10.15.24); and it was more difficult for freedmen[136] or slaves[137] to sue for abusive language.[138]

---

amid the homes of honest folk, fearless in its threatening. Stung to the quick were they who were bitten by a tooth that drew blood; even those untouched felt concern for the common cause, and at last a law was carried with a penalty, forbidding the portrayal of any in abusive strain. Men changed their tune, and terror of the cudgel led them back to goodly and gracious forms of speech" (*Ep.* 2.1.152–54 [Fairclough, LCL]). On the sense of *occentare*, see the detailed argument of Eduard Fraenkel, "Anzeige von Beckmann, *Zauberei und Recht in Roms Frühzeit*," *Gnomon* 1 (1925): 185–200.

[131] According to Suetonius, Augustus proposed that anyone who gave out under a false name books or songs indended to defame (*ad infamiam*) should be prosecuted (*Aug.* 55).

[132] On *iniuria* generally, see Max Kaser, *Das römische Privatrecht* (Munich: C. H. Beck, 1955), 3.520–22; on oral and writen *iniuria*, see Theodor Mommsen, *Römisches Strafrecht* (Berlin: Akademie-Verlag, 1899), 794–95.

[133] J. A. Crook, *Law and Life of Rome* (London: Thames and Hudson, 1967), 252. Abusing a senator might be a different matter. Annia Rufilla was tried before the Senate in A.D. 21 for her abuse of a senator (Tacitus, *Ann.* 3.36), but "a non-senator who had been subjected to like abuse would have had to proceed against his tormentor by the cumbrous processes of the civil law," that is, in a suit for *iniuria* (Peter Garnsey, *Social Status and Legal Privilege in the Roman Empire* [Oxford: Clarendon, 1970], 32). On Vespasian's *decretum* permitting citizens to return a senator's abuse (Suetonius, *Vesp.* 9.2), cf. Garnsey, *Social Status*, 200n1.

[134] Veyne, "Roman Empire," 169.

[135] *convicium contra bonos mores fieri videtur, si obscaeno nomine aut inferiore parte corporis nudatus aliquis insectatus sit* (Paulus, *Sententiae*, 5.4.21); cf. Veyne, "Folklore," 21.

[136] Praetors need not hear complaints from freedmen that their masters abused them verbally (*Digest*, 47.10.15.2).

[137] If a slave "be put to shame by some act or lampoon," the praetor's investigation "should take into account the standing of the slave" (*Digest*, 47.10.15.44).

[138] On social status and *iniuria*, see Garnsey, *Social Status*, 199–203.

III. Religious Rites

When Plato said he would prohibit uttering indecent things in holy places, he had specific contemporary practices in view. The religious rites that incorporated foul language were numerous, and were well enough established that Aristotle, although he wanted to ban foul language outright, felt he must make an exception in their case:

> And since we banish saying any such thing, we must clearly also ban seeing indecent paintings and stories. Let the rulers take care that there be neither statue nor painting that depicts such activities, except in the case of those gods to whom the law[139] grants even scoffing [τὸν τωθασμόν].[140] But for these cases, the law grants that men of adequate age may worship the gods on behalf of themselves and the children and women. (*Pol.* 1336b12–19)

One could wish that Aristotle had said more about the roles of women. On the one hand, his sense that women should not use or hear foul language was rather widespread in antiquity (as it has been ever since). But if Aristotle really intended to prohibit women from worshipping in rites involving obscene language, it is remarkable that he should have mentioned it so briefly, for the oldest and most famous of such rites, the Thesmophoria, were conducted by women alone. Women's foul language at the Thesmophoria was, in fact, proverbial. When Cleomedes wanted to deride Epicurus's philosophical argot,[141] he noted a few objectionable words[142] and claimed that they "resemble what is said by the women celebrating the Thesmophoria at Demeter's festivals" (*De motu circulari corporum caelestium* 2.91).

Considering evidence for and comments about foul language in various ancient cults (ritual aischrology) offers a glimpse into how foul

---

[139] W. L. Newman suggests this is "unwritten law" (*The Politics of Aristotle* [4 vols.; Oxford: Clarendon, 1887–1902], 3:491–92). Pausanias, describing the obscenity at the sanctuary of Mysian Demeter, says that the women do ὁπόσα νόμος ἐστὶν αὐταῖς, "all that is their law/custom" (*Descr.* 7.27.10).

[140] On the term τωθασμός, Hanns Fluck notes that "ohne Zusammenhang mit dem Kultischen verwendet, nur die Bedeutung von Scherz, Spott, Hohn hat, ohne jede Beimischung von Obszönem, was doch in dem von Aristoteles angeführten Ritus zweifellos vorhanden ist" (*Skurrile Riten in griechischen Kulten* [Endingen: Emil Wild, 1931], 12).

[141] On Epicurus's language, cf. n. 311 below.

[142] Including ληκήματα, which may mean "bouts of intercourse" or "cries of lovemaking" (Bain, "Six Greek Verbs," 70).

language was used and perceived.[143] For instance, there was a palpable sense of the abnormality of using such language; some explanation for it was required. The rites and their interpretations reveal that foul language could be potent, whether for promoting fecundity or warding off evil spirits or the evil eye. And ancient descriptions of the foul language in religious rites confirm that obscenities were frequently a source of laughter and fun.

The connection of foul language and humor is particularly prominent when ancient authors claim that aischrology was amusing and cheering for the gods. Paradigmatic is the worship of Demeter. Diodorus Siculus says of Sicily's ten-day autumnal festival for Demeter, "It is their custom during these days to indulge in coarse language [αἰσχρολογεῖν] as they associate one with another, the reason being that by such obscenity [αἰσχρολογία] the goddess, grieved though she was at the Rape of Core, burst into laughter."[144] The earliest reference to this myth occurs in the *Homeric Hymn to Demeter*, where it was the maid Iambe whose scurrilous comments pleased the goddess Demeter, who was then grieving for her daughter:

> There she [Demeter] sat, holding her veil before her face, and for a long time she remained there on the seat in silent sorrow. She greeted no one with word or movement, but sat there unsmiling, tasting neither food nor drink, pining for her deep-girt daughter, until at last dutiful Iambe with ribaldry and many a jest [χλεύηις... πολλὰ παρασκώπτουσα] diverted the holy lady so that she smiled and laughed and became benevolent. (*Hom. Hymn to Demeter* 197–204 [West, LCL])

The *Library* of Apollodorus gives a similar explanation for the jests at the Thesmophoria, the autumnal festival for Demeter celebrated by Greek women. Demeter, he says, angry and saddened over the abduction of her daughter, left heaven and came to Eleusis in the likeness of a woman.

---

[143] Furthermore, it has been suggested that Ephesians's prohibitions of crude language actually had in view the aischrology of the festivals of Demeter, a suggestion that can only be evaluated once we have some sense for the rites in question. This proposal (Larry J. Kreitzer, "'Crude Language' and 'Shameful Things Done in Secret' [Ephesians 5.4, 12]: Allusions to the Cult of Demeter/Cybele in Hierapolis?" *JSNT* 71 [1998]: 51–77) will be addressed specifically in chapter 4.

[144] ἔθος δ'ἐστὶν αὐτοῖς ἐν ταύταις ταῖς ἡμέραις αἰσχρολογεῖν κατὰ τὰς πρὸς ἀλλήλους ὁμιλίας διὰ τὸ τὴν θεὸν ἐπὶ τῇ τῆς Κόρης ἁρπαγῇ λυπουμένην γελάσαι διὰ τὴν αἰσχρολογίαν (*Bibl.* 5.4.7 [Oldfather, LCL]).

Some women were in the house, and when they bade her sit down beside them, a certain old crone, Iambe, joked (σκώψασα) the goddess and made her smile. For that reason they say that the women break jests (σκώπτειν) at the Thesmophoria. (Apollodorus, *Bibl.* 1.5.1 [Frazer, LCL])

In the "Orphic" versions of this myth,[145] Iambe is replaced by Baubo, who relieves Demeter's mourning by uncovering her genitals,[146] an act analagous to speaking obscenities in that it exposes what should be hidden.[147]

Various rites involving ritual aischrology were explained by etiologies similar to that of Demeter and Iambe. For instance, the *maledicta* in the rites of Heracles at Lindus were thought to commemorate the abusive remarks that once made Heracles laugh.[148] Similarly, in explaining

---

[145] As related by Clement, *Protr.* 20.1–21.2; Eusebius, *Praep. ev.* 2.3.31–35; and Arnobius, *Adv. Nat.* 5.25–26. The references to Baubo are collected and thoughtfully analyzed by Maurice Olender, "Aspects of Baubo: Ancient Texts and Contexts," in *Before Sexuality: The Construction of Erotic Experience in the Ancient Greek World* (ed. David M. Halperin, John J. Winkler, and Froma I. Zeitlin; Princeton: Princeton University Press, 1990), 83–113. Cf. also N. J. Richardson, *The Homeric Hymn to Demeter* (Oxford: Clarendon, 1974), 215–16.

[146] Clement, *Protr.* 20.3: ἀναστέλλεται τὰ αἰδοῖα καὶ ἐπιδεικνύει τῇ θεῷ.

[147] At times nakedness and foul language are combined. In one account, Iambe herself is said to make Demeter laugh both by joking *and* gesture (Olender, "Aspects of Baubo," 89). Language and exposure are also combined in the Egyptian worship of Artemis. Herodotus says that, sailing toward Bubastis, women shouted obscenities and exposed themselves (*Hist.* 2.59–60; cf. also *Hist.* 5.82–83).

[148] So Lactantius says that the rites are celebrated "not with words of good omen [*non* εὐφημίᾳ] (as the Greeks term it), but with revilings and cursing [*sed maledictis et execratione*]. And they consider it a violation of the sacred rites, if at any time during the celebration of the solemnities a good word shall have escaped from any one even inadvertently. And this is the reason assigned for this practice, if indeed there can be any reason in things utterly senseless. When Hercules had arrived at the place, and was suffering hunger, he saw a ploughman at work, and began to ask him to sell one of his oxen. But the ploughman replied that this was impossible, because his hope of cultivating the land depended altogether upon those two bullocks. Hercules, with his usual violence, because he was not able to receive one of them, killed both. But the unhappy man, when he saw that his oxen were slain, avenged the injury with revilings,—a circumstance which afforded gratification to the man of elegance and refinement. For while he prepares a feast for his companions, and while he devours the oxen of another man, he receives with ridicule and loud laughter the bitter reproaches with which the other assails him. But when it had been determined that divine honours should be paid to Hercules in admiration of his excellence, an altar was erected in his honour by the citizens, which he named, from the circumstance, the yoke of oxen; and at this altar two yoked oxen were sacrificed, like those which he had taken from the ploughman. And he appointed the same man to be his priest, and directed him always to use the same revilings in offering sacrifice, because he said that he had never feasted more pleasantly. Now these things are not sacred, but sacrilegious, in

the obscene songs at the rowdy New Year's festival of Anna Perenna,[149] Ovid describes how Anna tricked Mars when Mars wanted her to arrange a tryst for him with Minerva. Instead of complying with Mars's wishes, Anna pretended to be Minerva; when Mars realized this, he was humiliated. "The new goddess laughed at dear Minerva's lover. Never did anything please Venus more than that. So old jokes and obscene sayings are sung [*ioci veteres obscenaque dicta canuntur*], and people love to remember how Anna choused the great god."[150] Here it appears that Ovid is straining to apply an etiology akin to the myth of Demeter and Iambe to the aischrology of Anna Perenna. The very awkwardness of his explanation—Anna tricked Mars; this pleased Venus; *therefore* people sing obscene songs!—attests to the prominence of the idea that ritual aischrology must somehow delight the gods. According to Plutarch, Xenocrates did not think too highly of such festivals; but he nevertheless imagined that "obdurate and morose natures"—if not proper gods and daimons—were *enjoying* the rites:

> Such festivals as have associated with them either beatings or lamentations or fastings or scurrilous language or obscene speech [αἰσχρολογίαν][151] have no relation to the honours paid to the gods or to worthy daimons, but he [Xenocrates] believes that there exist in the space about us certain great and powerful natures, obdurate, however, and morose, *which take pleasure* in such things as these, and, if they succeed in obtaining them, resort to nothing worse. (*Mor.* 361B [Babbit, LCL, adjusted])

---

which that is said to be enjoined, which, if it is done in other things, is punished with the greatest severity" (*Div. Inst.* 1.21 [*ANF* 7:36]). For a similar explanation of rites for Heracles, see Conon, Tale 11 (Malcolm Kenneth Brown, *The Narratives of Konon* [Munich: K. G. Saur, 2002], 108–111).

[149] Ovid, *Fast.* 3.675–76: "Now it remains for me to tell why girls chant obscene songs [*cantent obscena*]; for they assemble and sing certain scurrilous verses [*certaque probra canunt*]" (Frazer, LCL). Ovid offers the fullest ancient description of the festival (*Fast.* 3.523–696); it is also mentioned by Macrobius, *Saturnalia*, 1.12.6; and there is a puzzling reference to "virginal blood" in connection to the festival in Martial, *Epig.* 4.64.16–17. For analysis of the limited evidence, see Kurt Latte, *Römische Religionsgeschichte* (Beck: Munich, 1967), 137–38; Howard Hayes Scullard, *Festivals and Ceremonies of the Roman Republic* (London: Thames and Hudson, 1981), 90. Carole Newlands's insightful analysis of Ovid's rhetoric concerning the festival also sheds much light on the festival itself ("Transgressive Acts: Ovid's Treatment of the Ides of March," *Classical Philology* 91 [1996]: 320–38).

[150] Ovid, *Fast.* 3.693–96 (Frazer, LCL, adjusted).

[151] The comments nicely fit the Thesmophoria, which included "beatings" (women hit each other with a scourge made of bark), lamentations and fastings (on the second day they fasted and sat on the ground in lamentation for Kore), and, of course, foul language.

Augustine also reveals this assumption that *someone* must be enjoying such language: "Who could fail to realize what kind of spirits they are which could *enjoy* such obscenities?" (*Civ.* 2.4).[152]

But not all the explanations for the aischrology in Demetrian worship focus on delighting the goddess. A scholion to Lucian's *Dialogue of the Courtesans* describes the Haloa[153] as "a feast in Athens which included mysteries of Demeter and Kore and Dionysus," which was held at "the cutting of the vine and the tasting of the wine already set aside." At this festival, "shameful male forms" were presented as a sign of human procreation "because Dionysus gave wine as a stimulating drug to promote sexual intercourse." The scholiast gives an explanation for the handling of the ἄρρητα ("unmentionables"), and he continues:

> On this day there is also a women's ceremony conducted at Eleusis, at which much joking and scoffing takes place [παιδιαὶ λέγονται πολλαὶ καὶ σκώμματα]. Women process there alone and are at liberty to say whatever they want to: and in fact they say the most shameful things to each other [τὰ αἴσχιστα ἀλλήλαις λέγουσι]. The priestesses covertly sidle up to the women and whisper into their ear—as if it were a secret—recommendations for adultery. All the women utter shameful and irreverent things [αἰσχρὰ καὶ ἄσεμνα] to each other. They carry indecent images of male and female genitals. Wine is provided in abundance and the tables are loaded with all the foods of the earth and sea.... The archons set up the tables and leave them inside for the women while they themsleves depart and wait outside, showing to all inhabitants that the types of domestic nourishment were discovered by them [the Eleusinians] and were shared by them with all humanity. On the tables there are also genitals of both sexes made of dough. It is called the Haloa because of Dionysus' fruit, since *aloai* are vine shoots. (Schol. Luc. *Dial. Mer.* 7.4)[154]

In other locations, the worship of Demeter involved not whispered indecencies among women, but jeering *between* the sexes. Pausanias describes a seven-day festival in the sanctuary of the Mysian Demeter:

> On the third day of the festival the men withdraw from the sanctuary, and the women are left to perform on that night the ritual that custom

---

[152] Translated by Henry Bettenson, *Augustine: The City of God* (London: Penguin Books, 1972).

[153] On the Haloa, see Ludwig Deubner, *Attische Feste* (Berlin: Heinrich Keller, 1932), 60–67; H. W. Parke, *Festivals of the Athenians* (Ithaca: Cornell University Press, 1977), 98–100; Matthew Dillon, *Girls and Women in Classical Greek Religion* (London: Routledge, 2002), 120–24.

[154] Trans. J. J. Winkler, *The Constraints of Desire: The Anthropology of Sex and Gender in Ancient Greece* (New York: Routledge, 1990), 195.

demands. Not only men are excluded, but even male dogs. On the following day the men come to the sanctuary, and the men and the women laugh and jeer at one another in turn [γέλωτί τε ἐς ἀλλήλους χρῶνται καὶ σκώμμασιν]. (*Descr.* 7.27.9–10 [Jones, LCL])

Ritual abuse was a part of other festivals for Demeter, such as the Stenia, held two days before the Thesmophoria;[155] and initiates into the Eleusinian mysteries were mocked as they crossed the bridge over the Cephisus.[156] (Abuse was prominent in the rites of other gods as well.)[157]

The role of ritual aischrology has been interpreted in a variety of ways. Some scholars have claimed that the obscene words served to engender fertility through a sort of homeopathic magic; others have proposed an apotropaic function, so that the words were meant to turn away malevolent forces. Still others have emphasized that transgressing normal linguistic (and other) rules was a way to relieve social tensions. Considering the Thesmophoria in more detail will make it clear why such varied interpretations have been possible.

The Thesmophoria[158] was the most widely celebrated cultic event in honor of Demeter, a three-day festival held from the eleventh to

---

[155] On the abusive speech at the Stenia, see Fluck, *Skurrile Riten*, 15–17; on the festival more generally, cf. Deubner, *Attische Feste*, 52–53; Parke, *Festivals*, 88.

[156] For the evidence (which is meager), see Richardson, *Homeric Hymn*, 214, who cites Strabo, *Geogr.* 9.1.24; Hesechius s.v. γεφυρίς (γ469–70 Latte); Aristophanes, *Vesp.* 1362–3: ἵν' αὐτὸν τωθάσω νεανικῶς, οἵοις ποθ' οὗτος ἐμὲ πρὸ τῶν μυστηρίων ("so I can play teenage tricks on him, the same tricks he played on me when I stood for initiation" [Henderson, LCL]). Richardson calls the *Wasps*'s τωθάζειν "a general reference to αἰσχρολογία as a preliminary to the Mysteries" (*Homeric Hymn*, 215). Cf. also Parke, *Festivals*, 66.

[157] Apollonius of Rhodes reports that women mocked men in the worship of Apollo Aigletes on the Island of Anaphe. "When Medea's Phaeacian handmaids saw them [Jason and his men] pouring water for libations on the burning brands, they could no longer restrain laughter within their bosoms.... And the heroes delighted in the jests and attacked them with shameful words [αἰσχροῖς ἥρωες ἐπεστοβέεσκον ἔπεσσιν]; and merry railing and contention flung to and fro were kindled among them. And from that sport of the heroes such scoffs do the women fling at the men in that island whenever they propitiate with sacrifices Apollo the gleaming god, the warder of Anaphe" (*Argonautica* 4.1721–30 [Seaton, LCL, adjusted]). On this cult, see Martin P. Nilsson, *Griechische Feste von religiöser Bedeutung mit Ausschluß der Attischen* (Leipzig: Teubner, 1906), 176. In the *Narratives* of Conon one finds a similar etiology for the same cult (Tale 49; Brown, *Konon*, 338–343).

[158] For discussions of the Thesmophoria, see Dillon, *Girls and Women*, 110–20; Nilsson, *Griechische Feste*, 313–25; Parke, *Festivals*, 82–88; Walter Burkert, *Greek Religion* (trans. John Raffan; Cambridge: Harvard University Press, 1985), 242–46; Marcel Detienne, *The Gardens of Adonis: Spices in Greek Mythology* (trans. Janet Lloyd; Sussex: The Harvester Press, 1977), 72–98; Marcel Detienne, "The Violence of Well-Born Ladies: Women in the Thesmophoria," in Marcel Detienne and J.-P. Vernant, eds., *The Cuisine of Sacrifice*

the thirteenth of Pyanopsion, just before the autumn sowing. Men and unmarried women were excluded (as were the wives of foreigners); married women were *required* to attend, and their husbands were obligated to pay for their expenses.[159] The first day of the festival was called the "Road up," presumably for a procession up to the Thesmophorion, which in Athens is believed to have been near the Pnyx, the men's place of assembly.[160] The second day was called the "Fast," during which women sat on the ground and fasted in sympathy with Demeter, who in her sorrow over Persephone refused a chair at Eleusis. The third day was called *Kalligeneia*, day of "Fair Offspring," indicative of the goal of the festival.

At a festival prior to the Thesmophoria (possibly the Skira, in the summer)[161] women threw sacrificed piglets and dough models of snakes and of male genitals into caverns in the ground. At the Thesmophoria, women serving as "bailers," having purified themselves with three days of sexual abstinence, hauled up the contents from these pits, and set them on altars. This material was then to be scattered in the fields to promote the fertility of the crops, an activity Burkert calls "the clearest example in Greek religion of agrarian magic."[162] It is not known for certain when in the course of these three days the proverbial foul language was used,[163] which makes it that much more difficult to analyze its role.

In James Frazer's view, the obscene language was meant to bring fecundity to the women and to the fields by a sort of "homeopathic magic":

> We may suppose that these indecencies [from the Haloa], like certain obscenities which seem to have formed a part of the Great Mysteries at Eleusis, were no mere wanton outbursts of licentious passion, but were

among the Greeks (Chicago: University of Chicago Press, 1989): 129–47; H. S. Versnel, *Inconsistencies in Greek and Roman Religion*, vol. 2: *Transition and Reversal in Myth and Ritual* (Leiden: Brill, 1993), 228–88; Froma I. Zeitlin, "Cultic Models of the Female: Rites of Dionysus and Demeter," *Arethusa* 15 (1982): 129–57; Winkler, *Constraints*, 188–209.

[159] Zeitlin, "Models of the Female," 132.

[160] Parke, *Festivals*, 85; Dillon offers another interpretation of the name "Ascent," and a discussion of the possible location (*Girls and Women*, 113, 118–20).

[161] So Deubner, *Attische Feste*, 40–44; Versnel, *Inconsistencies*, 2:235; for an alternative view, see Winkler, *Constraints*, 196.

[162] Burkert, *Greek Religion*, 244.

[163] Dillon suggests the third as the most likely, when the "bawdiness and lewdness" would be connected with women's fertility on the day of "beautiful birth" (*Girls and Women*, 114); Zeitlin suggests the second ("Cultic Models," 138–39).

deliberately practised as rites calculated to promote the fertility of the ground by means of homeopathic or imitative magic. A like association of what we might call indecency with rites intended to promote the growth of the crops meets us in the Thesmophoria, a festival of Demeter celebrated by women alone, at which the character of the goddess as a source of fertility comes out clearly in the custom of mixing the remains.[164]

In a particularly rich essay, Froma I. Zeitlen has argued that by exposing what should be hidden and by provoking laughter the obscenities of the Thesmophoria had the function of "opening and release." In connection with the fertility theme of the festival, this "opening" and emptying signified an "intensification, as it were, of the receptacle, the reservoir of fertility that is woman." These same words or gestures (*anasyrma*) that would in other contexts be apotropaic, were here prostropaic, "directed back to the source, the female herself."[165]

Walter Burkert, on the other hand, interprets the Thesmophoria as a festival of "release,"[166] noting that the evidence "always points most conspicuously to the absurdity and buffoonery of the whole affair." "There is," Burkert claims, "a conscious descent to the lower classes and the lower parts of the anatomy, mirrored in the talk of mythical maids. Just as pomp and ceremony contrasts with everyday life, so does extreme lack of ceremony, absurdity, and obscenity; a redoubled tension arises between the two extremes, adding further dimensions to the festival."[167] In place of holy silence there is cursing, and the antagonism between the sexes "finds release in lampoonery."[168]

---

[164] James George Frazer, *The Golden Bough* (3d ed.; repr.; London: Macmillan, 1966), 5:1:62–63, citing the Scholiast on Lucian *Dial. meretr.* 7.4, quoted above. Frazer cited various examples of rites from around the world in which violating normal linguistic decorum serves to engender fertility (*Golden Bough*, 1:1:267–68). In a Ba-Thonga ritual meant to deal with droughts, women had special roles and men were excluded; if a man came, the women could beat him and put riddles to the man "which he would have to answer in the most filthy language borrowed from the circumcision ceremonies; for obscene words, which are usually forbidden, are customary and legitimate on these occasions" (ibid., 2:154; cf. ibid., 8:280). Cf. also E. E. Evans-Pritchard, "Some Collective Expressions of Obscenity in Africa," *Journal of the Royal Anthropological Institute of Great Britain and Ireland* 59 (1929): 311–31.

[165] "Cultic Models," 144–45.

[166] Burkert, *Greek Religion*, 104–5.

[167] Burkert, *Greek Religion*, 105.

[168] This is the "purgative" function Thalien M. de Wit-Tak assigns to the obscenities in the struggle between male and female choruses in *Lysistrata*, e.g. 362, 402, 800, 824 ("The Function of Obscenity in Aristophanes' *Thesmophoriazusae* and *Ecclesiazusae*," *Mnemosyne* 21 [1968]: 360). Richardson combines interpretations, claiming that the initiates at Eleusis were both "participating in rituals of purification and the stimulation of

Versnel notes that the Thesmophoria was above all a festival of reversal: women were autonomous, free of male supervision, able to stay away from their house all night performing secret rituals (including sacrifice),[169] perhaps even able to drink wine.[170] All of these elements constitute reversals of normal life. Furthermore, there are several features of the festival that seem to reflect life as it was before civilization and law:[171] meat was not cooked but dried in the sun.[172] The women slept in temporary huts[173] on woven mats, an imitation of primeval life.[174] Prisoners were released and the courts and councils were suspended, actions which suggest a period of *anomia*.[175] The women's foul language could be seen as yet another of the ritual activities that signaled, in Zeitlin's words, "a regressive state of affairs which prededed the establishment of social rules."[176] This line of interpretation is especially intriguing when one notes that the first Stoics, who sought to expose the irrationality of various civilized customs, also advocated foul language.

Certainly the function of foul language was not the same in every cult. In some cults the pleasure of a festive release from normal social restraints seems to have been more prominent; in others there was more emphasis on the prostropaic (or, as we will see, the apotropaic) effects of obscene words. According to the scholiast's description of the Haloa, women were speaking to women about sex at a harvest festival that involved the use of dough models of the sexual organs. This would seem quite amenable to a prostropaic interpretation, with the "shame-

---

fertility" and also "sharing in the sorrow of Demeter, and its relief by laughter, song, and dance" (*Homeric Hymn*, 217). For the carnivalesque nature of the Thesmphoria, see Wolfgang Rösler, "Über Aischrologie im archaischen und klassischen Griechenland," in *Karnevaleske Phänomene in antiken und nachantiken Kulturen und Literaturen* (ed. Siegmar Döpp; Trier: Wissenschaftlicher Verlag, 1993): 75–97.

[169] Detienne ("Violence of Wellborn Ladies") emphasizes both the existence of and the importance of sacrifice in these rites.

[170] Versnel, *Inconsistencies*, 2:240–41.

[171] Diodorus Siculus (*Bibl.* 5.4.7) says that the participants in the festival for Demeter "imitate the ancient manner of life" (μιμούμενοι τὸν ἀρχαῖον βίον).

[172] Plutarch, *Mor.* 298B; Nilsson, *Griechische Feste*, 319.

[173] Nilsson, *Griechische Feste*, 319n1.

[174] Note that huts were also used in the festival of Anna Perenna (Ovid, *Fast.*, 3.525–33). W. Warde Fowler, in an excursus on the use of huts, also argues that they represent a reminiscence of an earlier form of life (*The Religious Experience of the Roman People* [London: MacMillan, 1911], 473–77); cf. J. N. Bremmer and N. M. Horsfall, *Roman Myth and Mythography* (Bulletin for the Institute of Classical Studies; Supplement 52 [1987]): 80.

[175] Versnel, *Inconsistencies*, 2:243.

[176] Zeitlin, "Cultic Models," 142–43.

less" sexual suggestions, like the models of the genitalia, representing, and thereby promoting, fertility. The combination of nudity, sex, and obscenity in the Roman worship of Flora, goddess of flowers and vegetation, points in the same direction.[177]

In the case of other festivals, ancient descriptions support Burkert's claim that foul language fostered a playful release.[178] For instance, Horace connects the origin of ribald Fescinnine taunts to the harvest festivals with their "relaxing" of bodies and minds.[179] Ovid's description of the festival of Anna Perenna makes it clear that, whatever its origins, by his time it was quite a lot of fun—a day for people to drink too much and to sing the lubricious songs they had learned in the theater.[180] Iamblichus, adopting a more clinical tone, also suggests that obscenities in the sacred rites could be "cathartic," modifying the passions by allowing them to be exercised "in brief bursts and within reasonable limits." Thus, he says, "by viewing and listening to obscenities [θεάμασί τισι καὶ ἀκούσμασι τῶν αἰσχρῶν] we are freed from the harm that would befall us if we practised them."[181] This makes participating in the raucous festivals sound about as much fun as eating one's daily fiber; but it is noteworthy that Iamblichus, searching for something salubrious in the rites, landed on the idea that they provided a necessary release.[182]

---

[177] On the Floralia, Lactantius says: "besides licentiousness of words, in which every obscenity is poured forth [verborum licentiam, quibus obscenitas omnis effunditur], women are also stripped of their garments at the demand of the people"; he complains that the mimes were performed all too realistically (Inst. 1.20.10 [ANF 7.32]). Cf. the comments of Martial, Proem to Book 1 and Tertullian, Spect. 17.2–3. Further aspects of the worship that point to fertility include the release of hares and goats, both thought to be fertile (Scullard, Festivals and Ceremonies, 111).

[178] It should not be forgotten that rites that may have begun for one reason may well have been enjoyed later for another. Versnel notes that in contemporary Greek women's festivals, fertility has ceased to be a central theme, yet indecent behavior (involving male sexual organs) and foul language are still prominent (Versnel, Inconsistencies, 2:244).

[179] Ep. 2.1.139–48.

[180] Scullard, Festivals and Ceremonies, 90.

[181] De Mysteriis 1.11 (trans. Emma C. Clarke, John M. Dillon, and Jackson P. Hershbell, Iamblichus: De mysteriis [WGRW 4; Leiden: Brill, 2004]): 49–51).

[182] Iamblichus is responding to Porphyry's now lost Letter to Anebo. Porphyry's objections to such rites can be found in his Abstinence from Killing Animals, where he claims that the passions are aroused to such a degree through "obscene language and abuse [αἰσχρορρημοσύνης τε καὶ λοιδορίας]" that people lose their reason and act mad (Abstin. 1.33–34).

Other scholars who have understood ritual aischrology's chief function as promoting fertility have argued that the obscenities worked apotropaicly rather than prostropaically. H. Fluck and others have claimed that foul language brought fecundity by warding off malevolent forces.[183] Again, such an interpretation can find support in some, if not all, ancient descriptions. Plutarch thought foul language served to "*turn away* bad daimons" (δαιμόνων δὲ φαύλων ἀποτροπῆς ἕνεκα [*Mor.* 417C]). He quoted Xenocrates to the same effect: if the gloomy "natures" were allowed to enjoy such obscenities, they would "resort to nothing worse" (*Mor.* 361B). Augustine says that in the town of Lavinium foul language was used, in conjunction with a procession of a phallic statue, to protect the crops from spells: "A whole month was consecrated to Liber, during which time everyone used the most indecent language [*omnes verbis flagitiosissimis uterentur*].... This was how Liber had to be *placated* to ensure successful germination of seeds; this was how evil spells had to be *averted* from the fields [*sic videlicet Liber deus placandus fuerat pro eventibus seminum, sic ab agris fascinatio repellenda*]" (*Civ.* 7.21 [Bettenson]).

This popular belief that obscene language might ward off curses can be seen in an etymology for the name of the obscene songs sung at weddings (*Fescinnine verses*) that appeals to the songs' ability to ward off a spell (*fascinum*).[184]

Such an apotropaic use of foul language in agriculture is widely attested. Foul language was used in the plowing of the Rarian meadow at Eleusis.[185] Pliny says that basil is to be planted "with curses and insults" (*cum maledictis ac probris*) so that it will come up more abun-

---

[183] H. Fluck, *Skurrile Riten*, 33: "Wie ich gezeigt zu haben glaube, ist der τωθασμός, der die Aischrologie enthält, durchaus etwas Apotropäisches, das sich negativ als 'Böses vertreibent' auswirkt und dadurch zugleich positiv als 'dem Segen freie Bahn schaffend', welch letzteres jene Fruchtbarkeits- und Frauenfeste zum eigentlichen Inhalt haben, von denen wir oben gesprochen." Siems reached similar conclusions ("Aischrologia," 16), and apotropaic explanations are frequently made in passing (e.g. Lesky, *Geschichte der Griechischen Literatur*, 135, 272; Latte, *Römische Religionsgeschichte*, 138 (on Anna Perenna). Ludwig Deubner explicitly rejected Fluck's suggestion in an afterword to *Attische Feste*, but without much elaboration.

[184] *Fescennini versus qui canebantur in nuptiis, ex urbe Fescennina dicuntur allati, sive ideo dicti, quia fascinum putabantur arcere* (Festus *apud* Paul p. 76, cited from Adams, *Latin Sexual Vocabulary*, 4; see also ibid., 7). On the nature of the Fescinnine verses, cf. Horace, *Ep.* 2.1.139–48; cf. also George E. Duckworth, *The Nature of Roman Comedy: A Study in Popular Entertainment* (Princeton: Princeton University Press, 1952), 7–8.

[185] Brown, *Konon*, 111. For further references to foul language with planting seeds, see Henderson, *Maculate Muse*, 14.

antly.[186] Pliny adds that people sowing cumin "pray for it *not* to come up," which is perhaps suggestive as to how the language was imagined to operate. J. H. Mozley says, "The idea is that the gods are hostile on principle, and so you must ask the opposite of what you want. The gods…must be treated as the peasant treats his pig when he pulls it backwards to get it into the stye." [187]

There were other festive occasions during which foul speech seems to have functioned apotropaicly. Crass taunting was standard in Roman military triumphs,[188] a moment when the victors would have been especially vulnerable to the evil eye. (There was also a phallus under the victorious cart to protect against "envy.")[189] Martial says, "The garlanded soldiery will sport in festive insults as they accompany the laurel-bearing horses. Even for you, Caesar, it is lawful to hear jests and lighter verses, if the triumph itself loves jollity."[190] In Caesar's Gallic triumph, his soldiers shouted, "Men of Rome, protect your wives; we are bringing in the bald adulterer. You fucked away [*effutuisti*] in Gaul the gold you borrowed here in Rome."[191]

The belief that foul language (and the phallus) might protect some person or thing can be seen not only in collective activities, such as the triumphs or the rites from Lavinium, but also in individual acts. Jocelyn adduces examples from Corinth, England, Italy, and upper Moesia of the depiction of a phallus accompanied by "some kind of curse, threat or humiliating order,"[192] frequently directed against envy.[193] For instance, on a sixth-century B.C. Corinthian votive plaque a kiln is depicted, above which there is a figure with swollen penis and what appear to be the first letters of some form of λαικάζω.[194] The belief

---

[186] Pliny, *Nat.* 19.120 (on which, see Adams, *Latin Sexual Vocabulary*, 6).

[187] J. H. Mozley, *Ovid: The Art of Love, and Other Poems* (LCL; Cambridge: Harvard, 1947), 362.

[188] Cf. Suetonius, *Jul.* 49.4.

[189] Pliny, *Nat.* 28.7.39. The protective power of the phallus is widely attested (Pliny, *Nat.* 19.4.19; Diodorus Siculus, *Bibl.* 4.6.4; Varro, *L.L.* 6.5; more references in Gaston Vorberg, *Glossarium Eroticum* [Hanau: Müller and Kiepenheuer, 1965] s.v. *fascinum*).

[190] *festa coronatus ludet convicia miles,/inter laurigeros cum comes ibit equos./fas audire iocos leviora-que carmina, Caesar,/et tibi, si lusus ipse triumphus amat* (*Epig.* 7.8.7–10 [Shackleton Bailey, LCL]). Cf. also 1.4.3: "Even the triumphs of Emperors are wont to tolerate jests."

[191] Suetonius, *Jul.* 51 (Rolfe, LCL, adjusted). Suetonius records another triumph chant which mocked Caesar's passive relationship with Nicomedes (*Jul.* 49.4).

[192] Jocelyn, "A Greek Indecency," 16–17.

[193] Bain notes also a gold ring inscribed with πυγίσω σε, presumably to threaten "envy" (Bain, "Six Greek Verbs," 69).

[194] Described and analyzed by Jocelyn, "A Greek Indecency," 16–17.

that foul words could ward off malevolent forces can also be seen in
the use of "copronyms."[195] Explaining why parents would name their
son Κοπρεύς, Olivier Masson says that such a name is "fortement apo-
tropaïque, destiné à écarter le mauvais oeil et les esprits dangereux."[196]

This survey makes it clear enough that no one function or significance could be assigned to the foul language that was a part of various
religious rites. But a more general observation might be made about
the effects of there being such sanctioned occasions for transgressing
normal linguistic mores—namely, that the existence of sanctioned occasions for suspending the regular rules typically serves to reinforce the
"naturalness" of the rules themselves.[197] Obviously this does not mean
that the reinforced norms were inviolable, for plenty of foul language
was used outside religious rites. But rituals (and discourse about them)
that mark such speech as exceptional contribute to the maintainence
of the norms, thereby preserving the possibility of transgression at
other times.

Excursus: The Language of Some Love Charms

Having seen that obscenities could be used to promote fertility and to
protect from malevolent forces, it is somewhat surprising to find that
foul words were not particularly prominent in magical texts. In fact,
obscene and euphemistic terms are interspersed in the same spells in an
apparently random way, which suggests the authors were simply using
the words most familiar to them for the relevant activities or body parts.
For instance, in one papyrus, just after a recipe for "being able to fuck
a lot" (πολλὰ βι[ν]εῖν δύνασθαι) (PGM VII.182–83), one encounters
a euphemism for the penis: to "get an erection when you want one,"

---

[195] On Greek copronyms (including an Egyptian Saint Kopres), see Olivier Masson,
"Nouvelles notes d'anthroponymie grecque," ZPE 112 (1996): 145–50, and Friedrich
Bechtel, Die historischen Personennamen des Griechischen bis zur Kaiserzeit (Halle: Niemeyer,
1917), 611.

[196] Masson, "Nouvelles notes," 150. The eighth-century Byzantine emperor Con-
stantine V Copronymus received his surname not from his parents but from his
iconophile opponents.

[197] So Victor Turner, on rituals of status reversal: "Cognitively, nothing underlines
regularity so well as absurdity or paradox. Emotionally, nothing satisfies as much
as extravagant or temporarily permitted illicit behavior. Rituals of status reversal
accommodate both aspects. By making the low high and the high low, they reaffirm
the hierarchical principle" (The Ritual Process: Structure and Anti-Structure [Ithaca: Cornel
University Press, 1969], 176).

you spread a mixture of pepper and honey on "your thing" (σου τὸ πρᾶγμα, lines 185–86). This same pattern can be observed elsewhere.[198] Surely πέος could have been used if the most direct words were felt to be necessary for the potency of the spell. Furthermore, in these cases the obscene word (βινεῖν) simply designates what these spells are meant to achieve; it is not itself part of an incantation.[199]

In other spells, the obscene words may have suggested themselves for their specificity. On a second-century lead tablet, one Ammonion binds a Theodotis ἵνα μὴ δυνηθῇς ἑτέρῳ ἀνδρὶ συνμιγῆναι πώποτε μήτε βινηθῆναι μήτε πυγισθῆναι μήτε ληκάζειν μηδὲ καθ᾽ ἡδονὴν <ποιήσῃς> μεθ᾽ ἑταίρῳ ἀνθρώπῳ εἰ μὴ μόνος ἐγώ.[200] This comprehensive list moves from the most modest and all-encompassing ("not ever have intercourse with any other man") to the specific and lexically indecent ("not get fucked, nor buggered, nor suck"), and back again ("nor do anything for pleasure"). A few other spells use these same verbs when enumerating the various forms of sexual activity from which the desired woman should be prevented from engaging.[201] But most of the love charms use standard sexual euphemisms.[202] Nowhere does one find long lists of *synonyms* for specific sexual activities, as if the spell's efficacy depended on getting just the right word for intercourse; this can be contrasted with the obsessive effort to find the right names for the deities who were to execute the spell-caster's wishes.

---

[198] In a third- or fourth-century A.D. spell one finds πρὸς πολλὰ βεινῖν (P 11909 line 11) shortly after instructions for anointing τὸ αἰδοῖον (Hans-Albert Rupprecht, ed., *Sammelbuch Griechischer Urkunden aus Ägypten* [Otto Harrassowitz: Wiesbaden, 1983]).

[199] Cf. *PGM* III.15, with instructions for what to rub ἐν τῷ πρωκτῷ of a drowned cat.

[200] Robert W. Daniel and Franco Maltomini, eds., *Supplementum Magicum* (Opladen: Westdeutscher Verlag, 1992), 38.4–6.

[201] There are other instances in which *fellatio* is made explicit with the (misspelled) verb λαικάζειν: so a daimon is to bind one Heronous ὅπως μὴ βεινηθῇ, μὴ πυγισθῇ, μὴ λεικάσῃ (*SEG* 8.574; *Supplementum Magicum* 46.9–10); similarly *Supplementum Magicum* 49.21–22. As Jocelyn put it, "The trio of verbs refer with blunt brevity to the sexual use of the three apertures of the woman's body, a theme which often exercised the talents of more sophisticated users of the Greek language ("A Greek Indecency," 20). There was obviously some sort of formula, although λαικάζω could be left out: *PGM* IV.350–51: μὴ βινηθήτω, μὴ πυγισθήτω μηδὲ πρὸς ἡδονὴν ποιή/σῃ μετ᾽ ἄλλου ἀνδρός, εἰ μὴ μετ᾽ ἐμοῦ μόνου; and a lead tablet (*SEG* 26.1717: lines 8–9): ὅπως μὴ βινηθῇ, μὴ πυγισθῇ, μη/δὲν πρὸς ἡδονὴν ποίσῃ ἑταίρῳ ἀνδρὶ εἰ μὴ ἐμοὶ μόνῳ τῷ Σαραπάμμωνι.

[202] Cf. *PGM* XXXVI.150: "until she comes and attaches her female 'nature' to my male 'nature'" (τὴν θηλυκὴν ἑαυτῆς φύσιν τῇ ἀρσενικῇ μου κολλήσῃ).

Thus the same vocabulary that appears in sexual threats, boasts, taunts, advice,[203] or in explanations of sexual preference,[204] shows up also in magic formulae seeking sexual favors.[205] We are not at all far from magical papyri when, in a first-century "letter" (P.Oxy 3070), Apion and Epimas inform Epaphroditus that things will go better for him if he lets them πυγίσαι him. (Lest this be too subtle, they repeat the proposition and include in the right margin of the papyrus a crude drawing, which they label ψωλή and φίκις.)[206] Probably if Apion and Epimas had written a spell to get what they wanted from Epaphroditus, they would also have used πυγίζω.[207] (And had they achieved their desire and then wanted to publicize the fact, they would have used the same word on a wall.)

IV. COMEDY

Anyone who has read Aristophanes does not need to be informed that obscene language is used generously. Aristophanes "exploits to the utmost the humour of excretion and every kind of genital friction, using in their literal sense words which are debarred from prose and tragedy."[208] Of the three writers of Comedy chosen as models by the Alexandrian critics (Cratinus, Eupolis, and Aristophanes), only Aristo-

---

[203] In a third-century A.D. Phrygian grave inscription, the deceased advises the reader to enjoy the pleasures of life while he still can: λοῦσαι, πίε, φαγέ, βείνησον (Philippe Le Bas and William Henry Waddington, eds., *Inscriptions Grecques et Latines recueillies en Asie Mineure* [2d ed.; New York: Olms, 2005], 977; *CIG* 3846; cited by Bain, "Six Greek Verbs," 57.

[204] A clay disk from Priene explains: I. φιλῶ γυνέκα βινο[υ]μένη[ν] καλῶς II. φιλῶ γυνέκα ἄκρα κελητίζοσας (meant: ουσαν) III. φιλῶ γινέκα εἰς τὰ γωνάτια εὑείσχι[ον] (F. Hiller von Gaertringen, *Inschriften von Priene* [Berlin: Georg Reimer, 1906], #317). For Latin, cf. *CIL* 4.1830: *futuitur cunnus [pil]ossus multo melius [qu]am glaber E[ad]em continet vaporem et eadem v[ell]it mentulam.*

[205] The word βινεῖν may have been used just as unconsciously when it appears in the list of rules for an Egyptian religious guild: a member will be fined if he βινῖ (*sic*) someone else's wife (*Sammelbuch* 6319.45). Bain suggests that the word here might have been jocular, or might reflect the low level of education of club members ("Six Greek Verbs," 58).

[206] P. J. Parsons, ed., *The Oxyrhynchus Papyri* XLII (London: The Egypt Exploration Society, 1974), 163, and plate 8. The demand of Apion and Epimas is formulated the same way in graffiti (*CIL* 4.2425: *dos pugiza*) and in the *Priapea.*

[207] Cf. Seneca's report that Mamercus Scaurus "had proposed, using an obscene word [*obsceno verbo*], an act that he was more ready to submit to" (Seneca, *Ben.* 4.31.4 [Basore, LCL]).

[208] Kenneth Dover, "Evaluative Terms," 94.

phanes's works survive whole; but obscene language is evident in the fragments of the other poets as well.[209] Jeffrey Henderson summarizes the language and flavor of Old Comedy:

> To a significant degree, the invective, obscenity, and colloquial styles of Old Comedy preserve the ethos of iambic poetry, which had flourished in the archaic period, and elaborate the carnivalesque festivity of the fertility cults, particularly those of Demeter and Dionysus. Old Comedy also features the open (though grotesquely stylized) display of human sexual, excremental, and gustatory functions. In the classical period, iambus, comedy, and the fertility cults were the only permissible public outlet for this sort of language and display.[210]

The linguistic liberty would not last forever. As we shall discuss further below, in the fourth century, obscene language largely disappeared from the comic stage (recall Aristotle's reference to "contemporary comedy's" use of innuendo). But as Kenneth Dover nicely observes, the most challenging question is not, Why did the fourth-century poets make less use of the obscene vocabulary?, but rather, "[W]hat enabled the Greeks of the late archaic and early classical periods to achieve a considerable rupture of the inhibitions which are manifested in so many cultures and were operative in the early archaic period[?]"[211] Homer, for instance, although he considered sex something good, never gives the details of sexual contact in the way he gives "precise descriptions of cooking meat or stabbing through a chink in an adversary's armour."[212]

If comedy partook of the general license of the Dionysiac festivals, its *literary* precedent for abusive and obscene language was iambic poetry. Itself likely developing out of the verbal abuse of fertility cults,[213] iambic was a genre of seventh- and sixth-century Ionia. It can be recognized "in explicitly sexual poems, in invective which goes beyond the witty

---

[209] "In fragments of the other Old-Comedy writers the same sort of obscenities occur as in the works of Aristophanes" (de Wit-Tak, "Function of Obscenity," 358); so Henderson, *Maculate Muse*, 12. The author of a life of Aristophanes actually claimed that Cratinus and Eupolis wrote *more* shamefully that Aristophanes (Quadlbauer, "Dichter," 49, 52). For general bibliography on obscenity in Comedy, see Andreas Willi, "The Language of Greek Comedy: Introduction and Bibliographical Sketch," in *The Language of Greek Comedy* (ed. Andreas Willi; Oxford: Oxford University Press, 2002), 10–11.

[210] Jeffrey Henderson, *Aristophanes: Acharnians. Knights* (LCL; Cambridge: Harvard University Press, 1998), 27–28.

[211] Dover, *Greek Popular Morality*, 207.

[212] Ibid.

[213] So Albin Lesky, *Geschichte der Griechischen Literatur* (3d ed.; Bern: Francke, 1971 [1956]), 135. Aristotle says that speaking in iambics could simply mean abusing someone (*Poet.* 1448b32, noted by Lesky).

banter...in elegy, and in certain other sorts of vulgarity."[214] Aristotle says that those poets who chose to dwell on unworthy men and actions wrote mocking poetry in iambic trimeter, from which comedy developed; what Homer's *Iliad* and *Odyssey* were to tragedy, his *Margites*[215] was to comedy.[216] Ralph M. Rosen has demonstrated that the writers of Old Comedy were "conscious of the iambographic provenance of their invective,"[217] and the obscenities in iambic fragments resemble those of Old Comedy.[218]

The harshness of some iambic can be seen in the stories about Archilochus and Hipponax. According to the tradition, Archilochus was to mary one Neobule, but her father Lycambes broke off the engagement. In retaliation, Archilochus wrote such biting attacks against both of them (and Neobule's sister) that they committed suicide.[219] And Hipponax, after two sculptors made an unflattering sculpture of him, "unsheathed such bitter verses that some believe he drove them to the noose."[220]

After a man named Corax killed Archilochus, he was told by oracle

---

[214] M. L. West, *Studies in Greek Elegy and Iambus* (Untersuchungen zur antiken Literatur und Geschichte 14; Berlin: Walter de Gruyter, 1974), 25; cf. K. J. Dover, "The Poetry of Archilochos," in *Archiloque* (Entretiens sur l'antiquité classique 10; Geneva: Foundation Hardt, 1964), 183–222.

[215] A burlesque attributed to Homer, describing the comical mishaps of one Margites. (For a reconstruction of some of the plot, see West, *Studies*, 30, 172.)

[216] Aristotle, *Poet.* 1448b38–a2.

[217] Ralph M. Rosen, *Old Comedy and the Iambograhic Tradition* (American Classical Studies 19; Atlanta: Scholars Press, 1988), 2. Rosen notes "obscenity, verbal violence and humor" as features that connect Archilochus and Hipponax to each other and both of these poets to Old Comedy (p. 1); on αἰσχρολογία in particular, cf. 26, 30. See also Edwards, "Popular Grotesque," 97 ("[Comedy's] roots, though distant by then, were in fertility rites, apotropaic magic, and the mocking laughter of the *komos* and iambic poetry").

[218] So B. M. W. Knox, who notes that "not until Aristophanes do we encounter so varied a scatological vocabulary again" (*The Cambridge History of Classical Literature* [2 vols.; ed. P. E. Easterling and B. M. W. Knox; Cambridge: Cambridge University Press, 1985], 1:162). For a list of obscene words from iambic fragments, see Henderson, *Maculate Muse*, 17–23. Henderson notes that the "outright obscenities" are limited to trimiter fragments, the epodic fragments prefering metaphors for sexual topics (Jeffrey Henderson, "The Cologne Epode and the Conventions of Early Greek Erotic Poetry," *Arethusa* 9 [1976]: 161).

[219] Evidence in Gerber, *Greek Iambic Poetry*. On the power of invective more generally, see Robert C. Elliott, *The Power of Satire: Magic, Ritual, Art* (Princeton: Princeton University Press, 1960), 1–15. Henderson compares the iambic use of direct language to the words on *tabulae defixionum* (*Maculate Muse*, 19n70).

[220] Pliny, *Nat.* 36.4.12. For his part, Pliny denies the story: "This is untrue, since later they made several statues in neighbouring islands."

to leave the temple of Apollo since he had "killed the servant of the Muses."[221] This oracle received a good deal of attention in antiquity, and the surviving reactions give some indication of the content of Archilocus's poetry, as well as the sensibilities of later readers. Dio Chrysostom cited Apollo's approval of Archilochus as evidence that it is good to revile people's stupidity.[222] Others were scandalized that the god would call the author of such offensive verse a "servant of the Muses."[223] Origen thought it absurd that someone who squandered his talent on a subject matter so "base and lewd" should have won such a label.[224] The Cynic Oenomaus said Archilochus "makes use of every kind of foul and unspeakable language against women, language which no man of discretion would even bear to hear...."[225] The Spartans banned Archilochus's writings as "immoral and immodest" with their "obscene insults" (obscenis maledictis).[226] And the Emperor Julian, when urging priests to keep themselves pure from using or hearing indecent language, specified what he had in mind: "Accordingly we must banish all offensive jests and all licentious intercourse. And that you may understand what I mean by this, let no one who has been consecrated a priest read either Archilochus or Hipponax or anyone else who writes such poems as theirs" (Ep. 89b [300C; Wright, LCL]).[227] Such diverse evaluations parallel the ancient reactions to the scabrous invective of comedy, with some approving its abuse as pedagogical and others rejecting it as too sullied by obscenity to be of use.

If iambic poetry provided comedy a literary antecedent for foul invective, the bawdy festivals of Dionysus provided it with a carnivalesque atmosphere in which such language could flourish.[228] Plutarch

---

[221] Galen, Protrept. 9.22 (cited by Gerber, Greek Iambic Poetry, 40–41).

[222] Dio Chrysostom, 1 Tars. 11–12; cf. Aelius Aristides, Or. 46, who notes that even though Archilochus wrote a "disagreeable" genre in iambic, Apollo defended him because he focused his defamation on bad people.

[223] AP 7.352, where the female victims of his verses ask the muses why they favored an unholy man.

[224] Cels. 3.25.

[225] ἄνδρα παντοίαις κατὰ γυναικῶν αἰσχρορρημοσύναις καὶ ἀρρητολογίαις, ἃς οὐδ' ἀκοῦσαί τις σώφρων ἀνὴρ ὑπομείνειεν, ἐν τοῖς οἰκείοις ποιήμασι κεχρημένον (Oenomaus apud Eusebius, Praep. ev. 5.32.2–33.9, cited from Gerber, Greek Iambic Poetry, 44–45).

[226] Valerius Maximus, Facta et dicta memorabilia 6.3 ext. 1.

[227] Epistle 89b in Joseph Bidez and Franz Cumont, L'Empereur Julien (Paris: Les belles Lettres, 2d ed., 1960), 1:168.

[228] Halliwell, "Comic Satire and Freedom of Speech," 69–70; idem, "Aristophanic Satire," Yearbook of English Studies 14 (1984): 6–20; idem, Aristophanes: Birds, Lysistrata, Assembly-Women, Wealth (Oxford: Clarendon Press, 1997), xvii–xxi, xlv. As mentioned

describes "jubilation," "din," "crude exultation," and vile hymns as part of the Dionysia,[229] and wagons carried mockers who insulted the participants.[230]

Some scholars have pointed to the carnivalesque context of the Dionysian festivals as the key for the liberty to transgress normal standards of linguistic and visual decorum. Drawing especially on Bakhtin's analysis of Rabelais,[231] Kenneth Reckford argues that when Aristophanes was separated from "the festive experience of life," he ceased to be understood and appreciated.[232] Ancient sources do indeed speak of the "license" afforded by the holiday.[233] At the very least, the bawdiness of the Dionysia can be said to have "contributed to the growth of obscenity as a standard and accepted element in the comic performances."[234]

But although Dionysiac festivity let obscenity flourish in Old Comedy, Old Comedy was not simply a matter of amusement. Aristophanes himself boasted that he had elevated his genre above the insipid and

---

above, iambic poetry itself probably also had connections to cultic practice—perhaps specifically the cult of Dionysus (West, *Studies*, 23–24).

[229] Plutarch, *Mor.* 1098B–C (Einarson and de Lacy, LCL): "So too when slaves hold a Saturnalian feast or go about celebrating the country Dionysia, you could not endure the jubilation and din, as in their crude exultation they act and speak like this" (καὶ γὰρ οἱ θεράποντες ὅταν Κρόνια δειπνῶσιν ἢ Διονύσια κατ' ἀγρὸν ἄγωσι περιιόντες, οὐκ ἂν αὐτῶν τὸν ὀλολυγμὸν ὑπομείναις καὶ τὸν θόρυβον, ὑπὸ χαρμονῆς καὶ ἀπεριοκαλίας τοιαῦτα ποιούντων καὶ φθεγγομένων). The song Plutarch quotes mentions Phoebus being "hymned vilely" (ὑμνεῖτο δ' αἰσχρῶς). Cf. Plutarch, *Mor.* 527D. We have a portrait of the Rural Dionysia in Aristophanes's *Acharnians* (241–79), where Dicaeopolis's slaves carry the phallus and he sings an obscene song to Phales. Diodorus Siculus says that Priapus or Ithyphallus was honored in the rites of Dionysus, carried in "with laughter and jest" (*Bibl.* 4.6.4).

[230] Arthur Pickard-Cambridge, *The Dramatic Festivals of Athens* (2d ed.; revised by John Gould and D. M. Lewis; Oxford: Clarendon Press, 1968), 12–13; Lesky, *Geschichte der Griechischen Literatur*, 272.

[231] Mikhail Bakhtin, *Rabelais and His World* (trans. Helene Iswolsky; Cambridge: M.I.T. Press, 1968).

[232] Reckford, *Old-and-New Comedy*, 383.

[233] Lucian has Philosophy say that she does not take Comedy to court for his abuse because the language is customary for the festival (*Pisc.* 14, 25; *Pisc.* 26 mentions "the sanction of a holiday"). For further ancient references to the license of the festival, see Halliwell, "Comic Satire and Freedom of Speech," 69n77.

[234] Henderson, *Maculate Muse*, 17, who goes on to say that "the use of obscene language to expose individuals and thus to make them comic was a standard feature of the cults as well as the comedies that were eventually part of them, and there can be little doubt that the suspension of the ordinary taboos and restrictions of society in cult prepared the way for the same extraordinary freedom enjoyed by comedy as part of the artistic side of the Dionysian festivals." Halliwell argues that the "special festival setting" of comic performances effectively removed them from the sphere of the laws of slander ("Comic Satire and Freedom of Speech," 54).

toothless humor of other comic poets both by the ingenuity of his wit and by his willingness to attack the likes of Cleon.[235] Scholars have pointed out that Old Comedy did, in fact, play an important part in the life of the democracy.[236] Henderson points out that the comic poets' "techniques of persuasion and abuse are practically identical with those used in political and forensic disputes," confirming that Comedy was "an organic feature of the sovereignty of the *demos*."[237] And A. T. Edwards notes that both Plato's sense that Aristophanes's *Clouds* prejudiced the public against Socrates (*Apology* 18b4–20c2) and Cleon's legal actions against Aristophanes's abuse belie Reckford's claim that "[f]estive mockery did not count in the ordinary world."[238] The dramatic festivals were not simply autonomous carnivals; they were an expensive and deliberate part of the democracy.[239]

But even allowing for Comedy's role in the democracy, one might wonder how the copious *obscenity* contributed to such an elevated civic responsibility. Henderson is surely right to note that foul language was

---

[235] See especially *Peace* 736–61, where the Chorus Leader claims that Aristophanes got rid of others' "poor, lowbrow buffoonery" (κακὰ καὶ φόρτον καὶ βωμολοχεύματ' ἀγεννῆ [748]) and created a "great art," attacking powerful men, courageously battling Cleon for the sake of the audience (on this passage, see Edwards, "Aristophanes' Comic Poetics," 169–70). On the superiority of Aristophanes's humor (in his own estimation), cf. *Vesp.* 55–57, 66; *Acharn.* 738; more generally, J. M. Bremer, "Aristophanes on his own Poetry," in *Aristophane* (ed. J. M. Bremer and E. W. Handley; Entretiens sur l'antiquité classique 38; Geneva: Foundation Hardt, 1993), 125–72. In *Clouds*, the Chorus Leader complains that despite all of the "hard work" of this "most sophisticated of my comedies," he was defeated by "vulgar men" (ὑπ' ἀνδρῶν φορτικῶν [*Nub.* 524]). He blames his defeat on having aimed to please the more sophisticated viewer, and promises that he will not "deliberately betray the intelligent" (*Nub.* 524–27). Unlike his opponents' plays, his new comedy is "decent" (σώφρων) and "hasn't come with any dangling leather stitched to her, red at the tip and thick, to make the children laugh" (*Nub.* 537–39). Here Aristophanes might have his tongue in his cheek (Reckford, *Old-and-New Comedy*, 396), for elsewhere he rejects defecation on stage (*Nub.* 296 and *Ran.* 5–8) but nevertheless employs it (e.g. *Eccl.* 316–73; see Bremer, "Aristophanes on his own Poetry," 168).

[236] A. T. Edwards, "Historicizing the Popular Grotesque," 89–117; idem, "Aristophanes' Comic Poetics: Τρύξ, Scatology, σκῶμμα," *TAPA* 121 (1991): 157–79 (Edwards cites some of the studies that have played down any serious political aim for Aristophanes's work [178n52]); Jeffrey Henderson, "The *Demos* and Comic Competition," in *Nothing to do with Dionysos?* (ed. J. J. Winkler and F. I. Zeitlin; Princeton: Princeton University Press, 1990), 271–313; Werner Jaeger, *Paideia: The Ideals of Greek Culture* (trans. Gilbert Highet; 3 vols.; New York: Oxford University Press, 1939), 1:360–70.

[237] Henderson, "The *Demos* and Comic Competition," 272–73.

[238] Edwards, "Popular Grotesque," 93, quoting Reckford, *Old-and-New Comedy*, 479.

[239] Henderson, "The *Demos* and Comic Competition," 274. Henderson claims that the laws against "unspeakable allegations" applied also to comedy (*Aristophanes*, 18), *contra* the arguments of Halliwell ("Comic Satire and Freedom of Speech"; idem, *Aristophanes: Birds*, xix–xx).

central to Comedy's ability "to expose, deflate, and provoke."[240] When the Sausage-Seller says that Cleon "can go suck his own dick" (*Knights*, 1010) and tells him to his face, "I'll fuck your arse-hole like a sausage skin" (*Knights*, 364 [Henderson, LCL]), Aristophanes is attacking a real political figure. Similarly, when a lizard defecates into Socrates's mouth (which was agape as he studied the stars), Strepsiades's resultant delight ("I like that, a gecko shitting on Socrates!") ridicules Socrates and his philosophizing.[241] Nonetheless, it is hard to escape the impression that much of the coarse language serves simply to entertain.[242] What was the *political* function of having slaves talk about masturbation (*Knights* 24, 29)? How was the city served by mentioning humongous farts— and calling the god who did not mind their smell a "shit-eater"?[243] It is difficult to explain purely in terms of Comedy's civic role why Aristophanes should devote a full sixty lines to Blepyrus's need to defecate (*Eccl.* 313–73). As Edwards notes, on the comic stage "[f]eces are intrinsically funny."[244]

Plutarch acknowledged that the comic poets rebuked their audience in ways that were potentially edifying, but in his view "the admixture of drollery and scurrility [συμμεμιγμένον δὲ τὸ γελοῖον αὐτοῖς καὶ βωμολόχον] in them, like a vile dressing with food, made their frankness ineffective and useless, so that there was nothing left for the authors but a name of malice [κακοηθεία] and coarseness [βδελυρία], and no profit for the hearers from their words."[245] He could not see what was so witty about Aristophanes, and concluded that the comic poet must have written his "indecent and wanton lines" for people without

---

[240] Henderson, *Aristophanes*, 28.

[241] *Nub.* 169–73; Edwards, "Aristophanes' Comic Poetics," 164.

[242] D. A. Russell, *Ancient Literary Criticism* (Oxford: Clarendon Press, 1972), 10.

[243] Aristophanes, *Plut.* 693–697, 700ff.

[244] Edwards, "Aristophanes' Comic Poetics," 164. The comments at *Nub.* 295–97 make it clear that talking about and depicting defecation were standard ways to raise a laugh. In de Wit-Tak's reckoning, five of the nine scatological obscenities in *Thesmophoriazusae* exist simply "for the pleasure of using the word" ("Function of Obscenity," 365).

[245] Plutarch, *Mor.* 68C (Babbitt, LCL). Cf. *Mor.* 711F–712A, where Old Comedy is rejected as an inappropriate post-prandial entertainment because "it has so little squeamishness in admitting jests and buffoonery that it is shockingly overloaded, nakedly indecent, and larded with words and phrases that are improper and obscene" (ἥ τε πρὸς τὰ σκώμματα καὶ βωμολοχίας εὐχέρεια δεινῶς κατάκορος καὶ ἀναπεπταμένη καὶ γέμουσα ῥημάτων ἀκόσμων καὶ ἀκολάστων ὀνομάτων [Minar, LCL]). On the ancient evaluation of Comedy, cf. Franz Quadlbauer, "Die Dichter der griechischen Komödie im literarischen Urteil der Antike," *Wiener Studien* 73 (1960): 40–82.

self-restraint, the slanderous and bitter ones for the malicious and malignant.[246] Marcus Aurelius, on the other hand, admired the way Old Comedy made a pedagogical use of blunt language (*Med.* 11.6).

The obscenity in comedy was not limited to any one type of character: men, women, the choruses, and above all, the heroes[247] use obscene words. Women use obscenities less than men,[248] and tend to use sexual rather than scatological words.[249] They also tend not to use obscenities in the presence of men.[250] When an old woman threatens to "beat the shit" out of a magistrate (ἐπιχεσεῖ πατούμενος [*Lys.* 440]), his reaction indicates just how shocking such language was ("Beat the shit out of me?... Tie her up first, the one who talks like that!"). McClure notes that this female, as an old woman, is a stock character in Old Comedy, "independent, lecherous, and found of drink"—the crone, whose speech is often coarse and abusive.[251] We get an interesting glimpse of the sense of modesty ascribed to a female character when a woman finds herself unable to utter any but the first letter of λαικάζειν: "Poor thing, you're already itching for the Ionian toy [i.e. a dildo], and I think you also want to do the L, like the Lesbians" (δοκεῖς δέ μοι καὶ λάβδα κατὰ τοὺς Λεσβίους [*Eccl.* 920; Henderson, LCL]). What she wanted to say was δοκεῖς δέ μοι καὶ λαικάζειν.[252]

At times, the characters who most lard their speech with obscenities are being characterized as buffoonish or lascivious.[253] Jocelyn, commenting

---

[246] οὐδενὶ γὰρ ὁ ἄνθρωπος ἔοικε μετρίῳ τὴν ποίησιν γεγραφέναι, ἀλλὰ τὰ μὲν αἰσχρὰ καὶ ἀσελγῆ τοῖς ἀκολάστοις, τὰ βλάσφημα δὲ καὶ πικρὰ τοῖς βασκάνοις καὶ κακοήθεσιν (*Mor.* 854D). He expresses a more mild attitude in passing at *Mor.* 1065E–66A, saying that the vulgar lines in comedies do not spoil the pleasantness of the whole.

[247] K. J. Dover notes that the comic heroes were characterized by "language uninhibited to a degree which was not tolerated in a serious setting" (*Greek Popular Morality*, 19). On the hero's obscenity, cf. also Henderson, *Maculate Muse*, 13.

[248] Laura McClure, *Spoken Like a Woman: Speech and Gender in Athenian Drama* (Princeton: Princeton University Press, 1999), 38, 208–9.

[249] McClure, *Spoken Like a Woman*, 209.

[250] Alan Sommerstein, "The Language of Athenian Women," in *Lo spettacolo delle voci* (Francesco de Martino and Alan Sommerstein, eds.; Bari: Levante, 1995): 79.

[251] McClure, *Spoken Like a Woman*, 211. Similarly, it is an ugly old woman who tells Epigenes, "Buck up and get moving; you can shit when we get in the house" (*Eccl.* 1062 [Henderson, LCL]). Still in the Middle Ages it was old women who were "implicated strongly in obscene language" and "perceived to be habitual offenders" (Jan M. Ziolkowski, "The Obscenities of Old Women: Vetularity and Vernacularity," in Ziolkowski, *Obscenity*, 73).

[252] Jocelyn notes that by the first century B.C., λάβδα σοι λέγω was a variant of λαικάζειν σοι λέγω ("A Greek Indecency," 17, 34, citing Varro, *Men.* 48). We might compare, "F- off."

[253] De Wit-Tak, "The Function of Obscenity," 363, 365.

on the particularly obscene word λαικάζειν and its cognates, notes
that "none of the comic personages who use them is demonstrably
a free-born, city-dwelling, property-owning, conventionally educated
male."[254] Those who use this word are rather "coarsely spoken slaves,"
"a professional μάγειρος," and "men of agricultural background."[255]

A similar pattern can be seen in later uses of obscenities. A word such
as βινεῖν was often put on the lips of unsophisticated speakers. In one of
the handful of obscenities from the *Philogelos*, it is a slave, whose speech
reveals him to be uneducated,[256] who delivers the punchline: "I fucked
[ἐβίνησα] a dancer, but my lady was inside" (*Philogelos* 251). It is also
the slave, Aesop, who mockingly advises his mistress to procure a good
looking lad, since she looks like "she is itching to screw" (G *Vita* 32 has
κινητιᾶν; the W *Vita* has βινητιῶσα). And in the fragmentary "novel"
from a second-century papyrus (P.Oxy 3010), it is a *gallus*, speaking in
Sotadean meter characterized by several "vulgarisms of language,"[257]
who advises his friend Iolaus on how he can βινεῖν (line 30).

In the fourth century, Comedy ceased to be as openly obscene.
"Totally uninhibited language was the norm in Aristophanic comedy;
by the late fourth century it was seldom heard on the comic stage."[258]
Dover notes that at this time, more serious literature "tended to be
circumspect, even coy, in expression, although not reticent in content,"[259]
and cites the way Demosthenes and Xenophon circled around sexual
activity.[260] The same sense of taboo now applied to comedy as well. As
mentioned earlier, in Menander's *Phasma*, a slave hesistates to say χέζω.[261]
Dover points out that a "slave character in comedy fifty years earlier
would probably not have apologized for using the word 'shit'."[262]

---

[254] Jocelyn, "A Greek Indecency," 14.

[255] Ibid.

[256] Andreas Thierfelder, *Philogelos: Der Lachfreund* (Munich: Heimeran, 1968),
195n13.

[257] P. J. Parsons, ed., *The Oxyrhynchus Papyri* XLII (London: Egypt Exploration
Society, 1974), 34.

[258] Dover, *Greek Popular Morality*, 206. So Siems: "und vor allem die αἰσχρολογίαι in
personam, wie sie in der Alten Komödie vorgebracht wurden, sind in der Mittleren
und Neuen Komödie, wenn auch nicht ganz verschwunden, so doch sehr selten
geworden" (Siems, "Aischrologia," 11). Cf. Willi, "Language of Greek Comedy," 11,
with further bibliography.

[259] Dover, *Greek Popular Morality*, 206.

[260] Demosthenes, *Fals. leg.* 19.309; Xenophon, *Hier.* 1.4.

[261] *Phasma*, 39–43; cf. Menander, *Sam.* 47–50 (see 2n10 above).

[262] Dover, *Greek Popular Morality*, 206n4.

While there is a clear trend toward more polite language in Menander, foul language did not disappear completely.[263] Menander has the cook Sicon utter the abusive and obscene οὐ λαικάσει,[264] rendered loosely as "bugger off."[265] There are other indecencies in Menandrian fragments;[266] but Jocelyn notes that "[p]ersons of the educated class in Menander's scripts do in fact without exception speak very decorously about sexual matters (cf. *Dysc.* 858, *Epitr.* 478–9, *Sam.* 47–50, *Sicyon.* 371–3)."[267]

Why did obscenity gradually disappear from the comic stage? There are references to comedy losing its right to abuse,[268] but the putative efforts at censorship pertained to ridiculing people by name (ὀνομαστὶ κωμῳδεῖν), not to decency of expression. Because Henderson sees obscenity as integral to comedy's function in the democracy, he also explains the near disappearance of obscenity as a result of changing political realities: "Without its function in the humor of abuse and exposure, obscenity becomes mere smut and disappears...."[269] But as was noted above, a significant role for obscenity was simply humor; and it can hardly be the case that foul language stopped making people laugh, for as it left the comic stage, it flourished in mime. Ultimately, it

---

[263] Bain notes that new discoveries have shown later comic writers were "less inhibited linguistically than was once believed" ("Six Greek Verbs," 53; cf. 55).

[264] On this expression, see Jocelyn, "A Greek Indecency," 40–41, 64–65, who gives other references to scholarly literature on this particular passage and a thourough evaluation of the tone and register of the phrase. Cf. also Bain, "Six Greek Verbs," 75–76. For the same expression, cf. D. L. Page, *Greek Literary Papyri* (2 vols.; LCL; Cambridge: Harvard University Press, 1942), 36–37, where it is used in annoyance in response to an archaic word: οὐκὶ λαικάσει, / ἐρεῖς σαφέστερόν θ' ὃ βούλει μοι λέγειν (reference from E. W. Handley, ed., *The Dyskolos of Menader* [Cambridge: Harvard University Press, 1965], 288).

[265] *Dysk.* 892 (trans. Maurice Balme, *Menander: The Plays and the Fragments* [Oxford: Oxford University Press, 2001], 39). This "vulgäre Beschimpfung" is used in response to Getas's question (τιμωρίαν [βούλ]ει λαβεῖν ὧν ἀρτίως ἔπασχες;), because Sicon (now tipsy) thinks Getas has used πάσχειν in an obscene sense (Franz Stoessl, *Menander: Dyskolos* [Paderborn: Ferdinand Schöningh, 1965], 234–35).

[266] E.g. κινητιᾶν (*Dysk.* 461); for other words and other comics, see Bain, "Six Greek Verbs," 55.

[267] Ibid., 64n315; so Adams: "such obscenities as were admitted were probably confined largely to lower-class characters" (*Latin Sexual Vocabulary*, 218). In ancient evaluations of Menander, he was frequently distinguished from Aristophanes for his avoidance of αἰσχρολογία (Quadlbauer, "Dichter").

[268] Cf. Horace, *Ars* 281–84; Cicero, *Resp.* 4.11; for a summary and evaluation of the evidence for restricting comedy's right to abuse, see Halliwell, "Comic Satire and Freedom of Speech in Classical Athens," 54–66; there is further bibliography in Csapo and Slater, *Context of Ancient Drama*, 165, 176–78, 415–16.

[269] Henderson, *Maculate Muse*, 29.

is difficult to say more than that there was a "gradual shift in notions of public decorum,"[270] a shift that Peter Green connects to social change in Athens and "an upsurge of middle-class urban *pudeur*."[271]

V. New Forms of Comic Drama

Obscenity may have left the comic stage, but it lived on in new dramatic contexts, above all in mime. In these short skits with scenes from the less noble elements of everyday life[272] the language was suited to its subjects. In the hands of Sophron of Syracuse (fl. *ca.* 450 B.C.), mime became something that even a Plato could praise[273]—despite the fact that some of Sophron's lines were judged "shameful" by others.[274] Some of the fragments of mime which survive in Egyptian papyri confirm the moralists' complaints about their language and content. For example, P.Oxy. 413 contains a mime featuring a deity called κυρία Πορδή ("Lady Fart").[275] The first thirty-six lines of this mime are badly damaged, yet one finds πορδή twice in the first two lines (out of three legible words!), and ἐν τῶι πρωκτῶι μου in line 6. Within the space of seven

---

[270] O'Higgins, *Women and Humor*, 102; cf. W. L. Newman, *The Politics of Aristotle*, 3.491–92.

[271] Peter Green, *Classical Bearings: Interpreting Ancient History and Culture* (New York: Thames and Hudson, 1989), 140. Green sees this "middle-class, mealy-mouthed" morality as winning out over "peasant earthiness" on the one hand and "aristocratic insouciance" on the other (145).

[272] Athenaeus (*Deipn.* 14.621C) gives two typical types of mime: "sometimes women who are adulteresses and procuresses, sometimes a man drunk and going on a revel to his lover." For a concise and well-documented introduction to mime, see I. C. Cunningham, *Herodas: Mimiambi* (Oxford: Clarendon, 1971), 3–9.

[273] Athenaeus, *Deipn.* 11.504B. Diogones Laertius says Plato brought Sophron's mimes to Athens and imitated their style (3.18); a copy was even found under his pillow! Cunningham suggests that while Plato "the philosopher and moralist would doubtless have condemned Sophron as a corrupting influence (one need mention only Fr. 24), Plato the man...was impressed by the mimes, and introduced them to Athens" (*Herodas: Mimiambi*, 11). Further references in Rudolf Pfeiffer, *History of Classical Scholarship* (Oxford: Clarendon Press, 1968), 265n4.

[274] Demetrius (*Eloc.* 151) gives two examples (fragments 52 and 24 from George Kraibel, ed., *Comicorum Graecorum Fragmenta* [Berlin: Weidmannsche Verlagsbuchhandlung, 1899]) of Sophron making jokes by means of innuendo (e.g., fragment 24 says that widows enjoy various sorts of fish, including σωλῆνες, which means "tube-fish," but is also slang for the penis); Demetrius finds such jokes αἰσχρά.

[275] P.Oxy. 413 recto and verso column 4 are printed as fragment 6 in I. C. Cunningham, *Herodae: Mimiambi* (Leipzig: Teubner, 1987); verso columns 1–3 are printed as fragment 7.

partially preserved lines the tone is clearly established, and it is no surprise to find a river called Ψώλιχος in line 27. The first three columns on the opposite side include a monologue "by a terrifying specimen of the 'weaker sex'"[276] who orders her slave brought in ἵνα με βινήσηι ("in order to fuck me" [column 2, line 3]), and when he refuses, asks whether her κύσθ(ος) really seemed so much rougher a task than all the work in the fields.[277] In general the vulgar language of mime was notorious. Plutarch said its coarse language made it unsuitable for entertainment for a dinner party.[278]

One third-century Hellenistic mimographer, Herodas,[279] modeled himself on Hipponax,[280] so that the substance of mime was expressed in the meter of iambic (hence *mimiamboi*).[281] In what survives from Herodas, the subjects are earthy and frank but the language is more circumspect than some other fragments of mime. In one mime, a nasty woman, angry with her slave-lover for sleeping around, brings up his "unmentionable tail" (τὴν ἀνώνυμον κέρκον, 5.45) while raving about his punishment. In another, two women discuss an impressive scarlet dildo (6.18). It is not entirely clear who was reading such works[282]—or even whether they were written to be read or to be performed.[283] One person we know for sure *was* reading Herodas is the Roman Pliny the Younger, who mentions Herodas favorably.[284]

---

[276] Cunningham, *Herodas: Mimiambi*, 8.

[277] Column 2, line 16. The plots, such as they can be discerned, are summarized by Cunningham, *Herodas*, 8–9.

[278] Plutarch, *Mor.* 711F–712A; cf. Martial, *Epig.*, 8. Introduction. Peter Green says mimes "tend to be brassily obscene, with a more than Aristophanic relish for taboo words" (*Alexander to Actium: The Historical Evolution of the Hellenistic Age* [Berkeley: University of California Press, 1990], 244).

[279] Or "Herondas" (for the dating of his life—and spelling of his name—cf. Lesky, *Geschichte der Griechischen Literatur*, 838).

[280] Lesky, *Geschichte der Griechischen Literatur*, 142, 838; Green, *Alexander to Actium*, 244.

[281] Cunningham, *Herodas*, 13.

[282] Giuseppe Mastromarco claims that most now believe Herondas "designed his mimiambi for the social and cultural élite of the Hellenistic society" (*The Public of Herondas* [trans. M. Nardella; Amsterdam: J. C. Gieben, 1984], 95, cited by Green [*Alexander to Actium*, 794n104]); Green himself suspects there was something in this literature for everyone.

[283] Cunningham thinks it probable that "the author intended his work to be recited...at gatherings of literary people, perhaps symposia..." (*Herodas*, 16).

[284] In a letter to his friend Arrius Antoninus: "I thought I was reading Callimachus or Herodes or better if such exists" (Pliny, *Ep.* 4.3.3 [Radice, LCL]).

The Roman comic stage included several genres which overlapped in style and subject matter.[285] Plautus's and Terence's *palliatae*—"drama in a Greek cloak" (*pallium*)—were adaptations of Greek New Comedy; like their models, they avoided primary obscenities. Augustine said of Roman comedies: "Their subject matter is often immoral, as far as action goes; but, unlike many other compositions, they are at least free from verbal obscenities" (*Civ.* 2.8 [Bettenson]). In the prologue of *Captives*, Plautus even draws attention to the fact that his play contains "none of those off-color lines that should not be spoken."[286] Plautus had more of Aristophanes's taste for the bawdy than did Terence,[287] but he achieved his humor with *double entendre*[288] or sexual situations in place of primary obscenities. So for instance, in *Casina*, the slave Olympio describes having frisked Chalinus in the dark—under the false impression that it was his new bride Casina:

> "While I'm searching for her sword to see if she has one, I got hold of a hilt. On second thoughts, though, she didn't have a sword, for that would have been cold." "Go on." "But I'm ashamed to." "It was not a radish, was it?" "No." "Or a cucumber?" "Heavens! Certainly not!...It was full grown, whatever it was." (*Cas.* 909–914)[289]

Plautus and Terence were still being performed in the time of Horace, but the comic stage was ultimately won over by the coarser Atellanae

---

[285] *OCD*, s.v. "comedy, Latin," 371.

[286] *neque spurcidici insunt versus immemorabiles* (*Capt.* 56). I have cited the translation of Palmer Bovie (David R. Slavitt and Palmer Bovie, eds., *Plautus: The Comedies* [vol. 1 of *Complete Roman Drama in Translation*; ed. David R. Slavitt and Palmer Bovie; Baltimore: Johns Hopkins, 1995], viii). Richard More takes the line as tongue-in-cheek ("none of those filthy jokes that everyone *hates* to repeat" (Richard More, *Plautus: The Comedies*, 1:191).

[287] Duckworth, *Roman Comedy*, 292–95.

[288] Cf. the "misunderstanding" in *Truculentus* 259–62:

Ataphium: *comprime sis eiram.*

Truculentus: *eam quidem hercle tu, quae solita es, comprime, impudens, quae per ridiculum rustico suades stuprum.*

Astaphium: *Eiram dixi: ut decepisti! dempsisti unam litteram.*

The Latin pun plays on *eira* (= *ira*, "wrath") and *era* ("mistress"). Truculentus takes Astaphium to be saying to him, "Screw your mistress" (*comprime eram*), instead of "check your rage" (*comprime eiram*). So she repeats herself and explains, "you took out one letter!" See James Tatum, *Plautus: The Darker Comedies* (Baltimore: Johns Hopkins University Press, 1983), 209n6. Duckworth (*Roman Comedy*, 352n53) and Adams (*Latin Sexual Vocabulary*, 219) offer further examples of Plautine sexual metaphors and plays on words.

[289] Trans. Richard Beacham in Slavitt and Bovie, eds., *Plautus: The Comedies*. For more evidence of the comic potential of "swords," cf. Adams, *Latin Sexual Vocabulary*, 20–21.

and mime.[290] A popular form of native Italian comedy,[291] the Atellanae were apparently "grotesque" and "full of broad humour and indecent references."[292] A wide range of the population appreciated their humor. The vulgar Trimalchio says he once bought some comic actors, but preferred them putting on Atellan farces (Petronius, *Sat.* 53). But even Sulla composed "satyric comedies" in Latin, which are often assumed to have been Atellanae.[293] As in other dramatic forms, it was an attack on an important person, not obscene language, that could prove an author's downfall. The "amusing *double entendre*" that got a writer of Atellan farces burned under Caligula[294] must have somehow insulted the emperor.

Roman mime was performed at the Floralia in or after 173 B.C.,[295] but it could also be performed "in the street or in the *triclinium*, in public or intimate gathering."[296] There seem to have been no restrictions on its use of obscene language;[297] Martial claimed that epigram such as his aimed at "the verbal license of mime" (*mimicam verborum licentiam* [*Epig.*, 8]).[298] Even those who disapproved of the content admitted mime was funny.[299] Passing references indicate that the titles of mimes basically parallel the titles of Atellanae,[300] and that adultery was often grist for the plot. In the reign of Tiberius the inhabitants of Massilia banned mime since their themes consisted mostly of "the enactment of illicit

---

[290] *OCD* 371; Ludwig Friedländer, *Roman Life and Manners Under the Early Empire* (trans. Leonard A. Magnus; 4 vols.; New York: Barnes & Noble, 1968), 2:90–92; Elaine Fantham, "The Missing Link in Roman Literary History," *Classical World* 82 (1988–89): 159; Csapo and Slater say that mime replaced Attelan farce about the middle of the first century B.C. as the *exodia* (*Context of Ancient Drama*, 371).

[291] Duckworth, *Roman Comedy*, 10–13.

[292] Friedländer, *Roman Life and Manners*, 2:91; similarly Duckworth, *Roman Comedy*, 11. A reference to Attelan obscenity in Quintilian (*amphibolia neque illa obscena, quae Atellani e more captant, Inst.* 6.3.47]) depends on an emendation of *obscena* from *obscura*. W. Beare has argued that the emendation is unnecessary, but nevertheless notes that, on the basis of fragments and titles, we could have guessed that "they were on occasion *obscenae*" ("Quintilian VI.iii.47 and the *Fabula Atellana*," *Classical Review* 51 [1937]: 213–15).

[293] Athenaeus, *Deipn.* 6.261C, cited by T. P. Wiseman, "Satyrs in Rome? The Background to Horace's *Ars Poetica*," *JRS* 78 (1988): 2.

[294] Suetonius, *Cal.* 27.

[295] See Fantham, "Missing Link," 155n10; N. Horsfall, "The Literary Mime," in *The Cambridge History of Classical Literature*, 2:293ff.

[296] Fantham, "Missing Link," 154.

[297] Horsfall, "Literary Mime," 293; Friedländer, *Roman Life and Manners*, 2:109.

[298] See also Ovid, *Trist.* 2.497; Quintilian, *Inst.* 6.3.29.

[299] Quintilian, *Inst.* 6.3.8–9.

[300] Fantham, "Missing Link," 157.

intercourse."³⁰¹ The elder Seneca, Juvenal, Tertullian, and Minucius Felix all mention mimes about adultery.³⁰²

By the reign of Augustus, mime had become extremely popular.³⁰³ When Ovid wanted to defend his own poetry, he appealed to the tenor and terms of the mime as well as to the fact that *everybody* watched them:

> What if I had written mimes with obscene jokes [*obscena iocantes*], which always contain passages on illicit love...? These are watched by girls ready to marry, by matrons, men and boys—and most of the senate attends. It's not enough that their ears should be besmirched by impure language [*incestis vocibus*]: their eyes have to get used to seeing much that is shameful.... Augustus, look at the accounts of the games you support—you will find that you have paid a lot for much that is of just this character. You have watched such things often in person, often put the show on yourself (so affable is your greatness in every sphere); with those eyes that are at the service of the world you have viewed adultery on the stage—without getting upset. (*Trist.* 2.497–514 [Wheeler, LCL])

VI. Literary Obscenities

Just as obscene language was used aggressively to attack others in iambic poetry and Old Comedy, it was used in the same way in some other genres of literature that attacked and lampooned. Menippus of Gadara was known as ὁ σπουδογέλοιος, "the serious jester" (Strabo, *Geogr.* 16.2.29); Lucian says Menippus "laughed while he bit" (γελῶν ἅμα ἔδακνεν [*Bis acc.* 33]). Menippus bequeathed these traits to the whole satirical tradition. Ennius set out "to mix the useful with the sweet"; and Horace said he wanted to "speak the truth with a laugh" (*ridentem dicere verum* [*Serm.* 1.1.24]). Menippus's works do not survive, and of the genre that bears his name (Menippean Satire), only Seneca's

---

³⁰¹ Valerius Maximus, *Facta et dicta memorabilia*, 2.6.7: *quorum argumenta maiore ex parte stuprorum continent actus* (cited by R. W. Reynolds, "The Adultery Mime," *CQ* 40 [1946]: 79).

³⁰² Seneca, *Controv.* 2.4; Juvenal, *Sat.* 6.41–44; 8.196–97; Tertullian, *Apol.* 15; Minucius Felix, *Octav.* 37.12 (references from Reynolds, "The Adultery Mime," 79).

³⁰³ Elaine Fantham, *Roman Literary Culture: From Cicero to Apuleius* (Baltimore: Johns Hopkins University Press, 1996), 146. On the frequency of public performances, see Friedländer, *Roman Life and Manners*, 2:11–12, and Csapo and Slater, *Context of Ancient Drama*, 209.

Apocolocyntosis survives intact. But the tone of *that* work,[304] occasional references to lewd language,[305] and titles of lost works (e.g. Varro's *Triphallus*),[306] suggest that, while it was less lexically coarse than Old Comedy, it had some freedom to use risqué expressions.

Lucian saw himself as heir to the mocking tradition of both Old Comedy and Menippus (*Bis acc.* 33).[307] Lucian makes far less use of primary obscenities than his Old Comic models,[308] but he uses καταπύγων, as well as the "novel and poetic form"[309] λαικαλέος, for a man who cannot help but notice anyone who is "well-hung" (πεώδης and πόσθων).[310] In one dialogue Lucian says that when Odysseus "had entered into the Epicurean life" on Calypso's island, he had it in his power "to live in idleness and to luxuriate and to βινεῖν the daughter of Atlas" (*Par.* 10), a use of βινεῖν so blunt that some have wondered if Lucian was trying to caricature an Epicurean way of speaking about sex.[311]

---

[304] E.g. the depiction of the death of Claudius: *Ultima vox eius haec inter homines audita est, cum maiorem sonitum emisset illequae facilius loquebatur, vae me, puto concacavi me* ("His last utterance heard among the living was this: when he had emitted a great sound from that part with which he found it easier to speak, he said, 'Oh, my, I think I shat myself' " [*Apoc.* 4]). The narrator comments that Claudius may indeed have soiled himself since he "certainly shat up everything else" (*omnia certe concacavit*).

[305] Varro, *Men.* 10: *pueri obscenis verbis novae nuptulae aures returant.*

[306] For similar titles, see Fantham, *Roman Literary Culture*, 52–53.

[307] The nature of the relationship between Lucian and Menippus has been variously assessed (see the literature cited by Raymond Astbury, "Petronius, P. Oxy. 3010, and Menippean Satire," *Classical Philology* 72 [1977], 22n4).

[308] E.g. πρωκτός occurs only at *As.* 56, and then in a proverb (Jocelyn, "A Greek Indecency," 55n171).

[309] Jocelyn, "A Greek Indecency," 28.

[310] *Lex.* 12. Lucian uses καταπύγων elsewhere (e.g. *Adv. ind.* 23, where the content shows that he means the word in its literal sense), as well as its derivative, καταπυγοσύνη (*Gall.* 32).

[311] The suggestion that Lucian is here caricaturing Epicurus is made by Jocelyn, "A Greek Indecency," 55n171, and Bain, "Six Greek Verbs," 55n32. The ancient comments about Epicurus's style are gathered by Hermann Usener, *Epicurea* (Leipzig: Teubner, 1887), 88–90, and discussed by Eduard Norden, *Die antike Kunstprosa* (Leipzig: Teubner, 1898), 123–25. Diogenes Laertius reports that Epicurus "used the proper [or "ordinary"] terms for things" (κέχρηται δὲ λέξει κυρίᾳ κατὰ τῶν πραγμάτων [*DL* 10.13]). Cleomedes (*De motu* 2.91) offers the lengthiest criticism of his style: "Since, in addition to other things, his style is also a corrupt motley, making use of expressions like 'stable states of the flesh' and 'hopeful hopes' concerning it, and calling tears 'glistenings of the eyes' and having recourse to phrases like 'holy screechings' and 'ticklings of the body' and 'wenchings' and other bad mischiefs of this kind. One may say that these expressions derive in part from brothels, in part they are similar to those spoken by women celebrating the Thesmophoria at the festivals of Demeter, and in part they issue from the midst of the synagogue and the beggars in its courtyards. These are Jewish and debased and much lower than reptiles [ἐπεί γε πρὸς τοῖς ἄλλοις καὶ τὰ κατὰ τὴν ἑρμηνείαν αὐτῷ ποικίλως διεφθορότα ἐστί, σαρκὸς εὐσταθῆ καταστήματα

Even without primary obscenities, Lucian could be gleefully graphic in his invective. So when he attacks the man who had criticized him (the "Mistaken Critic"), Lucian says that he had earned the nickname "Sore Throat" in Egypt after a sailor stuffed his mouth. The nickname became "Cyclops" in Italy after he performed "an obscene parody of Homer." He played an "eager to be fucked [βινητιῶν] Polyphemus,"[312] while a hired youth played Odysseus, coming at him with his "bar straight," ready to put out his eye. Lucian says that the "mistaken critic" set his mouth wide and "strove to engulf [his] Noman whole, along with his crew, his rudder, and his sails" (*Pseudol.* 27). Large sections of this essay consist of this sort of attack on his critic's sexuality; and although Lucian pretends to be "ashamed to tell" such stories (αἰσχύνομαι διηγεῖσθαι [*Pseudol.* 27; cf. 20]), he insists his target warranted it.

Latin satire tended to avoid primary obscenities, but it did not shy away from blunt images. Lucilius's *libertas verborum*[313] included "words of the utmost obscenity";[314] he could call himself *improbus* (1026) and he adopts the role of the cynic dog, and of a muck raker: "he (grubs about) in the dung on the ground, in the filth of the byre and the pig-shit."[315] Horace (65–8 B.C.) used obscene words in the first book of the *Sermones*, for instance, when attributing the Trojan War to Helen's

---

λέγοντι καὶ τὰ περὶ ταύτης πιστὰ ἐλπίσματα καὶ λίπασμα ὀφθαλμῶν τὸ δάκρυον ὀνομάζοντι καὶ ἱερὰ ἀνακραυγάσματα καὶ γαργαλισμοὺς σώματος καὶ ληκήματα καὶ ἄλλας τοιαύτας κακὰς ἄτας· ὧν τὰ μὲν ἐκ χαμαιτυπείων ἄν τις εἶναι φήσειε, τὰ δὲ ὅμοια τοῖς λεγομένοις ἐν τοῖς Δημητρίοις ὑπὸ τῶν Θεσμοφοριαζουσῶν γυναικῶν, τὰ δὲ ἀπὸ μέσης τῆς προσευχῆς καὶ τῶν ἐπ' αὐλαῖς προσαιτούντων, Ἰουδαϊκά τινα καὶ παρακεχαραγμένα καὶ κατὰ πολὺ τῶν ἑρπετῶν ταπεινότερα]" (trans. Menahem Stern, *Greek and Latin Authors on Jews and Judaism* [3 vols; Jerusalem: The Israel Academy of Sciences and Humanities, 1980], 2:157–58). Cleomedes was probably writing sometime in the first two centuries of the common era (so Alexander Jones, "The Stoics and the Astronomimcal Sciences," in *The Cambridge Companion to the Stoics* [ed. Brad Inwood; Cambridge: Cambridge University Press, 2003], 333).

[312] Bain notes that the desiderative βινητιᾶν is almost always used with the sense βούλομαι βινεῖσθαι ("Six Greek Verbs," 61).

[313] Mentioned in Cicero, *Fam.* 12.16.3.

[314] Michael Coffey, *Roman Satire* (2d ed.; Bristol: Bristol Classics Press, 1989), 6, who notes that Lucilius was not as extreme as Martial. H. P. Obermayer, citing *inbubinare* ("defile with mentruaual blood") and *inbulbitare* ("defile with excrement"), says that "Die Obszönitäten bei Lucilius sind bemerkenswert und stehen dem ordinären Sprachgebrauch mancher Inschr. (CIL 10,1,4483) in nichts nach" ("Pornographie, IV. Rom," *DNP* 11:170).

[315] *hic in stercore humi stabulique fimo atque sucerdis* (E. H. Warmington, *Remains of Old Latin* [4 vols.; LCL; Cambridge: Harvard University Press, 1967], 3:350, fragment 1081); translation by A. S. Gratwick, *Cambridge History of Classical Literature*, 2:164.

cunnus (*Serm.* 1.3.107; cf. also 1.2.36, 70). Yet after this book, Horace "changed his view about the propriety of such words," and "the lexical decency of [his second book of *Sermones*] set the pattern for later satire."[316] Juvenal (*ca.* A.D. 60–after 130) did not shy away entirely from "the coarser elements of the Latin sexual language," but avoided outright obscenities.[317] Publishing his satires in the second and third decades of the second century, he rued the loss of freedom of speech.[318] But by this Juvenal means the freedom to abuse people *by name*, for Juvenal was clearly free to be graphic in his abuse, whether it is a pathic's "smooth anus" (*podice leui* [*Sat.* 2.12]), the dangers of a flattering Greek's "organ" (*inguen* [*Sat.* 3.109]), "the unheard of length of your dangling tool" (*longi mensura incognita nerui* [*Sat.* 9.34]), or the fact that the only path up the social ladder leads right through a "rich old woman's *vesica.*"[319] The genre seemed not to permit using the strongest obscene terms, but Juvenal was still able to find expressions that might offend some readers.[320]

VI.A. *Epigram*

Catullus and Martial claimed that epigram demanded strong language;[321] their writings certainly delivered it. Both Catullus and Martial revel in blunt and obscene terms, using them to abuse and to amuse. Martial even mocks the writer of epigram whose chaste poems have no "cock."[322] Greek epigrams, while often dealing with sexual topics in imaginative (some would say disgusting) ways, made less frequent use of obscene

---

[316] Adams, *Latin Sexual Vocabulary*, 221; so Coffey, *Roman Satire*, 95.

[317] Adams, *Latin Sexual Vocabulary*, 221.

[318] *Sat.* 1.151–56.

[319] Literally "bladder," but here used contemptuously for her vagina (Susanna Morton Braund, *Juvenal: Satires Book 1* [Cambridge: Cambridge University Press, 1996], 85).

[320] For instance, when he speaks of an insatiable woman's "rigid vulva" (*rigidae tentigine volvae* [*Sat.* 6.129]); or of a slave cramming his "cock [*penem*] up your guts" (*Sat.* 9.43). For representative instances where Juvenal avoids "explicit obscenity through metaphor [or] synecdoche," see Braund, *Juvenal*, 26; on Juvenal's "rhetorical exploitation of obscenity," see Green, *Classical Bearings*, 240–55.

[321] Catullus, *Carm.* 16.7–11; Martial *Ep.* 1.1; 1.35; 8 Prologue.

[322] "You write all your epigrams in chaste language, there is no cock in your poems. I admire, I commend. You are the purest of the pure. Whereas no page of mine lacks lubricity. These then let naughty youths read and easy girls, an old fellow too, but one with a mistress to plague him. But *your* language, Cosconius, so respectable and pure, should be read by boys and maidens" (*Ep.* 3.69 [Shackleton Bailey, LCL]).

terms.[323] The whole Palatine Anthology has just six uses of βινῶ;[324] words such as πέος (which occurs twice)[325] or πρωκτός[326] are not common.

The exceptionally coarse sexual invective of Catullus and Martial has been richly analyzed by Amy Richlin with the metaphor of the garden guardian Priapus.[327] Priapus was the ithyphallic god whose statues were placed in gardens and orchards to ward off thieves. In the *Priapea*, a book of epigrams dealing with Priapus, potential thieves were warned in witty, filthy epigrams that Priapus would assault their every orifice with his gigantic member.[328] In lieu of actual activity, the god attacks with his lusty and shameless words.[329] Richlin suggests that the obscene verbal assaults of Catullus and Martial are similar: their obscene words are a sort of sexual assault.[330] Catullus 37 illustrates Richlin's point perfectly, as Catullus threatens a group of men first with *irrumatio* (37.8), and then with drawing "penises on the front of the tavern" (*frontem tabernae sopionibus scribam* [37.9–10]).[331]

---

[323] Ritter claimed that the obscenities in Catullus could be attributed to his Greek *Bildung*, since Greeks, he said, were free of the Romans' self-consciousness ("Übertriebene Scheu," 572). In fact, Greek epigram made less use of lexical indecency, prefering "figurative terminology" (Adams, *Latin Sexual Vocabulary*, 219). If Catullus was not simply innovative in his use of indecency, he was following Latin, not Greek, epigram (Richard W. Hooper, *The Priapus Poems: Erotic Epigrams from Ancient Rome* [Urbana: University of Illinois Press, 1999], 19). E. E. Sikes proposed yet another source for Martial's obscenity: "The grossness may be a legacy from Fescennine verses—or from the bestial side of human nature" ("Latin Literature of the Silver Age," in *The Cambridge Ancient History* [ed. S. A. Cook, F. E. Adcock, and M. P. Charlesworth; 12 vols.; Cambridge: Cambridge University Press, 1936], 11:725).

[324] Jocelyn, "A Greek Indecency," 55nn168–169. Bain suggests that when βινῶ was used, there was "a desire to provoke or else to characterize plain speaking" ("Six Greek Verbs," 56). The specificity of the word is necessary for Strato's clever argument "from nature" about the superiority of pederasty over sex between man and woman (*AP* 12.245; cf. P. G. Maxwell-Stuart, "Strato and the Musa Puerilis," *Hermes* 100 [1972]: 215–40); and the bluntness seems apt for the succinct ἁδὺ τὸ βινεῖν ἐστί (*AP* 5.29).

[325] E.g., *AP* 12.240, where the tone fits the topic (impotence).

[326] The word itself is important in *AP* 12.6, for Strato has discovered that πρωκτός has the same numerical value as χρυσός.

[327] *The Garden of Priapus: Sexuality and Aggression in Roman Humor* (New Haven: Yale University Press, 1983).

[328] E.g., *Priapea* 13, 22, 74. Poem 13 is illustrative: *Percidere puer, moneo, futuere puella. / barbatum furem tertia poena manet*, which is rendered creatively by Hooper as "Girl, watch your cunt; boy, keep your ass from grief. / Another threat awaits the bearded thief" (*Priapus Poems*). For more on Priapus, see W. H. Parker, *Priapea: Poems for a Phallic God* (London: Croom Helm, 1988).

[329] In addition simply to *using* obscene language throughout the poems, Priapus also makes the indecency of his language an explicit topic (e.g., 1, 2, 3, 7, 8, 29, 38, 41, 67, 68).

[330] Richlin, *Garden*, 66.

[331] For another reference to drawing a phallus "as a mark of contempt" (Adams, *Latin*

The obscenities in Catullus and Martial contribute above all to an aggressive and abusive humor.[332] Volusius's *Annals* are "shitty" (*Annales Volusi, cacata carta* [Catullus 36.1]); Aemilius's mouth, which smells as bad as his ass, is like "the cunt of a pissing mule in heat [*in aestu meientis mulae cunnus*]" (Catullus 97.7–8). In the same spirit Martial tells one Zoilus, "you spoil the bathtub washing your arse. To make it filthier, Zoilus, stick your head in it."[333] Martial frequently targets specific sexual practices. He accuses a pretentious philosopher of wanting "to have a stiff cock in your soft rump (an expensive taste for the smelly and a discreditable one for the hairy). You know the origins and authorities of the schools: tell me, Pannychus, to be sodomized—what sort of dogma is that?" (*Ep.* 9.47.8 [Shackleton Bailey, LCL]; cf. 9.27). But sometimes the obscenity is less aggressive. Catullus can use *fututio* in an erotic context (proposing "bouts of fucking" [32.8]); and often Martial's obscenities are simply funny or clever. It is difficult to find any grander purpose in epigrams like, "When you hear applause in a bath, Flaccus, you may be sure that Maro's cock is there."[334] Here we are not far removed from the muse that inspired "There once was a man from Nantucket" (which at least rhymes).

Such poetry was read aloud in homes, at private dinner-parties,[335] and at "grander affairs to which the educated public was invited."[336] Poetry readings were, according to Juvenal, all too frequent: he listed as one of the hazards of the city—alongside fires and collapsing houses—the danger of "poets reading their work in August,"[337] a comment which fits well with Petronius's portrait of Eumolpus subjecting people to his poetry in the theater, the baths, and at the dinner table (*Sat.* 89–93). Juvenal portrays people filling their own recitations with slaves and

---

Sexual Vocabulary, 64), cf. the graffito from Pomeii: *ut merdas edatis, qui scripseras sopionis* ("may you eat shit, you who draw dicks on the wall" [*CIL* 4.1700]). On the conventions in Catullus 37, see Brian A. Krostenko, "*Arbitria Urbanitatis*: Language, Style, and Characterization in Catullus cc. 39 and 37," *Classical Antiquity* 20 (2001): 239–72.

[332] For analysis of Catullus 42 as representing the conventions of, and itself embodying, *convicium*, see Eduard Fraenkel, "Two Poems of Catullus," *JRS* 51 (1961): 46–51, and Usener, "Italische Volksjustiz," 20–21.

[333] *Zoile, quod solium subluto podice perdis,* / *spurcius ut fiat, Zoile, merge caput* (*Ep.* 2.42 [Shackleton Bailey, LCL]).

[334] *audieris in quo, Flacce, balneo plausum,* / *Maronis illic esse mentulam scito* (Martial, *Ep.* 9.33 [Shackleton Bailey, LCL]). For a narrative treatment of the same theme, cf. Petronius, *Sat.* 92.

[335] Martial, *Ep.* 3.45; 4.6; 11.52.16–18; Juvenal, *Sat.* 11.179–81.

[336] Braund, *Juvenal*, 75; cf. Pliny, *Ep.* 1.13.

[337] *Sat.* 1.1; 3.9.

clients. Pliny the Younger defends his public reading of his own light
verse by noting that no *matronae* were present (*Ep.* 5.3). The idea that
women (and children) should be protected from indecent language was
certainly widespread,[338] but it is not clear that it was taken very seriously.[339] Martial says that Lucretia blushes and puts his book away
when Brutus is present, but when Brutus leaves, she will read (*Ep.*
11.16). If children used foul language in the presence of their parents,[340]
they had to have heard these words somewhere. Quintilian, in fact,
confirms that they learned them at home! "We taught them, they heard
it all from us.... Every dinner party echoes with obscene songs [*omne
convivium obscenis canticis strepit*]" (*Inst.* 1.2.7–8 [Russell, LCL]).[341]

VI.B. *Tales of Sexual Adventures and Sex Manuals*

When Ovid wanted to excuse his *Ars Amatoria*, he had no trouble listing
other authors who had dealt frankly with erotic topics. "Why refer to
the poetry of Ticidas or of Memmius, in whom things are named—
with names devoid of shame?" (*Trist.* 2.433–34); "Sisenna translated
Aristides and was not harmed for inserting lewd jests into his story."[342]
In addition to Aristides, Ovid mentions Eubius ("author of an impure
narrative [*Eubius, impurae conditor historiae*]"), an unnamed author of new
Sybaritica, and the others who "did not remain silent about their own
sexual activities." He adds that, thanks to the generous patronage of
"our leaders," all of these works had joined the "monuments of learned
men" and become quite public (*Trist.* 2.413–20).

---

[338] Demosthenes 21.79; Varro, *Men.* 10–12; Plutarch, *Rom.* 20.3 (Romulus forbade
"uttering any shameful word in the presence of a woman" (αἰσχρὸν δὲ μηδένα μηδὲν
εἰπεῖν παρούσης γυναικός); Martial, *Ep.* 5.2; 11.15.1–2; 11.16.9–10; Juvenal 11.166;
Priapea 8; Tertullian, *Spect.* 21.2; Augutine, *Civ.* 2.4–5.

[339] For Rome, cf. Thomas A. J. McGinn, *The Economy of Prostitution in the Roman World:
A Study of Social History and the Brothel* (Ann Arbor: University of Michigan Press, 2004),
124–28. Henderson (*Maculate Muse*, 34) and Csapo and Slater (*Context of Ancient Drama*,
286–87) argue that women were part of the audience for Old Comedy.

[340] Seneca, giving typical examples of naughty behavior by children, says that
a child "does not refrain from rather obscene words" (*verbis obscenioribus non pepercit*
[*Const.* 11.2]).

[341] Similarly Plutarch reports (disapprovingly) that οἱ πολλοί have mimes performed
even when women and children are on hand (*Mor.* 712E).

[342] *vertit Aristiden Sisenna, nec obfuit illi / historiae turpis inseruisse iocos* (*Trist.* 2.443–44).
The *turpis iocos* may simply *be* the Milesian tales that he wrote (rather than jokes added
to a history or narrative), such that the whole phrase means that "Sisenna's main literary occupation, historiography, was diversified by the composition of improper verse"
(D. R. Shackleton Bailey, "Notes on Ovid's Poems from Exile," *Classical Quarterly* 32
[1982]: 392).

There was obviously a market for salacious tales that were bawdier than the novels (which tended to treat erotic episodes modestly).[343] In Pseudo-Lucian's *Amores*, Lycinus says that Theomnestus has been delighting him all day with "the sweet persuasion of his wanton stories" (ἡ τῶν ἀκολάστων σου διηγημάτων αἱμύλη καὶ γλυκεῖα πειθώ), so that he felt like Aristides himself, enchanted by the *Milesian Tales* (*Am.* 1). The Romans even brought along Aristides's "licentious" Milesian books (ἀκόλαστα βιβλία τῶν Ἀριστείδου Μιλησιακῶν) on military campaign, a fact for which the Parthians mocked them![344]

In addition to racy stories about sexual adventures, there were also illustrated "sex manuals," perhaps most famously those of Philaenis, dubbed by Baldwin the "doyenne of ancient sexology."[345] Also popular were the works of Elephantis.[346] Suetonius, enumerating Tiberius's debaucheries on Capreae, says that he had rooms furnished with indecent pictures and statuary, as well as the erotic manuals of Elephantis, so that his needs might be adequately met (*Tib.* 43).

Such literature was naturally expected to arouse. Martial advises having a girl present when reading Mussetus's *pathicissimi libelli* and the *Sybaritica*, lest one propose marriage to one's hands (*Ep.* 12.95). A medical writer recommended reading *fabulae amatoriae* to overcome impotence.[347] Without possessing such texts[348] it is impossible to determine the exact language used; but with or without obscene language, it could have achieved such a purpose: Eumolpus's story about seducing a handsome boy in Pergamon (Petronius, *Sat.* 85–87) is free from lexical indecency, yet had its effect on Encolpius (*erectus his sermonibus* [*Sat.* 88.1]).

---

[343] On sex manuals in general, see Holt N. Parker, "Love's Body Anatomized: The Ancient Erotic Handbooks and the Rhetoric of Sexuality," in *Pornography and Representation in Greece and Rome* (ed. Amy Richlin; New York: Oxford University Press, 1992), 90–107.

[344] Plutarch, *Crass.* 32.

[345] B. Baldwin, "Philaenis: The *Doyenne* of Ancient Sexology," *Corolla Londoniensis* 6 (1990): 1–7, who addresses the argument of K. Tsantsanoglou, that Philaenis's book was merely a παίγνιον (Tsantsanoglou, "The Memoirs of a Lady from Samos," *ZPE* 12 [1973]: 183–95). Cf. Lucian, *Pseud.* 24; Clement, *Protr.* 61.2; Polybius, *Hist.* 12.13.1, where she is named alongside one Botrys and "the other obscene writers" (τῶν ἄλλων ἀναισχυντογράφων).

[346] Cf. Martial 12.43 (*molles Elephantidos libelli*); *Priapia* 4 (*obscaenas rigido deo tabellas / ductas ex Elephantidos libellis / dat donum Lalage rogatque temptes / si pictas opus edat ad figuras*); and Philodemus, *Epigram* 38.6: "taking the positions described by Elephantis" (David Sider, *The Epigrams of Philodemos* [New York: Oxford University Press, 1997]).

[347] Theodore Priscian, *Logicus* 34, cited by H. P. Obermayer, "Pornographie, IV. Rom," *DNP* 11:170.

[348] Except for the very fragmentary P.Oxy 2891, on which see Tsantsanoglou, "Memoirs," and Baldwin, "*Doyenne*."

VI.C. *Ovid's* Culpa

Given the abundance and popularity of such literature dealing so
explicitly with sexual topics, it is puzzling that Ovid should have been
banished (A.D. 8) for having composed the *Ars Amatoria*.[349] William
Alexander thinks Augustus was upset, in light of his attempt to restore
the stern virtues of early Roman life, by Ovid's "flippant *attentat contre
les moeurs*."[350] But the offending work, *Ars Amatoria*, had appeared years
before the exile (*Trist.* 2.545–46). Why so long between its publication
and the *relegatio*? Either Augustus was angry all along, "on the lookout
for some means of taking vengeance, just waiting, as it were, for the
opportunity to strike,"[351] or the poems were not really the reason for
Ovid's banishment. Fantham proposes that, whatever the exact nature
of Ovid's indiscretion, it was convenient for him and Augustus to act as
though it was a matter of the *Ars Amatoria*.[352] In any event, the nature
of Ovid's protest suggests that there was at least some *plausibility* in the
idea that a poet might be punished for indecent writings. It is worth
noting that in the two books Martial dedicated to Domitian, he was
"careful to observe almost perfect propriety."[353]

Conclusion

A person in the ancient Mediterranean world encountered foul language
on a variety of occasions. When, for reasons that are not clear, foul language ceased to appear in Middle Comedy, it resurfaced in other forms
of comic drama, most notably in mime. Foul language could be used
in light-hearted conversation and in several genres of poetry. A wide
range of religious festivals included scurrilous and obscene language, and
foul language played an apotropaic role in military triumphs, planting
seeds, and even the naming of a child. Foul language was also used in
abuse, whether written in poems or on walls, or shouted in the streets.

---

[349] Ovid protests that he is not the only one to have written tender love poetry, but
he was the only one to have paid a penalty for it (*Trist.* 2.361–62). His list of authors
who were not banished for *their* erotic texts suggests that this is the reason for his
punishment (*Trist.* 2.361–420).

[350] William H. Alexander, "The *Culpa* of Ovid," *Classical Journal* 53 (1957–58):
320.

[351] Alexander, "The *Culpa* of Ovid," 320–21.

[352] Fantham, *Roman Literary Culture*, 111–25.

[353] Sikes, *Cambridge Ancient History*, 11:725.

Because such abuse was intended to humiliate its victim, it often used humor to invite others to laugh down the intended target. Athenian law prohibited using a number of words, but obscene words were not on the list. Roman law, on the other hand, did forbid using words that were obscene and violated public mores. But far more important than laws were social codes that put limits on the use of obscene language in most settings and literary genres. The obscene words so common in Martial or on the walls of Pompeii are absent from Virgil and Cicero (though Cicero knows them all and can playfully allude to them [*Fam.* 9.22]). Aristophanes's obscene vocabulary shows up in mime, in graffiti, on the lips of slaves, and in the occasional indecent proposal; but is carefully avoided in Greek oratorical and historical writings and, with a few exceptions, even in Greek epigram. Such patterns of appearance confirm the impression that ancients felt foul speech was not normally acceptable.

Having examined some of the locations where foul language was used, we are in a better position to consider what it would have meant in cultural terms for some individual or some group of people to use or avoid such language.

CHAPTER TWO

SPEECH, CHARACTER, AND SELF-DEFINITION

I. Speech as it Relates to Character

For Greeks and Romans, speech was an indicator of one's character and place in society. *Talis oratio, qualis vita*: "As the speech, so the life."[1] One woman's charming speech was an important enough virtue to be recorded on her epitaph.[2] When Theophrastus wanted to describe different "characters," he frequently focused on how they spoke. In addition to those character types that were defined by speech ("Dissembling," "Idle Chatter," "Garrulity," "Rumor-mongering," "Griping," "Slander"), Theophrastus also used speech habits to illustrate "Boorishness" (he talks too loud), "Shamelessness" ("a tolerance for doing and *saying* shameful things"),[3] "Grouchiness" ("If he stumbles on the street, he is apt to curse the stone"), and, best of all, "Bad Taste" ("While eating he relates that he's drunk some hellebore that cleaned him inside out, and that the bile in his stool was blacker than the soup that is on the table" [Rusten, LCL]). Something as small as a misspoken salutation— saying "Be well!" when the time of day called for "Greetings!"—could cause considerable embarrassment, and might be taken as proof of bad breeding.[4]

---

[1] So Seneca quotes what he says had become a proverb among the Greeks: *talis hominibus fuit oratio qualis vita* (*Ep.* 114.1). Quintilian also calls it a Greek saying (*Inst.* 11.1.30), and Cicero says that it originated with Socrates (*Tusc.* 5.47). Plutarch said that words—even more than physical traits—reveal character (*Cat. Maj.* 7.2); cf. Juvenal, *Sat.* 4.81–83.

[2] "Stranger, what I have to say is brief: Stand by and read it though. This is the uncomely catacomb of a comely woman. Her parents named her the name Claudia. Her husband with all her heart she loved. She bore two sons. The one of them she leaves on the earth, the other lies beneath it. *Her speech was charming* [*sermone lepido*], her gait attractive. She kept the house, she wove the wool. I have spoken. You may go" (*CIL* 6.15346 [trans. Brian A. Krostenko, *Cicero, Catullus, and the Language of Social Performance* (Chicago: The University of Chicago Press, 2001), 71]).

[3] Cf. Aristotle, *Magna moralia* 1193a1–2: "Modesty [αἰδώς] is a mean between shamelessness [ἀναισχυντία] and extreme shyness; it concerns both actions *and words*."

[4] So Lucian in *A Slip of the Tongue in Greeting*. The whole piece is lighthearted; nevertheless, Lucian says that he was humiliated by his mistake (1); that another person had "almost died for shame" when making similar mistakes (8); and that some would

There were many potential speech errors, and many character flaws they could betray. The Elder Seneca, for instance, believed the youth of his day lacked eloquence *because* they lacked moral probity.[5] In an epistle on the connection between speech and life, the Younger Seneca concurs: "Exactly as each individual man's actions seem to speak, so people's style of speaking [*genus dicendi*] often reproduces the general character of the time, if the morale of the public has relaxed and has given itself over to effeminacy. Wantonness in speech is proof of public luxury [*argumentum est luxuriae publicae orationis lascivia*]" (*Ep*. 114.2 [Gummere, LCL]). Although Seneca names *lascivia* here, his concern is not with indecent topics or words, but rather with a lax, unmanly style. To demonstrate the correlation between life and language, Seneca reviews the moral failings of Maecenas and then quotes several of his lines. What is objectionable in the writings is their "misleading word order" and "inverted" and "nerveless" expression (*Ep*. 114.8). Similarly, the philosopher Demonax claimed he could detect something effeminate and ill-bred in Favorinus's "laxity of rhythm."[6]

In general, foul language—whether used in humorous abuse, casual conversation, or erotic discussions—was contrasted with nobility, self-restraint, high-mindedness, and high social status. A second-century A.D. rhetorical treatise from Oxyrhynchus embodies this general impression: "Take no pleasure saying anything obscene or reckless, for that is mean and comes from a dissolute character; on the contrary, avoiding foul language is high-minded and is an ornament of speech."[7] Since people of high social status frequently claimed special moral gravity, certain sorts of jokes or erotic writings were thought inappropriate for their character. On the other hand, it was precisely these people who had the education and leisure to compose texts that they might also find themselves forced to defend.

Turning first to the views about humor, it is clear that lower forms of joking, especially those that used obscene words or themes, were associated with a lack of moral seriousness or upper-class refinement. Plato warned that anyone who regularly entered into those battles of

---

take his blunder as proof of "ignorance, bad training or idiocy" (17). All this for a slip of the tongue that was εὔφημον and merely οὐκ ἐν καιρῷ!

[5] *Controversiae*, 1 Preface 8–9.
[6] Lucian, *Demon*. 12.
[7] [τι] δὲ μηδὲν αἰσχρὸν [μ]ηδὲ προπετὲς ἀδέ[ως] λέγε; καὶ γὰρ μικρ[ο]π[ρ]επὲς τὸ τοιοῦ[τον] κ[α]ὶ ἀκολάστω ἤθεος· τὸ δὲ φεύγεν τὰς αἰσχρολογίας μεγ[αλ]οπρεπὲς καὶ κόσμος λόγω (P.Oxy 3.410.71–79).

words that involved abusive humor would lose his "earnestness" and "high-mindedness."[8] So Dio Chrysostom saw in the Alexandrians' love of theatrical abuse and scurrility a lack of σπουδή (*Alex.* 32.4). This intuition has its reflex in oratorical books. Demetrius warned that the wrong sorts of jokes could reveal one's character, and could display a lack of self restraint.[9] Cicero said that when using humor in oratory, the speaker "should emphasize his *gentlemanliness* and *modesty* by avoiding foul words and obscene subjects."[10] Cicero encouraged orators to employ humor, but insisted that it be decorous.[11] Cicero also urged orators to avoid even the incidental obscenities that formed from the infelicitous conjunction of words,[12] a topic on which Quintilian dwelt at length and with considerably more caution.[13]

---

[8] ὅ τις ἐθιζόμενος οὐδεὶς πώποτε ὃς οὐ τοῦ σπουδαίου τρόπου ἤτοι τὸ παράπαν διήμαρτεν ἢ μεγαλονοίας ἀπώλεσε μέρη πολλά (Plato, *Leg* 11; 935B).

[9] *Eloc.* 171: ἔστι δὲ καὶ τοῦ ἤθους τις ἔμφασις ἐκ τῶν γελοίων καὶ ἢ παιγνίας ἢ ἀκολασίας.

[10] *praestet idem ingenuitatem et ruborem suum verborum turpitudine et rerum obscenitate vitanda* (*De or.* 2.242). Later he adds that the obscenity of the comedian is "not only not worthy of the courtroom, but is hardly fit for the dinner table of *free men*" (*non solum non foro digna sed vix convivio liberorum* [*De or.* 2.252]).
Cicero himself had a reputation for ignoring his own advice. Quintilian reports that he was regarded as having been too keen to raise a laugh (*Inst.* 6.3.2–3). Three books of Cicero's jests were published posthumously and drew some criticism for some for their content (Quintilian, *Inst.* 6.3.5). Quintilian can only believe that the worse ones were merely common property, not the invention of the great orator (Quintilian, *Inst.* 6.3.4). On Cicero's wit, cf. Krostenko, *Language of Social Performance*, 202–32.

[11] "The orator ought to use humor in such a way that it not be clownish for being too frequent (*ut nec nimis frequenti ne scurrile sit*), nor like a mime's humor for being off-color (*nec subobsceno ne mimicum*), nor reprehensible for being impudent (*nec petulanti ne improbum*), nor unfeeling...nor should the humor be inappropriate (*alienum*) to the orator's persona, or that of the judges, or to the occasion. These are examples of impropriety (*indecorum*). With these exceptions, he will make use of wit (*sal*) and humor (*facetiae*) in a way that I have seen none of the latter-day Atticists do, despite the fact that doing so is quite in accord with the Attic character" (*Or. Brut.* 98–99; cited from Krostenko, *Language of Social Performance*, 226).

[12] Cicero, *Or.* 154 (discussing contractions generally): "Is it not perfectly plain why we say *cum illis*, but use *nobiscum* rather than *cum nobis*? If the latter were used the letters would coalesce and produce an obscene meaning, as they would have done in this sentence unless I had place *autem* between *cum* and *nobis*" (*Quid, illud non olet unde sit, quod dicitur cum illis, cum autem nobis non dicitur, sed nobiscum? Quia si ita diceretur, obscenius concurrerent litterae, ut etiam modo, nisi autem interposuissem, concurrissent* [Hubbell, LCL]).

[13] "But since I have undertaken first to indicate faults, let us begin with what is called *cacemphaton*. This consists either (1) in a phrase perverted by bad usage so as to give an obscene meaning, as by those who (if you can believe it) get a laugh out of *ductare exercitus* and *patrare bellum*, which are respectable but old-fashioned expressions in Sallust (this is not, in my judgement, the writers' fault but the readers', but it is none the less to be avoided, inasmuch as our moral decline has led to the loss of respectable

Quintilian lists among the lower vices "affectation of buffoonery" and "disregard for modesty in regard to unseemly or indecent things or words"; these are faults, he says, found in those who are trying too hard to raise a laugh.[14] He felt that the sorts of jokes one encountered in popular drama were altogether inappropriate for orators.[15] For Quintilian, class concerns are paramount. One reason that he does not want jokes to be a central part of an orator's repertoire is that the upper class has no way to control them: even *rustici* can be funny, and there is no good way to teach humor (*Inst.* 6.3.13–14).

People of rank and refinement were not *supposed* to talk like the vulgar freedmen in Petronius's *Satyricon*,[16] although they evidently could not help laughing at, and even making, the same sorts of jokes. Suetonius finds Vespasian's quick wit part of his affability, but adds that his jokes were often "of a low and buffoonish kind, so that he did not even refrain from obscene expressions [*etsi scurrilis et sordidae, ut ne praetexta-tis quidem verbis abstineret*]."[17] Philo reports that Macro had to instruct Gaius that, as "sovereign of the earth," he really should not take such visible pleasure from the obscene jokes of the mimes (*Leg.* 42–44). In the Priapic poetry we can also see both this view that obscene humor

---

words, and we have to yield even to vices if they are winning); or (2) in a collocation of words which has an unfortunate sound: if we say *cum hominibus notis loqui* ('to speak with well-known men'), without the inserted *hominibus*, we find ourselves falling into something objectionable, because the last letter of the first syllable (*m*), which cannot be pronounced without closing the lips, either forces us to pause in a very unbecoming way, or, if joined to the next letter (*n*), is assimilated to it. Other collocations have similar consequences; to pursue them would amount to dwelling willingly on a fault which we say is to be avoided. Division also, however, can cause offence to modesty, for instance, the use of the nominative *intercapedo*" (*Inst.* 8.3.43–47 [Russell, LCL]).

[14] *Humiliora illa vitia: summissa adulatio, adfectata scurrilitas, in rebus ac verbis parum modestis ac pudicis vilis pudor, in omni negotio neglecta auctoritas; quae fere accidunt iis, qui nimium aut blandi esse aut ridiculi volunt* (*Inst.* 11.1.30 [Russell, LCL]).

[15] *Inst.* 6.3.46–48; cf. 6.3.29: "As for obscenity, it should not merely be banished from his language, but should not even be suggested."

[16] E.g. "'Go fuck yourself [*frigori laecasin dico*],' I say to the cold weather" (*Sat.* 42, using a non-literal, but dynamically equivalent, English expression); "He was an old lecher. I honestly don't think he left the dog alone" (*Sat.* 43); "But if we had any balls at all, he wouldn't be feeling so pleased with himself" (*Sat.* 44); "I used to bang [*debattuere*] my mistress so much that even the old boy suspected me" (*Sat.* 69); "not let people run up and shit on my monument [*ne in monumentum meum populus cacatum currat*]" (*Sat.* 71). Translation by J. P. Sullivan, *Petronius*: The Satyricon; *Seneca*: The Apocolocyntosis of the Divine Claudius (London: Penguin Books, 1998).

[17] *Vesp.* 22 (Rolfe, LCL). Suetonius says that "[Vespasian] also quoted Greek verses with great timeliness, saying of a man of tall stature, and monstrous parts: 'Striding along and waving a lance that casts a long shadow [*Iliad* 7.213]'" (*Vesp.* 23.1 [Rolfe, LCL]). If this is an example of Vespasian's better efforts, one can imagine what his coarser jokes were like.

was something unrefined *and* the undeniable fact that even the most educated people clearly enjoyed (and composed) it. The actual author of these poems obviously possessed considerable mastery of the Latin language; but the obscenities in the poems are regularly connected to the god's rusticity and ignorace (e.g. poems 3, 38, 41, 68).

Aside from the temptation to engage in low humor, rhetors were also faced with how best to depict the real or imagined sexual degeneracy of an opponent without saying things that would reflect badly on themselves. Orators found it best to avoid,[18] and urged others to avoid,[19] primary obscenities. To describe certain sexual activities too directly would compromise one's own modesty[20] or one's claim to proper *paideia*. When Polybius addresses the historian Timaeus's "filthy accusation" (αἰσχρολογία) against Demochares, he presents it as evidence of Timaeus's lack of *paideia*:

> Timaeus says that Demochares had played the whore with the upper parts of his body; that he was, in short, no longer fit to blow the holy fire; that in his practices he had actually exceeded the "Memoirs" of Botrys and Philaenis and the other shameless writers. Such abuse and such narrations are the sort that not only no educated man [πεπαιδευμένος ἀνήρ], but not even any of those who work in a brothel would make. (*Hist.* 12.13.1–2)[21]

---

[18] Aeschines, *Against Timarchus* 37–38 (Adams, LCL): "I beg you to pardon me, fellow citizens, if, compelled to speak about habits which by nature are, indeed, not noble, but are nevertheless his, I be led to use some expression that is as bad as Timarchus's deeds [ἐξαχθῶ τι ῥῆμα εἰπεῖν ὅ ἐστιν ὅμοιον τοῖς ἔργοις τοῦ Τιμάρχου]. For it would not be right for you to blame me, if now and again I use plain language [εἴ τι σαφῶς εἴποιμι] in my desire to inform you; the blame should rather be his, if it is a fact that his life has been so shameful [αἰσχρῶς] that a man who is describing his behaviour is unable to say what he wishes without sometimes using expressions that are likewise shameful"; *Against Ctesiphon* 162 (Adams, LCL): "What he used to do there or what was done to him, is a scandal that is in dispute, and the story is one that would be quite improper for me to repeat [καὶ τὸ πρᾶγμα οὐδαμῶς εὔσχημον ἐμοὶ λέγειν]"; cf. *Against Timarchus* 52. Cf. also Demosthenes 4.12; 19.309. Further references in Halliwell, "Uses of Laughter," 289n39.

[19] Pseudo-Aristotle, *Rhetorica ad Alexandrum* 1441b21 (cited above, p. 2n9); Pseudo-Isocrates *Demon.* 15: "You should not think it good even to mention that which is shameful to do" (ἃ ποεῖν αἰσχρόν, ταῦτα νόμιζε μηδὲ λέγειν εἶναι καλόν).

[20] So the Elder Seneca said that the orator "must stay far from any obscenity either of words or of meanings. It would be better to remain silent about certain matters, even to the detriment of one's cause, than to express them to the detriment of one's modesty" (*longe recedendum est ab omni obscenitate et verborum et sensuum; quaedam satius est causae detrimento tacere quam verecundiae dicere* [*Controv.* 1.2.23]).

[21] Cf. Polybius, *Hist.* 31.6.4, where Gaius Sulpicius Gallus's willingness to accept "any kind of foul and abusive language against the king" (πᾶσαν ἐπιδεχόμενος αἰσχρολογίαν καὶ λοιδορίαν) reflects badly on him, and *Hist.* 8.11.8, where Theopompus's αἰσχρολογία is indefensible.

Even if the stories were true, says Polybius, Timaeus had no business
putting them in a history (*Hist.* 12.14.2), for historians must consider not
so much what opponents deserve as what is appropriate for themselves
to say (*Hist.* 12.14.4).

The outrageous language of comedy and satirical writings could be
defended as a useful tool in exposing society's failings.[22] When Aelius
Aristides wanted to attack what he found to be the "hateful," "dissolute,"
and "shameful" language of the theater, he anticipated that his audience might believe that such lampooning should be tolerated because
it had a positive moral effect (*Or.* 29.16, 29), and that such humor was
in fact "urbane" (ἀστεῖον, *Or.* 29.32). Horace admired the way the old
comic poets—and Lucilius as a Latin successor—used great *libertas* in
exposing faults with their biting humor (*Serm.* 1.4.1–8). But in general,
the use of foul abuse was criticized as ignoble[23] more often than it was
defended as necessary.

If we turn from the language of humor to that of eros, we find the
same contrast of lewd talk and moral seriousness, but also the attempt
to redefine the discussion. In the case of the risqué vocabulary of erotic
poetry, sophisticated authors frequently complained that prudery about
sexual language bespoke bad breeding; only the unlettered would fail
to grasp the conventions of poetry, or would be ignorant of who had
used such language in the past, or would think that one's poetry was
an indication of one's morals.

Clearly such literature was often thought to reflect badly upon the
person accused of reading or writing it. So Quintilian (*Inst.* 10.1.63)
says of Alcaeus that he "*stooped* to love poetry, though his talents were
more suited to higher things" (*in amores descendit, maioribus tamen aptior*
[Russell, LCL]). Epictetus says that reading lewd writings reveals a
loss of modesty and nobility.[24] Lucian was not flattering his "mistaken

---

[22] Grant, *Ancient Rhetorical Theories*, 53–59; Quadlbauer, "Dichter," 58, 70.

[23] Representative is the comment of Aelian (*Suda* 1.376.11) that Archilochus was
"a *noble* poet in other respects if one were to take away his foul mouth and slanderous
speech and wash them away like a stain" (Ἀρχίλοχον γοῦν, ποιητὴν γενναῖον τἄλλα,
εἴ τις αὐτοῦ τὸ αἰσχροεπὲς καὶ τὸ κακόρρημον ἀφέλοι καὶ οἱονεὶ κηλῖδα ἀπορρύψειεν
[Gerber, *Greek Iambic Poetry*, LCL]).

[24] "Man, you used to be modest [ὑπῆρχες αἰδήμων], and are no longer so; have
you lost nothing? Instead of Chrysippus and Zeno you now read Aristeides and
Evenus.... But formerly you used never to think of any of these things [fancy clothes
and perfumes], but only where you might find decent discourse [εὐσχήμων λόγος], a
worthy man, a noble thought [ἐνθύμημα γενναῖον]. Therefore you used to sleep as a
man, to go forth as a man, to wear the clothes of a man, to utter the discourse that

critic" when he suggested that he learned his obscure words "from the Tablets of Philaenis, which you keep in hand" (*Pseudol.* 24).

Pliny the Younger mentions his efforts at poetry several times in his letters, often defending how a man so serious[25] or of such status could have written such light poems. Pliny was informed that there had been much discussion about his poetry, and that some felt he deserved censure for having held a public reading (*Ep.* 5.3.1). Pliny can only imagine that his critics were ignorant of the fact that even "the most learned, serious, blameless" men had written such verse. Anyone who knows whom Pliny is imitating—he gives a very long list of senators—should recognize that such a pursuit is not inappropriate for a man of his rank.[26] Pliny made a similar appeal to precedent when he told Plinius Paternus that some of the poetry he was sending might strike him as indelicate (*petulantiora* [*Ep.* 4.14.4]). Pliny suggests that a well-educated person should already recognize that the use of direct terms for sexual topics was acceptable; to refrain from using them would have more to do with a lack of courage than a sense of propriety.

> Your learning ought to tell you how many *distinguished* and *serious* men [*summos illos et gravissimos viros*] in dealing with such themes neither avoided lascivious subjects [*lascivia rerum*] nor refrained from expressing them in plain language [*ne verbis quidem nudis abstinuisse*]. If I have shrunk from this, it is not because my principles are stricter than theirs (why should they be?) but because I am less courageous; and yet I know that the best rule for this kind of thing is the one in Catullus, when he says that "the true poet should be chaste himself, though his poetry need not be, for it must be relaxed and free from restraint if it is to have wit and charm." (Ep. 4.14.4–5 [Radice, LCL])

Other poets would also appeal to precedent when their poetry called into question their seriousness[27]—at times with drastic effect. Martial

---

was suitable for a good man [λόγους ἐλάλεις πρέποντας ἀνδρὶ ἀγαθῷ].... Is not self-respect [αἰδώς] lost, is not decency [εὐσχημοσύνη] lost?" (*Diatr.* 4.9.6–9).

[25] *Ep.* 7.4.1: "You say that you have read my hendecasyllables, and you want to know how a *serious* [*severus*] man like me came to write them; and I am *not frivolous*, I admit" (Radice, LCL).

[26] Pliny does not seem to have been overly anxious about what he read, for he acknowledges the mimes of Herodas (*Ep.* 4.3.3) as well as comedy, farce, and Sotadic verse (*Ep.* 5.3.2) (on the emendation *Sotadicos* for *Socraticos*, see A. N. Sherwin-White, *The Letters of Pliny: A Historical and Social Commentary* [Oxford: Clarendon, 1966], 317).

[27] Cf. Martial, *Epig.* 8Prologue: "Although epigrams appearing to aim at the verbal license of mime have been written even by men of the *strictest morals and the highest station* [*a severissimis quoque et summae fortunae viris*], I have not allowed these here to talk as wantonly as is their custom" (Shackleton Bailey, LCL).

had several ways of defending his epigrams,[28] but at one point he quotes a poem of Augustus in which Augustus had used *futuere* four times and *pedicare* and *mentula* once each (all in the space of six lines!). Martial concludes, "Augustus, you surely absolve my witty little books, knowing how to speak with Roman candor [*Romana simplicitate*]."[29] It is striking that, although Pliny and Martial can list senators and emperors as writers of lewd verse, foul language continued to be depicted as something lowly and undignified. This widely held sentiment was not arrived at empirically.

Just as crass jokes or erotic poetry were often seen as unsuitable for those of high status, they were also inappropriate for the philosopher, with his pretense to dignified self-mastery. So Epictetus tells his disciples that it would be better not to attend poetry readings, and if they go, to guard their dignity and tranquility (*Ench.* 33.11). As had Aristotle, Epictetus warned against telling or even listening to the wrong sorts of jokes, lest one lose the respect of others; he goes beyond Aristotle by explaining what to do if αἰσχρολογία was used in one's presence:

> Do not try to provoke laughter, for this is liable to slip into vulgarity, and will lessen your neighbor's respect for you. And it is also dangerous to proceed into foul language [αἰσχρολογίαν]. When, therefore, such speech is used, if the situation is appropriate, rebuke the person who has gone so far; but if it is not appropriate, make it clear that you dislike such speech by remaining silent, blushing, and frowning. (*Ench.* 33.15–16)

This sort of frown or furrowed brow is precisely the reaction certain poets know that they might encounter, and which they ask readers to put aside.[30]

The stern disapproval Epictetus hoped to see in his disciples was embodied by Cato the Younger, who, in 55 B.C., had to leave the

---

[28] For a list of Martial's *apologiae*, see Richlin, *Garden*, 228n4.

[29] Martial, *Ep.* 11.20 (Shackelton Bailey, LCL). On the rhetoric of "candor" (*simplicitas*) in the defense of blunt language, cf. Petronius, *Sat.* 132; *Priapea* 3, 38; Apuleius, *Apol.* 11. In another poem, Martial cited Lucan to the same effect: "He did not blush to say in wanton verse [*lascivo versu*]: 'If I'm not even sodomized [*pedicor*], Cotta, what am I doing here?'" (*Ep.* 10.64 [Shackleton Bailey, LCL]).

[30] Martial, *Ep.* 1.4.12: *pone supercilium*; *AP* 12.2.6: τούτοις δ' ὀφρύες οὐκ ἔπρεπον; *Priapea* 1: *pone supercilium*; cf. Petronius, *Sat.* 132: *constricta spectatis fronte Catones*. Plutarch assumes brows will furrow over improper talk (*Mor.* 68C–D). Unlike a frown or furrowed brow, the blush was supposedly unfeignable; but one could aquire the modesty from which it would naturally flow (cf. Philo, *Her.* 128: divine wisdom "implants modesty and discretion [αἰδῶ καὶ σωφροσύνην]; and a blush [ἐρυθριᾶν], where the matter calls for blushing, is the clearest proof of the presence of these qualities" [Colson, LCL]).

Floralia because the actors could not carry on in his presence.[31] Martial opens his epigrams, in fact, by asking "Cato" to leave, so that he can speak as freely as he likes. And when Encolpius berates his impotent penis, he is aware that "it's improper to give you your real name when *talking seriously*,"[32] and that it is shameful to have words with "a part of the body that more *dignified* people [*severioris notae homines*] do not even think about." He finally defends his freedom of speech to the "Catos" of the world.

The Roman sense that a philosopher should be troubled by immoral talk can be seen in Eumolpus's tale about how he seduced a boy in Pergamon. "Whenever any mention was made at the table of taking advantage of pretty boys, I flared up so violently and I was so stern about my ears being offended by obscene talk that the mother especially regarded me as a real old-world philosopher."[33] Cicero's comments about Philodemus—whose epigrams include one of the rare uses of βινεῖν in Greek epigram[34]—reveal the same sense of incompatibility between philosophy and erotic poetry:

> He [Philodemus] proceeded to compose a poem so witty, neat, and elegant, that nothing could be cleverer. *Anyone who wishes is at liberty to find fault with him for this poem;* but let him do so gently, not as though with *a low and bare-faced rogue* [*non ut improbum, non ut audacem, non ut impurum*], but as with a poor little Greek, a parasite, a poet.... Had he been luckier in the sort of pupil he found [i.e. someone other than Piso], he might have turned out a *steadier* and more *irreproachable* character [*austerior et gravior*]; but chance led him into a style of writing which was *unworthy of a philosopher*, if, that is to say, philosophy is correctly described as comprising the whole theory of virtue and duty and the good life. (*Pis.* 70–72 [Watts, LCL])

The view that love poetry was incompatible with philosophical pretensions even played a part in the trial of Apuleius of Madauros, whose opponents presented the fact that he composed lighter works and love poems as evidence, along with his long hair and possession of a mirror, that he lacked the self-restraint required of a Platonic philosopher.[35]

---

[31] Valerius Maximus, *Facta et dicta memorabilia*, 2.10.8; cf. Seneca, *Ep.* 97.8; Plutarch, *Cat. Min.* 19; cf. Adams, *Latin Sexual Vocabulary*, 223.

[32] *nam ne nominare quidem te inter res serias fas est* (*Sat.* 132 [Sullivan]).

[33] *quotiescunque enim in convivio de usu formosorum mentio facta est, tam vehementer excandui, tam severa tristitia violari aures meas obsceno sermone nolui, ut me mater praecipue tanquam unum ex philosophis intueretur* (Petronius, *Sat.* 85 [Sullivan]).

[34] Cicero says he cannot read the poems in court (*Pis.* 71).

[35] Apuleius complains that they presented his poetry "as though it were the work of an unrestrained carouser" (*quasi improbi comisatoris* [*Apol.* 10]). He asks several times

Apuleius read his works again for the court, to show he was not
ashamed of those lines his opponents had read "as though they were
the most wanton imaginable" (*quos illi quasi intemperantissimos postremum
legere* [*Apol.* 9]). He makes the standard defenses of his poems (including one poem that expresses his attraction to the *pueri* of his friend),
such as citing other Greeks and Romans who wrote verse like his. But
he suspects his opponents will cavil that the authors cited were not
philosophers (*at philosophi non fuere* [*Apol.* 9]). And even after Apuleius
adds three philosophers to his list, he must prove that such verse is
suitable for a *Platonic* philosopher (*Apol.* 10). In Apuleius's opinion, this
charge only reveals his opponents' ignorance, for he can cite erotic
epigrams composed by Plato himself. Apuleius plays up the topic of
his opponents' lack of learning and culture throughout this section
(and, indeed, throughout the entire *Apology*). More literate men, he says,
would never have thought that "playing at verse" was any indicator of
character.[36] Do they not know the famous lines from Catullus 16, that
a poet may be chaste even if his lines are wanton? Do they not know
that the Emperor Hadrian said the same thing?[37] Reminding the court
of the conventions and pedigree of erotic verse does more than simply
exonerate Apuleius's poetry. Apuleius's copious references to Greek and
Latin literature continue throughout the whole of the *Apology*, effectively
separating himself and Claudius Maximus, the learned proconsul who
heard the case, from this unlettered family who lived on the edge of
the civilized world.[38]

---

what in his poetry is not fitting *for a philosopher* (*Quaeso, quid habent isti versus re aut verbo
pudendum, quid omnino quod philosophus suum nolit videri?* [*Apol.* 6]; *crimen haud contemnendum
philosopho* [*Apol.* 7]); and says that if he has written "bad poems" it is the crime not of
a philosopher, but of a poet (*si malos, crimen est, nec id tamen philosophi, sed poetae* [*Apol.* 9]).
   It has been argued that the prosecution presented the poems as evidence of magic—
mala carmina in the sense of "evil incantations" rather than "bad poems" (Adam Abt,
*Die Apologie von Apuleius von Madaura und die antike Zauberei: Beiträge zur Erläuterung der Schrift
de magia* [Giessen: Alfred Töpelmann, 1908]: 96–97; Vincent Hunink, *Pro se de magia:
apologia* [2 vols.; Amsterdam: J. C. Gieben, 1997], 2:43–45). Horace makes a similar
play on *mala carmina* and *bona carmina* (*Sat.* 2.1.82–84). Obviously, this would explain
the relevance of the poems to a trial about magic. But the poems hardly appear to
be "magical" (*pace* Hunink), and there is ample evidence that Apuleius is representing
the charge accurately enough, that is, that his opponents see in poetry full of longing
for two boys evidence of intemperate lust.
   [36] *ullum specimen morum sit versibus ludere* (*Apol.* 11).
   [37] Apuleius says that Hadrian wrote "you are lascivious in verse, but pure in mind"
(*lascivus versu, mente pudicus eras* [*Apol.* 11]).
   [38] As noted by Keith Bradley, "Law, Magic, and Culture in the *Apologia* of Apuleius,"
Phoenix 51 (1997): 213–14.

Apuleius again connects his opponents' prudery to their ignorance when addressing the charge that he had been searching for two fish with obscene names (*duas res marinas impudicis uocabulis* [*Apol.* 33]). Tannonius Pudens wanted to convey that the fish were named after the male and female genitalia, but could not bring himself to use the words, and, for all his oratorical prowess (Apuleius says with a sneer), could not figure out how else to designate them. For the male fish, Tannonius finally resorted to some "nasty and squalid circumlocution"; unable to name the female, he sought refuge in passage from the writings of Apuleius in which Apuleius had described the posture of a statue of Venus (*Apol.* 33).[39] The episode reveals the sense of shame Tannonius Pudens felt about describing sexual matters, a sense of shame that Apuleius chastises as of a piece with his lack of culture.

In the case of Catullus's frequently cited claim that verse need not reflect life,[40] it was not obscenity or lack of eloquence that led Aurelius and Furius to criticize him. They found his lines *molliculi* (a bit soft) and thought him *parum pudicum* (not entirely chaste); because they read in his poems of *milia multa basiorum* (many thousands of kisses) they thought him not much of man (*male me marem putatis*). When Ovid,[41] Martial,[42] Pliny,[43] and Apuleius[44] cite or allude to Catullus to distinguish their verse from their own lives, they seem primarily defensive about their own obscene topics and words. But Catullus 16 itself suggests that Aurelius and Furius thought Catullus's writings were *effeminate*, not *indecent*. It is rather ironic that the lines so frequently quoted to demonstrate that a poet can be pure even if his words are indecent occur in the middle of a poem which begins and ends with Catullus threatening his critics with anal and oral rape (*pedicabo ego vos et irrumabo* [16.1, 14]). Catullus is not concerned to prove himself a properly serious gentleman (Pliny), or to stay on the good side of the authorities (Ovid, Martial), or to

---

[39] Tannonius also criticized Apuleius for this description: *hic etiam pro sua gravitate vito mihi vortebat, quod me nec sordidiora dicere honeste pigeret* (*Apol.* 34).

[40] 16.5–6: "For the sacred poet ought to be chaste himself, but his poems need not be" (*nam castum esse decet pium poetam/ipsum, uersiculos nihil necesse est*).

[41] Ovid, *Trist.* 2.354: *vita verecunda est, Musa iocosa mea.*

[42] Martial, *Ep.* 1.4: "My page is wanton, but my life is virtuous [*lasciva est nobis pagina, vita proba*]"; *Ep.* 11.15.11–13: "Remember, Apollinaris, that these are Saturnalian verses. This little book does not have my morals [*mores non habet hic meos libellus*]" (Shackleton Bailey, LCL).

[43] *Ep.* 4.14.

[44] *Apol.* 11.

show himself a true philosopher (Apuleius); Catullus was letting his critics know that he would show them he was a man.

II. Speech as it Defined Specific Groups

The notion that habits of speech corresponded to character was applicable for groups as well as for individuals. Certain manners of speaking were associated with specific philosophical schools and were felt to express their ethos.

An excellent example of the way a style of speaking could *say* something about a group is furnished by the Pythagoreans' strict mastery of the tongue.[45] Pythagoreans were notorious for following some peculiar precepts—precepts whose rationale and significance could be a source of bemusement. For instance, everyone knew Pythagoreans avoided beans, but were not quite sure why.[46] But in the case of the Pythagoreans' requirement of five years of silence,[47] there was widespread agreement that this demonstrated an outstanding self-mastery (ἐγκράτεια). In the ancient rhetoric of self-mastery, the tongue is often listed alongside the belly and the sexual organs[48] as a source of desire in need of restraint. Inscribed on Anacharsis's statue was, "Bridle the tongue, the belly, the genitals."[49] Philo lists the same three areas of the body—slightly more discreetly: "Now philosophy teaches us the control of the belly and the parts below it, and control also of the tongue."[50] And Musonius Rufus

---

[45] It is not clear to what extent actual Pythagorean communities actually existed in antiquity. For the relevant ancient references and modern debate, see John Dillon and Jackson Hershbell, *Iamblichus: On the Pythagorean Way of Life* (Atlanta: Scholars Press, 1991): 14–16.

[46] For various rules, cf. D.L. 8.17–18, 24; for evidence of how seriously the no-bean policy was taken, cf. D.L. 8.39–40; *VP* 190–94.

[47] D.L. 8.10; Iamblichus, *On the Pythagorean Life*; for a joke on the Pythagoreans' proverbial silence, see Lucian, *Demon.* 14.

[48] Cf. Xenophon's portrayal of Socrates as the most self-controlled (ἐγκρατέστατος) with respect to sex, food, and wine (*Mem.* 1.2.1; cf. 1.3.14–15).

[49] γλώσσης, γαστρός, αἰδοίων κρατεῖν (D.L. 1.104). Plutarch relates the story about Anacharsis, when he lay down to sleep, covering his genitals with his left hand and his mouth with his right, since "the tongue needs the stronger restraint [χαλινός]" (*Mor.* 505A).

[50] φιλοσοφία δὲ ἐγκράτειαν μὲν γαστρός, ἐγκράτειαν δὲ τῶν μετὰ γαστέρα, ἐγκράτειαν δὲ καὶ γλώττης ἀναδιδάσκει (*Congr.* 80). Cf. *Spec.* 2.195: "because of the self-restraint [δι᾽ ἐγκράτειαν] which it [the Day of Atonement] entails; always and everywhere indeed he exhorted them to shew this in all the affairs of life, in controlling the tongue and the belly and the organs below the belly [διά τε γλώττης καὶ γαστρὸς

lists these three areas of temptation when he promised that philosophy would engender self-control.[51] Theophrastus defined garrulity as
akrasia of speech.[52] When Plutarch vowed to avoid anger and wine, he
also vowed he would *continently* (ἐγκρατῶς) keep his speech courteous
and avoid evil words.[53] The Christian monastic movement attached a
similar interpretation to silence, setting it alongside fasting, celibacy,
and limited sleep.[54]

In this rhetoric, the tongue is treated like the source of an appetite.
Clement of Alexandria said that "ἐγκράτεια applies not only to sexual
pleasures, but to everything for which the soul *lusts wickedly* because it is
not satisfied with the necessities; ἐγκράτεια *concerns the tongue*, property
and its use, and desire."[55] Plutarch suggests that a person tempted to
speak should ask himself, "What object is my tongue *panting for?*"[56] Philo
likewise speaks of "desire" moving into the tongue (*Spec.* 4.90).

Given this widespread view that the tongue must be controlled to
obtain self-mastery, it is not surprising to find the Pythagoreans explaining their silence in these terms. In their view, maintaining silence was
the same type of discipline as avoiding unlawful intercourse with
concubines, abstaining from wine, and limiting food and sleep. "The
commands about silence... train in self-control, for the hardest kind
of control is that of the tongue."[57] Pythagoras himself "was never
known to over-eat, to indulge in sex, or to be drunk. He would avoid

---

καὶ τῶν μετὰ γαστέρα]." Cf. *Spec.* 2.49: "tongue, belly and organs of generation [τὰ
γεννητικά]."

[51] "He would be master of tongue, belly, and the pleasures of sex" (ἐγκρατὴς μὲν
εἴη ἂν γλώσσης, γαστρός, ἀφροδισίων [Lutz, Frag. 16]). Cf. Frag. 8, which claims
that philosophy accustoms one to "control one's tongue" (ἐθίζει δὲ γλώττης κρατεῖν).
For further examples of this triad of desires, see Gustav Gerhard, *Phoinix von Kolophon*
(Leipzig: Teubner, 1909), 285–86.

[52] Theophrastus, *Char.* 7.1 (Rusten, LCL): "Garrulity, should you like to define
it, would seem to be an inability to control one's speech" (ἡ δὲ λαλιά, εἴ τις αὐτὴν
ὁρίζεσθαι βούλοιτο, εἶναι ἂν δόξειεν ἀκρασία τοῦ λόγου). Cf. Pseudo-Aristotle, *Virt.
vit.* 1251a16–21 (Rackham, LCL): "To profligacy [ἀκολασία] belongs choosing harmful
and base pleasures and enjoyments... and being *fond of laughter and mockery and jokes and
levity in words and deeds* [τὸ φιλογέλοιον εἶναι καὶ φιλοσκώπτην καὶ φιλευτράπελον καὶ
τὸ ῥᾳδιουργὸν εἶναι ἐν τοῖς λόγοις καὶ ἐν τοῖς ἔργοις]."

[53] ἐγκρατῶς προσέχων καὶ διαφυλάττων μετ' εὐφημίας ἵλεω καὶ ἀμήνιτον ἐμαυτόν,
ἁγνεύοντα καὶ λόγων πονηρῶν... (*Mor.* 464C).

[54] Douglas Burton-Christie, *The Word in the Desert: Scripture and the Quest for Holiness in
Early Christian Monasticism* (New York: Oxford University Press, 1993), 136–50.

[55] *Strom.* 3.4.1–2. Cf. *Strom.* 3.59.2.

[56] Plutarch, *Mor.* 514E; cf. *Mor.* 510A, where the tongue is "inflamed and throbbing."

[57] Iamblichus, *VP* 195; similarly 68, 71–72. Apollonius of Tyana's silence is played
up as a sign of his great self-control (Philostratus, *Life of Apollonius* 1.14–16).

laughter and all pandering to tastes such as insulting jests and vulgar tales [σκωμμάτων καὶ διηγημάτων φορτικῶν]."⁵⁸ The connection of silence with self-control was sufficiently widespread that we find Josephus describing the silence of the Essenes,⁵⁹ and Philo the silence of the Theraputae,⁶⁰ in terms like that of the Pythagoreans.⁶¹ Silence is one of the traits that constitutes and communicates these groups' solemnity and self-control.

The Pythagorean rules for speech went beyond the requirement of a period of silence. Pythagoras called it seemly to limit laughter, and advised against saying anything in anger (D.L. 8.23). Pythagoreans should, in fact, keep themselves pure of *all* evil speech, including belligerent complaining, fighting, slandering, or anything vulgar and clownish.⁶² Pythagoreans avoided swearing by the gods,⁶³ and were "sparing in their use of the gods' names."⁶⁴ Even regular conversation was subject to regulation: "no conversation should happen negligently and at random"⁶⁵ and there was "a right way and a wrong way of talking to [different] people" which varied with age, status, kinship, and favors done.⁶⁶

---

⁵⁸ D.L. 8.19–20 (Hicks, LCL, adjusted).

⁵⁹ Josephus says of the Essenes: "Before the sun is up they utter no word on mundane matters" (οὐδὲν φθέγγονται τῶν βεβήλων [*B.J.* 2.128]). They eat in silence (*B.J.* 2.130), and "no clamour [κραυγή] or disturbance [θόρυβος] ever pollutes their dwelling; they speak in turn, each making way for his neighbour" (*B.J.* 2.132–33; cf. 146). This silence appears "as some awful mystery" to those outside, but is due, says Josephus, "to their invariable sobriety and to the limitation of their alloted portions of meat and drink to the demands of nature" (*B.J.* 2.133 [Thackeray, LCL]), so that their silence not only exhibits their self-control, but is enabled by it. Control of the belly has enabled them to control their tongues.

⁶⁰ *Contempl.* 31, 75, 77, 80.

⁶¹ For the comparison of the Pythagoreans and the Essenes (noted by Josephus, *A.J.* 15.371) and Therapeutae, see Dillon and Hershbell, *Iamblichus*, 15 (with bibliography).

⁶² *VP* 171, where these prohibitions of bad speech are again related to self-control (avoiding "luxury" and leading a "sensible and manly life"): ὅθεν <παρήγγελλεν> ἐκ παντὸς εἴργειν τε καὶ ἀπωθεῖσθαι τὴν τρυφὴν καὶ συνεθίζεσθαι ἀπὸ γενετῆς σώφρονί τε καὶ ἀνδρικῷ βίῳ, δυσφημίας δὲ πάσης καθαρεύειν τῆς τε σχετλιαστικῆς καὶ τῆς μαχίμου καὶ τῆς λοιδορητικῆς καὶ τῆς φορτικῆς καὶ γελωτοποιοῦ.

⁶³ "They should deal in words which would be trustworthy without oaths" (Iamblichus, *VP* 46).

⁶⁴ They were even reluctant to name Pythagoras, preferring for him the circumlocution "he who discovered the Tetract of our wisdom" (*VP* 150). Cf. Julian, *Orat.* 6.196C: οὐ μὰ τὸν ἐν στέρνοισιν ἐμοῖς παραδόντα τετρακτύν.

⁶⁵ *VP* 233.

⁶⁶ *VP* 180.

Whereas the Pythagoreans' regimine of the tongue constituted part of the quest for self-mastery, the Cynics used *their* speech in the aim of another of ancient philosophy's chief goals: the life in accordance with nature.

II.A. *Cynics and Shameless Speech*

The Cynics were not known for their doctrines the way the Pythagoreans or Academics or Epicureans were,[67] but even without a set of well-developed theoretical positions, the Cynics were easily recognized by their characteristic behavior. By begging, rebuking, publicly masturbating, engaging in sex, farting, urinating, and defecating[68] (hence the title "dog"), the Cynics set themselves against polite conventions and in favor of a "hard primitivist" interpretation of the philosophical motto, "live according to nature."[69] The Cynic wanted to unmask unnatural cultural conventions, as is summed up in Pseudo-Diogenes's words to Crates: "For nature is great, but since it has been banished from life by opinion, we are bringing it back for the salvation of humanity."[70] Hence actions that transgressed societal norms recovered and displayed for others life as nature meant it to be. The Cynics disregarded personal appearance (or, as it often seemed to their critics, they gave great care to appearing poor and disheveled).[71] They were determined to cure people of their unnatural sense of shame. When Metrocles of Maroneia farted while rehearsing a speech, he was so humiliated that he

---

[67] On the Cynics' hostility to learning, cf. Ronald F. Hock, "Cynics and Rhetoric," in *Handbook of Classical Rhetoric in the Hellenistic Period 330 B.C.–A.D. 400* (ed. Stanley E. Porter; Leiden: Brill, 1997), 759. Some said the Cynics represented a way of life, not a school of thought (Varro *apud* Augustine, *Civ.* 19.1.2–3; D.L. 6.103; Julian, *Or.* 6.181D).

[68] For public masturbation, D.L. 6.46; Dio Chrysostom, *Or.* 6.216–20; *Ep. Diog.* 44; *AP* 5.302; public defecation, Dio Chrysostom, *Or.* 8.36; Julian, *Or.* 6.202C; farting, Epictetus, *Diatr.* 3.22.80; Julian, *Or.* 6.202C; urinating (on people), D.L. 6.46; cf. 6.56.

[69] John Moles, "The Cynics," in *The Cambridge History of Greek and Roman Political Thought* (ed. Christopher Rowe and Malcolm Schofield; Cambridge: Cambridge University Press, 2000), 421.

[70] Diogenes, *Ep.* 6, 2.

[71] When Antisthenes wore his cloak so that the torn part showed, Socrates pointed to it and said, "I see your love of fame peeping through your cloak" (D.L. 6.8); cf. Lucian, *Peregr.* 4, 34; *Demon.* 48, 13 (references from Miriam Griffin, "Cynicism and the Romans: Attraction and Repulsion," in *The Cynics: The Cynic Movement in Antiquity and Its Legacy* [ed. R. Bracht Branham and Marie-Odile Goulet-Cazé; Berkeley: University of California Press, 1996], 197n24).

shut himself up at home, intending to starve himself to death. Crates
the Cynic paid him a visit and pointed out that what had happened
was entirely natural (κατὰ φύσιν), and finally cheered Metrocles up by
farting himself (D.L. 6.94).

Given that Diogenes the Cynic, in his Herculean[72] effort to overthrow
conventions, went so far as to *perform* publicly the "works of Demeter
and of Aphrodite" (D.L. 6.69), it would have been strange indeed if
he had observed the taboos against *discussing* them. And in fact, the
Cynics "censured and ridiculed" those who believed there was something shameful in obscene words.[73] (Diogenes also thought people mad
[μαίνεσθαι] for treating an extended middle finger so differently from
an extended forefinger.)[74] Both the reports about their language and
some of the surviving sayings themselves confirm that their disregard
for normal linguistic decorum was yet another aspect of Cynic shamelessness (ἀναίδεια).

The Cynic habit of haranguing people in public was notorious.[75]
Diogenes called freedom of speech (παρρησία) the greatest thing in
the world,[76] and the Cynics delivered their frank rebukes even when
they were unwelcome or painful. When Antisthenes[77] was asked why he
was so bitter in reprimanding people, he said that physicians were the
same with the sick.[78] In the original "talking cure," it was apparently
the doctor's words that were to bring healing.[79] The Cynics' willingness

---

[72] Hercules was a model of convention-rejecting liberty for the Cynics (D.L. 6.71).
One time Diogenes gave a lecture on Hercules's cleaning the dung from the Augean
stables and was moved by his topic to defecate in front of his audience (Dio Chrysostom, *Or.* 8.36)!

[73] Cicero, *Off.* 1.128.

[74] D.L. 6.35. Cf. Epictetus, 3.2.11, where Diogenes infuriates a sophist by pointing
to him with his middle finger.

[75] A. J. Malherbe, "Gentle as a Nurse," in *Paul and the Popular Philosophers* (Minneapolis: Fortress, 1989), 38; Grant, *Ancient Rhetorical Theories*, 53–56; Gerhard, *Phoinix von
Kolophon*, 33–45. Ancient authors regularly assume readers are familiar with the style of
the Cynic abuse (e.g. Lucian, *Peregrin.* 3; cf. Aulus Gellius, *Noc. att.* 9.2.6).

[76] D.L. 6.35.

[77] Diogenes Laertius claimed that Antisthenes was the first Cynic (D.L. 6.2), but was
aware that there was debate about Cynic origins (cf. D.L. 6.13). Certainly Antisthenes
shared many of the Cynics' traits.

[78] D.L. 6.4; cf. 6.19 (biting with words).

[79] On the medical imagery of Cynic *parrhesia*, cf. Abraham Malherbe, "Medical
Imagery in the Pastoral Epistles," in *Paul and the Popular Philosophers*, 121–36; David E.
Fredrickson, "ΠΑΡΡΗΣΙΑ in the Pauline Letters," in *Friendship, Flattery, and Frankness of
Speech: Studies on Friendship in the New Testament World* (ed. John T. Fitzgerald; NovTSup
82; Leiden: Brill, 1996), 164–65.

to ignore cultural conventions meant that they would rebuke even the most powerful or reputable people. Antisthenes called Plato Σάθων ("Dick") and wrote a book about him by that title.[80] When Alexander the Great asked Diogenes what he should do for him, Diogenes replied, "Get out of my light."[81] Demetrius told Nero, "You threaten me with death, but nature threatens you."[82] Diogenes is recorded as arguing with prominent philosophers (Plato, Aristotle) and rulers (Philip, Alexander). No doubt some of these encounters have been fabricated (some involve chronological impossibilities);[83] but they represent the cheeky audacity central to the Cynics' sense of themselves.[84]

At times Cynics used their bitter and frank speech to *convey* their message; but not infrequently, inappropriate speech-acts *were* the contravention of cultural norms that formed the *content* of the Cynic gospel.[85] The Cynics' shamelessness was didactic because it "denied the ontological basis of social conventions.... Bad manners were culturally significant."[86] All the gross things that came out of the Cynic's body—

---

[80] Athenaeus, *Deipn.* 5.220D–E and 11.507A. Diogenes Laertius mentions the book: Σάθων ἢ περὶ τοῦ ἀντιλέγειν (D.L. 6.16). The tone of the word Σάθων is not completely clear. Several ancient lexicographers said that the word was a nickname for a baby boy. But the passage in *Deipn.* says Antisthenes acted ἀσυρῶς καὶ φορτικῶς ("lewdly and vulgarly") in so naming his work. Diogenes Laertius also says that Antisthenes was angry with Plato when he wrote it, and that afterwards they continued to be estranged from one another (D.L. 3.35). Σάθων is occasionally attested as a male name (Bechtel, *Personennamen*, 482; other references in Pierre Chantraine, *Dictionnaire étymologique de la langue grecque, histoire des mots* [Paris: Éditions Klincksieck, 1968], s.v. σάθη [4:984]; P. M. Fraser and E. Matthews, *A Lexicon of Greek Personal Names: The Aegean Islands, Cyprus, Cyrenaica* [Oxford: Clarendon, 1987], 1.1400); but although "Dick" is a personal name in English, it would still be viewed as insulting for one philosopher to title a book about his or her colleague *Dick*. Cf. also Catullus's use of *mentula* for Mamurra (Catullus 105).

[81] D.L. 6.38.

[82] Epictetus, *Diatr.* 1.25.22.

[83] D. R. Dudley, *A History of Cynicism from Diogenes to the Sixth Century A.D.* (London: Methuen & Co., 1937), 28–29.

[84] Cf. D.L. 2.129–30 (Menedemus infuriating the tyrant Nicocreon in Cyprus with his criticism) and Suetonius, *Vesp.* 13 (the Cynic Demetrius and Vespasian).

[85] On the avoidance of euphemism as of a piece with Cynic shamelessness, cf. L. P. Wilkinson, *Classical Attitudes to Modern Issues* (London: William Kimber, 1978), 103. For a more general treatment of words as speech-acts in Cynicism, cf. F. Gerald Downing, "Words as Deeds and Deeds as Words," *Biblical Interpretation* 3 (1995): 129–43.

[86] Derek Krueger, "The Bawdy and Society," in Branham and Goulet-Cazé, *The Cynics*, 239. Similarly Abraham Malherbe says: "The Cynic shamelessness is part of this rejection of opinions and conventions, and is the mark of the doggish philosopher" ("Self-Definition among Cynics," in *Paul and the Popular Philosophers*, 15); cf. also Dudley, *Cynicism*, 30–31.

spit, urine, fecal matter, *or words*—helped in the mission to "deface the common currency."[87]

We can see something of a lesson when Antisthenes attacked a common Cynic target, superstition: "When he [Antisthenes] was being initiated into the Orphic mysteries, the priest said that those admitted into these rites would be partakers of many good things in Hades. 'Why then,' said he, 'don't you die?'"[88] The reply is unpleasant (for the priest), but implicit in it is an argument pertinent to initiatory rites ("if death were *really* so good for initiates...").[89] But it is harder to find any such message in the similar punch-line fathered on Diogenes: "He was asking alms of a bad-tempered man, who said, 'Yes, if you can persuade me.' 'If I could have persuaded you,' said Diogenes, 'I would have persuaded you to hang yourself.'"[90] Here we are closer to the sort of abusive remark that earned the Cynics their reputation for simply being nasty. Dio Chrysostom complained about the Cynics who thought that any sort of abuse (λοιδορία) counted as bold criticism (παρρησία). He lamented that there were Cynics all around who "string together rough jokes and much tittle-tattle and that low badinage that smacks of the market-place."[91] In Lucian's *Runaways*, a personified Philosophy complains to Zeus about the Cynics' shamelessness and "novel terms of abuse" (13); she says that their mouths are full of "defiled filth" (ὁ μιαρὸς βόρβορος, 20).

The "defiled filth" could apparently include indecent language.[92] Lucian,[93] Marcus Aurelius,[94] and Pseudo-Demetrius[95] linked the language and style of the Cynics to that of Old Comedy. Demetrius

---

[87] On the oracle's advice that Diogenes deface the currency, cf. D.L. 6.20 and the discussion in Dudley, *Cynicism*, 20–23. The Emperor Julian said that the Pythian God enjoined two precepts: τὸ Γνῶθι σαυτὸν καὶ Παραχάραξον τὸ νόμισμα (*Orat.* 6.188A; cf. 7.208D). The observation about all the things that come out of the Cynic's body was made by Krueger, "Bawdy," 236–37.

[88] D.L. 6.4 (Hicks, LCL).

[89] The distinction between the tone of the words and the content of the lesson is explicit in Pseudo-Plutarch, *Lib. ed.* 5C: "With coarseness of speech, but with substantial truth [φορτικῶς μὲν τοῖς ῥήμασιν ἀληθῶς δὲ τοῖς πράγμασι], [Diogenes] advises and says, 'Go into any brothel to learn that there is no difference between what costs money and what costs nothing'" (Babbitt, LCL).

[90] D.L. 6.59 (trans. Hicks); cf. Lucian, *Demon.* 24, for essentially the same joke.

[91] σκώμματα καὶ πολλὴν σπερμολογίαν συνείροντες καὶ τὰς ἀγοραίους ταύτας ἀποκρίσεις (*Alex.* 9 [Cohoon, LCL]).

[92] Kindstrand, *Bion*, 44.

[93] *Bis ac.* 33.

[94] *Med.* 11.6.

[95] *Eloc.* 259–61.

illustrated the resemblance with an example,[96] and concluded that "the form of the Cynic speech is like a dog that fawns at the same time as it bites." And many of the surviving *chreiai* are crude—although lexically restrained in comparison to Old Comedy.

Antisthenes may have said his biting rebukes were like a physician's bitter remedies, but what curative medical function was his *parrhesia* performing when he told those who were asking him for a song to "Play the flute!"?[97] Or again, when Diogenes heard that Didymon (Δίδυμων) the flute-player had been caught in adultery, he said, "he should be hanged by his name"—i.e., he should be hanged ἐκ τῶν διδύμων, "by his balls" (D.L. 6.51).[98] A book of school exercises preserves the following unedifying "humor": "On seeing an Ethiopian shitting [χέζοντα], [Diogenes] said: 'Such is a pierced kettle.'"[99]

Here, as in so many *chreiai*, the Cynic does not deliver any special wisdom through his harsh language; rather, the brazenness of the utterance is itself the reason the story is passed on. The medium is the message. Violating polite linguistic conventions is of a piece with violating other cultural norms; the speech is itself a counter-cultural act.

---

[96] Diogenes got an erection while wrestling with a handsome lad and exclaimed, "Don't worry, son, I am not like you in *that* way" (*Eloc.* 261).

[97] εἰπόντος αὐτῷ τινος παρὰ πότον, "ᾆσον," "σὺ δέ μοι," φησίν, "αὔλησον" (D.L 6.6). It may be an over-imaginitive interpretation, but one wonders if a gesture accompanied the comment, giving it the sense of "Play *my* flute." That there was a potential humor in flute-playing as a reference to *fellatio* is certain (Menander, *Perik.* 485; Archilochus *apud* Athenaeus, *Deipn.* 10.447b; Athenaeus, *Deipn.* 13.591f); but αὐλέω plus the dative of person is not in itself unusual (cf. Xenephon, *Sympos.* 2.21: ἐμοὶ αὐλησάτω; Matt 11:17: ηὐλήσαμεν ὑμῖν).

[98] Further occurrences of this *chreia* are listed by Ronald F. Hock and Edward N. O'Neil, *The Chreia in Ancient Rhetoric* (Atlanta: Scholars Press, 1986), 313. Other examples from Diogenes could be adduced; cf. D.L. 6.53 and 6.56, where the words used are not themselves obscene but the tone is coarse.

[99] Cited by H. I. Marrou, *A History of Education in Antiquity* (trans. George Lamb; London: Sheed and Ward, 1956), 156; the text is printed in Hock and O'Neil, *Chreia*, 321. On the jocular tone of χέζω, cf. *Vita Aesopi* (*Vita* G) 67, where Xanthos asks why "when we shit [ἐπὰν χέζωμεν], do we frequently look at our own excrement?" Aesop explains that it is because once a man "shat out his own brains" (τὰς ἰδίας φρένας ἔχεσεν). The word also provides the humor in a few places in the *Philogelos*. A young husband, asked whether he takes orders from his wife or if she obeys him, answers that his wife has such fear of him that when he opens his mouth she shits (χέζει) (*Philogelos* 250; for the humor, such as it is, see Thierfelder, *Philogelos*, 278). In another joke (*Philogelos* 184) a patient asks his irritable doctor, "Why is it that I'm shitting blood and bile [χολάς]?" The doctor, understanding χολᾶς for χολάς ("Why is it that I'm shitting blood and you get upset?"), answers, "Even if you shat out your guts, I wouldn't be upset." (The joke has two versions, one with two more polite terms [κάθημαι and ἐκβάλλω] for χέζω).

Many Cynics were remembered for their style of speaking. The third-century Cynic Bion of Borysthenes was known as "theatrical, good at tearing things up with his jokes, using vulgar names for things."[100] His style of talking is noted as one aspect of his Cynic shamelessness (ἀναισχυντία).[101] A similar Cynic wit is still recognizable in the jabs of the second-century A.D. philosopher Demonax. When the eunuch Favorinus asked what qualifications Demonax had for philosophy, Demonax replied, "Balls."[102] When a handsome young aristocrat pressed Demonax for the solution to a logical problem, Demonax replied, ἕν οἶδα, τέκνον, ὅτι περαίνει ("I know one thing, lad: you're getting poked!").[103]

The Cynics themselves survive above all in such *chreiai*.[104] Even in second- and first-century B.C. Rome, when there seems to have been less of a Cynic presence, the Cynic stereotype was still known.[105] Generations of school children studied Cynic *chreiai* as part of learning to read and write.[106] The *chreia* of Diogenes about the Ethiopian survives in a fourth-century A.D. papyrus book in which the student has copied out these sayings (P.Bour. 1).[107] Dio Chrysostom noted that "the mass

---

[100] ἦν δὲ καὶ θεατρικὸς καὶ πολὺς ἐν τῷ γελοίως διαφορῆσαι, φορτικοῖς ὀνόμασι κατὰ τῶν πραγμάτων χρώμενος (D.L. 4.52).

[101] D.L. 4.54. On Bion's use of foul language and its Cynic antecedents, cf. Kindstrand, *Bion of Borysthenes*, 44–55.

[102] Lucian, *Demon.* 12; cf. Lucian, *Eunuch.* 12 ("they should strip him…and determine by inspection whether he has the balls to practice philosophy" [εἰ δύναται φιλοσοφεῖν τά γε πρὸς τῶν ὄρχεων]).

[103] Demonax plays on the fact that the word περαίνω was used in logic, but also meant "to penetrate" sexually. The form περαίνει could be third-person active (relating to the logical problem) or second-person passive. The young man's fury at the "pun" confirms he understood the offensive second sense (Lucian, *Demon.* 15).

[104] Margarethe Billerbeck says that these *chreiai* are "the oldest stratum of the Cynic tradition," and that they represent Diogenes "as the Dog in all his aspects of shamelessness (*anaideia*) and in his unrestraned freedom of speech (*parrhesia*)" ("The Ideal Cynic from Epictetus to Julian," in Branham and Goulet-Cazé, *The Cynics*, 205). Dudley notes that all the traditions about Diogenes agree that he was "remarkable for his powers of ridicule and repartee" (Dudley, *Cynicism*, 28–29). Naturally one cannot have a great deal of confidence in the historicity of any given saying (on which cf. Hock and O'Neil, *Chreia*, 41–47), but the cumulative effect of the *chreiai* coheres well with the comments about how Cynics spoke.

[105] Miriam Griffin, "Cynicism and the Romans," 190–91.

[106] Krueger, "Bawdy," 223; on the *gnomai* and *chreiai* in school (and Diogenes' place in the *chreiai*), see Teresa Morgan, *Literate Education in the Hellenistic and Roman Worlds* (Cambridge: Cambridge University Press, 1998), 120–51.

[107] Hock discusses this document and lists many other educational texts that contain *chreiai* attributed to Diogenes ("Cynics and Rhetoric," 764–65).

of ordinary people retain a clear memory of the sayings ascribed to Diogenes."[108]

Although such biting sayings express the Cynics' scorn for a variety of practices, probably the preponderance of them attack men for perceived effeminacy.[109] Since it was thought that the handsome Menedemus of Eretria was "getting serviced" by his friend Asclepiades, Crates touched him on the thighs and said, "Asclepiades is in there" (D.L. 6.91). When Diogenes saw a good-looking youth sleeping unguardedly, he nugdged him and said, "Get up, lest someone poke a spear in your backside while you sleep" (D.L. 6.53; cf. Lucian, *Dem.* 50).

These sorts of jokes were obviously not the sole property of the Cynics. Diogenes himself would have been proud of the lines attributed to Arcesilaus and Menedemus (cited above, p. 22). Athenaeus includes a long list of the sordid accusations philosophers made, noting that they were "more abusive than the comic poets."[110] But although there are plenty of examples of this sort of aggressive wit from philosophers of various schools, no group could rival the Cynics for the *reputation* of outrageous speech. Unless it was the Stoics.

II.B. *Stoics*

According to Diogenes Laertius, Zeno of Citium first studied with the Cynic Crates, but his sense of modesty prevented him from fully adopting Cynic shamelessness.[111] Despite Crates's best efforts to help him overcome this character flaw (D.L. 7.3), Zeno was ultimately to go his own way and found the Stoa. But his sense of modesty did not keep him from writing a *Republic* with strongly Cynic features (D.L. 7.4). As had the *Republic* and tragedies of Diogenes, Zeno's work endorsed cannibalism and did away with all sexual restrictions (anyone, he advised, should be allowed to διαμηρίζειν anyone else [Sextus Empiricus, *Pyr.* 3.245]—including, should the occasion arise, one's own mother).[112]

---

[108] Dio 72.11 (cited in F. Gerald Downing, *Cynics, Paul and the Pauline Churches: Cynics and Christian Origins II* [London: Routledge, 1998], 50).

[109] Cf. Gerhard, *Phoinix von Kolophon*, 140–55. This trend led Gerhard to identify the anonymous treatise found in P. Heid. 310 as a Cynic work (cf. κίναι[δος] line 120 and κατα[πύγων] or κατά[πυγος] in line 130).

[110] *Deipn.* 5.220–21; cf. Plutarch, *Mor.* 1086E–F.

[111] αἰδήμων δὲ ὡς πρὸς τὴν Κυνικὴν ἀναισχυντίαν (D.L. 7.2–3).

[112] Zeno reportedly saw nothing wrong with a man "rubbing his mother's μόριον with his own" (Sextus Empiricus, *Pyr.* 3.205). Even Oedipus, Zeno argued, did nothing

Such doctrines will have been enough to earn his work its reputation for "shameful and impious" content.[113] Apparently its language, as well as its content, was the source of offense. In Plutarch we encounter a complaint about Zeno having included a discussion of "thigh-spreading" in such a treatise,[114] and Philodemus says that Zeno, along with his partners in crime, were pleased to use words "nakedly and unreservedly and all of them!" (ἀποκεκ[α]λυμμένως [τοῖς ὀ]νόμασι χρῆσθαι καὶκε[ραίως] καὶ πᾶσ[ι]ν [*Stoic.* 18]).[115] The authenticity and doctrines of Zeno's *Republic* were affirmed by Cleanthes and Chrysippus,[116] but would later prove to be a source of embarrassment for some Stoics.[117]

Chrysippus, the third head of the Stoa, apparently took seriously Zeno's dictum that the "wise man will speak bluntly." For instance, Chrysippus offered a philosophical interpretation of some ancient representation of Hera fellating Zeus.[118] According to Origen, Chrysip-

---

wrong in "rubbing" (τρίβειν) Jocasta: after all, if some *other* part of her body had been causing her pain, he could have rubbed it with his hands (*Pyr.* 3.246). Cf. D.L. 7.131 and, for the Cynics, D.L. 6.72. Malcolm Schofield sums up the ethics: "This is pure Cynicism" ("Social and Political Thought," in *The Cambridge History of Hellenistic Philosophy* [ed. Keimpe Algra et al.; Cambridge: Cambridge University Press, 1999], 758).

[113] Philodemus says that nothing αἰσχρόν nor ἀσεβές could be found in Epicurus, but that Zeno's *Republic* was full of both (*Stoic.* column 11).

[114] "'As for me, by the dog,' he said, 'I could wish that Zeno had put all of his "thigh-spreading" in some playful symposium and not in something so earnest as his *Republic*'" (ὡς ἔγωγε, νὴ τὸν κύνα, καὶ τοὺς Ζήνωνος ἂν ἐβουλόμην, ἔφη, διαμηρισμοὺς ἐν συμποσίῳ τινὶ καὶ παιδιᾷ μᾶλλον ἢ σπουδῆς τοσαύτης ἐχομένῳ συγγράμματι, τῇ Πολιτείᾳ, κατατετάχθαι [Plutarch, *Mor.* 653E]).

[115] Zeno, Philodemus says, was "full of shameful, offensive doctrines" (ὡς ἀνάμεστος αἰσχρῶ[ν δογμάτων] εἶναι κα[ὶ] βαρυλόγων [*Stoic.* 14]). For βαρύλογος, cf. Pindar, *Pyth.* 2.55, where it is used in reference to the infamous Archilochus (Tiziano Dorandi, "Filodemo. Gli Stoici [PHerc. 155 E339]," *Cronache Ercolanesi* 12 [1982]: 118).

There is a certain irony in Philodemus, the author of obscene epigrams, chastising the Stoics for their language. The importance of genre is paramount. Philodemus surely felt that certain words were not out of place *in such writings*. Note that in Plutarch's dialogue, Zopyrus defends Epicurus's treatment of sexual congress as being appropriately placed in his *Symposium*, since it is not shameful to discuss such things over wine; and Zopyrus's complaint about Zeno is that he put *his* discussion of "thigh-spreading" in a serious genre (Plutarch, *Mor.* 653B–E).

[116] D.L. 7.34; 7.131, 188; Plutarch, *Mor.* 1044B–E; Philodemus, *Stoic.* 15. See the discussion in Schofield, "Social and Political Thought," 758–59. For the possibility of Stoics even in the time of Zeno reacting negatively to the *Republic*, cf. Goulet-Cazé, *Les* Kynica *du stoïcisme*, 20.

[117] The reaction to Zeno's work by later Stoics is discussed below. On Zeno's *Republic* and the reaction to it, see Andrew Erskine, *The Hellenistic Stoa: Political Thought and Action* (London: Duckworth, 1990), 9–42; Goulet-Cazé, *Les* Kynica *du stoïcisme*, 9–68.

[118] Origen says that this portrait was on Samos, the *Clementine Homilies* say it was in Argos: Origen, *Cels.* 4.48; *Clementine Homilies* 5.18=*SVF* 2.1072 ("And when Chrysippus

pus (whom he dubs ὁ σεμνὸς φιλόσοφος) interpreted this portrait as a representation of the way the *spermatikos logos* goes from God (Zeus) into matter (Hera). What Origen described as "Hera giving Zeus the unmentionable" (ἀρρητοποιοῦσα ἡ ῞Ηρα τὸν Δία) was apparently discussed by Chrysippus in the grossest terminology.[119] Diogenes Laertius describes the reaction to Chrysippus's language as follows:

> There are some who inveigh against Chrysippus for having written much in a way that was shameful and unrepeatable. For in his treatise *On the Ancient Physiologues*, he relates the activites of Hera and Zeus quite shamefully, saying things at about line 600 which no one could repeat without defiling his mouth. They say that he has fashioned the account in the most obscene manner, and even if he is extolling the principles of physics, it is in any event better suited to whores than to gods. (D.L. 7.188)[120]

So there is evidence that the founding fathers of Stoicism were capable of overstepping the bounds of linguistic propriety.[121] Their own *justification* for this freedom is preserved in the writings of Cicero. In a letter to his Epicurean friend Paetus, prompted by Paetus's use of the term *mentula* ("dick"), Cicero offers a "Stoic lecture" (*schola Stoica*) on obscene language:

---

describes the image in Argos in his *Amatory Epistles*, he defiles Hera's face with Zeus's penis"). Theophilus also chimed in on the topic (*Autol.* 3.8=*SVF* 1073).

[119] Jocelyn suspects Chrysippus might even have used λαικάζω or λαικάστρια ("A Greek Indecency," 27).

[120] εἰσὶ δὲ οἵ κατατρέχουσι τοῦ Χρυσίππου ὡς πολλὰ αἰσχρῶς καὶ ἀρρήτως ἀναγεγραφότος. ἐν μὲν γὰρ τῷ Περὶ τῶν ἀρχαίων φυσιολόγων συγγράμματι αἰσχρῶς τὰ περὶ τὴν ῞Ηραν καὶ τὸν Δία ἀναπλάττει, λέγων κατὰ τοὺς ἑξακοσίους στίχους ἃ μηδεὶς ἠτυχηκὼς μολύνειν τὸ στόμα εἴποι ἄν. αἰσχροτάτην γάρ, φασί, ταύτην ἀναπλάττει ἱστορίαν, εἰ καὶ ἐπαινεῖ ὡς φυσικήν, χαμαιτύπαις μᾶλλον πρέπουσαν ἢ θεοῖς.

Malcolm Schofield interprets this passage differently, and translates ἃ μηδεὶς ἠτυχηκὼς μολύνειν τὸ στόμα εἴποι ἄν with "things nobody who had the misfortune to soil his lips would say," suggesting that this is "an allusion to the act of fellatio which was the subject of the picture Chrysippus claimed to be interpreting" (*The Stoic Idea of the City* [Cambridge: Cambridge University Press, 1991], 5n5). Schofield's interpretation of the passage is too intricate to discuss in full, but the important point for my topic is that ἃ μηδεὶς ἠτυχηκὼς μολύνειν τὸ στόμα εἴποι ἄν refers to defiling the mouth by repeating what Chrysippus had written. It is true, as Schofield notes, that fellatio was typically connected with an "impure mouth." But what sense would it make to say that fellators, of all people, would be "unable to say" what Chrysippus had written? ἀτυχέω refers here not to "misfortune," but to "failing" to do something ("no one who said them would have failed to defile his mouth").

[121] So Andrew Erskine comments: "complete freedom of speech in sexual matters," along with other Cynic elements, "were a feature of mainstream Stoicism in the third century and cannot be limited to the early career of Zeno" (*Hellenistic Stoa*, 14).

I like your modesty!—or rather your freedom of language. But after all, this found favour with Zeno, a clever man, no getting away from it, though our Academy is mightily at loggerheads with him—but as I say, the Stoics hold it proper to call everything by its name. Their argument runs like this: There is no such thing as obscene or indecent language. For if there is anything shocking in obscenity, it lies either in the matter or in the word; there is no third possibility. Now it does not lie in the matter. Accordingly, there are accounts of the actual process, not only in Comedy (for example *The Demiurge*: 'T' other day, as luck would have it...'—you know the solo, you remember Roscius—'so she left me bare': the whole speech is guarded as to the words, but pretty shameless as to the matter) but in Tragedy too. What else is this bit: 'When one woman' (mark it now) 'sleeps in two beds'? Or 'His daughter's (?) bed / This man dared enter?' Or 'Me, a virgin all unwilling, Jupiter did rudely force.' 'Force' is very good. And yet it means the same as the other word,[122] which nobody would have tolerated. You see therefore that, although the matter is the same, there is not thought to be any indecency because the words are different. Therefore it does not lie in the matter.

Much less does it lie in the words. For if that which is signified by a word is not indecent, the word which signifies it cannot be indecent either. You say 'seat,'[123] using a transferred word: why not use the proper one? If it's indecent, you should not use the first even; if not, you should use the second. The ancients used to call a tail a penis—hence 'penicillus'[124] from the similarity. But nowadays 'penis' is an obscene word. And yet Piso Frugi in his *Annals* complains of young men being 'devoted to the penis.' What you call by its proper name in your letter he more guard-edly called 'penis'; but because many others did the same, it became no less obscene a word than the one you have employed. Again, 'When we[125] wanted to meet you' is an ordinary enough phrase. Is it obscene? I remember an eloquent Consular once saying in the Senate 'Shall I call this or that[126] the more reprehensible?' Most obscene, was it not? no, you say, for he didn't intend it so. Very well then, obscenity does not lie in the word; and I have shown that it does not lie in the matter. Therefore it lies nowhere.

'Provide for the continuation of your family.' What a respectable phrase! Fathers even ask their sons to do it. But they dare not utter the word for

---

[122] I.e. *futuit* (D. R. Shackleton Bailey, *Cicero: Epistulae Ad Familiares* [2 vols.; Cambridge: Cambridge University Press, 1977], 2:331).

[123] Using the word *anus*, "ring," a metaphor for *culus* (on *anus*, see Adams, *Latin Sexual Vocabulary*, 115–16); on the "proper word," *culus*, see Adams, *Latin Sexual Vocabulary*, 110–12.

[124] Meaning "paintbrush."

[125] *Cum nos* pronounced like *cunnos*.

[126] *illam dicam*, which when pronounced would produce (*il*)*landicam*, "clitoris" (cf. Adams, *Latin Sexual Vocabulary*, 97–98).

this 'provision.' Socrates was taught the lute by a very celebrated player whose name was Connus. Do you think that obscene? When we say 'terni'[127] there's nothing to shock; but when we say 'bini'[128] is it obscene? 'Yes,' you say, 'to a Greek.' Then there is nothing in the word, since I know Greek, and I still say to you 'bini,' and you behave as though I spoke in Greek instead of in Latin.[129] Take 'ruta' and 'menta'; both all right. But if I want a word for 'little mint' corresponding to 'rutula,'[130] I can't have it. 'Tectoriola'[131] is a nice enough word. Try to make a diminutive from 'pavimentum' in the same way: you can't.[132] Don't you see that it's all nonsense, that indecency does not exist either in word or matter, and therefore does not exist at all?

So we utter obscenities when we use respectable words. Take 'divisio.' A respectable word, wouldn't you say? But it contains an obscenity,[133] just like 'intercapedo.' Are these words obscene? Our practice is really comical. If we say 'he throttled his father,' we don't apologize; but if we say something about Aurelia or Lollia, an apology is due. Indeed even quite innocent words have come to count as obscene. 'Battuit,'[134] somebody says: shameless! 'Depsit':[135] much more so! Yet neither word is obscene. The world is full of fools. 'Testes' is a perfectly respectable word in a court of law, elsewhere not too respectable. Lanuvian bags are respectable, Cliternian not.[136] Why even an action is sometimes respectable, sometimes indecent, is it not? It's shocking to break wind. Put the culprit naked in the bath, and you won't blame him.

So there you have a Stoic lecture: 'The Sage will speak bluntly [ὁ σοφὸς εὐθυρρημονήσει].' What a multitude of words out of one of yours, to be sure! I like you to have no inhibitions when you are addressing me. For myself, I adhere (and shall so continue, since it is my habit) to the modesty of Plato. That is why I have written to you in guarded language

---

[127] "Three each."

[128] "Two each," but *bini* sounds like the Greek βινεῖ.

[129] I.e. Cicero's interlocutor cannot claim that *bini* is only obscene when said among those who know Greek (βινεῖ), because *he* knows Greek, and yet may innocently say *bini*. Hence obscenity cannot lie in the word.

[130] "Little rue." The corresponding diminutive for "little mint" from *menta* would be *mentula*, "dick."

[131] Diminutive of *tectorium*, "wall plaster." This is a *hapax legomenon*.

[132] The resulting *pavimentula* would contain *mentula*.

[133] I.e. *vissio*, "fart softly."

[134] "He pounds"; cf. Petronius, *Sat.* 69.3; and Adams, *Latin Sexual Vocabulary*, 147, 168.

[135] "He kneads"; see Adams, *Latin Sexual Vocabulary*, 153–54, 168.

[136] Shackleton Bailey notes that the meaning of this comment is not entirely clear: "*coleus*, connected with *culleus*, 'bag' (cf. κολεός, κουλεός), usually = 'testicle'; but apparently *colei Lanuvini* were something special and not indelicate" (*Cicero: Epistulae Ad Familiares*, 2:334). Adams calls *coleus* "The obscene word for 'testicle,'" but says of Cicero's comment, "the implication of the passage is uncertain" (*Latin Sexual Vocabulary*, 66).

on a theme which the Stoics handle with complete freedom. But they also say that we ought to break wind and belch with equal unconstraint. So let us respect the Kalends of March![137]

Remember me kindly and keep well. (*Fam.* 9.22 [Shakelton Bailey, LCL, slightly altered])

Cicero had been working on his *Paradoxa Stoicorum* and other philosophical texts around the time he wrote this letter (dated between 46 and 44 B.C.), and he took Paetus's use of the word *mentula* as an opportunity to write this rather light-hearted explanation of the Stoics' treatment of obscene words. The argument is not terribly complicated, and the letter goes on longer than necessary simply because Cicero was clearly enjoying coming up with examples. In short, the Stoics argue that there can only be something obscene in words or in their referents; they then demonstrate from how people normally speak that there is nothing obscene in either, which implies that obscenity is in fact nowhere (*turpitudinem nec in verbo esse nec in re, itaque nusquam esse*). They conclude, therefore, that it makes no sense not to use the "real words."

Showing the non-obscenity of words is made easier here by treating words as purely acoustic phenomena, such that to enunciate the relevant phonemes is to have said the word.[138] If a word is treated in this way, then obscenity certainly cannot inhere in words, for people reproduce the sounds of "obscene" words without causing any offense. The examples of *bini* and "Connus" anticipate the objection that the sounds of obscene words should only count as obscene for speakers or hearers who know the relevant language. Cicero points out that he *does* know Greek—and he knows βινεῖ would be obscene in Greek—and yet he can still say *bini*. "Connus" provides a similar example, for if it can be uttered by a Latin-speaker when referring to the Greek musician, then obscenity cannot inhere in the homophonous word *cunnus*. This leaves as the only alternative that obscenity lies in the referent. But since sexual and scatological topics can be invoked without causing

---

[137] A festival for married women. In other words, "Let's not offend the ears of the matrons" (Wendt, *Ciceros Brief an Paetus*, 17; Shackleton Bailey, *Cicero: Epistulae Ad Familiares*, 2:334).

[138] Normally Stoics distinguished signifier (the spoken words "Cato is walking"), signification (the state of affairs which a competent hearer can apprehend from these words), and the external object (the man Cato walking). The signifier and the name-bearer are corporeal (a sound and a person), but the significations, or "sayables" (λεκτά), are not (Sextus Empiricus, *Math.* 8.11–12; cf. D.L. 7.56–57, and further texts and discussion in Long and Sedley, *Hellenistic Philosophers*, 1.195–202).

offense ("provide for the continuance of the family," "sleeping in two beds," etc.), it cannot lie in the referent. So the prevailing conventions of polite speech are absurd (*nihil esse nisi ineptias*) and ridiculous (*ridicule*), and "the world is full of fools" (*stultorum plena sunt omnia*).

II.B.1. *The Linguistic Roots of the Stoic Ethics of Foul Language*

The argument fits nicely both with the Stoic critique of conventional taboos and with their interest in linguistics (more specifically, with their adherence to a form of linguistic naturalism). If Zeno and Chrysippus, like the Cynics, called into question the wrongness or shamefulness of leaving a body unburied, or refraining from certain forms of sexual intercourse, why not also demonstrate that the taboo against certain words was irrational?[139] While the Stoics shared the Cynics' interest in counter-cultural or "paradoxical" teachings, they differed from the Cynics in that they viewed not only ethics but also physics and logic as critical areas of investigation. The Stoics, in fact, paid particular attention to the realm of logic, and broke new ground both in their development of reasoning ("logic" in our sense) and in grammar and linguistics.[140] The Stoics' criticism of euphemism coheres rather well with their conviction that the same *logos* that structures the universe also structures language.[141] Since language is part of nature, words are related naturally to their objects. The Stoics believed that the relationship between words and referents was not a matter of convention but of nature.[142] As a result of this naturalist view of language, the Stoics held that "there was one proper word for each thing."[143] One implication is that it was *natural* to use the real names, not euphemisms.

---

[139] The argument even bears a certain resemblance to Zeno's argument that there was nothing shameful in incest. If there would have been nothing shameful in Oedipus's touching another part of Jocasta, why should there be shame in what actually transpired? Similarly, if there is nothing inherently shameful in telling the story of Oedipus with "polite" words, why should there be something shameful in using the proper words? Body parts are just body parts; words are just words.

[140] On Stoic linguistic theory, cf. Michael Frede, "Principles of Stoic Grammar," in *The Stoics* (ed. John M. Rist; Berkeley: University of California Press, 1978), 17–75; A. A. Long, *Hellenistic Philosophy: Stoics, Epicureans, Sceptics* (2d ed.; Berkeley: University of California Press, 1986), 131–39; A. A. Long and D. N. Sedley, *The Hellenistic Philosophers* (2 vols.; Cambridge: Cambridge University Press, 1987), 1:183–236; F. H. Sandbach, *The Stoics* (London: Chatto & Windus, 1975), 99–100.

[141] So Goulet-Cazé, *Les Kynica du stoïcisme*, 49n149.

[142] Origen, *Cels.* 1.24; *SVF* 2.146.

[143] Krostenko, *Language of Social Performance*, 136. Cf. also Frede, "Stoic Grammar," 45.

Because the idea that words are related "by nature" to their referents strikes most people today as rather bizarre, it is worth emphasizing just how widespread the idea was, and how seriously its implications could be taken.[144] An incipient "naturalist" view of language can already be seen in King Psammetichus's experiment to determine the oldest race.[145] Psammetichus had two infants kept apart from any language and waited to see what their first utterance would be. It was *bekos*. When this was determined to be the Phrygian word for bread, the Egyptians conceded that the Phrygians were older than themselves (Herodotus, *Hist.* 2.2). The premise of this experiment is that there is something *natural* about language—that a human infant, when kept from the vagaries of any specific language, will use a certain word for a certain thing.

The debate among Greek philosophers predates Plato's *Cratylus*, but it is difficult to reconstruct precisely the arguments.[146] Heraclitus (*fl. ca.* 500 B.C.) believed that words were related to their referent by nature, but his reasons are imperfectly known.[147] Democritus (born *ca.* 460–457 B.C.) argued for a form of conventionalism.[148] Plato appears to have been undecided about the debate. In his *Cratylus*, Hermogenes claims that names signify only by convention;[149] Cratylus claims names

---

[144] The debate about whether words were related to things by nature or by convention was begun before Socrates and would last throughout antiquity. It is frequently mentioned as a popular and long-standing debate (e.g. Aulus Gellius, *Noct. att.* 10.4). For a survey, see Eugenio Coseriu and Bimal K. Matilal, "Der φύσει-θέσει-Streit/ Are words and things connected by nature or by convention?" in *Sprachphilosophie: ein internationales Handbuch zeitgenössischer Forschung* (ed. Marcelo Dascal et al.; 2 vols.; Berlin: Walter de Gruyter, 1996), 2:880–900; Christopher Shields, "Language, Ancient Philosophy of," in *Routledge Encyclopedia of Philosophy* (ed. Edward Craig; 10 vols.; London: Routledge, 1998), 5:356–61.

[145] R. J. Hankinson, "Usage and Abusage: Galen on Language," in *Language* (ed. Stephen Everson; Cambridge: Cambridge University Press, 1994), 167n2.

[146] Coseriu, "Der φύσει-θέσει-Streit," 2:881.

[147] G. S. Kirk denies that Heraclitus had a specific "Sprachtheorie" (*Heraclitus: The Cosmic Fragments* [Cambridge: Cambridge University Press, 1962], 116–22), but allows that for Heraclitus the names of things "give some indication of their nature" (118); similarly cautious is Coseriu: "Von Heraklit nur soviel, daß er den Parallelismus von Sein, Denken und Sprache behauptet" ("Der φύσει-θέσει-Streit," 2:883).

[148] Words cannot be connected to their referents by nature, claimed Democritus, because there are homonyms (what does a *chest* of drawers have to do with a man's *chest?*) and there are synonyms (how could multiple words all be connected *by nature* to the same thing?). Besides, different languages use different words to refer to the same things (Shields, "Language," 5:357).

[149] Hermogenes says that there is no correctness of names "other than convention and agreement" (ξυνθήκη καὶ ὁμολογία [384D]); names belong to things "by habit and custom" (νόμῳ καὶ ἔθει [384D]).

signify by nature;[150] Socrates refutes them both and the dialogue ends without a clear solution. Aristotle came down definitively on the side of convention,[151] but his was the minority position throughout the Hellenistic period. Like the Stoics, the Epicureans affirmed a natural relationship between names and objects. Epicurus tried to overcome the most serious objection to naturalism, namely that different ethnic groups use different names for the same things, by claiming that, due to their differing environments, people received somewhat different impressions and let out correspondingly different sounds.[152] Other Epicureans, such as Lucretius[153] and Diogenes of Oenoanda,[154] would reiterate this view forcefully.

The Stoics were well-known for their defense of linguistic naturalism. So when Origen addresses "the profound and mysterious issue of the nature of names," he cites the Stoics as the representatives of the claim that names exist "by nature" (*Cels.* 1.24). The Stoics seem to have inherited from Heraclitus the view that the same *logos* that structures reality also governs patterns of thought and hence speech.[155] Their

---

[150] According to Hermogenes, Cratylus asserts that "everything has a right name of its own, which comes by nature, and that a name is not whatever people call a thing by agreement [ξυνθέμενοι],...but that there is a kind of inherent correctness in names [ὀρθότητά τινα τῶν ὀνομάτων], which is the same for all men, both Greeks and barbarians" (*Crat.* 383A–B [Fowler, LCL]). At the end of the dialogue Cratylus says he sides with Heraclitus (*Crat.* 440E).

[151] "No word exists by nature" (φύσει τῶν ὀνομάτων οὐδέν ἐστιν [*Int.* 16a27–28]); Origen, *Cels.* 1.24: ὡς οἴεται Ἀριστοτέλες, θέσει ἐστὶ τὰ ὀνόματα.

[152] "Thus names too did not originally come into being by coining, but men's own natures underwent feelings and received impressions which varied peculiarly from tribe to tribe, and each of the individual feelings and impressions caused them to exhale breath peculiarly, according also to the racial differences from place to place. Later, particular coinings were made by consensus within the individual races, so as to make the designations less ambiguous and more concisely expressed" (D.L. 10.75–76 [Long and Sedley]). See also J. M. Rist, *Epicurus: An Introduction* (Cambridge: Cambridge University Press, 1972), 72–73, who rightly notes that Epicurus allows for a measure of "convention" secondary to the initial, natural stage.

[153] "It was nature that compelled the utterance of the various noises of the tongue, and usefulness that forged them into the names of things.... So to think that someone in those days assigned names to things, and that that is how men learnt their first word, is crazy" (5.1028–90 [trans. Long and Sedley]).

[154] Diogenes says of the possibility that someone simply coined and taught names, "it is absurd, indeed absurder than any absurdity, not to mention impossible" (10.2.11–5.15 [trans. Long and Sedley]).

[155] Long, *Hellenistic Philosophy*, 131. On Heraclitus's influence on Stoicism, cf. A. A. Long, "Heraclitus and Stoicism," in *Stoic Studies* (ed. A. A. Long; Cambridge: Cambridge University Press, 1996), 35–57; E. Zeller, *Stoics, Epicureans, and Sceptics* (trans. Oswald J. Reichel; repr.; New York: Russell & Russell, 1962), 393–94.

conviction that words are related by nature to their referents can be
seen in the their appeals to etymology.[156] Chrysippus, who wrote two
works on etymology,[157] noted that in saying the first syllable of the
Greek word for "I," *ego*, the chin pointed towards the chest; he took
this as evidence for his claim that the center of consciousness was in
the heart rather than the head.[158] This sort of inference only makes
sense if words are not arbitrary, if the Greek *ego* is related *by nature* to
its referent.

Long concludes that "for the Stoics the whole world is the work of
immanent *logos* or reason, and in his power of articulate thought a man
is supposed to have the means to formulate statements which mirror
cosmic events. Language is part of nature and provides man with the
medium to express his relationship with the world."[159]

If, then, Stoics believed that words are related by nature (φύσει) to
their referent, then the Stoic sage who aims to live "according to nature"
(κατὰ φύσιν) should use the real, *natural*, names. It is worth noting that
when Cicero describes the Stoics' argument, he does not say that they
advocate using "foul" or "obscene" words. Rather, he says, the Stoics
argue that since there is no *obscenitas* or *turpitudo* in words, it would be
better to use things' *own names* (*sua nomina*). "The Stoics hold it proper
to call everything *by its name* [*suo nomine*]" (*Fam.* 9.22.1). To use the
euphemism *anus* (Latin for "ring") is to apply an *alienum nomen*, and it

---

[156] So Origen, *Cels.* 1.24: "This [naturalism] is the basis on which they introduce
some elements of etymology."

[157] Diogenes Laertius records two works of seven and four volumes (D.L. 7.200).

[158] *SVF* 2:884. Similarly, Publius Nigidius proved that words were φύσει from the
fact that in saying *vos* ("you"), the lips point at the other person (Aulus Gellius, *Noct.
att.* 10.4).

[159] Long, *Hellenistic Philosophy*, 125. Even Zeno's interest in the parts of speech may
suggest this sense of cosmic connectedness between speech and being. Epictetus says
that Zeno described the philosopher's task as "keeping his reason right" (τὸ ὀρθὸν ἔχειν
τὸν λόγον [*Diatr.* 4.8.12]). This entails understanding τὰ τοῦ λόγου στοιχεῖα, which
Frede argues must mean not "the elements of reason" but "the parts of speech." Frede
notes also P.Herc. 1020 = *SVF* 2:131, where Chrysippus says, "philosophy, whether it is
the care for, or the knowledge of, right reason, is the discipline concerned with reason
(*logos*). For if we are completely familiar with the parts of speech (*logos*) [τῶν τοῦ λόγου
μορίων] and their syntax, we will make use of it (i.e., the *logos*) in an expert way. By
logos I mean the one that by nature belongs to all rational beings" (Frede, "Stoic Grammar," 60). Clearly for Zeno and Chrysippus part of the value of studying the parts of
speech lay in their aid in analyzing fallacies; but "the way Epictetus and Chrysippus
speak suggests some 'deeper connection'" (Frede, "Stoic Grammar," 61).

would be better to use its *own* name (*cur non suo potius?* [*Fam.* 9.22.2]).[160] If there should be nothing artificial in speech,[161] the sage will use the real words. Thus Zeno's dictum, "The sage will speak bluntly," coheres very nicely with Stoic linguistic theory.[162]

To return to Cicero's letter to Paetus, it should be noted again that Cicero clearly finds the Stoic argument amusing (he gives far more examples of obscene words than necessary to make the relevant points). Presumably he was not the only one. No doubt Stoics must have relished pointing out the irrationality of yet another cultural practice. Cicero quipped elsewhere that the Stoics put forth their doctrines mostly "for sake of argument."[163] Clearly part of the pleasure of philosophy was the ability to ask unanswerable questions. We might consider Lucian's ridiculous Stoic Heteomocles boasting that he could shut the mouths of other philosophers "with a single syllogism"—that he need not even mention such problems as "the horns," "the heap," or "the mower" (*Symp.* 23), which they could not possible solve. It is not difficult to imagine other Stoics using their stance on foul language similarly. Perhaps early Stoics, who reflected extensively about ethics *and* linguistics, noticed the strangeness of avoiding "real" names.[164] In time, this might have become a Stoic argument like "the horns" or "the mower"—the sort of unanswerable riddle that the likes of Heteomocles would put to other philosophers: "So answer me this: Is there something obscene in the matter or in the word?"

Excursus: Bryson the Megarian

The Stoics were not the only ones to deny the possibility of obscene language. Aristotle mentions and refutes a similar argument of the

---

[160] Similarly, trying to make babies is an act that has "its own name" (*eius operae nomen* [*Fam.* 9.22.3]). It was not only Stoics who spoke as if the impolite words for sexual parts were the parts' *own* names. Cf. Cicero, *Off.* 1.127: "neither body parts nor their functions are called by *their own names* [*suis nominibus*]"; Arnobius, *Adv. nat.* 3.10: *genitalium membrorum…foeditates, quas ex oribus verecundis infame est* suis appellationibus *promere* (quoted from Adams, *Latin Sexual Vocabulary*, 1n4).

[161] So Chrysippus: περιῃρηκέναι γὰρ ἐν τῇ φωνῇ τὸ πλάσμα καὶ τῷ εἴδει (D.L. 7.118).

[162] Wilkinson, *Classical Attitudes*, 103.

[163] Cicero, *Mur.* 62. Cf. Plutarch, *Mor.* 472A.

[164] Recall Diogenes's sense of how odd it was that the middle finger should be treated so differently from the others (D.L. 6.35).

Megarian philosopher Bryson (*ca.* 400 B.C. to *ca.* 340).[165] (It is not inconceivable that Bryson's argument influenced Zeno and the Stoics, for Zeno studied with Stilpo and Diodorus Cronus, leaders of the Megarian school,[166] and Megarians made an impact on Stoic logic.)[167] Aristotle's refutation, in the midst of a discussion of metaphor, does not mention the context or the motivation of Bryson's claim:

> Metaphors should also be derived from things that are beautiful, the beauty [κάλλος] of a word consisting, as Licymnius says, in its sound or sense, and its ugliness [αἶσχος] in the same. There is a third thing, which refutes the sophistical argument; for it is not the case, as Bryson said, that no one ever uses foul language [αἰσχρολογεῖν], if the meaning is the same whether this or that word is used; this is false; for one word is more proper than another, more of a likeness, and better suited to putting the matter before the eyes. Further, this word or that does not signify a thing under the same conditions; thus for this reason also it must be admitted that one word is fairer or fouler [κάλλιον καὶ αἴσχιον] than the other. Both, indeed, signify what is fair or foul, but not *qua* fair or foul; or if they do, it is in a greater or less degree. Metaphors therefore should be derived from what is beautiful either in sound, or in signification, or to sight, or to some other sense. For it does make a difference, for instance, whether one says "rosy-fingered morn," rather than "purple-fingered," or, what is still worse, "red-fingered."[168] (Aristotle, *Rhetoric* 1405b5–21 [Freese, LCL])

Aristotle says that poetry must be both clear and well fitted to its topic. Having stated that metaphors should be drawn ἀπὸ καλῶν, Aristotle has to address what exactly comprises the beauty or ugliness of words. In contrast to Licymnius, who claimed a word's beauty depended either

---

[165] On Bryson and the Megarian school, see Klaus Döring, *Die Megariker* (Amsterdam: Verlag B. R. Grüner N.V., 1972), who has gathered and commented on Bryson's fragments (62–67, 157–66).

[166] Sandbach, *The Stoics*, 22.

[167] Long, *Hellenistic Philosophy*, 9.

[168] μεταφοραὶ γὰρ αἰνίττονται, ὥστε δῆλον ὅτι εὖ μετενήνεκται. καὶ ἀπὸ καλῶν· κάλλος δὲ ὀνόματος τὸ μέν, ὥσπερ Λικύμνιος λέγει, ἐν τοῖς ψόφοις ἢ τῷ σημαινομένῳ, καὶ αἶσχος δὲ ὡσαύτως. ἔτι δὲ τρίτον, ὃ λύει τὸν σοφιστικὸν λόγον· οὐ γὰρ ὡς ἔφη Βρύσων οὐθένα αἰσχρολογεῖν, εἴπερ τὸ αὐτὸ σημαίνει τόδε ἀντὶ τοῦ τόδε εἰπεῖν· τοῦτο γάρ ἐστι ψεῦδος· ἔστι γὰρ ἄλλο ἄλλου κυριώτερον καὶ ὁμοιωμένον μᾶλλον καὶ οἰκειότερον τῷ ποιεῖν τὸ πρᾶγμα πρὸ ὀμμάτων. ἔτι οὐχ ὁμοίως ἔχον σημαίνει τόδε καὶ τόδε, ὥστε καὶ οὕτως ἄλλο ἄλλου κάλλιον καὶ αἴσχιον θετέον· ἄμφω μὲν γὰρ τὸ καλὸν καὶ τὸ αἰσχρὸν σημαίνουσιν, ἀλλ' οὐχ ἧ καλὸν ἢ οὐχ ἧ αἰσχρόν· ἢ ταῦτα μέν, ἀλλὰ μᾶλλον καὶ ἧττον. τὰς δὲ μεταφορὰς ἐντεῦθεν οἰστέον, ἀπὸ καλῶν ἢ τῇ φωνῇ ἢ τῇ δυνάμει ἢ τῇ ὄψει ἢ ἄλλῃ τινὶ αἰσθήσει. διαφέρει δ' εἰπεῖν, οἷον ῥοδοδάκτυλος ἠὼς μᾶλλον ἢ φοινικοδάκτυλος, ἢ ἔτι φαυλότερον ἐρυθροδάκτυλος.

on its sound or its sense, Aristotle adds ὄψις ("appearance" or "aspect"), and develops this idea in contradistinction to the claim of Bryson.[169]

Bryson's argument claims that so long as two words point to the same referent, it makes no difference which word is chosen.[170] This clearly resembles the view of the Stoics—although they argued not simply that it makes no difference, but that one *ought* to use the "real" terms. Döring says that Bryson must, from his premises, have claimed that the ugliness of a word can only lie in the topic (*Sache*), not in the choice of word.[171] Döring suggests Bryson's goal was to counter those (e.g. Plato, Xenocrates) who were opposing the use of αἰσχρὰ ὀνόματα.[172] But Bryson may simply have wanted to note the oddity of the fact that, even when multiple expressions have the same referent, they are not all considered obscene.[173] In any event, Aristotle disagreed with Bryson's analysis. He claimed that different words refer to the same referent *in different ways*, more or less directly, or with different perspectives; therefore an expression can be attractive or repulsive, even when it points to the same thing.[174]

II.B.2. *Changes in Stoic (and Cynic) Views of Obscene Speech*

If one knew nothing about the Stoics apart from what could be gathered from Cicero's letter to Paetus and the comments in *De Officiis*, the frank use of terms would appear to mark the boundary between the Stoics (and Cynics) and others. And as late as the fifth century, the argument against the existence of obscenity could be described as the *Stoic* claim.[175] But we do know more about the Stoics. First of all, we

---

[169] Döring, *Die Megariker*, 165; Siems, "Aischrologia," 12.

[170] Quintilian was familiar with a similar argument (*Inst.* 8.3.38–39, cited below, p. 109).

[171] Döring, *Die Megariker*, 165.

[172] Döring, *Die Megariker*, 165. Perhaps Bryson was partial to the notoriously crass Megarian humor (Aristotle, *Eth. nic.* 1123a21ff.)—humor that even Aristophanes thought base (*Vesp.* 57; *Ach.* 738).

[173] Sandbach says that the leaders of the Megarian school "were greatly interested in logical puzzles and the invention of arguments that seemed to lead to paradoxical conclusions" (*The Stoics*, 22).

[174] Döring, *Die Megariker*, 165.

[175] Jerome describes the Stoic view of foul language just as Cicero described it in his letter to Paetus and in *Off.* 1.127–28, on which Jerome was probably depending: "*Recteque contra Babylonem inverecundis utitur nominibus, licet nulla sit turpitudo humani corporis membrum vocare nomine suo... disputant Stoici multa re turpia prava hominum consuetudine verbis honesta esse ut parricidium, adulterium, homicidium, incestum et cetera his similia; rursumque re honesta nominibus videri turpia ut liberos procreare, inflationem ventris crepitu digerere, alvum relevare stercore,*"

know that the Stoics argued the naturalness of several things that they did not put into practice. Zeno and Chrysippus may have defended cannibalism or incest in their treatises, but they did not feel obligated to practice them.[176]

But beyond the fact that we are not sure to what degree Stoics acted on their belief about foul language, not all Stoics even agreed with Zeno's argument. From the second century B.C. onward, some Stoics clearly did not approve of foul language: they advised against it in their ethical writings; they deleted offensive passages from older Stoic texts; and one Stoic even detected and criticized an impropriety in an innocent line from Virgil. Although in his letter to Paetus Cicero treats the Stoa as a whole, in De Officiis he says that it was only "*some* Stoics" who were practically Cynics and who ridiculed those who would not use direct language (*Off.* 1.128). Furthermore, when Cicero wrote against foul language in *De Officiis*, he was following a *Stoic* work, namely, Panaetius of Rhodes's Περὶ τοῦ καθήκοντος.[177] Since we also know of other Stoics who were opposed to using or even tolerating foul language,[178] several questions emerge. First, why in his letter to Paetus and in *De Officiis* does Cicero label the use of obscenity a "Stoic" posi-

---

vesicam urinae effusione laxare: denique non posse nos ut dicimus a ruta rutulam sic ὑποκοριστικὸν *mentae facere*" ("Rightly does he use immodest words against Babylon. One may mention a part of the human body by its own name without there being any indecency. The Stoics point out that many things offensive in their reality are, because of twisted human convention, perfectly acceptable when put in words, such as parricide, adultery, murder, incest, and the like. On the other hand, things that are actually decent in reality seem offensive when it comes to their names, such as the procreation of children, breaking wind, going to stool, or relaxing the bladder by the effusion of urine. Finally, they point out that we are not able to make the diminutive of *mint* in the way we say *rutula* from *ruta*" (*In Isa.* 47.3 [*PL* 24.455A], cited by Wendt, *Ciceros Brief an Paetus*, 11, and Shackleton Bailey, *Cicero: Epistulae Ad Familiares*, 2:331).

[176] Cf. Rist, *Stoic Philosophy*, 68–69: "However close many of Zeno's theories in the *Politeia* and in others of his works are to those of the Cynics, he did not practise what he preached in the same way."

[177] Cf. Cicero, *Att.* 16.11.4; *Off.* 1.6; 3.7–10, 20. Cicero occasionally notes where he is *not* following Panaetius (e.g. *Off.* 1.7b–8, 152–61; 2.86–90). On Cicero's use of Panaetius, cf. Andrew R. Dyck, *A Commentary on Cicero, De Officiis* (Ann Arbor: University of Michigan Press, 1996), 17–29; J. M. Rist, *Stoic Philosophy*, 173, 186); A. A. Long, *Hellenistic Philosophy*, 114; F. H. Sandbach, *The Stoics*, 126. In his commentary on *De Officiis*, Dyck frequently uses "Cicero/Panaetius," expressing the inevitable uncertainty as to the degree that Cicero is preserving his source.

[178] For instance Cato. In addition to the episode of the Floralia, there is the comment from Plutarch that when Cato wrote iambic verses against Scipio, he used Archilochus's bitterness, but not his licentiousness or puerility (τῷ πικρῷ προσχρησάμενος τοῦ Ἀρχιλόχου, τὸ δὲ ἀκόλαστον ἀφεὶς καὶ παιδαριῶδες [*Cato Min.* 7.3]).

tion, when he was obviously aware that not all Stoics held it? Second, how did some Stoics come to abandon and even oppose their school's original position?

We can take up the second question first by considering how Panaetius reconceived what it meant to live a life in accordance with *nature*. We recall that Diogenes the Cynic originally made "life according to nature" the means for attaining happiness (D.L. 6.71). Most ancient philosophers agreed life should be lived "according to nature"; the question was how this should be interpreted.[179] For Diogenes, the motto meant "hard primitivism,"[180] and Diogenes appealed to primitive man, animals, and uncivilized barbarians as models of what was "natural."[181] The earliest Stoics adopted a similar conception. Chrysippus, for instance, urged people to learn from the behavior of animals that there was nothing unnatural in sex, birth, and death in holy places.[182] "Nature" is what the animals do; where human behavior is at variance, it has fallen prey to mere opinion.

But Cicero's Stoic model Panaetius understood "nature" in a fundamentally different way,[183] and as a result, he marks something of a shift in the Stoics' advocacy of objectionable behavior, including offensive speech. Born to an aristocratic family in Rhodes, Panaetius studied with Crates of Mallos at Pergamon and later with Diogenes of Babylon and Antipater of Tarsus at Athens. He knew leading Romans, such as Scipio Aemilianus and C. Laelius.[184] He accompanied Scipio on an embassy to Rhodes and Pergamum, and later stayed at his home in Rome.[185] He was clearly comfortable with Roman rule,[186] and as the Stoic scholarch from 129 until his death in 110, he "tried to adapt Stoic

---

[179] Moles, "The Cynics," 421.

[180] Ibid.

[181] Long, *Hellenistic Philosophy*, 110.

[182] Plutarch, *Mor.* 1045A–B.

[183] "De la définition du *télos* traditionelle dans l'ancien stoïcisme: 'vivre en accord avec la nature', il donne une interprétation toute nouvelle" (Marie-Odile Goulet-Cazé, *L'Ascèse Cynique* [Paris: J. Vrin, 1986], 174). For a summary of Panaetius's innovations, cf. Rist, *Stoic Philosophy*, 173–200.

[184] Cicero, *Fin.* 2.24; Erskine, *Hellenistic Stoa*, 213.

[185] Erskine, *Hellenistic Stoa*, 213.

[186] Erskine notes other prominent Roman friends and discusses Panaetius's father's relationship to Roman rule. Max Pohlenz (*Antikes Führertum: Cicero De Officiis und das Lebensideal des Panaitios* [Leipzig: Teubner, 1934]) emphasized the role of Panaetius's time in Rome and contact with Scipio (which Pohlenz called decisive for Panaetius's life), but Dyck argues that Panaetius wrote a thoroughly Greek work, his admiration for Scipio (*Off.* 2.76) notwithstanding (*Commentary*, 24–28).

ethics to the requirements of the life of the Roman *grands seigneurs* with whom he associated, by putting into the foreground the more active and brilliant virtues of magnanimity, benevolence, and liberality."[187] In Cicero's estimation, Panaetius avoided the "gloom and harshness" of other Stoics.[188]

For Panaetius, the what is "proper" or "fitting" (πρέπον, which Cicero translates with *decorum*) is precisely what fits a human's superiority "in those respects in which his nature differs from that of the rest of the animal creation."[189] Temperance, self-control, and the deportment that suits a gentleman are all derived from nature.[190] Gone is the older assumption that a philosopher must inure himself to "opinion" to discover truth. When Antisthenes was told that many people praised him, he assumed he must have done something wrong.[191] This sense of swimming against the popular current is palpable in the older Stoics (Chrysippus thought all existing law codes were mistaken)[192] and lived on as a Stoic ideal (Seneca, *Const.* 14.4). But for Panaetius, the propriety taught by nature will win the *approbation* of others "by the order, consistency, and self-control it imposes upon every word and deed."[193] Not only is indifference to public opinion condemned, but in speech, movement, and posture, nature directs people *to seek* the approval of those they live with (*Off.* 1.126; cf. 1.137). *Vox populi, vox naturae.* Not only must one observe justice by not wronging others, but one must also observe modesty (*verecundia*) by not wounding their feelings.[194] Even when—or perhaps *especially* when—relaxing, people must be on their guard not to violate modesty.[195] Thus one's sense

---

[187] Von Fritz, *OCD²* 774, cited by Green, *Alexander to Actium*, 642. Roman aristocrats must have found the Stoic program more palatable when Panaetius rejected the classic Stoic position that virtue alone is sufficient for happiness; one also needs, said Panaetius, health, strength, *and money* (D.L. 7.128; see Rist, *Stoic Philosophy*, 7–10).

[188] *Fin.* 4.79. Panaetius explained the duties that applied to those who were making moral progress but had not yet achieved the perfection of the Stoic "sage" (cf. Cicero, *Off.* 1.46; 3.15–16, and Rist, *Stoic Philosophy*, 197). Long (*Hellenistic Philosophy*, 213–16) points out that there are older Stoic antecedents for concern with the duties of imperfect humanity.

[189] *Off.* 1.96.

[190] *Off.* 1.96–98.

[191] D.L. 6.8.

[192] Erskine, *Hellenistic Stoa*, 208.

[193] *Off.* 1.98 [Miller, LCL].

[194] *Iustitiae partes sunt non violare homines, verecundiae non offendere; in quo maxime vis perspicitur decori* (*Off.* 1.99).

[195] "And even when they wish to relax their mind and give themselves up to enjoyment they should beware of excesses and bear in mind the rules of modesty [*caveant*

of modesty is elevated as a teacher and guide.[196] Just as nature put the "ugly" parts of the body out of view,[197] so also "all right-minded people keep out of sight what Nature has hidden and take pains to respond to Nature's demands as privately as possible" (*Off.* 1.126–27 [Miller, LCL]). The doggish behavior of a Diogenes is now ruled out by nature itself. Where Zeno had urged that "no part of the body be hidden away,"[198] Cicero/Panaetius "contrives to enlist 'nature' on the side of codes of dress conventional in society."[199]

For Cicero/Panaetius, "nature" has various lessons for the proper ways to speak. Speech is one of the most basic bonds among humans (*Off.* 1.50), and must be decorous so as to avoid giving offense, lest it divide rather than unite. Although humankind was not created for play or joking, jokes may be enjoyed like "sleep or other relaxations" when more serious tasks have been completed (*Off.* 1.103). But even within this more limited scope of joking, the jokes must not be "excessive or immodest, but refined and witty."[200] Jokes offer evidence of the character, and the right kind must be chosen if the "light of an upright disposition" (*probi ingenii lumen*) is to shine forth, for at no time should one's speech reveal a moral defect.[201] Jokes can be divided into two types: one is "low, wanton, shocking, obscene," the other is "refined, urbane, clever, witty."[202] Cicero/Panaetius concludes that it is easy to distinguish between the "refined" and the "vulgar" (*facilis igitur est distinctio ingenui et illiberalis ioci* [*Off.* 1.104]), but the explanation actually confuses matters, for it begins by making appropriate joking a matter of *timing*, and finishes with reference to the *content* and *language*: "The one kind, if done at the right time, as when the mind is relaxed, is worthy of the most serious person; the other is unworthy of any gentleman, if

---

intemperantiam, meminerint verecundiae]. And this will be easier, if the young are not unwilling to have their elders join them even in their pleasues" (*Off.* 1.122 [Miller, LCL]).

[196] *retinenda igitur est huius generis verecundia, praesertim natura ipsa magistra et duce* (*Off.* 1.129).

[197] Of course, only if clothing is involved!

[198] D.L. 7.34.

[199] Dyck, *Commentary*, 302; cf. Erskine, *Hellenistic Stoa*, 207n12. Cicero, *Off.* 1.148: "But no rules need to be given about what is done in accordance with the established customs and conventions of a community; for these are in themselves rules."

[200] *Ipsumque genus iocandi non profusum nec immodestum, sed ingenuum et facetum esse debet* (*Off.* 1.103).

[201] *in primisque provideat, ne sermo vitium aliquod indicet inesse in moribus* (*Off.* 1.134).

[202] *Duplex omnino est iocandi genus, unum illiberale, petulans, flagitiosum, obscenum, alterum elegans, urbanum, ingeniosum, facetum* (*Off.* 1.104).

base subjects or obscene words are employed."[203] Apparently there is
no time—not even in relaxation—when a gentleman (*liber*) can appropriately use obscenity in his jokes; and jokes that would be appropriate
on a light topic or at dinner are inappropriate at other times.[204] The
whole discussion is clearly geared toward the upper classes. The same
adjective used for vulgar jokes (*illiberalis*) is used to describe the means
of livelihood that are beneath a gentleman.[205]

Just as sane people follow nature's lead by covering their private parts,
so they must avoid referring to them by their real names. "In the case
of those parts of the body which only serve Nature's needs, neither
the parts nor the functions are called by their real names. To perform
these functions—if only it be done in private—is nothing immoral; but
to speak of them is indecent. And so neither public performance of those
acts nor obscene mention of them is free from indecency."[206] Cicero/
Panaetius knows that this goes directly counter to the Cynic and older
Stoic claim, for it is in this context that he states:

> But we should give no heed to the Cynics (or to some Stoics who were
> practically Cynics) who censure and ridicule us for holding that the mere
> mention of some actions that are not immoral is shocking, while other
> things that are immoral we call by their real names. Robbery, fraud, and
> adultery, for example, are immoral in deed, but it is not obscene to name
> them. To beget children is in deed morally right; to speak of it is obscene.
> And they assail modesty with a great many other arguments to the same
> purport. But as for us, let us follows Nature and shun everything that is
> offensive to our eyes or our ears.[207]

---

[203] *Alter est, si tempore fit, ut si remisso animo, <vel gravissimo> homine dignus, alter ne libero
quidem, si rerum turpitudo adhibetur aut verborum obscenitas* (*Off.* 1.104, following Dyck's text
[*Commentary*, 266]).

[204] *turpe enim valdeque vitiosum in re severa convivio digna aut delicatum aliquem inferre sermonem*
(*Off.* 1.144).

[205] *Off.* 1.150, where the wrong sort of trades are *illiberales* and *sordidi*.

[206] *quarumque partium corporis usus sunt necessarii, eas neque partes neque earum usus suis
nominibus appellant; quodque facere turpe non est, modo occulte, id dicere obscenum est. Itaque nec
actio rerum illarum aperta petulantia vacat nec orationis obscenitas* (*Off.* 1.127). Dyck notes that
petulantia ("offensive rudeness, scurrility" [*OLD*, s.v. 2]) is here "one step removed from
insanity" (the previous line has just mentioned "all right-minded people" [*qui sana mente
sunt*]). Cf. Cicero, *Orat.* 2.305.

[207] *Nec vero audiendi sunt Cynici, aut si qui fuerunt Stoici paene Cynici, qui reprehendunt et irri-
dent, quod ea, quae turpia non sint, verbis flagitiosa ducamus, illa autem, quae turpia sint, nominibus
appellemus suis. Latrocinari, fraudare, adulterare re turpe est, sed dicitur non obscene; liberis dare
operam re honestum est, nomine obscenum; pluraque in eam sententiam ab eisdem contra verecundiam
disputantur. Nos autem naturam sequamur et ab omni, quod abhorret ab oculorum auriumque appro-
batione, fugiamus* (*Off.* 1.128 [Miller, LCL, adjusted]).

One of Panaetius's innovations in the treatment of "nature" was his view that there is both a universal human nature and also a nature peculiar to each individual.[208] Morality and decorum are derived from the nature common to all,[209] but a person's style of speech can accord with his or her unique *persona*, which includes the possibility of being pretty funny (some have *multus lepos* [*Off.* 1.108]). Aware that this distinction between universal and individual natures might appear to justify extravagant behavior for those who claimed their personality demanded it, Cicero/Panaetius reiterates that there will be no more Socrateses or Aristippuses, men who "did or said things contrary to their cities' manners and conventions."[210] In other words, one's special personal nature can never justify behavior outside the bounds of what is fitting for humanity as a whole. Cynics may well have been appealing to Socrates as an example,[211] for immediately after mentioning Socrates comes the abrupt denunciation: "the Cynic's whole system of philosophy must be rejected, for it is inimical to modesty, without which nothing can be upright, nothing morally good."[212]

When we turn from Cicero's adaptation of the Stoic Panaetius to Stoic philosophers such as Musonius Rufus and his pupil Epictetus, we find a similar appreciation for modesty. Musonius and Epictetus both commended a sense of modest respect of societal norms, which they contended were not opposed to, but rather derived from, human nature. The sense of modesty or shame, which Cynics labored so hard to undo, was reinstated as a natural and healthy part of a human being. Musonius commends αἰδώς frequently,[213] claiming that philosophy

---

[208] *duabus quasi nos a natura indutos esse personis* (Cicero, *Off.* 1.107). In all Panaetius distinguishes four *personae* (*Off.* 1.115 mentions the third and fourth): 1) that of all humans as rational agents; 2) each individual's nature (temperament, appearance); 3) the *persona* defined by external circumstances (being rich or poor affects who one is, but is different from being born a serious person); 4) the *persona* of personal choice, such as one's chosen life-style. Cf. Dyck, *Commentary*, 269; A. A. Long, *Stoic Studies*, 164–66.

[209] *Off.* 1.107.

[210] *Off.* 1.148.

[211] For Socrates's reputation for being willing to take a conversation in indecent directions, cf. Xenophon, *Mem.* 1.30; Plato, *Gorg.* 494E; *Symp.* 221D–E. His bluntness and irony were commemorated by Timon (D.L. 2.19). On Socrates's image among Stoics and Cynics, cf. Long, *Stoic Studies*, 1–8.

[212] *Cynicorum vero ratio tota est eicienda; est enim inimica verecundiae, sine qua nihil rectum esse potest, nihil honestum* (*Off.* 1.148 [Miller, LCL]).

[213] Cf. Lutz, fragments 4, 8. Billerbeck suggests that Musonius, like Cicero, may have been influenced by Panaetius's Περὶ τοῦ καθήκοντος (Margarethe Billerbeck, *Vom Kynismus: Epiktet* [Leiden: Brill, 1978], 67).

"presents modesty [αἰδώς] as the greatest good."[214] Epictetus chastises the unbathed philosopher on the grounds that he has insulted others and ignored social convention (*Diatr.* 4.11). For Epictetus, a sense of shame is critical—even for the Cynic (*Diatr.* 3.22.15).[215] The sense of shame is not contrary to nature; it is a human possession *by nature*.[216] It was precisely those things that separate humans from the animals that must belong to human nature. "Nature says, 'Wash your teeth.' Why? In order that you may be a human being, and not a beast or a pig" (*Diatr.* 4.11.11).[217]

Epictetus criticized the way abusive speech and other aspects of Cynic shamelessness had become an end in themselves: "But no, you say, what makes a Cynic is...to revile tactlessly [λοιδορεῖσθαι ἀκαίρως] the people he meets or to show off his fine shoulder."[218] A Cynic must issue rebukes, but he will do so as a father (*Diatr.* 3.22.96, 82), with charm and wit (*Diatr.* 3.22.90).[219] Epictetus will tolerate no foul language.[220] In all of this, Epictetus follows and expands upon Musonius, who warned, "One begins to lose his hesitation to do unseemly things when one loses his hesitation to speak of them."[221]

In short, philosophers such as Epictetus wanted to cleanse the Cynic in order to cleanse the image of the Stoic. Miriam Griffin argues that "the new, sanitized Cynic ideal helped Stoicism to shed unacceptable features of its historical heritage (Cynic and Stoic) and to exploit Cynic notions that appealed to the Romans."[222] A Roman appreciation for propriety seems also to have contributed to the domestication of some strands of Cynicism and to the Stoics' separating themselves from

---

[214] ὁ τὴν αἰδῶ μέγιστον ἀποφαίνων ἀγαθόν (Lutz, frag. 3; 42.24–25). For similar sentiments, cf. Spicq, "αἰδώς, ἀναίδεια," *TLNT* 1:41–44.

[215] Cf. Billerbeck, *Vom Kynismus*, 67–68.

[216] *Diatr.* 2.10.22: οὐδὲν ἔχομεν αἰδῆμον φύσει; Ἔχομεν. This whole lecture by Epictetus on τὰ καθήκοντα treats the human as a "gentle, social being" (*Diatr.* 2.10.15) who ceases to be human as soon as he damages his natural self-respect and dignity. Similar sentiments are frequent in his lectures (*Diatr.* 1.5.5, 9; 1.28.20; 3.7.27; 4.1.126; 4.5.21). Cf. Seneca, *Ep.* 11; 25.2.

[217] Cf. Epictetus, *Diatr.* 1.4.18; 1.28.20; 2.10, 14f.; 3.7.27.

[218] Epictetus, *Diatr.* 3.22.50.

[219] For Cynics' different approaches to rebuking, see Malherbe, "'Gentle as a Nurse': The Cynic Background to 1 Thessalonians 2," in *Paul and the Popular Philosophers*, 35–48.

[220] *Ench.* 33.15–16 (cited above, p. 74); *Diatr.* 4.4.46 (cited below, pp. 166–67); cf. *Diatr.* 4.3.2: the philosopher has gained αἰδώς in place of αἰσχρολογία.

[221] Ἀρχὴ τοῦ μὴ κατοκνεῖν τὰ ἀσχήμονα <πράττειν> τὸ μὴ κατοκνεῖν τὰ ἀσχήμονα λέγειν (Lutz, fragment 26).

[222] "Cynicism and the Romans," 204.

their Cynic past and from the more outlandish elements of their own founders.[223] Epictetus's tirades against the Cynics' shameless talk are a case in point.[224] The voice of this sanitized Cynic can be heard in the tone of the Cynic Epistles, as when Diogenes writes to Metrocles, "It is not only bread, water, a bed of straw, and a threadbare garment that teach temperance and endurance, but also, if I may put it this way, the shepherd's hand" (*Ep.* 44, 1–2). The once outrageous Diogenes now apologizes for a veiled reference to masturbation!

Perhaps it is in this context that we have an answer to the question raised earlier, namely, why would Cicero, even as he follows a Stoic author, argue for avoiding obscene language as though he were *countering* the Stoics? Could he have had polemical intentions? To quote Griffin again: "We might surmise that Stoics or those favorable to them ascribed the embarrassing parts of the Stoic heritage to the Cynics or to the Cynic influence on their founders while critics of the Stoa might identify these same notions as Stoic without qualification."[225] We should note the way Cicero concludes his letter to Paetus: "But they [the Stoics] also say that we ought to break wind and belch with equal unconstraint."[226] In a similar way, Philodemus tries to link the Stoics to ugly Cynic traits.[227]

Jaap Mansfeld argued that in the Hellenistic period there were "two different views concerned with the continuity between Cynics and Stoics, viz. one (the tradition preferred by Diog. Laert.) emphasizing dignified ethics, the other (sort of tucked away by him) immoral and obscene ideas."[228] The Stoics were eager to link themselves to Socrates (according to Philodemus they even wanted to be called "Socratics");[229]

---

[223] It is interesting to note the Emperor Julian's comment: "When [the Stoics] saw that the cities of Greece were averse to the excessive plainness and simplicity of the Cynic's freedom of manners [τὸ λίαν ἀκραιφνὲς καὶ καθαρὸν τῆς ἐλευθερίας τοῦ κυνός], they hedged him about with screens as it were, I mean with maxims on the management of the household and business and intercourse with one's wife and the rearing of children, to the end, I believe, that they might make him the intimate guardian of the public welfare" (6.185C–D [Wright, LCL]).

[224] On Epictetus's opposition to indecent speech, cf. Adolf Friedrich Bonhöffer, *The Ethics of the Stoic Epictetus* (trans. William O. Stephens; New York: Peter Lang, 2006 [1894]), 96–97.

[225] "Cynicism and the Romans," 192.

[226] *Fam.* 9.22.4.

[227] Goulet-Cazé, *Les* Kynica *du stoïcisme*, 24–25. Cf. Plutarch's criticism of the Stoics for approving of Diogenes's public masturbation (*Mor.* 1044B).

[228] Jaap Mansfeld, "Diogenes Laertius on Stoic Philosophy," *Elenchos* 7 (1986): 346, cited by Schofield, *Stoic Idea*, 11n19.

[229] Σωκρατ[ι]κοὶ καλεῖσθαι θέ[λο]υσιν (*Stoic.* col. 13).

but the line from Socrates to Zeno included Antisthenes, Diogenes, Crates.[230] This lineage made the Stoics heirs of ideas that were difficult for the later Stoa to defend. Evidence of their attempt to "sanitize" the Cynic elements can be seen in how later Stoics reacted to their predecessors' writings. As was mentioned before, Zeno's *Republic* was a source of embarrassment for later Stoics. Philodemus reports that the Stoics of his day (first century B.C.) tried to excuse the *Republic* on the grounds that Zeno was just a young man when he wrote it (*Stoic.* 9).[231] Philodemus says that even those "noble souls" who accepted the *Republic* made some defense for the things Zeno had written about διαμηρίζειν (*Stoic.* 15). Others even denied he had written the *Republic*, and one Stoic deleted some of Zeno's offensive lines: "Isidorus likewise affirms that *the passages disapproved by the school were expunged from [Zeno's] works by Athenodorus the Stoic*, who was in charge of the Pergamene library; and that afterwards, when Athenodorus was detected and compromised, they were replaced."[232] The expunger in question was the Stoic Athenodorus Cordylion.[233] Athenodorus's work would have been at the beginning of the first century B.C.—not far from the time that Philodemus was mentioning Stoics' anxiety about Zeno's *Republic*. Presumably Athenodorus, like the others Philodemus describes, was trying to eradicate "any trace of Cynicism" from Zeno's book.[234]

Just how wide a gap lay between Zeno's approach to foul language and that of some later Stoics can be seen in the first-century A.D. Stoic Annaeus Cornutus. According to Aulus Gellius, Annaeus Cornutus criticized Virgil's discreet description of the union of Vulcan and Venus (*Aen.* 8.404–406)—a passage other poets had actually praised for its modesty![235]

---

[230] Dudley, *Cynicism*, 25; Goulet-Cazé, *Les* Kynica *du stoïcisme*, 17–18, 20–21.

[231] For Stoic excuses, see Philodemus, *Stoic.* 9–15, and commentary by Goulet-Cazé, *Les* Kynica *du stoïcisme*, 13–20; Malcolm Schofield, "Epicurean and Stoic Political Thought," in *The Cambridge History of Greek and Roman Political Thought* (ed. Christopher Rowe and Malcolm Schofield; Cambridge: Cambridge University Press, 2000), 443 and 443n18; cf. idem, "Social and Political Thought," 759n45. For continued reservations about Zeno's writings, cf. Clement, *Strom.* 5.58.2.

[232] D.L. 7.34. On this passage, see Schofield, *Stoic Idea*, 4n5; David Hahm, "Diogenes Laertus VII: On the Stoics," *ANRW* 36.6 (1992): 4133n135; and Goulet-Cazé, *Les* Kynica *du stoïcisme*, 22–23.

[233] See Sandbach, *The Stoics*, 142; *RE* 2.2045, s.v. "Athenodorus," no. 18; Rudolf Pfeiffer, *History of Classical Scholarship*, 236n6; Schofield, *Stoic Idea*, 9. Athenodorus became a friend of the younger Cato when Cato visited Pergamum in 67–66 B.C. (Plutarch, *Cat. Min.* 10). Here is a common spirit: the one removes offensive lines from Zeno, the other is a man in whose presence the mimes of Flora could not speak freely.

[234] Schofield, *Stoic Idea*, 10.

[235] Aulus Gellius says that many poets praised Virgil for describing "an act that

But Annaeus Cornutus, a man in many other respects, to be sure, lacking neither in learning nor taste, nevertheless in the second book of the work which he compiled *On Figurative Language*, defamed the high praise of all that modesty by an utterly silly and odious criticism. For after expressing approval of that kind of figurative language, and observing that the lines were composed with due circumspection, he added: "Virgil nevertheless was somewhat indiscreet in using the word *membra*." (Aulus Gellius, *Noct. att.* 9.10.5–6 [Rolfe, LCL])[236]

It seems that under the Empire there were enough Stoics who opposed foul language that people did not typically think of foul talk as a Stoic trait. Plutarch liked neither the Stoics nor foul language, but he does not typically criticize the former for their use of the latter. When Lucian paints a nasty caricature of Heteomocles the Stoic, he still portrays him as reluctant to describe pederasty.[237] Quintilian mentions people who "do not think it necessary to avoid obscenity, on the ground that no word is shocking in itself and that, if the thing meant is disgusting, it comes to be understood by whatever name it is called";[238] but he does not identify them as Stoics.[239]

---

nature's law bids us conceal with a modest paraphrase" (*rem lege naturae operiendam verecunda quadam translatione verborum* [*Noct. att.* 9.10.1–2]). They admired Virgil's ability to speak "of those sacred mysteries of chaste intercourse in so many and such plain words, which yet were not indecent [*non praetextatis*], but pure and honorable" (Rolfe, LCL, adjusted).

[236] This would appear to have been quite prissy indeed, for in this passage *membra* was not even referring to the sexual organs; and even if Virgil *had* used the word in that sense, *membrum* was a euphemism that even someone like Tertullian could employ (*Adv. Val.* 1.3).

[237] *Symp.* 26: "If it were not shameful for me to say such things [αἰσχρὸν ἦν ἐμὲ λέγειν τὰ τοιαῦτα], I might have told you something more.... But it is wrong to make trouble at a wedding and to defame others, especially with charges so unseemly [αἰσχραῖς αἰτίαις]."

[238] *Inst.* 8.3.38–39 (Russell, LCL). The argument Quintilian attributes to these people resembles the claim of the Stoics and that of Bryson: "[Words] are not however without ornamental quality, unless they are beneath the dignity of the subject on which we have to speak—obscenities set out in crude terms are of course an exception. I say this to warn those who do not think it necessary to avoid obscenity, on the ground that no word is shocking in itself and that, if the thing meant is disgusting, it comes to be understood by whatever name it is called. For my part, I shall content myself with our modest Roman ways, and follow the tactful procedure of answering such speakers by silence" (*sed ne inornata sunt quidem, nisi cum sunt infra rei, de qua loquendum es, dignitatem, excepto si obscena nudis nominibus enuntientur. Quod viderint, qui non putant esse vitanda, quia nec sit vox ulla natura turpis et, si qua est rei deformitas, alia quoque appellatione quacunque ad intellectum eundem nihilominus perveniat. Ego Romani pudoris more contentus, ut iam respondi talibus, verecundiam silentio vindicabo*).

[239] Where Cicero said he would maintain his *Platonic* modesty, Quintilian says here that he would maintain "modest *Roman* ways" (*Romani pudoris more* [*Inst.* 8.3.39]).

So there existed plenty of Stoics who opposed obscene language. Were there any who continued to advocate it? Cicero says that Posidonius made a list of all the actions that were so repulsive that they should not be done even to save one's country. There is no way to know exactly what sort of words Posidonius used,[240] but Cicero finds them "so shocking, so obscene, that it seems indecent even to mention them" (*sed ita taetra quaedam, ita obscena, ut dictu quoque videantur turpia* [*Off.* 1.159]). Hecaton of Rhodes, a pupil of Panaetius, had no problem recording a *chreia* of Cleanthes that plays on διαμηρισμός: "When an attractive young man said, 'If one who strikes into the stomach 'stuffs the stomach,' then one who strikes into the thigh 'stuffs-the thighs.' Cleanthes replied, 'You can have your thigh-spreadings, young man; analogous words don't always signify analogous things.'"[241]

Having begun this examination of Stoicism with its founder, Zeno, it is fitting to bring it to a close with the Emperor Marcus Aurelius.[242] He praised the bold speech of Old Comedy and Cynicism: "And after Tragedy the Old Comedy was put on the stage, exercising an educative freedom of speech [παιδαγωγικὴν παρρησίαν], and by its very *directness of utterance* [δι᾽ αὐτῆς τῆς εὐθυρρημοσύνης][243] giving us no unserviceable warning against unbridled arrogance. In a somewhat similar vein Diogenes also took up this rôle" (*Med.* 11.6 [Haines, LCL]). Aurelius himself could use strong, if not obscene, language, especially in passages where he sought to strip reality of any comforting illusions.[244] Human life is transient, "yesterday, a drop of snot [μυξάριον]; tomorrow, embalmed

---

[240] I. G. Kidd notes that "Posidonius was perfectly capable of deliberately vulgar language in indignant invective" (I. G. Kidd, *Posidonius* [Cambridge: Cambridge University Press, 1999], 3:66), citing as an example his use of σιληπορδῶν: "Athenion...now *farts* his way arrogantly through town and country" (quoted in Athenaeus, *Deipn.* 5.212C–D; trans. Kidd, *Posidonius*, 2:871).

[241] φησὶ δ᾽ ὁ Ἑκάτων ἐν ταῖς Χρείαις, εὐμόρφου μειρακίου εἰπόντος, εἰ ὁ εἰς τὴν γαστέρα τύπτων γαστρίζει, καὶ ὁ εἰς τοὺς μηροὺς τύπτων μηρίζει, ἔφη, σὺ μέντοι τοὺς διαμηρισμοὺς ἔχε, μειράκιον· αἱ δ᾽ ἀνάλογοι φωναὶ τὰ ἀνάλογα οὐ πάντως σημαίνουσι πράγματα (D.L. 7.172). It is difficult to convey the play on words: γαστρίζω is a word, μηρίζω is not, διαμηρισμός is the word associated with Zeno. For διαμηρίζω, cf. Aristophanes, *Av.* 669: "I'd gladly spread her thighs!"

[242] On Aurelius's Stoicism, see F. W. Bussell, *Marcus Aurelius and the Later Stoics* (Edinburgh: T. & T. Clark, 1910); Anthony Birley, *Marcus Aurelius: A Biography* (New Haven: Yale University Press, 1987).

[243] On the connection of εὐθυρρημοσύνη to obscene language, cf. 5n26.

[244] Cf. R. B. Rutherford, *The Meditations of Marcus Aurelius: A Study* (Oxford: Clarendon, 1989), 22, 143–47.

meat or ash."[245] Aurelius considers the animal nature of humankind with its "eating, sleeping, copulating, excreting, and so on...".[246] Sexual intercourse is charmingly described as the "friction of an entrail and a convulsive expulsion of snot."[247] And quoting the line from Menander he says, "for all his wealth, he has no place to shit."[248]

So far I have been looking primarily at the uses of and views about obscene language among Greeks and Romans. But to situate the Christians' ethics of obscene speech, we should also consider the relevant biblical passages and the ways in which decency of language was being treated in Jewish circles.

---

[245] *Med.* 4.48. For ancient Jewish and Christian parallels to this description of life, cf. Allan and Burridge, *Euphemism and Dysphemism*, 55.

[246] οἷοί εἰσιν ἐσθίοντες, καθεύδοντες, ὀχεύοντες, ἀποπατοῦντες, τὰ ἄλλα (*Med.* 10.19).

[247] ἐντερίου παράτριψις καὶ μετά τινος σπασμοῦ μυξαρίου ἔκκρισις (*Med.* 6.13).

[248] ὑπὸ τῆς εὐπορίας οὐκ ἔχειν, ὅποι χέσῃ (*Med.* 5.12).

CHAPTER THREE

JEWISH SCRIPTURE AND EARLIEST CHRISTIANITY

The Mosaic Law's great concern that nothing abominable enter Israelite mouths[1] was not exactly matched by concerns about disgusting things coming out. Naturally, the Pentateuch does contain various rules pertaining to speech, including prohibitions against false witness (Exod 20:13), false oaths (Lev 6:3), blasphemy (Exod 22:27; Lev 24:10–16), using the Lord's name in vain (Exod 20:7),[2] and cursing parents (Lev 20:19; cf. Prov 19:20), leaders (Exod 22:27), or the deaf (Lev 19:14).[3] But biblical law nowhere addresses the decency of language *per se*.[4]

The Hebrew prophets occasionally criticized how the people spoke, but they focused on sins other than speaking obscenely. Isaiah explained the Lord's displeasure with Israel as a response to the fact that every mouth "spoke folly" (וכל־פה דבר נבלה [Isa 9:16]). The word נבלה could be used with reference to what was sexually unacceptable (Judges 19:23), and the rabbis would later explain Isaiah's "speaking folly" (דבר נבלה) as *indecent* language (נבלות פה), but only because נבלות פה had come to refer to obscene speech.[5] In its original context in Isaiah, "speaking folly" refers to prophets and dignitaries leading the people astray with "senseless, irreligious language" (BDB s.v.), which is roughly how the LXX understood the verse (πᾶν στόμα λαλεῖ ἄδικα). Similarly, in Isa 32:6 the statement "the fool speaks folly" (נבל נבלה ידבר) means, as the same verse goes on to say, that fools "utter error concerning the Lord."

---

[1] Nothing "detestable" (שקץ, Lev 11:10–13, 20, 23, 41–42) or "abominable" (תועבה, Deut 14:3) was to be eaten.

[2] Cf. Lev 19:12 (swearing profanes the name) and Lev 20:4 (God's name is defiled when Israelites worship Molech).

[3] The same verb (קלל) is used for the deaf, for parents, and in the context of blasphemy (Exod 22:27 and Lev 24:11, 14–15). For a discussion of its meanings, see Jacob Milgrom, *Leviticus: A New Translation and Commentary* (3 vols.; AB 3–3B; Garden City: Doubleday, 1991–2001), 2108–9.

[4] Other ancient Near Eastern laws do not seem to have addressed "obscene" speech, either. For ancient Near Eastern laws about cursing, cf. Martha T. Roth, *Law Collections from Mesopotamia and Asia Minor* (Atlanta: Scholars Press, 1995), 20 (a law that orders the offender's mouth to be scoured with salt), 202, 203; for a Middle Assyrian law about a woman saying something disgraceful or blasphemous, cf. 155.

[5] *b. Shabbat* 33a (the text is quoted below, p. 117).

But in addition to giving rules or advice *about* words, the sacred writings were also composed *of* words. On the whole, the language of scripture is discreet and euphemistic. Many of the ancient Hebrew euphemisms are still used in English—sometimes with the memory of their provenance preserved (e.g. "she knew him in the *biblical* sense").[6] In addition to "knowing," the Bible expresses sexual congress with a variety of euphemisms, such as "go in to" (Gen 6:4; 16:2); "approach" (Gen 20:4; Lev 18:14); "touch" (Gen 20:6); "lie with" (Gen 19:32); and "go up to the bed" (Gen 49:4).[7] The rabbis also saw the phrase "eating bread" in Gen 39:6 (*Gen. Rab.* 86.6) as a euphemism for sexual intercourse,[8] and "eating" alludes to the adulteress's activity in Prov 30:20. The Bible speaks of "covering the feet" for relieving oneself (Judges 3:24; 1 Sam 24:3). It uses "nakedness" (Gen 9:22), "feet" (Exod 4:25),[9] and "thighs" (Gen 24:2) to refer to the genitals.

At times it is unclear if a phrase is meant to be a euphemism. For instance, the phrase "to play with" may imply sexual activity, for when Abimelech saw Isaac "playing with" Rebecca (מצחק את רבקה [Gen 26:8]),[10] he was able to infer that she was not his sister. Of course, one of the consequences of using euphemistic language is that, once innocent expressions have been used often enough to designate something else, they are then themselves liable to be misunderstood in other contexts. So when the Queen of Sheba "came to Solomon" (ותבא אל־שלמה [1 Kings 10:2]) and he gave her "all her desire" (כל־חפצה [10:13]), some readers got the wrong idea.[11]

Philo was proud of the way Moses avoided an overly explicit discussion of certain topics for the sake of decency.[12] And in the twentieth

---

[6] The rabbis assembled lists of biblical euphemisms, calling the phenomenon *kinnah ha-katuv*, "Scripture used a euphemistic expression" (L. I. Rabinowitz, "Euphemism and Dysphemism," *Encyclopaedia Judaica*, 6:960).

[7] E. König, "Style of Scripture," in *Dictionary of the Bible* (Extra vol.; ed. James Hastings; New York: Charles Scribner's Sons, 1904), 164; cf. the delightful and erudite essay of Marvin H. Pope, "Bible, Euphemism and Dysphemism in the," *ABD* 1:720–25. Cf. also Stefan Schorch, *Euphemismen in der hebräischen Bibel* (OBC 12; Wiesbaden: Harrassowitz, 2000).

[8] Rabinowitz, "Euphemism and Dysphemism," *Encyclopedia Judaica*, 6:961.

[9] Cf. Isa 7:20, where "hair of the feet" means "pubic hair."

[10] Edward Ullendorff suggests "sporting with" ("The Bawdy Bible," *BSOAS* 42 [1979]: 430); BDB has "conjugal caresses."

[11] Ullendorff gives examples of how it was misunderstood ("The Bawdy Bible," 427–28).

[12] Philo, *Spec.* 2.129–132. Moses avoided specifying clearly the parents' rights should their children die because to "speak plainly" about such a thing would have been to introduce a "sinister thought" (129); instead Moses avoided "undisguised terms"

century, E. König would cite biblical euphemisms as proof that "The writers of Scripture sought to give to their words that ennobling effect which springs from regard to *purity* or chastity."[13] But, as König himself admits, the Bible is not always euphemistic. Changes in the patterns of use for specific words, as well as in mores more generally, meant that later Jews and Christians have not always been comfortable with the "purity" of their own holy texts. The Mishnah actually specifies the biblical passages that should be avoided in public reading, or that should be read (in Hebrew) and left untranslated (*Megillah* 4.10). For the most part these passages involve material that might be deemed shameful to important biblical figures or might be otherwise theologically problematic, rather than passages with specific words that were offensive.[14] The Talmud, however, expands on the Mishnah by listing a dozen indelicate Hebrew words from scripture that should be replaced by other expressions (*b. Megillah* 25a). The Talmud says that whatever was written לגנאי ("disgracefully") should be read לשבח ("politely").[15] Where שגל ("rape")[16] is written, שכב ("lie with") should be read; in place of עפלים (traditionally understood as "hemorrhoids"),[17] one should say טחורים;[18] for חריונים ("dove's dung"),[19] דביונים; for מחראות ("latrine"),[20] מוצאות.[21] The terms of Rabshakeh's taunt ("eating their own dung and drinking their own urine" [2 Kings 18:27 = Isa 36:12]) were to be replaced: חריהם[22] with צואתם and שיניהם with מימי רגליהם.

(γυμνοῖς ὀνόμασι, 131) and wrote "decently" (πρεπόντως, 130). This is perhaps more like the rabbinic concern with "opening one's mouth to the devil"—saying something inauspicious—than with *decency*. On the decency of scriptural language, cf. Basil of Caesarea, *Letter* 160.3 ("the divine scripture passed by in silence [ἀπεσιώπησε]" sundry forms of immorality, "preferring not to befoul its own dignity by naming shameful things"). For medieval comments on scriptural euphemism, cf. Carla Casagrande and Silvana Vecchio, *Les Péchés de la langue: Discipline et éthique de la parole dans la culture médiévale* (trans. Philippe Baillet; Paris: Cerf, 1991), 282.

[13] E. König, "Style of Scripture," 164.

[14] In fact, the Mishnah demands that prudery not prevent one from reading Lev 18:6–18 literally; the reader should not substitute "shame" for "nakedness" (*m.Meg.* 4.9).

[15] In the Masoretic text, the suggestions in *b. Meg.* 25 are given as the *qere*.

[16] Deut 28:30; Isa 13:16; Jer 3:2; Zech 14:2.

[17] Deut 28:27; 1 Sam 5:6, 9, 12; 6:4, 5. Cf. *HALOT*, s.v.: "the layer of subcutaneous fat around the testicles, perinaeum, wild growth of tissue in the vulva, thickening of flesh in the anus."

[18] 1 Sam 6:11, 17.

[19] 2 Kings 6:25; 2 Kings 18:27 = Isa 36:12.

[20] 2 Kings 10:27.

[21] Ullendorff says "the *ketib* is 'place of excrements', while the *qere* means 'place one goes out to, privy'" ("Bawdy Bible," 444).

[22] Isa 36:12 has a different spelling (חראיהם).

Why these expressions and not others caused offense is often impossible to say.[23] Since both חרא and the cognates חריונים and מחראות were to be replaced, one suspects that words from this root had come to sound offensive (perhaps roughly like "shit" and the cognate place thereof, "the shitter").[24] But whereas שין was to be replaced, the related verb שתן, "urinate,"[25] caused no offense when used in the expression "one who urinates upon the wall" (משתין בקיר).[26]

I have already mentioned that the Talmud advised against reading aloud some of the Bible's impolite words. Other rabbinic literature exhibits a similar concern for avoiding offensive expressions. Some rabbinic euphemisms avoid what would be inauspicious, summarized by the expression, "A man should not open his mouth to Satan" (b. Ber. 19a).[27] Thus when something bad is predicted for Israel, rabbinic texts can replace "Israel" with "the enemies of Israel" (b. Suk. 29a; Lev. Rab. 25.1),[28] or can negate the sentiment ("and every trouble which shall not come on Israel").

In addition to avoiding such ominous expressions, rabbis also warned against indecent language. In b. Shabbat 33a, the words נבלות פה are

---

[23] Cf. the comments of Saul Lieberman, *Hellenism in Jewish Palestine* (New York: Jewish Theological Seminary of America, 1950), 32–34; and A. Tal, "Euphemisms in the Samaritan Targum of the Pentateuch," *Aramaic Studies* 1 (2003): 109–30 (especially 120–24).

[24] *HALOT* has *cacavit* for חרא. Cf. Benjamin Urrutia, "Rab-Shakeh's Verbal Aggression and Rabbinical Euphemism," *Maledicta* 5 (1981): 103–4. The euphemistic צאה, on the other hand, needed no replacement in Deut 23:14 or Ezek 4:12. Cf. 11QTemple XLVI, 15.

[25] Either the hiphil of שתן or the qal with reflexive -t- of שין (cf. *HALOT* s.v. שין).

[26] 1 Sam 25:22, 34; 1 Kings 14:10; 16:11; 21:21; 2 Kings 9:8 (the LXX uses οὐρέω). Many English translations (e.g. NASB, NIV, NRSV, NKJV) simply render this earthy expression "male." But as Robert Alter notes, in the case of 1 Sam 25:22, the "edge of vulgarity seems perfectly right for David's anger" (*The David Story* [New York: Norton, 1999], 156). Furthermore, Peter J. Leithart ("Nabal and His Wine," *JBL* 120 [2001]: 525–27) observes that 1 Sam 25 plays on the "pissing" in ways that would be obscured by less literal translations. For instance, Nabal's heart would later stop "while the wine was going out of him" (1 Sam 25:37); hence Nabal is not only a fool (*nabal*) but a wineskin (*nebel*).

[27] On this phenomenon of "opening the mouth to Satan," cf. Joshua Trachtenberg, *Jewish Magic and Superstition: A Study in Folk Religion* (Cleveland: Meridian Books, 1961), 56–60.

[28] This occurs already in 2 Sam 12:14, where it might represent a euphemism original to the Bible rather than simply a scribal emendation. For a discussion of this passage (and an Egyptian inscription with a similar euphemism), see Carmel McCarthy, *The Tiqqune Sopherim* (Orbis Biblicus et Orientalis 36; Göttingen: Vandenhoeck & Ruprecht, 1981), 183–87.

connected to the "folly" (נבלה) of Isa 9:16 in a comment on obscene language:

> As a punishment for obscenity [נבלות פה], troubles multiply, cruel decrees are proclaimed afresh, the young of Israel's enemies die, and the fatherless and widows cry out and are not answered; for it is said, "Therefore shall the Lord not rejoice over their young men, neither shall he have compassion over their fatherless and their widows: for every one is profane and an evil-doer, and every mouth speaketh folly [כל פה דובר נבלה]. For all this his anger is not turned away, but his hand is stretched out still" [Isa 9:16]. What is meant by, "but his hand is stretched out still"?—Said R. Ḥanan b. Rabbah: All know for what purpose a bride enters the bridal canopy, yet against whomsoever who speaks obscenely [כל המנבל פיו] [thereof], even if a sentence of seventy years' happiness had been sealed for him, it is reversed for evil. Rabbah b. Shila said in R. Ḥisda's name: He who puts his mouth to folly [כל המנבל את פיו], Gehenna is made deep for him, as it is said, "A deep pit is for the mouth [that speaketh] perversity." (Soncino)

The saying of R. Ḥanan b. Rabbah is found also in *b. Ketubbot* 8b, using the language of Isa 9:16 to condemn obscene talk (המנבל פיו) or letting a foolish word go from one's mouth (ומוציא דבר נבלה מפיו). In keeping with this principle, one finds in rabbinic texts[29] euphemistic expressions for sexual organs,[30] sexual intercourse,[31] the toilet,[32] urine,[33] defecation,[34] and masturbation.[35]

Amidst all this modesty it is interesting to note that *b. Megillah* 25b mentions the opinion that foul language *could* perhaps be employed towards idolaters. Although, as mentioned above, the Talmud states that the word מחראות of 2 Kings 10:27 was to be replaced by the more polite מוצאות, the Talmud adds that R. Joshua b. Korha disagreed and said that the actual word should be read because it was a term of

---

[29] See Rabinowitz, "Euphemism and Dysphemism," *Encyclopaedia Judaica*, 6:961–62, from whom the following examples are taken.

[30] The penis was "the organ" (*b. B. Meṣ* 84a) and the vagina "that place" (*b. Nid.* 20a).

[31] "The usage of the bed" (*tashmish ha-mittah, b. Yoma* 8.1) or simply *tashmish* (*b. Ketub.* 65b).

[32] "The house of water" (*t. Meg.* 3.2) or "the house of the chair" (*b. Tam.* 1.1; *b. Ber.* 25a).

[33] "The jet" (*b. Ber.* 25) or "the water of the feet" (as in the *qere* of 2 Kings 18:27 and Isa 36:12).

[34] "Having need of his apertures" (*b. Giṭ.* 70) or "turning aside" (*b. Toh.* 10.2; *b. Ber.* 62a).

[35] "By way of limbs" (*b. Nid.* 13b).

opprobrium for idolatry (שהוא גנאי לעבודת כוכבים).[36] To this is added
Rabbi Nahman's opinion that "All gibing [ליצנותא] is forbidden save
gibing at idolatry, which is permitted." Several passages are adduced
that could be read in such way as to mock idols:

> As it is written, "Bel boweth down, Nebo stoopeth" [Isa 46:1] and the text
> goes on, "They stoop, they bow down together, they cannot deliver the
> burden," etc. R. Jannai learns the same lesson from here: "The inhabit-
> ants of Samaria shall be in dread for the calves of Beth Aven, for the
> people thereof shall mourn over it and the priests thereof shall tremble
> for it, for its glory, because it is departed from it" [Hos 10:5]. Read not
> "its glory" [כבודו], but "its burden" [כבידו]. (Soncino)

To this are appended two other opinions in favor of using nasty expressions against idolaters: "R. Huna b. Manoah said in the name of R. Aḥa
the son of R. Iḳa: It is permitted to an Israelite to say to an idolater,
Take your idol and shove it in your *shin tof*.[37] R. Ashi said: It is permis-
sible to abuse a person of ill fame with the term *gimel shin*."[38]

I. Prophetic Scatology

These rabbis who allowed the use of crass language when chiding sinners were, in a sense, faithful to a strand of prophetic discourse that
used vulgar images to chastise Israel. Isaiah promised that the Lord
would leave the daughters of Zion with scabs on their heads and their
vaginas laid bare (Isa 3:17; 7:20).[39] Ezekiel narrated the people's religious
history in terms of a despised baby, navel cord uncut, thrown aside and
weltering in its own blood (Ezek 16:4–6). Ezekiel is shockingly explicit
in his use of the metaphor that represents idolatry as sexual infidel-

---

[36] The biblical text in question refers to worship of Baal: "Then they demolished
the pillar of Baal, and destroyed the temple of Baal, and made it a latrine to this day"
(2 Kings 10:27).

[37] I.e. שת, "butt," a biblical word, which the Talmud preferred to spell out.

[38] The meaning of *gimel shin* is not so clear; Rashi explains it as *gaifa shaita*, "adulterer," "madman."

[39] The meaning of פת in Isa 3:17 is not entirely certain (*HALOT* has "brow, forehead"
but notes that it might mean "female pudenda"). Pointing to the use of the word in
1 Kings 7:50, where it may refer to the sockets in which doors turn, J. Cheryl Exum
argues that the use in Isaiah is "an obscene reference to the woman's vagina" (*Plotted,
Shot and Painted: Cultural Representations of Biblical Women* [Sheffield: Sheffield Academic
Press, 1996], 105, cited by Yvonne M. Sherwood, "Prophetic Scatology: Prophecy and
the Art of Sensation," *Semeia* 82 [1998], 193n16).

ity. When he depicts unfaithful Israel as a loose woman, he does not merely state that she was interested in men (as the RSV would have it: "you offered yourself to every passer-by"), but makes her posture explicit: "you spread your legs."[40] Not content to say that this craven woman longs for a handsome foreign lover, Ezekiel says that she wants his massive "flesh" and bestial seminal emissions (Ezek 23:20).

Ezekiel 8:17 was also understood in antiquity to be indecent. Its meaning is obscure and it was already interpreted in two different (but equally offensive) ways in rabbinic texts.[41] As Ezekiel enumerates Israel's abominations, he describes men with their backs to the temple, worshipping the sun in the court of the Lord (8:16). Yahweh is the speaker, and asks angrily, "Is it not bad enough that the house of Judah commits the abominations done here? Must they fill the land with violence, and provoke my anger still further? See, they are putting the branch to their nose! [והגם שלחים את הזמורה אל אפם]." Because it is Yahweh who is angry and offended, the suffix of "nose" may have been changed from "my nose" to "their nose"—a common scribal emendation. But it is still unclear what it meant that they "put a זמורה to his nose."[42] Some readers understood this either as a reference to a phallus or a fart.[43] The latter interpretation was suggested by the fact that the men Ezekiel sees have turned their backs to the temple.[44] One begins to see why the prophets—like Diogenes the Cynic—were called madmen.[45]

Yvonne M. Sherwood has brilliantly explored both the prophets' grotesque imagery and dignified commentators' discomfort with finding such a mess between the bindings of the Sacred Bible.[46] Even

---

[40] Ezek 16:25: ותפשקי את־רגליך (LXX: διήγαγες τὰ σκέλη σου).

[41] McCarthy, *The Tiqqune Sopherim*, 91–97. McCarthy's evidence suggests that, despite what the rabbis saw in this passage, it might *not* have been a lewd idiom originally (*contra* Ullendorff, "Bawdy Bible," 441).

[42] For explanations other than those of the rabbis, see Leslie C. Allen, *Ezekiel 1–19* (WBC 28; Dallas: Word Books, 1994), 121–22, 145–46; *HALOT* s.v. זמורה.

[43] Ullendorff: "and they stick their penis in my nose" or "something like 'and they fart in my face'" ("Bawdy Bible," 441). Cf. Walther Zimmerli, *Ezekiel* (trans. Ronald E. Clements; 2 vols.; Philadelphia: Fortress, 1979), 1:244–45.

[44] "'With their backs to the Temple of the Lord.' It teaches that they uncovered themselves and committed a nuisance towards that which is below [a euphemism for heaven, i.e., God]." (*b. Yoma* 77a).

[45] Hos 9:7; Jer 29:26; 2 Kings 9:11; cf. D.L. 6.54, where Diogenes is called a "Socrates gone mad."

[46] Yvonne M. Sherwood, "Prophetic Scatology: Prophecy and the Art of Sensation," *Semeia* 82 (1998): 183–224. It was apparently not Sherwood's purpose to evaluate the exact register of Hebrew words used in the Bible, but rather to show the extreme

Ullendorff, who clearly relishes uncovering what he refers to as the "bawdy" elements of scripture, goes out of his way to reassure his readers that the prophets "did not offend good taste when dealing with subjects of such delicacy."[47] König had to acknowledge the need to "explain and to excuse certain passages in Ezekiel."[48] The sexual language has even been raised to a theological problem, calling into question whether God could have inspired such lurid descriptions.[49] As Sherwood notes, the Bible has been asked to represent a gospel of gentility even though its texts do not always fit with later notions of civilized decorum.[50]

II. WISDOM LITERATURE AND BEN SIRACH

For Jewish wisdom literature, as exemplified by the Book of Proverbs, right use of speech is paramount: "Death and life are in the power of the tongue" (Prov 18:21). Proverbs commends silence,[51] good words,[52] and discretion,[53] and praises the tongue of the righteous;[54] it warns against

---

distress that the prophets have caused genteel readers by the crudity of their language. Hence she gives the grossest possible English translations to make her point, a practice which unfortunately may at times confuse the prophets' metaphors, which are certainly shocking and often disgusting, with the register of their language, which is much more difficult to ascertain. She mocks using a word like "dung" to translate פרש; but she does not explain why "shit" is more appropriate (197). Is there evidence that פרש bothered later readers the way חרא did? Again, what would suggest that the tone of נבלות in Hos 2:12 is best reproduced by "cunt" (197n21)?

[47] "The Bawdy Bible," 447. He says at another point: "The Old Testament may at times be bawdy both in substance and expression; it is never lascivious, salacious or sly" (433).

[48] E. König, "Style of Scripture," 164–65.

[49] When the Reverend Jimmy Swaggart and the Muslim apologist Ahmed Deedat debated the inspiration of the Bible (Baton Rouge, Louisiana), Deedat asked why, if God was the author, there was so much foul sexual material. To make his point, Deedat offered Swaggart $100 to read Ezekiel 23 with the full, robust expression Swaggart brought to other biblical texts. Swaggart had no choice but to take the challenge, but after a few minutes of scanning the text which he was handed by Deedat—an NIV translation in which Deedat had actually highlighted Ezek 23:20 ("whose genitals were like those of donkeys and whose emission was like that of horses")—Swaggart read— very quickly and in a monotone—from his own Bible.

[50] "Prophetic Scatology," 200.

[51] Prov 11:12, 13; 12:16; 13:3.

[52] Prov 12:14, 18, 25; 13:2; 15:23.

[53] Prov 5:12; 12:23; 15:1, 4.

[54] Prov 10:20, 31, 32.

scoffing,[55] babble,[56] perverse speech,[57] deceit,[58] gossip,[59] rashness,[60] and slander,[61] to name just a few potential failings. In short, a sage should be characterized by the ability to speak well.[62] In general this advice is supported by appeals to the practical consequences that attend good or bad speech. Some of these consequences are quite general, but others suggest a special concern with impressing one's social betters. When Proverbs warns that "the perverse tongue will be cut off" (Prov 10:31)[63] or promises that the king will delight in righteous words (Prov 16:13), one can see the concerns of those whose well-being depended on their superiors' good graces.[64] One should not give offense by being garrulous, or by getting caught in gossip or slander or lies. Qohelet advised, "Do not curse the king, even in your thoughts, or curse the rich, even in your bedroom; for a bird of the air may carry your voice, or some winged creature tell the matter" (Eccl 10:20). It is all fine and good to win the admiration of one's neighbors by timely speech; but far more pressing is avoiding any verbal activity that might offend those with power—especially those with the power to cut out the tongue! Ultimately, "to watch over mouth and tongue is to keep out of trouble" (Prov 21:23).

Given the concern to guard against every slip of the tongue, it is striking that Proverbs nowhere addresses "foul language," which, as we have seen from Greek and Latin sources, clearly had the potential to offend. But in the Greek translation of Sirach, a book that exhibits

---

[55] Prov 1:22; 3:34; 9:7–8.

[56] Prov 10:8b; 10:10b, 19; 13:3.

[57] Prov 2:12 (contrast 8:6–9 on the straightness of the author's own words); 10:31, 32.

[58] Prov 4:24; 6:12, 17, 19; 12:17, 19, 22.

[59] Prov 18:8; 19:19; 26:22.

[60] Prov 12:18.

[61] Prov 10:18.

[62] William McKane, "Functions of Language and Objectives of Discourse according to Proverbs, 10–30," in *La Sagesse de l'Ancien Testament* (ed. Maruice Gilbert; 2d ed.; BETL 51; Leuven: Leuven University Press, 1990), 166–85.

[63] Cf. Prov 12:13; cf. 11:9, 11; 12:6.

[64] On the place of sages in Israelite society, cf. Joseph Blenkinsopp, *Wisdom and Law in the Old Testament: The Ordering of Life in Israel and Early Judaism* (OBS; Oxford: Oxford University Press, 1995), 9–17; on their possible relationship to the royal court, cf. R. N. Whybray, *The Book of Proverbs: A Survey of Modern Study* (History of Biblical Interpretation Series; Leiden: Brill, 1995), 18–22; James L. Crenshaw, "Wisdom Literature," in *The Oxford Companion to the Bible* (ed. Bruce M. Metzger and Michael D. Coogan; New York: Oxford University Press, 1993), 801.

a range of concerns about speech similar to that of Proverbs,[65] we do find a warning against "course, foul language." To my knowledge this is the first mention of this type of speech from a Jewish author. Under the category of "Discipline of the Tongue" (παιδεία στόματος),[66] Sirach addresses the use of God's name in oaths (23:7–11), and then warns against "lewd stupidity" and "words of reproach":

12 ἔστιν λέξις ἀντιπαραβεβλημένη θανάτῳ
μὴ εὑρεθήτω ἐν κληρονομίᾳ Ιακωβ·
ἀπὸ γὰρ εὐσεβῶν ταῦτα πάντα ἀποστήσεται,
καὶ ἐν ἁμαρτίαις οὐκ ἐγκλισθήσονται.
13 ἀπαιδευσίαν ἀσυρῆ μὴ συνεθίσῃς τὸ στόμα σου·
ἔστιν γὰρ ἐν αὐτῇ λόγος ἁμαρτίας.
14 μνήσθητι πατρὸς καὶ μητρός σου,
ἀνὰ μέσον γὰρ μεγιστάνων συνεδρεύεις,
μήποτε ἐπιλάθῃ ἐνώπιον αὐτῶν
καὶ τῷ ἐθισμῷ σου μωρανθῇς
καὶ θελήσεις εἰ μὴ ἐγεννήθης
καὶ τὴν ἡμέραν τοῦ τοκετοῦ σου καταράσῃ.
15 ἄνθρωπος συνεθιζόμενος λόγοις ὀνειδισμοῦ
ἐν πάσαις ταῖς ἡμέραις αὐτοῦ οὐ μὴ παιδευθῇ. (Sir 23:12–15)

12 There is a manner of speaking comparable to death;
may it never be found in the inheritance of Jacob!
Such conduct will be far from the godly,
and they will not wallow in sins.
13 Do not accustom your mouth to lewd ignorance,
for therein lies sinful speech.
14 Remember your father and mother
when you sit among the great ones,
lest you forget yourself in their presence,
and your bad habit makes you a fool;
then you will wish that you had never been born,
and you will curse the day of your birth.
15 Those who are accustomed to using abusive language
will never become disciplined as long as they live. (NRSV, adjusted)

---

[65] Speech comes up constantly throughout the book: Sir 4:23–29; 5:11–6:1; 6:5; 7:11–14; 8:3–6; 9:17–18; 11:7–9; 13:11, 22; 14:1; 18:15, 18–19; 18:30–19:4; 19:10–12; 20:1–8, 18–19, 24–27; 21:7, 16, 27–28; 22:20–27; 23:7–15; 26:14, 27; 27:4–7, 13–15, 28; 28:12–26; 31:31–32:12.

[66] The heading is found in some mss. (G. H. Box and W. O. E. Oesterley, "Sirach," in *Apocrypha and Pseudepigrapha of the Old Testament* [ed. R. H. Charles; 2 vols.; Oxford: Clarendon, 1913], 1:394); cf. Sir 23:7: παιδείαν στόματος ἀκούσατε, τέκνα.

The passage is not entirely explicit about what type or types of speech it is rejecting.[67] Verse 13, which could be rendered literally, "Do not accustom your mouth to lewd stupidity," sounds like a reference to foul language. Those commentators who have understood the passage as addressing foul language[68] have not drawn attention to how unique a thought this would be in the context of Jewish Wisdom literature.[69] Other commentators have doubted it was about foul language at all.

Reference to other versions of the text does not elucidate the meaning of the Greek or give a clear indication of what the original Hebrew might have been. In fact, the Syriac and Latin versions do not suggest a concern with foul language. The Syriac[70] has a more general warning against teaching one's mouth "foolishness" (ܣܟܠܘܬܐ).[71] The Old Latin is a fairly literal translation of this Greek passage—except, unfortunately, for the verse that most interests us here:

---

[67] So Duesberg and Auvray: "D'après le contexte il s'agit de l'impureté en paroles. Mais en dépit de sa sévérité, ou peut-être à cause d'elle, l'auteur reste dans un certain vague et ne permet pas de préciser exactement la nature de la faute envisagée" (Hilaire Duesberg, O.S.B. and Paul Auvray, *L'Ecclésiastique* [Paris: Cerf, 1958], 112).

[68] Patrick W. Skehan and Alexander A. Di Lella, *The Wisdom of Ben Sira* (AB 39; New York: Doubleday, 1987), 323: "coarse talk," "indecent and lewd conversations or remarks," "improper speech"; Thomas H. Weber, "Sirach," in *The Jerome Bible Commentary* (Englewood Cliffs, New Jersey: Prentice-Hall, 1968), 548: "coarse talk and abusive language"; V. Ryssell, *Die Sprüche Jesus', des Sohnes Sirach*, in *Die Apokryphen und Pseudepigraphen des Alten Testaments* (ed. E. Kautzsch; Tübingen: Mohr, 1900), 1:342; Joseph Knabenbauer, S. J., *Commentarius in Ecclesiasticum* (Paris: P. Lethielleux, 1902), 257; Rudolf Smend, *Die Weisheit des Jesus Sirach* (Berlin: Georg Reimer, 1906), 208–209 (v. 13: "Gemeint sind etwa Zoten"; v. 15: "unanständige Reden"); Vinzenz Hamp, *Das Buch Jesus Sirach* (Würzburg: Echter-Verlag, 1951), 61; Otto Fridolin Fritzsche, *Die Weisheit Jesus-Sirach's* (Leipzig: S. Hirzel, 1859), 119: "Gemeint ist Ungezogenheit, Rohheit im Sprechen"; Box and Oesterley, "Sirach": "unseemly manner of speech"; Moshe S. Segal, *Sefer Ben Sira Hashalem* (Jerusalem: Mosad Byalik, 1958), 139 (Segal translates 23:13a פיד נבול אל תאלף). For further references, see A. J. Desečar, "La Necedad en Sirac 23, 12–15," *LASBF* 20 (1970): 266.

[69] John Ifeanyichukwu Okoye mentions this passage only in passing (*Speech in Ben Sira with special reference to 5,9–6,1* [Frankfurt am Main: Peter Lang, 1995], 60, 70–71). Jack T. Sanders (*Ben Sira and Demotic Wisdom* [SBLMS 28; Chico, Calif.; Scholars Press, 1983]) mentions no Egyptian parallels to this passage from Sirach.

[70] Usually held to be translated from the Hebrew in the fourth century (M. A. Nelson, *The Syriac Version of the Wisdom of Ben-Sira Compared to the Greek and Hebrew Materials* [SBLDS, 107; Atlanta: Scholars Press, 1988]; Benjamin G. Wright, *No Small Difference: Sirach's Relationship to Its Hebrew Parent Text* [SBLSCS 26; Atlanta: Scholars Press, 1989]).

[71] "Don't teach your mouth foolishness, for in it there are words of deceit." The Syriac at 23:15 refers to "idle words" (ܡܠܠܐ ܕܣܪܝܩܐ) rather than "words of reproach."

23:15 est et alia loquella contraria morti
non inveniatur in hereditate Iacob
16 etenim a misericordibus omnia haec auferentur
et in delictis non volutabunt
17 indisciplinose non adsuescat os tuum
est enim in illa verbum peccati
18 memento patris et matris tuae
in medio enim magnatorum consistis
19 ne forte obliviscatur te in conspectu illorum
et adsiduitate tua infatuatus inproperium patiaris
et maluisses non nasci
et diem nativitatis tuae maledicas
20 homo adsuetus in verbis inproperii
in omnibus diebus suis non erudietur.

For the Greek ἀπαιδευσίαν ἀσυρῆ (23:13) the Latin has the more general *indisciplinose*, thus rendering ἀπαιδευσία but not the adjective ἀσυρής.[72]

Even commentators who have seen foul language addressed in v. 13 have not always thought that vv. 12–15 all treat the same topic. Generally it is agreed that vv. 13 and 15 must describe a similar vice.[73] But v. 12 has often been understood as a reference to blasphemy. The phrase ἔστιν λέξις ἀντιπαραβεβλημένη θανάτῳ has been taken to mean "a type of speaking *meriting* death,"[74] and has thus suggested blasphemy, since Lev 24:16 prescribes death for blasphemers. If blasphemous speech is the subject in v. 12, it might also be the subject in v. 14, in which case "forgetting oneself" among the "great ones" (23:14) could mean some sort of irreligious talk.[75]

In an article devoted to Sir 23:12–15, A. J. Desečar argued that this entire section of Sirach addresses not indecent words but words that

---

[72] This led Smend to suggest that in 23:13 ἀσυρῆ was an addition of the translator or a gloss (*Weisheit*, 209).

[73] Both verses mention *paideia* (ἀπαιδευσίαν, παιδευθῇ), "word" (λόγος, λόγοις), and habituation (συνεθίσῃς, συνεθιζόμενος, cf. also v. 9); so presumably the content of the "words of reproach" (v. 15) is being described as "lewd and stupid" (v. 13). Some scholars suggest rearranging the verses (in the order 12, 14, 13, 15) to reflect this understanding (Smend, *Weisheit*, 208; Box and Oesterley, "Sirach," 1:394).

[74] "Une manière de parler qui mérite la mort" (Duesberg and Auvray, *L'Ecclésiastique*, 112); Burton Mack says, "the meaning of speech *comparable to death* is unclear. It may mean 'rivaling death' or 'meriting death' and so intend a reference to blasphemy, the punishment for which was death" (*The HarperCollins Study Bible* [ed. Wayne A. Meeks; San Francisco: HarperCollins, 1993], 1565).

[75] Smend, *Weisheit*, 209.

encourage abandoning pure Yahwistic religion.[76] In his view, not even the ἀπαιδευσία ἀσυρής of 23:13 (which he renders *baja grosería*) refers to impure language (*las palabras impuras*), since—as he righly notes—the latter sin is not mentioned anywhere else in the Hebrew Bible. Instead, Desečar argues that v. 12 refers to an indirect sort of blasphemy, namely, to arguing against traditional Israelite religion. Then vv. 13–15 explicate this sin, labeling such arguments for apostasy as "base stupidity" (23:13) and "words of reproach" (23:15). Desečar thinks "sitting among the great ones" (23:14) refers to dining with those Jewish aristocrats who advocated religious hellenization; in their presence there would be a great temptation to argue in favor of hellenization, and later the pangs of conscience for this lapse of fidelity would cause one to curse the day of one's birth (23:14).

Such an interpretation is improbable. In the first place, "base stupidity" (23:13) is not an apt expression for speech that urges departing from a more traditional to a more hellenized approach to the divine;[77] and a reference to "words of reproach" (23:15) is particularly out of place in this scenario (words reproaching whom?). Furthermore, μεγιστᾶνες are not portrayed so negatively in Sirach (cf. Sir 38:3; 39:4), and there is no reason to see them here as religiously compromised aristocrats. When Sirach addresses sitting at a table of the great (31:12–32:13), he worries not about "religious" fidelity, but about deportment that will reveal one's *paideia*.[78] The problem with a "word of reproach" in that context is that it is impolite, out of keeping with the spirit of the symposium:

> Do not reprove your neighbor at a banquet of wine,
> and do not despise him in his merrymaking;
> speak no word of reproach [λόγον ὀνειδισμοῦ] to him
> and do not distress him by making demands of him. (Sir 31:31)

I think Desečar is right to see all four verses of Sir 23:12–15 addressing one type of speech. But if we dispense with the idea that 23:12

---

[76] A. J. Desečar, "La Necedad en Sirac 23, 12–15," *Studii Biblici Franciscani Liber Annuus* 20 (1970): 264–72.

[77] Philo said that ἀπαιδευσία was a cause of inane twaddle (ληρεῖν [*Ebr.* 6, 11]); he mentions this in a discussion of how drinking leads to stupid talk (*Ebr.* 4). For "stupidity" of the mouth resulting in outbursts of temper, cf. Pseudo-Clement, *Epistulae de virginitate* 1.11.6: διὰ ἀπαιδευσίαν γὰρ γλώσσης ἐπέρχονται ὀργαί.

[78] On Sirach's view of manners and morals at meals, cf. Oda Wischmeyer, *Die Kultur des Buches Jesus Sirach* (BZNW 77; Berlin: de Gruyter, 1995), 102–19.

refers to blasphemy, all the elements in this section can be understood as referring to vulgar speech.[79] In v. 12, a "type of speech" is being *compared* with death.[80] Since the slip of the tongue described in 23:14 will make the speaker curse the day of his birth, it is not too great a stretch to suggest that Sirach likens this sort of speech to "death" (23:12).[81] Once the specter of the death penalty has been removed, there is no reason to read "blasphemy" into the passage, and the whole coheres as a warning against using foul language at a banquet.

The key phrase is ἀπαιδευσίαν ἀσυρῆ (13), whose flavor the NRSV captures quite well with "coarse, foul language." There might even be a sexual element in ἀσυρής, which can be used to designate "lewd" conduct or words.[82] Polybius uses ἀσυρής for a lewd life[83] and for some sort of nasty abuse.[84] It was "lewd and vulgar" (ἀσυρῶς καὶ φορτικῶς) when Antisthenes called Plato "Dick."[85]

Sirach is warning, then, against accustoming the mouth to "lewd" or "base" stupidity. This lewd stupidity describes the form of the "reproachful words" (λόγοις ὀνειδισμοῦ). Sirach elsewhere says that the way fools talk, laugh, and abuse is offensive, sinful, and grievous to hear (Sir 27:13–15; cf. 20:19). Stupid, lewd reproach characterizes the foolish, and, in fact, it makes one a fool (μωρανθῆς, 23:14). Nobody who speaks reproachful words will ever attain *paideia* (23:15). (Polybius, we recall, also said that there are certain filthy words of reproach that

---

[79] Othmar Schilling agrees that already in v. 12 there is a reference to indecent speech, and cites Eph 5:3 as expressing the same sentiment (*Das Buch Jesus Sirach* [Freiburg: Verlag Herder, 1956], 103); cf. Arthur F. Taylor, *Meditations in Ecclesiasticus* (London: James Clarke & Co. Limited, 1928), 154.

[80] LSJ s.v. ἀντιπαραβάλλω: "place side by side so as to compare or contrast"; for the passive with the dative, "measure oneself against, rival." The Syriac leaves out the reference to death ("There is another similar to this").

[81] "Social disasters of this sort make one wish one 'had never been born' (v 14e; cf. 3:11, 16; Jer 20:17–18) and curse the day of [one's] birth (v 14f; cf. Job 3:3–10; Jer 20:14)" (Skehan and Di Lella, *Wisdom of Ben Sira*, 324). Schilling suggested that behind the Greek of v. 12 might have been a wordplay on דבר, read first as "word" and then as "pestilence" (*Sirach*, 103). Such use of alliteration in formulating proverbs was not uncommon (cf. Prov 11:2; Eccl 7:1).

[82] LSJ, s.v., "lewd, filthy." Hamp renders the Greek "schmutzige Ungezogenheit" (*Sirach*, 61).

[83] *Hist.* 4.4.5 (of someone who had "renounced his claim to be a man"); in *Hist.* 18.55.8, βίος ἀσυρῆς is set beside ἀσέλγεια.

[84] *Hist.* 38.20.6 (accusations against Hasdrubal for breaking an oath, desertion, cowardice, and general baseness of soul are made μετὰ χλευασμοῦ καὶ λοιδορίας ἀσυροῦς καὶ δυσμενικῆς).

[85] See above, p. 83.

no educated person [πεπαιδευμένος] would make.)[86] Sirach's advice for how to behave at banquets mentions "words of reproach," "great ones," and the need to display *paideia*—all elements we find in 23:12–15. At a banquet one must be careful what one says when "the great" are present (32:9): the young should only speak when addressed (32:7); modest behavior wins approval (32:10); and one must not sin "through proud speech" (32:12). It is in this constellation of concerns—modesty, propriety, displaying good breeding through how one eats, drinks, and speaks—that Sirach addresses an especially grievous slip of the tongue: lewd abuse.

The habit of using lewd language could result in a slip of the tongue among the "great ones," and the presence of wine would make the banquet all the more dangerous for maintaining courteous speech.[87] For Sirach, with his intense concern for appearance, uttering lewd abuse amidst the prominent would be cause for overwhelming shame (23:14). One is to guard against this by remembering one's mother and father.[88] Verse 14 follows on verse 13 because bad habits might betray a person when he has his opportunity to sit among the grandees—that is, at precisely the worst moment for a lapse of discretion. This is just the sort of "slip" of the tongue that Sirach frequently worries about.[89] Sirach views every moment of speech as fraught with peril. Speech can win honor and renown (5:13a), but it can also lead to a fall (5:13b).[90] Again, since such a slip makes one wish he had never been born and

---

[86] Polybius, *Hist.* 12.13.1–2, cited above, p. 71. For Philo, also, the one who cannot control his tongue exhibits his lack of *paideia* (*Abr.* 20).

[87] Similarly *T. Jud.* 16.1–3 suggests that, when drinking, someone will forget discretion and utter reproachful words (λόγοι ὕβρεως), and *T. Jud.* 14.8 makes it clear that such speech will be indecent: "But if he exceeds the limit [of drink], wine casts the spirit of error into his mind and makes the drunkard become *foul mouthed* [αἰσχροῃμονεῖν] and lawless; yet rather than be ashamed, he boasts in his dishonorable action and considers it good."

[88] Schilling adds preciously, "especially the mother" ("Der Gedanke an die Träger des Lebens, vor allem wohl der Gedanke an die Mutter, sollte den Menschen bestimmen, Ehrfurcht zu haben vor dem Geheimnis des Lebens" [*Das Buch Jesus Sirach*, 103]).

[89] For "slipping" with the tongue (ὀλίσθημα or ὀλισθαίνειν), cf. Sir 14:1; 20:18; 21:7; 25:8; 28:26. Sir 20:18 can be compared with a similar saying attributed to Zeno (D.L. 7.26).

[90] On the peril of speaking among one's social superiors, cf. Philo, *Ebr.* 131: "We know that when servants are about to approach their masters, or sons their parents, or subjects their rulers, they will take careful thought to be sober that they may not transgress in word and deed, and thus either receive punishment for having shewn contempt for the dignity of their betters, or at the best become an object of scorn" (Colson, LCL).

curse the day of his birth, Sirach can quite appropriately liken such speech to "death" (23:12).

In retrospect, this passage is significant as the first surviving comment on foul speech in a Jewish text. It was apparently not quite so striking in antiquity. Not even Clement of Alexandria, who cites Sirach frequently in formulating his own speech ethics, makes reference to this passage. And in its Latin and Syriac (and presumably the original Hebrew) forms, it would not have spoken clearly against "stupid, lewd talk" at all. Nonetheless, the passage did not fade entirely from memory. In Hesychius's *Lexicon*, the word ἀσυρῆ is glossed as ἀκάθαρτα, with reference to Sir 23:13.[91]

III. JESUS

Of the many striking assertions about speech attributed to Jesus, none directly touches on the decency of language. The absence of instruction about foul language cannot be attributed to Jesus' having viewed speech as a trivial matter. To the contrary, he warned that even "every idle word" would be relevant to the final judgment (Matt 12.36–37).[92] Just as a tree is to be known by its fruits, so speech, as one of those "fruits," reveals a person's inner quality: "for from the abundance of the heart the mouth speaks [ἐκ γὰρ περισσεύματος καρδίας λαλεῖ τὸ στόμα αὐτοῦ]" (Luke 6:45b≈Matt 12:34b; cf. *Gos. Thom.* 45).[93] This claim does not so much encourage a specific regimen for the tongue (note that no advice is given for how one *ought* to speak) as it collapses

---

[91] Hesychius, *Lexicon*, 7957 (Kurt Latte, ed., *Hesychii Alexandrini lexicon* [Copenhagen: Munksgaard, 1953], 1.269).

[92] There have been various attempts to define ῥῆμα ἀργόν more precisely, but many commentators have stuck close to the literal sense: "words that achieve nothing," with the implication that words *ought* to do something positive (Adolf Schlatter, *Der Evangelist Matthäus* [3d ed.; Stuttgart: Calwer, 1948], 411; Robert H. Gundry, *Matthew: A Commentary on His Handbook for a Mixed Church under Persecution* [2d ed.; Grand Rapids: Eerdmans, 1994], 241; Hubert Frankemölle, *Matthäus: Kommentar* [2 vols.; Düsseldorf: Patmos, 1997], 2:149). In any event, thought, word, and deed are treated as indivisible and as appropriate criteria for divine judgment (Joachim Gnilka, *Das Matthäusevangelium* [HTKNT 1.1; Freiburg: Herder, 1986], 1:461). The sense of "pointless," "achieving nothing" can be seen in the saying of Pythagoras: "You should sooner throw a stone in vain than speak an idle word [αἱρετώτερόν σοι ἔστω λίθον εἰκῆ βάλλειν, ἢ λόγον ἀργόν]" (Stobaeus, *Ecl.* 3.34.11).

[93] The idea that trees are recognized by their fruit appears also in Matt 7:16–20, but without any reference to speech.

any potential gap between what one says and who one is: the tongue is destined to reveal what is in the heart.[94] Speech cannot change without the person being changed, as Jesus emphasizes in Matthew: "How can you speak good things, when you are evil?" (12:34a).

In a particularly famous and controversial saying[95] that could appear to touch on "unclean" language, Jesus says that "what comes out of the mouth" defiles (Matt 15:11; cf. *Gos. Thom.* 14). But on closer inspection it becomes clear that the saying has less to do with speech than with the defiling power of sin. In both Matthew and Mark, the Pharisees and scribes criticize Jesus' disciples for eating with unwashed hands, whereupon Jesus accuses the Pharisees of placing too high a value on human tradition (Matt 15:1–9; Mark 7:1–13), and then denies that what goes into the body defiles (Matt 15:11; Mark 7:15, 18). The Matthean version includes four references to "the mouth": Jesus say that it is not what goes into *the mouth* but what comes out of *the mouth* that defiles a person.[96] Everything that goes into the *mouth* goes into the belly and is then evacuated into the latrine,[97] but that which comes out of *the mouth* (τὰ δὲ ἐκπορευόμενα ἐκ τοῦ στόματος) comes from the heart, and these things defile (Matt 15:18).

Matthew's version would perhaps read more coherently if the sins that "come out of the mouth" were sins of the tongue: "it is not what goes into the mouth, but what comes out of the mouth that defiles a person: lies, gossip, cursing, slander, perjury, careless words, lewd humor." But as it stands, Matthew contrasts the food that goes into the mouth with "murders, adulteries, fornications, thefts, false-witnesses and slanders," not all of which so obviously come out of the mouth (15:19).[98] Thus Matthew's four additions of "the mouth" in this pericope (15:11 *bis*;

---

[94] François Bovon, *L'Évangile selon Saint Luc* (3 vols.; CNT 3a; Geneva: Labor et Fides, 1991), 1:331.

[95] James Dunn argues that the saying can be traced back to the historical Jesus (*Jesus, Paul, and the Law* [Louisville: Westminster/John Knox, 1990], 37–60).

[96] οὐ τὸ εἰσερχόμενον εἰς τὸ στόμα κοινοῖ τὸν ἄνθρωπον, ἀλλὰ τὸ ἐκπορευόμενον ἐκ τοῦ στόματος τοῦτο κοινοῖ τὸν ἄνθρωπον (Matt 15:11).

[97] πᾶν τὸ εἰσπορευόμενον εἰς τὸ στόμα εἰς τὴν κοιλίαν χωρεῖ καὶ εἰς ἀφεδρῶνα ἐκβάλλεται (Matt 15:17). Mark has "into the person" rather than "into the mouth" (πᾶν τὸ ἔξωθεν εἰσπορευόμενον εἰς τὸν ἄνθρωπον οὐ δύναται αὐτὸν κοινῶσαι ὅτι οὐκ εἰσπορεύεται αὐτοῦ εἰς τὴν καρδίαν ἀλλ᾽ εἰς τὴν κοιλίαν, καὶ εἰς τὸν ἀφεδρῶνα ἐκπορεύεται).

[98] The presence of ψευδομαρτυρίαι and βλασφημίαι makes the list resemble the second half of the Decalogue (murder, adultery/fornication, theft, false-witness/slander) more than a summary of "evil speech" (W. D. Davies and Dale Allison, Jr., *The Gospel According to Saint Matthew* [3 vols.; ICC; Edinburgh: T. & T. Clark, 1988–97], 2:536).

15:17, 18) are ill at ease with the overall thrust of the passage, which, as it stands in Matthew, cannot simply be read as "it is not what one *eats* but what one *says* that defiles."[99] It is unsurprising that the Matthean version was applied to speech by ancient interpreters,[100] but the text as it stands, even less than any logion behind it, is not focused on forms of speech that defile.

In fact, Jesus' *lack* of interest in "defiling speech" can perhaps be seen when comparing his comments on oaths with those of a contemporary such as Philo. In Matthew Jesus rejects oaths (Matt 5:33–37),[101] and chides the Pharisees for their fine distinctions between valid and invalid forms of swearing (Matt 23:16–22). The prohibition in Matthew 5 is presented as a demand for veracity in all speech, not simply speech under oath. This is also what motivated the Essenes' avoidance of oaths,[102] and Matthew 5 was sometimes understood this way by later

---

[99] Jesper Svartvik has proposed that the parallel passage (Mark 7:1–23) is better understood as a warning against "the perils of evil speech" than as a cleansing of foods (Jesper Svartvik, *Mark and Mission: Mk 7:1–23 in its Narrative and Historical Contexts* [ConBNT 32; Stockholm: Almqvist & Wiksell International, 2000], 411). But if the logion were originally about "evil speech," why has Matthew not listed more sins of the tongue? Why has Mark retained no reference to "the mouth"? Rather it appears that it is Matthew, who exhibits an intense concern with speech elsewhere, who has adapted a saying (without achieving perfect consistency) to emphasize what comes out *of the mouth*.

[100] Tertullian says, "But if we ought to abominate all that is immodest, on what ground is it right to hear what we must not speak? For all licentiousness of speech, nay, every idle word, is condemned by God. Why, in the same way, is it right to look on what it is disgraceful to do? How is it that the *things which defile a man going out of his mouth, are not regarded as doing so when they go in at his eyes and ears*—when eyes and ears are the immediate attendants on the spirit—and that can never be pure whose servants-in-waiting are impure?" (*Spect.* 17 [*ANF* 3:87]). John Chrysostom found here a statement about all sorts of "dirty" talk (slander, abuse, angry words, foul language, laughter, wittiness), talk that leaves stains that water alone cannot cleanse (*In Matt.* [PG 58:516]).

[101] Greek and Roman warnings against excessive swearing are not uncommon; cf. Plato, *Leg.* 11.917B; Epictetus, *Ench.* 33.5; Plutarch, *Mor.* 271C, 275C–D; Quintilian, *Inst.* 9.2.98 (*iurare, nisi ubi necesse est, gravi viro parum convenit*). Pythagoras forbade swearing by the gods: Iamblichus, *VP* 47 and D.L. 8.22 (μηδ' ὀμνύναι θεούς). Some have seen Socrates's swearing "by the dog" and Epictetus's use of "Another" as motivated by reverence. See the discussion in Th. Klauser, "Beteuerungsformeln," *RAC*, columns 219–24.

[102] Josephus, *B.J.* 2.135: "Any word of theirs has more force than an oath [ὅρκου]; swearing [ὀμνύειν] they avoid, regarding it as worse than perjury, for they say that one who is not believed without an appeal to God stands condemned already" (Thackeray, LCL). D.L. 8.22 attributes a similar motive to Pythagoras's prohibition of oaths. Cf. Philo, *Spec.* 2.2, 4, 8.

Christians.[103] What is absent in these Matthean passages is any comment like we find briefly in Sirach[104] and at greater length in Philo, about the *offensiveness* and *impurity* of filling one's speech with swearing. Philo, in particular, is horrified by the way some people swear "incessantly and thoughtlessly about ordinary matters [κατακόρως καὶ ἀνεξετάστως ὀμνύουσιν ἐπὶ τοῖς τυχοῦσιν]" (*Dec.* 92), and "make whole speeches consisting of a string of oaths and thus, by their misuse of the many forms of the divine name [τῷ τοῦ θεοῦ πολυωνύμῳ καταχρησαμένους ὀνόματι] in places where they ought not to do so, show their impiety" (*Dec.* 94 [Colson, LCL]).[105] Anyone who takes such matters lightly, says Philo, is "polluted and unclean [μιαρὸς καὶ ἀκάθαρτος]," and will be severely punished (*Dec.* 95). By contrast, Jesus seems far less concerned with the potential impurity of swearing.

In Matthew 5, Jesus addresses abusive speech, declaring both anger and insult—even calling someone ῥακά or μωρέ—to be as serious as murder (Matt 5:22). There has been considerable debate about the derivation and meaning of the words ῥακά and μωρέ, and it has been proposed that ῥακά (or ῥάχα)[106] might be a "crude" Greek word of abuse.[107] But there is general agreement that it is in fact a loanword, transliterating the Aramaic ריקה or ריקא[108] ("worthless" or "empty-head"),

---

[103] Justin, 1 *Apol.* 16.5: "Now concerning not swearing at all, *but always speaking the truth*, he gave the following command: 'Do not swear at all…'" (περὶ δὲ τοῦ μὴ ὀμνύναι ὅλως, τἀληθῆ δὲ λέγειν ἀεί, οὕτως παρεκελεύσατο· μὴ ὀμόσητε ὅλως…); *Apostolic Constitutions* 5.12: "For if our Lord commanded us not to swear by the true God, *that our word might be more trustworthy than an oath* [ὅπως ὁ λόγος ἡμῶν πιστότερος ᾖ τοῦ ὅρκου]…".

[104] "Their cursing and swearing make one's hair stand on end, and their quarrels make others stop their ears [λαλιὰ πολυόρκου ἀνορθώσει τρίχας / καὶ ἡ μάχη αὐτῶν ἐμφραγμὸς ὠτίων]" (Sirach 27:14). On the overuse of oaths, cf. also Sirach 23:9–11.

[105] Before taking an oath, one should be sure his tongue is pure from slander, "for it would be unholy for someone to utter any of the shameful words through the same mouth that brings forth the holiest name [οὐ γὰρ ὅσιον, δι' οὗ στόματος τὸ ἱερώτατον ὄνομα προφέρεταί τις, διὰ τούτου φθέγγεσθαί τι τῶν αἰσχρῶν]" (*Dec.* 93).

[106] So ℵ* D, W.

[107] Ernest Cadman Colwell, "Has *Raka* a Parallel in the Papyri?" *JBL* 53 (1934): 351–54. Colwell notes the abusive use of ῥαχά in the Zenon papyri (Preisigke, *Sammelbuch* 7638, 7 [257 B.C.]), and suggests the rarity of attestation may owe to the word's "belonging to the crude vocabulary of abuse" (354). Betz refers to this papyrus as evidence that the *semitic* term was being used already in Greek (Hans Dieter Betz, *The Sermon on the Mount: A Commentary on the Sermon on the Mount, including the Sermon on the Plain [Matthew 5:3–7:27 and Luke 6:20–49]* [Hermeneia; Minneapolis: Fortress, 1995], 220n171).

[108] BGAD, s.v. ῥακά; Joachim Jeremias, "ῥακά," *TDNT* 6:973–74; Robert A. Guelich, "Mt 5,22: Its Meaning and Integrity," *ZNW* 64 (1973): 39–40; so most recent commentators.

a common, and not very severe,[109] term of opprobrium.[110] The word may have been transliterated because "its emotional value could not be rendered exactly,"[111] because a literal translation (κενός) was not common in Greek invective,[112] or because the loanword was being used in a bilingual setting.[113] Since ῥακά appears to be a non-Greek word, it has been proposed that μωρέ might also be a transliteratation (for instance, of the Hebrew מורה),[114] or that μωρέ was meant not as a second term of opprobrium but rather as a gloss for ῥακά.[115] But "you fool!" was very common in Greek,[116] and it would have represented quite well any common Aramaic word for "fool."[117]

---

[109] Jeremias, *TDNT* 6:974.

[110] For examples of its use in rabbinic literature, see Str-B 1:278–79; Marcus Jastrow, *A Dictionary of the Targumim, the Talmud Babli and Yerushalmi, and the Midrashic Literature* (New York: The Judaica Press, 1971), s.v. ריקא. Michael Sokoloff says, "The masculine noun רק ('worthless person') derives from ריק, 'to pour out a liquid, empty'" (*Dictionary of Jewish Palestinian Aramaic of the Byzantine Period* [Ramat-Gan: Bar Ilan University Press, 1990], s.v. רקא).

[111] Gerard Mussies, "The Use of Hebrew and Aramaic in the Greek New Testament," *NTS* 30 (1984): 424.

[112] Robert A. Guelich, *The Sermon on the Mount: A Foundation for Understanding* (Waco, Texas: Word Books, 1982), 186. Cf. James 2:20.

[113] Guelich, "Mt 5, 22," 42; Davies and Allison, *Matthew*, 1:513; Gnilka, *Matthäusevangelium*, 154; slightly differently, Betz, *Sermon*, 220–21 (the word represents the "'lower' vernacular for the community of the SM"). Calling somebody "raka" was still being forbidden in the third-century Syriac *Didascalia apostolorum*, and knowledge of the word's *sense* was retained: "'For if one called a layman fool or raca, he is liable to the assembly' as one of those who rise up against Christ—because that he calls 'empty' his brother, him, in whom Christ dwells, who is not *empty but fulfilled*" (*Didascalia apostolorum* 6.25; trans. Arthur Vööbus, *The Didascalia Apostolorum in Syriac* [CSCO 402; Louvain: Secrétariat du CorpusSCO, 1979], 103). Jerome and Hilary also know the meaning to be "empty" (references in BGAD). Jeremias suggests a Syriac pronunciation might account for the spelling ῥακά in place of ῥηκά; but J. Payne Smith says the word came into Syriac *via* the Greek (*A Compendious Syriac Dictionary* [Oxford: Oxford University Press, 1903] s.v. ܪܩܐ).

[114] "Rebel," in Deut 21:18, used by Moses in Num 20:10; cf. T. W. Manson, *Sayings of Jesus* (Grand Rapids: Eerdmans, 1979), 155–56; C. C. Torrey, *The Four Gospels: A New Translation* (New York: Harper, 1933), 10; Morton Smith, "Notes on Goodspeed's 'Problems of New Testament Translation,'" *JBL* 64 (1945): 502–4.

[115] K. Köhler, "Zu Mt 5:22," *ZNW* 19 (1919): 91–95; Mussies, "The Use of Hebrew and Aramaic," 425 ("its field of meaning was roughly defined by μωρέ"); C. F. D. Moule, "Uncomfortable Words I. The Angry Word: Matthew 5.21f.," *Expository Times* 81 (1969): 12–13. Guelich adduces arguments against this proposal ("Mt 5:22," 41–42).

[116] See the examples in BGAD, s.v. μωρός, c.

[117] Jeremias proposes שטיא (*TDNT* 6:975); cf. Adolf Schlatter, *Der Evangelist Matthäus* (3d ed.; Stuttgart: Calwer, 1948), 169; and Guelich, *Sermon*, 188. Theodor Zahn (*Das Evangelium des Matthäus* [4th ed.; Leipzig: Deichert, 1922], 227n96) argued that Jesus himself used μωρέ since the Greek word had passed into Aramaic (for examples of which, see Str-B, 1:279–80; Guelich, "Mt 5:22," 41).

Since both of these words were fairly common terms for "fool," and since there is no evidence that saying μωρέ was any nastier than saying ῥακά,[118] it is not clear why the respective judgments seem to be increasingly severe: anger makes one liable to the proceedings of a local court, ῥακά to the "Sanhedrin," μωρέ to "the fire of Gehenna."[119] This has led commentators to suggest that these are simply three expressions for the death penalty;[120] that Matthew is deliberately showing the impossibility of making casuistic distinctions between anger and different angry expressions;[121] or that Matthew has added 5:22c (perhaps to gloss ῥακά), and has thereby confused what would originally have been a two-part saying to the effect that both anger and insult were as deserving of death as murder.[122]

Regardless of how one solves all the interpretive problems, the passage clearly enough addresses words used abusively in anger—as the Matthean Jesus himself illustrates by calling the scribes and Pharisees "fools" (Matt 23:17). Before God, Jesus claims, not only murder, but even hatred and its everyday verbal expression, are equally culpable. By condemning a term of abuse as mild and common as "fool," Jesus would have effectively excluded the more offensive epithets as well.

But although such a teaching would effectively exclude the angry use of the obscene vocabulary, it is obviously not a comment about the offensiveness of foul language *per se*. Nowhere do we find Jesus commenting on the purpose of language, or reflecting on the value of the social conventions that mark some words and expressions as offensive. There is no instruction about how to react when obscene humor was used (as it no doubt would have been in the theater at Sepphoris, an hour's walk from Jesus' hometown).[123] Perhaps most striking is the absence of anything like the rabbinic comments condemning lewd language about

---

[118] Guelich, *Sermon*, 168; Davies and Allison, *Matthew*, 1:515; Jeremias, *TDNT* 6:975; *contra*, e.g., Schlatter, *Matthäus*, 169; Betz, *Sermon*, 222.

[119] On the meaning of ἔνοχος ἔσται τῇ κρίσει ("liable to a court proceeding"), see Guelich, "Mt 5:22," 44–47.

[120] Jeremias, *TDNT* 6:975.

[121] Zahn, *Das Evangelium des Matthäus*, 228; Guelich, *Sermon*, 188.

[122] Davies and Allison, *Matthew*, 1:516.

[123] On the theaters of Caesarea and Sepphoris, see Richard A. Batey, "Jesus and the Theatre," *NTS* 30 (1984): 563–74; idem, *Jesus and the Forgotten City: New Light on Sepphoris and the Urban World of Jesus* (Grand Rapids: Baker, 1991), 83–103. For criticism of Batey's claim that the theater had been built in Jesus' lifetime, cf. Jonathan L. Reed, *Archaeology and the Galilean Jesus: A Re-Examination of the Evidence* (Harrisburg: Trinity Press International, 2000), 108.

sex, or the warnings that words could incite lust and speaking with
women could lead to sexual immorality,[124] or the *Didache*'s warning that
foul language will lead to adultery. Even when Jesus proposes drastic
measures against potential sources of lust (i.e. destroying the eye, the
hand, and the "foot" [Mark 9:43–48; Matt 5:27–32; 18:8–9]), he does
not mention the tongue or the ears. Given these other Jewish warnings
against foul language, the absence of any surviving comment from Jesus
is itself noteworthy and worth further consideration.

IV. JAMES

Jesus' concern with careless and abusive speech is reflected—and indeed
amplified—in some early Christian texts. The Epistle of James, which
knows Jesus' prohibition of oaths (James 5:12), is particularly anxious
about sins of the tongue. Some of what James says is commonplace for
Jewish wisdom literature[125] or Greek and Roman ethical writings. The
value of silence (James 1:19), for instance, is a widely attested theme in
Jewish and non-Jewish sources.[126] The treatment of speech in James is
extraordinary not for the content of its advice, but for the way it places
the tongue at the center of a cosmic battle. True religion, James says,
consists in keeping oneself unstained by the world (θρησκεία καθαρὰ
καὶ ἀμίαντος...αὕτη ἐστίν...ἄσπιλον ἑαυτὸν τηρεῖν ἀπὸ τοῦ κόσμου
[1:27]). James later explains that it is the tongue—which itself is "the
world of unrighteousness"—that stains the body (ὁ κόσμος τῆς ἀδικίας
ἡ γλῶσσα καθίσταται ἐν τοῖς μέλεσιν ἡμῶν, ἡ σπιλοῦσα ὅλον τὸ σῶμα
[3:6]). These are the only two uses of the σπιλ- root in James.

Here James's language departs from the hackneyed warnings about
the advantages of silence or the importance of being honest. When
Plutarch, for instance, speaks of the paradox that such a small part
of the body can ignite such a large fire, he means simply to say that

---

[124] *m. Abot* 1:5; *b. Ned.* 20a; *b. Ber.* 43b; *b. Ber.* 24a (just as seeing a woman is a sexual
incitement, so is hearing a woman's voice); *b. Meg.* 15a (simply saying "Rahab, Rahab"
leads to ejaculation); cf. Tal Ilan, *Jewish Women in Greco-Roman Palestine* (Tübingen:
Mohr, 1995), 126.

[125] William R. Baker sees James' speech-ethics in the context of Jewish wisdom
traditions (*Personal Speech-Ethics in the Epistle of James* [Tübingen: Mohr, 1995], 7–12).

[126] Luke Timothy Johnson, "Taciturnity and True Religion" in *Greeks, Romans, and
Christians: Essays in Honor of Abraham J. Malherbe* (ed. David L. Balch, Everett Ferguson,
and Wayne A. Meeks; Minneapolis: Fortress Press, 1990), 329–39.

"loose lips sink ships."[127] But when James likens the potency of this little part of the body to the spark and the forest fire (3:5), something more sinister is in view. The goal of religion is to maintain purity against a world that threatens it. James's shocking news is that that inimical world is already present in the human body in the form of the tongue. And the stakes run higher than one's own purity, for the tongue sets on fire "the cycle of nature" and is itself "set on fire by hell" (φλογίζουσα τὸν τροχὸν τῆς γενέσεως καὶ φλογιζομένη ὑπὸ τῆς γεέννης, 3:6).

Why is the tongue the thing through which the world defiles people?[128] In part James recoils at the thought that the tongue that is sanctified by blessing God should be profaned by cursing men. But the idea of chaos is also lurking here, for James says that the tongue is the one thing on earth that has not yet been tamed. The tongue, unlike the animals (!), has not come under human control in accordance with God's design for the world. The beasts are now subject to human nature; the tongue, however, *cannot* be mastered by humankind (3:7–8). Unlike the rest of creation, this little piece of flesh, built into human bodies, is immune to domestication. If the tongue could be stopped, a person would be perfect, gaining control over the entire body (3:2). As it stands, people are alienated from themselves. Their body is not under their own control; Hell uses their tongues to set Creation on fire, and their bodies are defiled as the flame passes through their mouths.

For all of James's hostility to "the world," the letter does not suggest an anxiety about interaction with unbelievers. James is not seeking to erect *social* barriers. He is trying to stop his readers from fighting and cursing one another. Such angry speech represents the invasion of the world into their bodies. The dangerous and defiling "world" is not "out there" where the pagans live; it is, to borrow a phrase from Moses, "near you—in your mouth." The addressees are chastised for their friendship with this world (4:4), for their laughter and happiness

---

[127] Cf. Plutarch, *Mor.* 507B.

[128] Other Jewish and Christian texts also worry about the defiling potential of various sorts of speech. Sirach says the whispering gossip "defiles" himself (μολύνει, Sir 21:28). Philo goes on at length about the defilement incurred through improper swearing (*Dec.* 92–95). The *Damascus Document* says those speaking against the divine statutes defile "their holy spirit": את רוח קדשיהם טמאו [CD V, 11–13]). In *Joseph and Asenath*, Asenath is terrified to invoke God's name because her mouth is defiled from eating idol sacrifices and from the names of the Egyptian gods (11.6; cf. 11.17–18; 12.5; 21.13–14; 21.19), and Joseph exhibits an almost visceral sense of repulsion at the prospect of kissing someone who has named foreign gods (8.5–6). Later her mouth must be "purified" (16.8–15).

(4:9), for thinking about the pleasures of life (4:3). Laughter and cursing are treated almost like sexual activities, constituting a "friendship" with the world that James views as adultery (4:4). In a sense, James has rhetorically configured "the world," "true religion," and "the tongue" in such a way that to use the tongue abusively (in cursing) is actually to grant "the world" access to one's mouth. Thus the male and female addressees are alike "adulteresses" (μοιχαλίδες).[129] In James's cosmology, abusive language is no longer the mark of a manly brio (think of Catullus 16), but rather a sexual humiliation. The moment one shouts an abusive *irrumabo*, one suffers *irrumatio*.

In none of this does James single out obscene language. But since James was appalled by the thought of *any* sort of cursing (3:9), fighting (4:1), or laughter (4:9), one can only guess what he would have said about verbal nastiness or humor that made use of tabooed words or obscene images. What I want to emphasize in the case of James's treatment of speech is the fact that he makes speech a cosmic issue involving hell and creation, and places the tongue at the center of the struggle for religious purity. This approach stands at some remove from the wisdom in Proverbs or Sirach or the *Didache*, with their emphasis on the social and ethical consequences that follow from inappropriate speech.

V. DIDACHE 3:3 AND THE TWO WAYS

The early Christian writings known as "church orders" include various instructions for how Christians are to speak. These rules about speech are found above all in the "Two Ways" material, where ethical instruction is given under the rubric of the "way of life and the way of death."[130] So, for instance, the Two Ways section in the *Didache*[131]

---

[129] The reading μοιχοὶ καὶ μοιχαλίδες in some manuscripts is probably secondary (Bruce M. Metzger, *A Textual Commentary on the Greek New Testament* [rev. ed.; London: United Bible Societies, 1975], 682–83).

[130] *Didache* 1:1: "There are two ways, one of life, the other of death, and between the two ways there is a great difference"; *Doctrina* 1:1: *Viae duae sunt in saeculo, vitae et mortis, lucis et tenebrarum; in his constituti sunt angeli duo, unus aequitatis, alter iniquitatis; distantia autem magna est duarum viarum*; cf. *Barn.* 18.1; *Apostolic Church Order* 4; *Apostolic Constitutions* 7.1.

[131] The *Didache* is mixed generically, but it is "a rule for ecclesiastical praxis, a handbook of church morals, ritual, and disciplines" (Kurt Niederwimmer, *The Didache* [trans. Linda M. Maloney; Minneapolis: Fortress, 1998], 2).

addresses perjury,[132] false witness,[133] evil speaking,[134] dishonesty,[135] how to speak to slaves,[136] cursing,[137] and foul language.[138] Concern with speech is far less pronounced in the *Didache* outside the Two Ways material (there is instruction for how to reprove one another,[139] and a reference to examining a prophet who is speaking in a spirit).[140]

Although no explanation for the relationship between the various church orders has won universal acceptance,[141] there is broad agreement that they are not simply dependent on each other, but rather, that some of them drew independently on a common Two Ways source.[142] There is also widespread agreement that this Two Ways tractate was originally a Jewish work[143] which itself underwent various changes, and was used

---

[132] *Did.* 2.3: οὐκ ἐπιορκήσεις.

[133] *Did.* 2.3: οὐ ψευδομαρτυρήσεις.

[134] *Did.* 2.3: οὐ κακολογήσεις.

[135] *Did.* 2.4–5: οὐκ ἔσῃ διγνώμων οὐδὲ δίγλωσσος: παγὶς γὰρ θανάτου ἡ διγλωσσία. οὐκ ἔσται ὁ λόγος σου ψευδής, οὐ κενός, ἀλλὰ μεμεστωμένος πράξει.

[136] *Did.* 4.9–11.

[137] The way of death is "full of cursing" (κατάρας μεστή [*Did.* 5.1]). The same phrase is used at *Barn.* 20.1 to describe "the Way of the Black One"; cf. Psa 10:7 (LXX 9:28) (cited in Rom 3:14): οὗ ἀρᾶς τὸ στόμα αὐτοῦ γέμει.

[138] *Did.* 3.3; 5.1.

[139] "Reprove each other not in wrath but in peace as you find in the Gospel" (ἐλέγχετε δὲ ἀλλήλους μὴ ἐν ὀργῇ, ἀλλ᾽ ἐν εἰρήνῃ ὡς ἔχετε ἐν τῷ εὐαγγελίῳ [*Did.* 15.3]). Compare this to Pythagoras's rule not to speak in anger, and to 1QS V, 25; CD IX, 3–4. For various Jewish interpretations of Lev 19:17 (on rebuking one's neighbor), cf. James L. Kugel, "On Hidden Hatred and Open Reproach: Early Exegesis of Leviticus 19:17," *HTR* 80 (1987): 43–61; cf. also *Apostolic Constitutions* 7.3.3.

[140] The *Didache* calls testing or examining a prophet who is speaking in a spirit the sin which cannot be forgiven (*Did.* 11.7).

[141] Cf. Niederwimmer, *Didache*, 4–54; Marcel Metzger, *Les Constitutions apostoliques* (3 vols.; Paris: Cerf, 1985–87), 1:13–54.

[142] W. Rordorf, "Un chapitre d'éthique judéo-chrétienne: les Deux voies," *Recherches de science religieuse* 60 (1972): 109–28; M. J. Suggs, "The Christian Two Ways Tradition: Its Antiquity, Form and Function," in *Studies in New Testament and Early Christian Literature: Essays in Honor of Allen P. Wikgren* [ed. David Edward Aune; NovTSup 33; Leiden: Brill, 1972], 60–74); for diagrams representing the various stages of this source, cf. Suggs, "Two Ways," 63, and John S. Kloppenborg, "The Transformation of Moral Exhortation in Didache 1–5," in *The Didache in Context: Essays on Its Text, History and Transmission* (ed. Clayton N. Jefford; Leiden: Brill, 1995), 92.

[143] Huub van de Sandt and David Flusser isolate the original Jewish form of the Two Ways and analyze it in considerable detail as a Jewish document (*The Didache: Its Jewish Sources and Its Place in Early Judaism and Christianity* [CRINT 3.5; Minneapolis: Fortress, 2002], 55–190); cf. Kloppenborg, "Transformation," 108: "The Christian Two Ways document (β) which is embedded in *Didache* 1–5 and the *Doctrina* represents an early Christian adaptation of a Jewish exemplar"; Bentley Layton, "The Sources, Date, and Transmission of *Didache* 1.3b–2.1," *HTR* 61 (1968): 379: "Its [the Latin *Doctrina*'s] lost Greek *Vorlage* was almost certainly a Jewish didactic work, used in the Hellenistic

in its various permutations by the authors of *Barnabas*, the *Didache*, and the *Doctrina apostolorum*.[144] The original function of the Two Ways is unfortunately difficult to determine with much precision.[145]

One of the changes that the Two Ways underwent was the addition of the discreet unit of sayings found in *Did.* 3.1–6.[146] This unit is distinguished from the rest of the *Didache* by its vocabulary[147] and by the form of the prohibitions, which changes from οὐ with the future (*Did.* 2.2–7) to the present imperative (μὴ γίνου).[148] The rhetoric of light and heavy sins in *Did.* 3.1–6 has ample parallels in other Jewish literature,[149] and is similar in both form and content to rabbinic Derekh Erets tractates.[150] So although the warning about foul language in *Did.* 3.3 survives in this Christian document, it seems entirely likely that it first functioned in Jewish instruction, was later incorporated into the Two Ways, and was then brought into the *Didache* and other Christian

---

synagogue before the *Didache* was compiled"; so Schürer, *Judaism*, 3:172n83. 1QS 3.13–4.26 is cited as an extant Jewish text with some similar features.

[144] Niederwimmer, for instance, places the first Christian recension of the Two Ways prior to the use *Barnabas* made of it; it was then further redacted (including the addition of the material in *Did.* 3.1–6) prior to its incorporation into the *Didache* and *Doctrina* (*Didache*, 40–41).

[145] "It probably belonged within the broader context of the community rules of Jewish religious communities (as did 1 QS, 1QSa in Qumran)" (Niederwimmer, *Didache*, 37); cf. Suggs, "Two Ways Tradition," 68.

[146] The *Epistle of Barnabas* has parallels to most of the Two Ways material from *Didache* 2–6 (including what comes just before and after *Did.* 3.1–6), but nothing like this section. Robert Kraft concludes, "Barnabas shows no clear knowledge of this material, and it is only in Did. 5:1 that there seems to be any significant relationship between 3:1–6 and the Two Ways ethic of the Didache....Thus this section probably was added to the Didache branch of the Two Ways soon after the Barnabas form had separated from the common stock, and it came to influence the list of vices in 5:1" (Robert A. Kraft, *Barnabas and the Didache* [vol. 3 of *The Apostolic Fathers*; ed. Robert M. Grant; New York: Thomas Nelson & Sons, 1965], 146); cf. van de Sandt and Flusser, *Didache*, 133; Niederwimmer, *Didache*, 94. For a synopsis of the texts which makes this relationship especially clear, see Jean-Paul Audet, *La Didachè: Instructions des apôtres* (Paris: J. Gabalda, 1958), 138–53.

[147] Of the twenty-five terms for vice in *Did.* 3.1–6, nineteen do not appear elsewhere in the document (R. H. Connolly, "The Didache in Relation to the Epistle of Barnabas," *JTS* 33 [1932]: 241–42).

[148] Audet, *Didachè*, 299–300.

[149] See Hubertus Waltherus Maria van de Sandt, "Didache 3,1–6: A Transformation of an Existing Jewish Hortatory Pattern," *JSJ* 23 (1992): 21–41; for further references, see Niederwimmer, *Didache*, 94n1.

[150] Van de Sandt and Flusser, *Didache*, 165–79; Kloppenborg describes it as "building a fence around the Torah" ("Transformation," 105n71); so C. Taylor, *The Teaching of the Twelve Apostles with Illustrations from the Talmud* [Cambridge: Deighton, Bell and Co., 1886], 23). On this section and parallels from *The Testaments of the Twelve Patriarchs*, cf. Kraft, *Barnabas and the Didache*, 146.

documents. (*Doctrina apostolorum* 3.1–6 omits the saying of *Did.* 3.3.[151] If the *Doctrina* preserves an earlier form of the Greek Two Ways, [152] then we might see the comment about foul language as a later addition. But when one notes that the lists of vices given in *Doctrina* 5.1–2 and *Did.* 5.1–2 show some correspondence with the vices warned against in 2.1–4.14,[153] and then notes that *Doctrina* includes *impudica loquela* at the point where *Did.* 5.1 has αἰσχρολογία,[154] it seems more likely that the *Doctrina* has somehow omitted the material we find in *Did.* 3.3[155] than that this unit of instruction originally lacked it.)

In *Did.* 3.1–6, the teacher addresses the pupil as "my child" (τέκνον μου), in the style of Jewish sapiential literature. In each case the teacher forbids a certain sin because it will lead to something worse. An admonition not to be a certain type of person ("do not be a liar") is followed with a reason which explains (ἐπειδή or γάρ) that that sin ("lying") leads to (ὁδηγεῖ πρός/εἰς) something more serious (e.g., "for lying leads to theft"). Then two or three other types of person are named ("and do not be a lover of money or vainglorious"), followed by the reason that "from all of these" (ἐκ γὰρ τούτων ἁπάντων) the more serious sins are begotten (γεννῶνται). To summarize this section's main points: anger leads to murder (3.2), lust leads to fornication (3.3), obscene language leads to adultery (3.3), omens and astrology lead to idolatry (3.4), lying leads to theft (3.5) and grumbling leads to slander (3.6).[156]

---

[151] (3.1) *Fili, fuge ab homine malo et homine simulatore.* (3.2) *Noli fieri iracundus, quia iracundia ducit ad homicidium, nec appetens eris malitiae nec animosus, de his enim omnibus irae nascuntur* (3.4) *Noli esse mathematicus neque delustrator, quae res ducunt ad vanam superstitionem; nec velis ea videre nec audire.* [This verse lacks the second half: we would have expected other sins and *de his enim omnibus vanae superstitiones nascuntur.*] (3.5) *Noli fieri mendax, quia mendacium ducit ad furtum; neque amator pecuniae, nec vanus, de his enim omnibus furta nascuntur* (3.6) *Noli fieri murmuriosus, quia ducit ad maledictionem. Noli fieri audax nec male sapiens, de his enim omnibus maledictiones nascuntur.* (The text of the *Doctrina* is taken from an appendix of *La Doctrine des douze apôtres* [ed. Willy Rordorf and André Tuilier; Paris: Cerf, 1978], 203–10.)

[152] Van de Sandt and Flusser think the *Doctrina* best represents the original Jewish form of the Two Ways, although it is "less reliable as far as the precise wording is concerned" (*Didache*, 112). Cf. E. J. Goodspeed, "The Didache, Barnabas and the Doctrina," *Anglican Theological Review* 27 (1945): 228–47.

[153] Rordorf and Tuilier, *Doctrine*, 166–67n1; Kraft, *Barnabas and the Didache*, 158.

[154] Cf. Audet, *Didachè*, 151; Leo Wohleb, *Die lateinische Übersetzung der Didache kritisch und sprachlich untersucht* (Paderborn: Schöningh, 1913), 67, 98–99.

[155] Van de Sandt ("Didache 3,1–6," 21n2) offers further arguments for the originality of *Did.* 3:3, and Van de Sandt and Flusser include *Did.* 3:3 in their reconstruction of the original Greek Two Ways (*Didache*, 122–28), noting that "the text of the Doctrina is also unsatisfactory in that it omits GTW 3:3" (*Didache*, 134).

[156] Cf. the chart in Niederwimmer, *Didache*, 95.

According to *Did.* 3.3, adultery is the outcome of being a foul-mouthed person and a "lifter of the eyes" (μηδὲ αἰσχρολόγος μηδὲ ὑψηλόφθαλμος· ἐκ γὰρ τούτων ἁπάντων μοιχεῖαι γεννῶνται). What verbal and ocular misdeeds are in view here, and why do they lead to adultery? Both αἰσχρολόγος[157] and ὑψηλόφθαλμος are rare words. Αἰσχρολόγος is obviously related to the more common αἰσχρολογία (*Did.* 5.1), so translators have understood αἰσχρολόγος as a speaker of some sort of indecent language.[158] If foul language was used above all in humor and in angry abuse, presumably angry abuse could safely be ruled out as an inducement to adultery. Jewish wisdom could warn about verbal abuse as the first step toward murder (cf. Sirach 22:24 and *Did.* 3.2b), but nasty accusations are clearly not in view here. Lewd humor might also seem irrelevant were it not for the fact that laughter was often seen as a precursor to sexual transgressions.[159]

But as we saw when discussing erotic fiction, there was ample evidence that hearing the tales of sexual adventures[160] could have an arousing effect (see above p. 63). Not only did Martial warn against reading erotica without a *puella* nearby (*Ep.* 12.95), but he and Catullus imagined that their own poetry possessed aphrodisiacal properties.[161] Juvenal could ask of some pillow talk, "Is there any crotch that's not in fact aroused by such a seductive and naughty phrase? It has fingers of its own" (*Sat.* 6.196–97 [Braund, LCL]).[162] And the language used by those in the grip

---

[157] BGAD refers to this passage, and both it and LSJ mention Pollux, *Onom.* 6.123; 8.80–81, where words beginning with αἰσχ- are listed. The word is used again in the parallel passages from the *Apostolic Church Order, Epitome*, and the *Apostolic Constitutions* (see below).

[158] Lake, "nor a speaker of base words" (LCL); Kraft, "neither be obscene in speech" (*Barnabas and the Didache*); Rordorf and Tuilier, "évite les propos obscènes" (*Doctrine,* 153); Audet, "ni non plus ordurier" (*Didachè*); Th. Klauser, "nec turpibus utaris verbis" (*Doctrina Duodecim Apostolorum. Barnabae Epistula* [Bonn: Peter Hanstein, 1940]); F. X. Funk, "neque verbis turpibus utaris" (*Doctrina Duodecim Apostolorum: Canones Apostolorum Ecclesiastici ac Reliquae Doctrinae de Duabus Viis Expositiones Veteres* [Tübingen: Laupp, 1887], 13); Niederwimmer says, "Αἰσχρολόγος is someone who likes to tell dirty jokes" (*Didache,* 97); Moulton and Milligan cite *Did.* 3.3 as an example of the way that "the adj. is generally associated with foul or filthy rather than abusive speaking in Col 3.8" (MM s.v.).

[159] E.g. Clement, *Paed.* 3.29.3, cited below, p. 231.

[160] Something that by Clement of Alexandria's definition (see p. 224), would certainly count as *aischrologia*.

[161] Catullus says verses "only then have wit and charm if they are a little soft and not too modest, and can stir up desire. And I'm not talking about in boys, but in these hairy men who cannot move their stiff groins" (16.7–11). Cf. Martial, *Epig.* 1.35.

[162] On the titillating capacity of words, see Adams, *Latin Sexual Vocabulary,* 7–8. For other references to the naughty talk of the bedroom, cf. the way Plautus has a bride

of love could be described as "shameful."[163] Furthermore, the fact that foul language could be used in fertility rites indicates that direct sexual terms were felt to have some sort of sexual potency (though in *most* of those rites the foul language was used abusively or humorously).

Because the *Didache* has linked being "a speaker of foul words" with being ὑψηλόφθαλμος, we might ask whether this latter term offers a clue as to how obscene speech would have functioned. This word, which is found only here[164] and in the later works that knew this text or its source,[165] can be understood as lifting up the eyes[166] in the sense of "leering,"[167] or in the sense of giving "bold gazes." On the former interpretation, the concern is that "uplifted eyes" will imbibe images that excite lust. On the latter, some movement of the eyes constitutes a seductive gesture (wink, wink). Both interpretations find ample ancient support.

In Akkadian and Hebrew the phrase "to lift the eyes towards" was an idiom that could mean "to desire," and specifically, to desire sexually.[168] *Syriac Menander* also seems to express sexual desire with this idiom: "For if you *raise your eyes* in your house, you will become very sad, / but if you *are chaste*, you shall be happy and fortunate" (350–51).[169] The antithetical parallelism suggests that "raising the eyes" is either a euphemism for engaging in sex (the opposite of chastity), or that the act of raising the

---

refer to her ignorance of the language of the wedding night: *virgo sum: nondum didici nupta uerba dicere* (*Dyscolus*, fragment 68). Ovid urges that "in the midst of play" indecent words (*improba verba*) should not be silenced (*Ars* 3.795–96; cf. *Ars* 2.723–24).

[163] Demosthenes said Theramenes "regales his fancy with things by which all are disgusted, with shameful language [αἰσχρορρημοσύνη]" (*Ep.* 4.11). In the *Shepherd of Hermas*, when Hermas sees a heavenly vision of Rhoda, she says that God is angry because Hermas sinned against her. Hermas then protests his innocence, "Did I ever say a *shameful word* to you?" (πότε σοι αἰσχρὸν ῥῆμα ἐλάλησα; [*Vis.* 1.1.7]), which I believe means, "Have I ever made an indecent or lewd comment?" The reader already knows that Hermas had desired Rhoda (1.1.4), and Hermas's own protest ("Did I not always respect you as a sister?" [1.1.7]) as well as Rhoda's response (she mentions his "wicked desire" (ἡ πονηρὰ ἐπιθυμία [1.1.8]) all suggest a *sexual* sense for αἰσχρὸν ῥῆμα.

[164] Niederwimmer says that the word is "characteristic of the language of the tractate" (*Didache*, 97n29), by which he must have in view the use of unfamiliar terms.

[165] E.g. the *Apostolic Church Order* and *Epitome*. The *Constitutions* has ῥιψόφθαλμος, which is not much more illuminating (LSJ offers "casting the eyes about").

[166] So Kirsopp Lake (LCL).

[167] Audet, "ni lorgneur" (*Didachè*, 305); Kraft, "nor have roving eyes" (*Barnabas and the Didache*, 147).

[168] Shalom M. Paul, "Euphemistically 'Speaking' and a Covetous Eye," *HAR* 14 (1994): 198–200. Cf. Gen 39:7; Ezek 23:27.

[169] Trans. T. Baarda, in Charlesworth, *OTP* 2:602.

eyes leads to the temptation that leads to sex (the text has just warned not to "glance at your maidservant in your house" [347].)[170]

The *Testament of Judah* speaks of wine leading the eyes into error; the wandering eyes let the mind be "confused by sordid thoughts" (ἐν διαλογισμοῖς ῥυπαροῖς), which in turn lead to *porneia* (*T. Jud.* 14.1–3).[171] The concern embodied in *Did.* 3.3 might be that obscene talk would contribute to such "dirty thoughts," just as, in the *Testament of Judah*, wine does.[172] Clement of Alexandria imagines desires being stirred by what the eyes see: "One who looks can slip, but the one who does not look cannot lust."[173] Keeping the eyes down protects against desire by preventing lust-inducing images from entering the soul, a thought that provides a fine commentary on Sir 23:4: μετεωρισμὸν ὀφθαλμῶν μὴ δῷς μοι, καὶ ἐπιθυμίαν ἀπόστρεψον ἀπ' ἐμοῦ:[174] "Do not give me upraised eyes [such that I would see and desire]; and keep desire from me" (my translation). The sexual power (and pleasure) of seeing is given an especially striking formulation in Achilles Tatius's *Leucippe and Clitophon*: "beholding a lover" is said to have "more pleasure than the actual actions [μείζονα τῶν ἔργων ἔχει τὴν ἡδονήν]," for it is a "sort of intercourse at a distance [ἔχει τινὰ μίξιν ἐν ἀποστάσει]," "a new way for bodies to intertwine [καινὴ γάρ ἐστι σωμάτων συμπλοκή]."[175]

These same authors who worry about how seeing will inspire lust also speak of the "upraised eyes" as though they are an inviting signal, a sign of unchastity. Sirach says that "A woman's unchastity can be

---

[170] Such sorts of warnings are not uncommon. Cf. Sirach: "Do not look intently at a virgin, or you may stumble" (9:5); "Turn away your eyes from a shapely woman" (9:8).

[171] For the eyes as the source of ἐπιθυμία, cf. *T. Reub.* 2.4.

[172] The difference between the *Didache* and the *Testament of Judah* is that the *Testament of Judah* sees the primary function of wine as removing a sense of shame (*T. Jud.* 14.4; 16.2). The resulting lack of shame makes room for sex *and* foul language; the *Testament of Judah* never has the foul language lead to sex. Interestingly, *Apostolic Constitutions* 7.6 adds "drunkard" to the *Didache*'s "foul-mouthed" and "lifter of the eyes."

[173] *Paed.* 3.83.1; cf. *Paed.* 3.77.1, where looking around at the theater brings up "erotic desires"; and *Paed.* 3.31–33, where the sights at the baths stir up lust. Valerius Maximus says that the Massilians ruled out mime, with its enactment of illicit sex, for concern that the habit of watching would lead to imitation (*Facta et dicta memorabilia*, 2.6.7).

[174] The expression μετεωρισμὸς ὀφθαλμῶν is often understood to mean haughtiness here (e.g. Smend, *Weisheit*, 205), but the second line suggests a closer connection with "lust."

[175] *Leucippe* 1.9.4, discussed by Simon Goldhill, "The Erotic Experience of Looking," in *The Sleep of Reason: Erotic Experience and Sexual Ethics in Ancient Greece and Rome* (ed. Martha C. Nussbaum and Juha Sihvola; Chicago: University of Chicago Press, 2002), 378.

seen in the raising of her eyes and her eyelids."[176] The reference to *eyelids* makes it clear that the eyes are not conceived as a passageway but rather as the means of communicating sexual interest (presumably they have been adorned with cosmetics).[177] The *Psalms of Solomon* speak of the man who, "with his eyes, *speaks* to every woman with a wicked signal."[178] For Clement of Alexandria the connection between the eyes and sex has, at times, as much to do with a lewd gesture as with the sights that enter the soul *via* the eyes; but the concepts are hardly kept distinct. He says that "quivering glances" and "ogling" and "winking" are "nothing other than adultery through the eyes, since lust attacks at a distance through them."[179] Women who flash the whites of their eyes are thereby putting themselves up for sale, for their "fornication is in the raising up of their eyes" (*Paed.* 3.70.4, citing Sir 26:9). It was not only in Christian and Jewish texts that certain "looks" betrayed sexual proclivities. The Pseudo-Aristotelian treatise *Physiognomics* connects "glittering" eyes to lasciviousness.[180]

Turning back from the "upraised eyes" to the "foul mouth," it seems we could also imagine language of a sexual nature leading to adultery either by communicating an interest or by stimulating desire—or both. Clement of Alexandria thought foul language could fire desire (e.g. *Paed.* 2.52.1). And John Chrysostom would describe "foul language" and "wit" as the vehicle of lust and fornication.[181] Similarly, the Emperor

---

[176] πορνεία γυναικὸς ἐν μετεωρισμοῖς ὀφθαλμῶν καὶ ἐν τοῖς βλεφάροις αὐτῆς γνωσθήσεται (Sir 26:9). This is sometimes understood as a "haughty stare" (Skehan and Di Lella, *Wisdom*, 344), but better as a seductive look (Smend, *Weisheit*, 235). In Sir 26:11 husbands are warned to be alert for their wives' "shameless eye"—some look they can apparently observe—for it is a precursor to her infidelity.

[177] The *Testaments of the Twelve Patriarchs* uses expressions similar to Sirach's for movement of the eyes, but it is less clear whether they refer to seeing or gesturing. Cf. *T. Iss.* 7.2: "I knew no woman besides my wife, nor did I commit *porneia* by raising my eyes (οὐκ ἐπόρνευσα ἐν μετεωρισμῷ ὀφθαλμῶν μου); cf. also *T. Benj.* 6.3.

[178] Or "of evil intercourse": ἐν ὀφθαλμοῖς αὐτοῦ λαλεῖ πάσῃ γυναικὶ συνταγῇ κακίας (*Ps. Sol.* 4.5).

[179] κλαδαραὶ δὲ ὄψεις καὶ τὸ ἐνιλλώπτειν, ὃ διὰ τῶν ὀφθαλμῶν βλεφαρίζειν ἐστίν, οὐδὲν ἀλλ᾽ ἢ διὰ τῶν ὀφθαλμῶν μοιχεύειν ἐστὶν ἀκροβολιζομένης τῆς ἐπιθυμίας δι᾽ αὐτῶν (*Paed.* 3.70.1).

[180] "But those whose eyes are glittering are sensual [οἱ δὲ τοὺς ὀφθαλμοὺς στιλπνοὺς ἔχοντες λάγνοι]" (*Physiogn.* 812b11).

[181] *Hom. Eph.* (PG 62:118): "Just as there he removed angry shouting, since it is the chariot of anger, so here foul language and wittiness, since they are the chariot of fornication" (ἀλλ᾽ ὥσπερ ἐκεῖ [i.e. Eph 4:31] τὴν κραυγὴν περιεῖλεν, ὄχημα οὖσαν τῆς ὀργῆς, οὕτω νῦν [Eph 5:3] τὴν αἰσχρολογίαν καὶ εὐτραπελίαν ὄχημα οὖσαν τῆς πορνείας). Chrysostom goes on to say that a tendency to joke often leads to fornication.

Julian warned priests about the way erotic stories would excite their lusts.[182] Rabbi Akiba said that "jesting and levity accustom a man to lewdness" (*m. Abot* 3:14), but as in *Did.* 3.3, the context provides little clue as to why exactly that would be so. Since Sirach and rabbinic texts could warn against conversation with women as endangering chastity,[183] it would be unsurprising to find that *lewd* conversation would be perceived as all the more dangerous.

In short, it is hard to determine whether the concern embodied in *Did.* 3.3 is that foul language would break down morals, incite one's own lust, or send seductive messages. Sexual language was conceived as functioning in all these ways. Perhaps the fact that the *Didache* warns against beaing a *speaker* of indecent words gives some small indication that the concern is with words as a means of communicating sexual interest rather than with *hearing*—and being aroused by—lewd talk, for we can contrast the way that the next verse warns against using incantations *and also* wanting "to see or *hear* such things" [*Did.* 3.4b]).

The *Didache*'s warning about foul speech leading to adultery was preserved relatively literally in later church orders.[184] But new contingencies required more to be said about indecent talk. Both the *Didascalia*[185] and

---

[182] Speaking of fiction that has erotic plots (ἐρωτικὰς ὑποθέσεις καὶ πάντα ἁπλῶς τὰ τοιαῦτα [301B]), Julian warns: "For words breed a certain sort of disposition in the soul, and little by little it arouses desires, and then on a sudden kindles a terrible blaze, against which one ought, in my opinion, to arm oneself well in advance" (ἐγγίνεται γάρ τις τῇ ψυχῇ διάθεσις ὑπὸ τῶν λόγων, καὶ κατ᾽ ὀλίγον ἐγείρει τὰς ἐπιθυμίας, εἶτα ἐξαίφνης ἀνάπτει δεινὴν φλόγα, πρὸς ἥν, οἶμαι, χρὴ πόρρωθεν παρατετάχθαι) (*Letter* 89b [301C]; Wright, LCL).

[183] See above, n. 124.

[184] The later church orders gave the Two Ways material a narrative setting by putting it on the lips of the various apostles as their words of wisdom at the Jerusalem Council. *Did.* 3:3b is often spoken by Simon, as in *Didascalia* 3.6: "Simon said, My son, do not speak obscenities, also do not be haughty of eye for from these adulteries arise" (trans. Arthur Vööbus, *The Didascalia Apostolorum in Syriac* [CSCO 402; Louvain: Secrétariat du CorpusSCO, 1979], 33). (In another manuscript this saying has been put in the mouth of James, who says, "My son, speak not foul and silly words, *for these take one far from God*, and be not haughty of eye, for everyone that is haughty of eye falleth before God. Do not covet the wife of thy friend; do not love sodomy; from these things come adulteries and the wrath of God" [Margaret Dunlop Gibson, *The Didascalia Apostolorum in English* (London: C. J. Clay and Sons, 1903), 14]). In the *Apostolic Church Order* 9, the text is very similar to *Did.* 3.3: Σίμων εἶπεν· Τέκνον, μὴ γίνου αἰσχρολόγος μηδὲ ὑψηλόφθαλμος· ἐκ γὰρ τούτων μοιχεῖαι γίνονται. The *Apostolic Constitutions* reorders the material found in *Did.* 3.3, and augments being a speaker of foul language and a lifter of the eyes with being a drunkard: οὐκ ἔσῃ αἰσχρολόγος οὐδὲ ῥιψόφθαλμος οὐδὲ μέθυσος· ἐκ γὰρ τούτων πορνεῖαι καὶ μοιχεῖαι γίνονται (7.6.4).

[185] On the *Didascalia*'s use of the *Didache*, cf. Richard Hue Connolly, "The Use of the *Didache* in the *Didascalia*," *JTS* 24 (1923): 147–57, and idem, *Didascalia Apostolorum* (Oxford: Clarendon, 1929), xxxviii.

the *Apostolic Constitutions* are aware of the possibility that unseemly talk and lewd songs might be part of the merriment of Sunday worship, and cite Psalm 2:10–11 as a scriptural demand for due reverence.[186] The *Didascalia* and the *Apostolic Constitutions* concede that Sunday is a day for rejoicing,[187] and hence had to specify that not even on Sunday should indecent talk and song be allowed. Perhaps here we have another glimpse at the enduring desire to include the bawdy in celebration and worship (cf. the medieval tradition of *risus paschalis*). In fact, indecent songs and dances continued to be a part of ecclesiastical festivities, a problem that the Third Council of Toledo (589) urged clerics to address. In the fourteenth century, Pope John XXII discovered that sexually suggestive songs were being used in the liturgy itself![188]

VI. PAUL

In the authentic Pauline letters there is no comment that directly addresses decency in language. Paul includes "revilers" (λοίδοροι) among those who will not inherit the kingdom of God (1 Cor 6:10), and urges

---

[186] The *Didascalia* explains: "On this account is it required of a Christian to keep himself from empty speech and from words of levity [ܪ̈ܟܣܐ ܡܠܐ] and impurity [ܛܢܦܘܬܐ ܡܠܐ]. Indeed, not even on Sundays—in which we rejoice and are glad—is it permitted to anyone to speak a word of levity or one (such) alien (thing) to the fear of God, as our Lord also teaches us in the Psalm through David, saying thus: 'And now, you kings, understand; and be instructed, all you judges of the earth. Serve the Lord in fear, and rejoice unto Him with trembling.'" (trans. Vööbus).

The *Apostolic Constitutions* is similar, but also includes the vocabulary of Col 3:8 and Eph 5:4: "Now we exhort you, brethren and fellow-servants, to avoid vain talk [ματαιολογίαι] and obscene discourses [αἰσχρολογίαι], and jestings [εὐτραπελίαι], drunkenness, lasciviousness, luxury, unbounded passions, with foolish discourses [μωρολογίαι], for not even on Sundays, your festive days, do we permit you to utter or do anything unseemly [ἄσεμνόν τι ἢ φθέγγεσθαι ἢ πράττειν]; for the Scripture somewhere says: 'Serve the Lord with fear, and rejoice unto Him with trembling'" (*Ap. Const.* 5.10 [*ANF* 7.442, modified]).

[187] On Sunday rejoicing, cf. *Barn.* 15.9. Philo gives a nice picture of the popular assumption about what belonged to a festive day: Speaking of the Day of Atonement, Philo expects that people will laugh at the thought of a "festival" (ἑορτή) that lacked the usual fun: copious food, strong drink, entertainers, "merriment and revelry with frolic and drollery [εὐφροσύναι τε καὶ κῶμοι σὺν ἀθύρμασι καὶ τωθασμοῖς]," as well as dancing to all the "instruments of the debilitated and invertebrate kind of music which through the channel of the ears awaken the unruly lusts" (*Spec.* 2.193 [Colson, LCL])

Theodoret contrasts the Christians' worship with the "procession and shameful activities and shameful speech" of pagans; he urges celebrating without drunkenness, revelry, or laughter, but with divine hymns and holy words (*Graecarum affectionum curatio* 8.69).

[188] James A. Brundage, "Obscene and Lascivious: Behavioral Obscenity in Canon Law," in Ziolkowski, *Obscenity*, 248–49.

that Christian revilers should be shunned (1 Cor 5:11).[189] Certainly foul language was used in reviling, but Paul is addressing a much broader category. Resisting the urge to respond in kind to abuse was difficult, the mark of a holy or especially self-restrained person.[190] The *Testament of Benjamin* says, "For if someone insults a pious man, he repents, for the pious man has mercy on the one who abused him, and is silent."[191] Paul exhorted believers to bless in the face of abuse (1 Cor 4:12; Rom 12:14)[192] as part of the effort to live at peace (Rom 12:18) and to leave judgment to God (Rom 12:17–21).

One passage in the undisputed Pauline epistles that could pertain to the corrupting power of "evil speech" is 1 Cor 15:33: φθείρουσιν ἤθη χρηστὰ ὁμιλίαι κακαί. Here Paul quotes a proverbial line, originally from Menander's *Thais*,[193] in the midst of a chapter about the resurrection body. Most translations and commentaries suggest that it is "bad company" that ruins "good morals" (RSV).[194] But ὁμιλίαι can also mean "conversations."[195] Clement of Alexandria and other early Christian writers associated this passage with the other NT injunctions for clean speech, reading ὁμιλίαι as "conversations."[196] When John of Damascus gathered Christian quotations for his chapter "On Foul

---

[189] Ephesians 4:25–5:5 mentions most of the vices named in 1 Cor 6:9–11, and one might see the speech sins of Eph 5:4 as Ephesians's interpretation of λοιδορία. But λοιδορία means "reproach" or "insult"; if Ephesians has an equivalent, it is βλασφημία (4:31), which, occurring as it does in the context of θυμός, ὀργή, and κραυγή, is virtually synonymous with λοιδορία.

[190] Plato said both the aggressor and the one acting in self-defense should be punished in cases of public abuse (*Laws* 11.935C). Epictetus says that avoiding λοιδορία was a sign of moral progress (*Diatr.* 4.4.46).

[191] ἐὰν γὰρ ὑβρίσῃ τις ἄνδρα ὅσιον, μετανοεῖ· ἐλεεῖ γὰρ ὁ ὅσιος τὸν λοίδωρον, καὶ σιωπᾷ (*T. Ben.* 5.4). Cf. also *T. Benj.* 6.4–5; *b.Giṭ* 36b.

[192] 1 Peter bases the ethic of not reviling on Jesus' own silence in the face of abuse: ὃς λοιδορούμενος οὐκ ἀντελοιδόρει (1 Pet 2:23); μὴ ἀποδιδόντες...λοιδορίαν ἀντὶ λοιδορίας (1 Pet 3:9).

[193] Fragment 187 in Alfred Koerte, *Menandri Quae Supersunt* (revised by Andreas Thierfelder; 2 vols.; Leipzig: Teubner, 1953), 2.74. Andreas Lindemann points out that attribution to Menander is not absolutely certain, and that, in any event, Paul is citing what had become a proverb (*Der Erste Korintherbrief* [HNT 9/1; Tübingen: Mohr, 2000], 353).

[194] Similarly Anthony C. Thiselton: "Belonging to bad gangs ruins reputable lifestyles" (*The First Epistle to the Corinthians: A Commentary on the Greek Text* [NIGTC; Grand Rapids: Eerdmans, 2000], 1222).

[195] BGAD, s.v., cites the scholia for Sophocles, *El.* 420: ἡ ὁμιλία λέγεται καὶ ἐπὶ συνουσίας καὶ ἐπὶ διαλέξεως, "the term ὁ. is used both of association and conversation." For examples, see BGAD, s.v. ὁμιλία 2. For indecent conversations, cf. Julian, *Ep.* 89b [300C] (πᾶσα δὲ ἀσελγὴς ὁμιλία), where the context—this follows references to "uttering," "hearing," and "joking"—indicates a linguistic element to ὁμιλία.

[196] Cf. Asterius Sophista, *Com. Psalm.* 8.20.10.

Language" (Περὶ αἰσχρολογίας), he opened with this passage.[197] Nevertheless, the context in 1 Corinthians 15 indicates that whether one understands "bad company"[198] or "bad conversations," the concern is not with indecent talk but rather with the sort of company or conversation that will corrupt well-formed Christian convictions. Epictetus says something very similar when he warns pupils not to consort with non-philosophers lest their talk melt down recently acquired doctrines like so much wax (*Diatr.* 3.16).[199]

If Paul did not address foul language explicitly, is there anything in his epistles that the authors of Colossians and Ephesians may have drawn on—or reacted to—when they argued against such language? On the whole, Paul seems to have favored respecting prevailing norms of decorum. He says that love is not "unseemly" (οὐκ ἀσχημονεῖ, 1 Cor 13:5);[200] and he commends decorous behavior (Rom 13:13; 1 Cor 14:40; 1 Thess 4:12). But from time to time scholars (and pastors) have asserted that Paul used off-color language in the case of the word σκύβαλα in Phil 3:8, claiming that this word had the register of *shit* or *crap*, rather than the RSV's "refuse."[201] Paul might also have used indecent language when he committed to writing his wish that those in favor of circumcision would "cut themselves off" (Gal 5:12). F. Gerald Downing, for instance, claims to see in both instances a Cynic-style crudeness: "Paul's coarseness at times would have sounded typically Cynic (in particular, the reference to gelding (Gal 5.12) and to shit (Phil 3.8))."[202] This is a proposal worth considering,[203] for if Paul's language was indecent by contemporary standards, then Ephesians's

---

[197] *Sacra parallela* (PG 95:1253).

[198] So Johannes Weiss: "ὁμιλίαι sind zunächst Gespräche, aber ebenso gut auch Umgang, und das allein paßt hier" (*Der Erste Korintherbrief* [KEK 5; Göttingen: Vandenhoeck & Ruprecht, 1910], 367n1).

[199] Cf. the saying of Solon, μὴ κακοῖς ὁμίλει (D.L. 1.60).

[200] Those in search of a Cynic Paul should read οὐκ εὐσχημονεῖ with p[46]: "love is not seemly"! (For a more likely sense for this variant, see BGAD, s.v. εὐσχημονέω.)

[201] Alternatively "filth" (New Jerusalem Bible); "rubbish" (NRSV and NIV); the Vulgate has *stercora*.

[202] Downing, *Cynics, Paul and the Pauline Churches*, 41.

[203] John Boswell also proposed that the tone of κοῖται was coarse, and hence that Paul's ἀρσενοκοῖται (1 Cor 6:9) would have sounded something like "male fuckers" (*Christianity, Social Tolerance, and Homosexuality: Gay People in Western Europe from the Beginning of the Christian Era to the Fourteenth Century* [Chicago: University of Chicago Press, 1981], 342). But he does not really establish that the tone was so striking (his reference to Rom 13:13 will hardly make the case). Patristic authors may have been unclear about the word's meaning, but they do not seem to have been bothered by its register, as they quote 1 Cor 6:9 often, without resorting to circumlocutions for ἀρσενοκοῖται.

and Colossians's comments against foul language could be seen as a reaction within Pauline Christianity.

VI.A. *Galatians 5:12*

In his contentious letter to the Galatians, Paul says he wishes that those who unsettle the churches would "mutilate themselves" (Gal 5:12, RSV). In fact, Paul's ἀποκόψονται seems to have a specific sort of "mutilation" in view, namely castration,[204] a fact recognized by most commentators[205] and translations.[206] Having mentioned circumcision in the preceding verse (Gal 5:11), Paul wishes those who demand his converts be circumcised would take off more than their own foreskin. This was not the only time Paul made the connection between circumcision and a more drastic removal of flesh: Phil 3:2–3[207] seems to depend on a similar connection.[208] Occasionally in gentile minds circumcision and castration were associated.[209] And in the geographical context of

---

[204] For this specific meaning of ἀποκόπτειν, cf. Deut 23:2, where the word is used to describe men with mutilated penises (Hebrew כרות שפכה): οὐκ εἰσελεύσεται θλαδίας καὶ ἀποκεκομμένος εἰς ἐκκλησίαν κυρίου. BDF §317 says that the middle voice has the sense of "to let oneself be..."; i.e., "get themselves emasculated."

[205] So M.-J. LaGrange, *Saint Paul Épitre aux Galates* (Ebib; Paris: Librarire Lecoffre, 1950), 143; Heinrich Schlier, *Der Brief an die Galater* (KEK 7; Göttingen: Vandenhoeck & Ruprecht, 1965), 240–41; Pierre Bonnard, *L'épitre de saint Paul aux Galates* (2d ed.; CNT 9; Neuchâtel: Delachaux & Niestlé, 1972 [1953]), 107; Franz Mußner, *Der Galaterbrief* (HTKNT 9; Freiburg: Herder, 1988), 363–64.

[206] The RSV's "mutilation" is made more specific by the NRSV: "castrate themselves." So NIV: "I wish they would go the whole way and emasculate themselves!"

[207] "Beware of the dogs, beware of the evil workers, beware of those who mutilate the flesh!" (βλέπετε τοὺς κύνας, βλέπετε τοὺς κακοὺς ἐργάτας, βλέπετε τὴν κατατομήν [Phil 3:2]).

[208] Concerning the play on περιτόμη and κατατομή, Hans von Campenhausen says (of Phil 3:2–3) "die Vorkämpfer einer kirchlichen περιτομή vielmehr ingrimmig als κατατομή gebrandmarkt werden" ("Ein Witz des Apostels Paulus und die Anfänge des christlichen Humors," in *Neutestamentliche Studien für Rudolf Bultmann* [ed. Walther Eltester; BZNW 21; Berlin: A. Töpelmann, 1954], 190, cited by Jakob Jónsson, *Humour and Irony in the New Testament* [Reykjavík: Bókaútgáfa Menningarsjóos, 1965; repr., Leiden: Brill, 1985], 268).

[209] Dio Cassius 80.11 has ἀποκόπτειν as the completion of περιτέμνειν. L. W. Barnard points out that Hadrian equated circumcision with castration and forbade both ("Hadrian and Judaism," *JRH* 5 [1969]: 285–98). The connection persists today. On 11 November 2002, Russia's President Vladimir Putin, enraged that Chechnyans had taken a Moscow theater hostage, vented his anger at a European Union summit meeting. He issued the following invitation to would-be Muslim radicals: "If you are determined to become a complete Islamic radical and are ready to undergo circumcision, then I invite you to Moscow. We are multi-confessional. We have experts in this sphere as well. I will recommend to conduct the operation so that nothing on you will grow again." A long silence followed and the translators actually never rendered these words into the languages of the diplomats and journalists in attendance (Michael

Galatia, the wish that the false teachers cut themselves off might have made an allusion to the cult of Cybele in North Galatia, since Cybele's priests, the *galli*, were castrated.[210]

While this interpretation has rarely been challenged by recent interpreters, many have found Paul's comment "rude" and "obscene"[211] or "coarse."[212] (Others have found it humorous.)[213] Writing at the turn of the twentieth century, W. M. Ramsay was deeply troubled by the thought that Paul "would have yielded so completely to pure ill-temper as to say what this favourite interpretation attributes to him."[214] Rather, proposed Ramsay, Paul merely wished that the false teachers in Galatia be "cut off" from the congregation.[215] He explains, "It would be mere affectation to try to deny or conceal that, on the current interpretation, Paul uses a piece of foul language in the ordinary style of the enraged Oriental, who, regardless of the utter unsuitability of the expression employed, heaps insult on his enemy, animate or inanimate, man or brute, seeking only to be foul and insulting, and all the better content the more he attains this end."[216]

Wines, "Why Putin Boils Over: Chechnya Is His Personal War," *New York Times*, 12 November 2002).

[210] So, e.g., J. Louis Martyn, *Galatians* (AB 33A; New York: Doubleday, 1997), 478; Jónsson, *Humour*, 230, 268.

[211] Martyn: "Saying that, in the case of the Teachers, castration is the true conclusion of the rite of circumcision, Paul paints a *rude, obscene,* and literally bloody picture at their expense" (*Galatians*, 478, emphasis added).

[212] A. W. F. Blunt: "The sense, *coarse* as it is, gains at any rate some point from the comparison which Paul has already made (4⁹) between Judaism and heathenism" (*The Epistle of Paul to the Galatians* [Oxford: Clarendon, 1947], 122, emphasis added).

[213] Andrie du Toit calls it "the prize example of a grim Pauline joke": "One can almost see the smile on the face of more than one staunch Galatian!" ("Vilification in Early Christian Epistolography," *Biblica* 75 [1994]: 410); cf. Jónsson, *Humour*, 230, 267–68.

[214] W. M. Ramsay, *A Historical Commentary on St. Paul's Epistle to the Galatians* (New York: G. P. Putnam's Sons, 1900): 438.

[215] Ramsay says he prefers the A.V. and R.V. to the trend he saw in recent commentators (437). Interpreters such as J. B. Lightfoot were in view; Lightfoot had said that the passage "will not admit the rendering of the A.V., 'I would they were even cut off.' On the other hand, the meaning given above ["mutilate themselves, like your priests of Cybele"] is assigned to ἀποκόψονται by all the Greek commentators, I believe, without exception (the Latin fathers, who read 'abscindantur' in their text, had more latitude), and seems alone tenable" (*Saint Paul's Epistle to the Galatians* [London: Macmillan, 1866], 207).

[216] *Galatians*, 438. Ramsay's elaboration is interesting: "the ancient peoples, and many of the modern peoples in the same regions, resort to foul language when they express anger, in circumstances where Anglo-Saxons have recourse to profane language." He explains the difference in a footnote: "The traveller in the East knows that the use of profane language, objectionable as it is, constitutes a really great step in civilisation and refinement, compared with the unutterable hatefulness of the style of objurgation used

For Ramsay, it is simply unthinkable that Paul should have spoken like an "enraged Oriental," hence Paul *cannot* be saying any such thing: "The scornful expression would be a pure insult, as irrational as it is disgusting."[217]

VI.B. *Philippians 3:8:* Σκύβαλα

Describing his new way of thinking about his own religious accomplishments, Paul tells the Philippians that he considers his old gains "loss." Then, putting it more strongly, he adds that he considers all he has lost "rubbish" (σκύβαλα).

> ἀλλὰ ἅτινα ἦν μοι κέρδη, ταῦτα ἥγημαι διὰ τὸν Χριστὸν ζημίαν. ἀλλὰ μενοῦνγε καὶ ἡγοῦμαι πάντα ζημίαν εἶναι διὰ τὸ ὑπερέχον τῆς γνώσεως Χριστοῦ Ἰησοῦ τοῦ κυρίου μου, δι᾽ ὃν τὰ πάντα ἐζημιώθην, καὶ ἡγοῦμαι σκύβαλα, ἵνα Χριστὸν κερδήσω.

> Yet whatever gains I had, these I have come to regard as loss because of Christ. More than that, I regard everything as loss because of the surpassing value of knowing Christ Jesus my Lord. For his sake I have suffered the loss of all things, and I regard them as rubbish, in order that I may gain Christ. (Phil 3:7–8, RSV)

More than just those scholars who fancy Paul a Cynic have thought that σκύβαλον was, if not indecent, at least vulgar.[218] More recent commentators have often agreed.[219] Spicq attempts to convey the "crudity" of the Greek by "It's all crap" ("c'est de la crotte").[220] Hawthorne says that "it is quite improper to weaken its meaning in any way by translation or by interpretation."[221] (It is rather ironic that he then renders σκύβαλα "unspeakable filth," which is neither unspeakable nor filthy.) Did Paul use a word that some would have found offensive or exceedingly vulgar? Did σκύβαλα sound more like *refuse* or *dung* or *crap* or *shit*?

---

by the angry Oriental" (438n1). Throughout Ramsay emphasizes the irrationality which is a sort of affront against language itself, robbing it of its communicative properties.

[217] *Galatians*, 438.

[218] Friedrich Lang calls it a "vulgar expression": "Die Wahl des vulgären Ausdrucks unterstreicht die Energie und Totalität dieser Abkehr" ("σκύβαλον," *TWNT*, 7.447).

[219] Against this reading is J. B. Lightfoot, who thinks it has the sense of "scraps" from the table, suited for the "dogs" mentioned at Phil 3:2 (*Saint Paul's Epistle to the Philippians* [4th ed.; London: Macmillan, 1913], 149). In Spicq's list of how the word has been rendered, this idea of something left over (e.g. "scrap," "sweepings," "rubbish") predominates (*TLNT* 3:263n1).

[220] Spicq, "σκύβαλον," *Lexique théologique du Nouveau Testament* (Fribourg: Cerf, 1991), 1401.

[221] Gerald F. Hawthorne, *Philippians* (WBC 43; Waco, Texas: Word Books, 1983), 139.

Σκύβαλον is a *hapax legomenon* in the New Testament, and in general restricted to later Greek.[222] The etymology of the word is uncertain;[223] the Suida relates it to "that which is thrown to the dogs."[224] BDAG rightly identifies the basic meaning of the word as "useless or undesirable material that is subject to disposal," hence *refuse, garbage*."[225] But the word is also used frequently for *excrement*.[226] In general, σκύβαλα is anything that is left over: the σκύβαλον of the sea is the "offal";[227] the σκύβαλον of food is excrement.[228] As English words such as *excrement, dung*, or *feces* remind us, even words referring to fecal matter are not necessarily offensive.

To determine the register of the word we must consider who used the word and in which contexts. As it turns out, the pattern of usage suggests anything but a vulgar or offensive term. It was used by Strabo,[229] Symmachus,[230] Ben Sirach,[231] the Sibylline Oracles,[232] Philo,[233]

---

[222] Chantraine says σκύβαλον and its cognate verbs are "termes familiers et tardifs" (*Dictionnaire étymologique*, 4:1022); so Marvin R. Vincent, *The Epistles to the Philippians and to Philemon* (ICC; New York: Charles Scribner's Sons, 1897), 101.

[223] Chantraine says, "Pour un Grec le mot devait évoquer βάλλω, mais cela ne débouche sur aucune étymologie" (*Dictionnaire étymologique*, 4:1022). Lang says simply that the "derivation has not been cleared up" (*TDNT* 7:445).

[224] κυσιβαλόν τὸ τοῖς κυσὶ βαλλόμενον (Spicq, *TLNT* 3:263n2).

[225] BDAG, s.v.; similarly Spicq gives this as the first meaning of the word (*TLNT* 3:263–64).

[226] Artemidorus, *Oniricriticon* 1.67; 2.14; Josephus, *B.J.* 5.571; and above all, in medical writers.

[227] θαλάσσης σκύβαλον, Achilles Tatius, *Leucippe et Clitophon* 2.11.5.

[228] The grammarian Aelius Herodianus even uses τὸ σκύβαλον after a list of related words, where it apparently has the function of καὶ τὰ λοιπά (which he uses after similar lists), "and so on," "and the *rest*": αἴρω ὅθεν καὶ αἵρεσις· αἱρετικὸς· αἱρεσιάρχης· αἶρα, τὸ σκύβαλον (J. F. Boissonade, *Herodiani partitiones* [Amsterdam: Hakkert, 1963 (1819)], 36).

[229] Describing a poor drainage system that results in "filth" accumulating on the streets (*Geogr.* 14.1.37).

[230] Symmachus used σκύβαλον for excrement at Ezek 4:12 and 15 (for the Hebrew לֵּג; LXX βόλβιτον).

[231] Describing what appears in a person's thoughts or speech (λογισμός and διαλογισμός) Ben Sirach uses σκύβαλα in synonymous parallelism with κοπρία ("manure"): ἐν σείσματι κοσκίνου διαμένει κοπρία, οὕτως σκύβαλα ἀνθρώπου ἐν λογισμῷ αὐτοῦ (27:4). The translations and commentaries vary considerably on this verse, but the sense must be something along the lines of "When a sieve is shaken, the refuse remains; so does a person's filth when he speaks." The tone is certainly not crass; and the text refers to what is filthy or defective in a person.

[232] At *Sib. Or.* 7.58 and 11.185 the word refers to the "refuse of war" (σκύβαλον πολέμου).

[233] Philo, in a discussion of sacrifice, uses σκύβαλα to describe the parts of the sacrifice which are to be left "as refuse" to the mortal race. "For as on the threshing-floor the wheat, barley, and other grain are gathered apart, while the chaff and husk and

Josephus,[234] the author of the *Acts of Paul* (in a passage dependent on Phil 3:8),[235] Plutarch,[236] Clement of Alexandria,[237] and the Chaldean Oracles.[238] Artemidorus, who avoided obscene terms even when giving detailed interpretations of sexual dreams,[239] used the word for "excrement."[240] And the vast majority[241] of the occurrences of σκύβαλον

---

any other refuse [τις ἄλλος φορυτός] are scattered elsewhither, so too in us there are the best, the profitable elements which provide that true nourishment, whereby right living is brought to its fullness. These it is which must be dedicated to God, while the rest which has nothing of the divine must be left as refuse to mortality [τὰ δὲ ἄλλα ὅσα μὴ θεῖα ὑπολειπτέον ὥσπερ σκύβαλα γένει τῷ θνητῷ]. It is from the former then that we must take for our offering" (*Sacr.* 109 [Colson, LCL]). Later in the same work he says of burnt-offerings that "nothing save the remains of food and hide [μηδὲν ἔξω τροφῆς σκυβάλων καὶ δέρματος]... should be left to created being"(*Sacr.* 139, changing Colson's "excrement" to "remains of food," for the sake of literalness). In this latter passage, joined with τροφή ("nourishment"), the word clearly has the *sense* of what is left over from the food, and thereby *refers* to excrement. It is difficult to imagine that in this context, discussing sacrifices to God, Philo would have chosen a word of low register. Nothing in Philo's other uses suggests a vulgar word: *Somn.* 2.22 (distinguishing the necessary things from the "superfluous"); *Virt.* 145 (on how oxen help cleanse the sheaves and separate the genuine and useful material from the "refuse"); *Prov.* 2.62 (rubbish and "refuse" accumulate in the corners of houses).

[234] *B.J.* 5.571.

[235] In the *Acta Pauli* 2.23, Paul says: οὐδὲν γάρ σε ταῦτα ὠφελήσει, ἐὰν μὴ θεὸν [αἰ]τήσῃ τὸν [τὰ] μὲν ὧδε δυνὰ σκύβαλα ἡγούμενον ("For these things will not help you at all unless you ask God, who considers that which is mighty here to be refuse") (C. Schmidt and W. Schubart, Πράξεις Παύλου, *Acta Pauli: Nach dem Papyrus der Hamburger Staats- und Universitätsbibliothek* [Glückstadt: J. J. Augustin, 1936], 29). This clearly resembles Phil 3:8 (note the use of ἡγέομαι).

[236] *Mor.* 352D (used parallel to the "surplus from food" [περίττωμα τροφῆς]); *Mor.* 693E (of filtering the dregs of wine, like any other sediment or "refuse").

[237] *Paed.* 2.39.3; *Paed.* 3.65.3 ("urine and excrement"); *Protr.* 34.1 ("the sea spit out pitiable refuse").

[238] Speaking of the soul's ascent and its depositing "the remains of matter" (τὸ τῆς ὕλης σκύβαλον), oracle 158 (Ruth Majercik, *The Chaldean Oracles: Text, Translation, and Commentary* [SGRR 5; Leiden: Brill, 1989], 108).

[239] Artemidorus is quite explicit when interpreting sexual dreams, since the meaning of the dreams often hinges on the specific positions and actions involved, but he always uses euphemistic terms. In *Onirocriticon* 1.78–80, sexual intercourse is described with such modest terms as συνουσία, ἀφροδίσια, μίγνυμαι, περαίνω, and περαίνομαι (κινῶ is used at 1.50); masturbation is χειροτονέω τὸ αἰδοῖον; manual stimulation is δέφω; fellatio is ἀρρητοποιῶ (one person dreamed that he was ὑπὸ τῆς μητρὸς ἀρρητοποιεῖσθαι [1.79], which, it turns out, is inauspicious—the man later lost his αἰδοῖον); sex with animals is ὀχεύω.

[240] *Onir.* 1.67; 2.26; 5.79.

[241] Dibelius also noted the use of the word on a *Skelettbecher*, where the "remains" of a person are mere "filth" (Martin Dibelius, *An Die Thessalonicher I II; An die Philipper* [3d ed.; HNT 11; Tübingen: Mohr, 1937], 89). For the use of σκύβαλος as a personal name, cf. Masson, "Nouvelles notes," 145–47.

are found in medical writers (e.g. Erasistratus,[242] Galen,[243] Soranus,[244] Diascorides Pedanius,[245] Aretaeus,[246] etc.), who, as was noted before, "scrupulously avoided"[247] offensive words in their writings. Thus it becomes clear that the word was not crude, vulgar, or of low register. None of these authors was working in genres that permitted disgusting or offensive vocabulary; they were obviously not choosing a word with the tone of the English *shit*.

Vincent noted that some patristic interpreters were embarrassed by this passage,[248] but what concerned them was not the register of Paul's term but rather his disparagement of the law.[249] Chrysostom was at pains to show that Paul did not mean that the Mosaic law was itself ζημία. He argues that σκύβαλον is more like chaff: it is cast away, but it is nonetheless useful for its own purpose.[250] But Chrysostom gives no indication that there was anything inappropriate in the tone of the word σκύβαλον, and in fact he himself uses the word.

To summarize: In the case of Galatians, there was never a question of Paul's having used a "proper obscenity." But Gal 5:12 does make the sort of terse, *cutting* play on words that characterizes many of the Cynic *chreiai*. Demonax's biting riposte to Favorinus (*Demon.* 12, cited above p. 86) struck Lucian as "well-directed and urbane" (εὐστόχως τε ἅμα καὶ ἀστείως). Perhaps Paul felt the same way about his own comment, and one suspects someone like Cicero might have agreed that it was just the sort of mordantly witty remark a man must occasionally employ for force. Others would not have been so impressed. When Plutarch urges that arrogance, ridicule, scoffing, and scurrility (ὕβρις, γελῶς, σκῶμμα, βωμολοχία) be banished from παρρησία, his examples

---

[242] Fragment 76 (I. Garofalo, *Erasistrati fragmenta* [Pisa: Giardini, 1988]).

[243] E.g. *Comp. medic.* (C. G. Kühn, *Claudii Galeni opera omnia* [Hildesheim: Olms, 1965 (1827)], 13:1046).

[244] E.g. *Gynaeciorum* 4.38.1

[245] E.g. *De simplicibus medicines* 1.68.4; *De Materia medica* 5.75.8.

[246] E.g. *De causis et signis diuturnorum morborum* 1.15.2.

[247] Bain, "Six Greek Verbs," 53. As noted above, Celsus explicitly stated that he wanted to avoid the *foediora verba* (*De medicina* 6.18.1; cf. 7.18.3). The word was actually later taken over by Latin medical writers (Adams, *Latin Sexual Vocabulary*, 244).

[248] Vincent, *Philippians*, 101.

[249] Erich Haupt, *Die Gefangenschaftsbriefe* (KEK 8/9; 8th ed.; Göttingen: Vandenhoeck und Ruprecht, 1902), 126.

[250] τὸ γὰρ σκύβαλον ἀπὸ τοῦ σίτου ἐστί, καὶ τὸ ἰσχυρὸν τοῦ σίτου τὸ σκύβαλον ἐστι, τὸ ἄχυρον λέγω. Ὥστε πρὸ τούτου χρήσιμον τὸ σκύβαλον ἦν (*Hom. Phil.* [PG 62:265]).

of these breaches of decorum are rude but not obscene. Plutarch might well have regarded Paul's comment in Gal 5:12 as evidence of malice (κακοηθεία) or coarseness (βδελυρία) (*Mor.* 68). In addition to the fact that Gal 5:12 might seem inconsistent with a spirit of charity,[251] it would also have sounded as coarse and offensive to some readers and hearers in the ancient world as it has to commentators more recently.

In the case of Phil 3:8, σκύβαλα simply did not have the register of *shit* or *crap*. The word *was* frequently used in medical texts for excrement; and to describe one's prior religious attainments with even so inoffensive a word as *excrement* is certainly forceful. But ultimately, there is little evidence that Paul spoke or wrote with a Cynic-style shamelessness such that we should read Ephesians and Colossians as reactions in the Pauline school in the way that later Stoics were reacting to Zeno and Chrysippus. However unpleasant he could be, by the standards of his time, Paul was not lexically indecent.

CONCLUSION

Many Christians and Jews in late antiquity took for granted that God disapproved of foul language. But when the rabbis and church fathers forbade such talk, they did not point to any clear "Thou shalt not" in their holy writings. The fact that the rabbis could appeal to Isa 9:16 was a coincidence, a result of the fact that the later Hebrew expression for speaking lewdly used the same consonants as Isaiah's expression for religiously misguided talk. In a slightly different way, when Tertullian or Clement of Alexandria or John Chrysostom applied Jesus' saying "that which comes out of the mouth defiles" to foul speech, it was not because Jesus had laid down a clear teaching on lexical propriety, but because their own sense that foul speech was "dirty" had made Jesus' words, in their Matthean form, apropos. Christians and Jews did not derive their morality of foul speech from their scriptures; and the Christians' aversion to foul speech did not stem from the teachings of Jesus.

The first place in Jewish literature that a concern with foul speech surfaces is in the wisdom tradition. Sirach 23:12–15 calls foul speech "sinful," and says that it is liable to humiliate a person if one has the habit of using it. The *Didache* represents the first clear Jewish or Christian warning that foul speech will lead to sexual sins (*Did.* 3.3).

---

[251] A criticism voiced already by Porphyry (Giancarlo Rinaldi, ed., *Biblia Gentium* [Rome: Libreria Sacre Scritture, 1989]: 674–75).

CHAPTER FOUR

COLOSSIANS AND EPHESIANS

The only two New Testament texts that explicitly mention foul language are Colossians and Ephesians. Although certainty is impossible, this study will work from the general scholarly consensus that Ephesians is a pseudonymous[1] epistle, written to one or more gentile churches in Asia Minor toward the end of the first century, and written with a knowledge of Colossians.[2] Colossians is also probably pseudonymous,[3]

---

[1] Markus Barth (*Ephesians* [2 vols.; AB 34–34A; Garden City: Doubleday, 1974]) and A. van Roon (*The Authenticity of Ephesians* [Leiden: Brill, 1974]) offer two of the lengthiest defenses of its authenticity. As far as authorship is concerned, I find attractive Nils Dahl's thesis that Ephesians was written by a disciple of Paul after the apostle's death, in an effort to call Pauline communities back to their Pauline foundations (*Studies in Ephesians: Introductory Questions, Text- and Edition-Critical Issues, Interpretation of Texts and Themes* [ed. David Hellholm, Vemund Blomkvist, and Tord Fornberg; WUNT 131; Tübingen: Mohr, 2000], 414).

[2] Most scholars who take one or both epistles to be pseudonymous agree that it is Ephesians that draws on Colossians. The literature on the question is extensive; for a survey with bibliography, see Markus Barth and Helmut Blanke, *Colossians* (trans. Astrid B. Beck; AB 34B; New York: Doubleday, 1994), 101–14. Ernest Best has recently called into question how sure we can be that this was the direction of influence (*A Critical and Exegetical Commentary on Ephesians* [ICC; Edinburgh: T. & T. Clark, 1998], 20–36); John Muddiman draws attention to the difficulties of assuming Ephesians drew directly on Colossians (*The Epistle to the Ephesians* [BNTC 10; London: Continuum, 2001]). Ephesians and Colossians are full of similarities but relatively little verbatim agreement, the exception being the 29 words in the same order in Ephesians 6:21–22 and Colossians 4:7–8, where the references to co-workers feel more at home in Colossians than in Ephesians. Furthermore, certain words, such as μυστήριον, οἰκονομία, and πλήρωμα, are common to both epistles, but are used differently (see C. Leslie Mitton, *The Epistle to the Ephesians: Its Authorship, Origin and Purpose* [Oxford: Clarendon Press, 1951], 244–45). It seems that the author of Ephesians knows the words of Colossians, but rearranges them and gives them new meanings. Although Goodspeed's argument that Ephesians is an introduction to the *Corpus Paulinum* written by Onesimus is no longer very popular, his view that the author of Ephesians knew Colossians extremely well but did not regularly consult it as he wrote would account reasonably well for the relationship between the two letters.

[3] For a survey and evaluation of the arguments marshaled against Pauline authorship, see Mark Kiley, *Colossians as Pseudepigraphy* (Sheffield: JSOT Press, 1986), 37–73; Outi Leppä, *The Making of Colossians: A Study on the Formation and Purpose of a Deutero-Pauline Letter* (PFES 86; Göttingen: Vandenhoeck & Ruprecht, 2003); R. McL. Wilson, *Colossians and Philemon* (ICC; London: T. & T. Clark International, 2005), 9–35 (Wilson expresses greater uncertainty about pseudonymity). For arguments in favor of the letter's

but it is very difficult to be precise about its date or purpose.[4] Since Colossians was probably written first, I will begin by considering its prohibition of αἰσχρολογία before turning to Ephesians's expanded treatment of foul speech.

I. Colossians 3:8

In drawing the ethical implications of having died and risen with Christ (Col 2:20–3:17),[5] Colossians urges the addressees to think about what is above, not what is on earth (μὴ τὰ ἐπὶ τῆς γῆς, 3:2), since their real life is hidden with Christ in God (3:3–4).[6] In addition to not thinking earthly things, they must also mortify what is earthly in them (νεκρώσατε οὖν τὰ μέλη τὰ ἐπὶ τῆς γῆς, 3:5),[7] which amounts to eliminating various sins ("fornication, impurity, passion, evil desire, and covetousness"). Colossians then explains that these are sins of the addressees' pre-Christian lives—sins which will face God's wrath (3:6). A new list of what not to do follows this warning of wrath: "But now put them all away: anger, wrath, malice, slander, and *foul talk* [αἰσχρολογίαν] *from your mouth*" (3:8, RSV). It is this last phrase that interests us. Anger, wrath, malice,

---

authenticity, see Peter T. O'Brien, *Colossians and Philemon* (WBC 44; Waco, Texas: Word Books, 1982), xli–liv.

[4] The authorship of Colossians is not as important for my interpretation as would be the occasion and purpose for the letter. On this question there have been many intriguing proposals, including the impressive work of Angela Standhartinger (*Studien zur Entstehungsgeschichte und Intention des Kolosserbriefs Studien zur Entstehungsgeschichte und Intention des Kolosserbriefs* [NovTSup 94; Leiden: Brill, 1999], 195–246); but it is difficult to feel enough confidence in any explanation of the letter's purpose that one could then build on that as a given.

[5] The language of Colossians here is often thought to reflect a baptismal catechism. So, e.g., Ehrhard Kamlah, *Die Form der katalogischen Paränese im Neuen Testament* (Tübingen: Mohr, 1964), 28; Gnilka, *Kolosserbrief*, 184. (It is interesting to note that the *Canons* of Hippolytus 15 prohibited baptising a person who "speaks of shameful things.") For detailed comparisons of Colossians's ethical exhortations and those of Jewish apocalyptic texts, see Allan R. Bevere, *Sharing the Inheritance: Identity and the Moral Life in Colossians* (JSNTSup 226; London: Sheffield Academic Press, 2003), 148–81.

[6] As Angela Standhartinger, among others, has noted, this contrast between "above" and "below" coheres well with the thought of the epistle as a whole ("Colossians and the Pauline School," *NTS* 50 [2004], 590–91); cf. Burton Scott Easton, "New Testament Ethical Lists," *JBL* 51 (1932), 6.

[7] For τὰ μέλη, "your members," cf. Rom 6:12–13; see also Siegfried Wibbing, *Die Tugend- und Lasterkataloge im Neuen Testament* (BZNW 25; Berlin: Alfred Töpelmann, 1959), 113.

slander—these are not difficult to understand.[8] But what would have been understood by "foul talk"? And why would "foul talk" have been listed among the deeds of the "old person" (3:7, 9)?

Because the mention of foul language is so brief, the place to start is with the word αἰσχρολογία itself. Αἰσχρολογία is used only here in the NT and does not occur in the LXX. Nevertheless, it is not otherwise particularly uncommon.[9] In many cases we do not know exactly what sort of talk it was that got labeled αἰσχρολογία, so it is not always clear what is shameful about it. But in general, two broad categories can be discerned. First, using primary obscenities (e.g. βινεῖν, λαικάζειν) could be labeled αἰσχρολογία, regardless of the context for the obscenities (humor, abuse). Second, αἰσχρολογία could also be used for abusive speech whose content (and perhaps also its choice of words) was deemed offensive. Beginning with Lightfoot, commentators have observed that αἰσχρολογία could mean either "filthy-talking" or "abusive language." Lightfoot rightly added that "the word can only mean abuse when the abuse is 'foul-mouthed.'"[10]

Aristotle used αἰσχρολογία in the first sense, of the obscene language of iambic and Comedy. This was language from which Aristotle thought children were to be protected,[11] and which was inappropriate for a gentleman to use or listen to.[12] Aristotle mentions this language occurring at festivals and being used in relaxing, light-hearted conversation. Absent from his several discussions is any mention of using foul language in anger (though he does recognize that a joke is a sort of abuse).

---

[8] Bevere treats most of these vices in detail, seeking to situate them in a Jewish context, but does not comment on αἰσχρολογια (*Sharing the Inheritance*, 182–203; cf. 171). Interestingly, several of the Jewish ethical lists (for example, in the *Testaments of the Twelve Patriarchs*, 1QS, or *Didache* 1–6), which Bevere considers to be the proper background for Colossians 3, also warn against foul language.

[9] *Contra* Alfred Wikenhauser, αἰσχρολογια is not a word that occurs "gar nicht oder nur spärlich" in secular sources ("Zum Wörterbuch des Neuen Testamentes," *BZ* 8 [1910]: 271). I am not sure what Theodor Nägeli meant by listing αἰσχρολογία among the "gewähltere Wörter" in Colossians (*Der Wortschatz des Apostels Paulus* [Göttingen: Vandenhoeck & Ruprecht, 1905], 84).

[10] *Saint Paul's Epistles to the Colossians and to Philemon* (rev. ed.; London: Macmillan, 1916), 212. Similar analysis is offered by Joachim Gnilka, *Der Kolosserbrief* (HTKNT 10/1; Freiburg: Herder, 1980), 184–85 (the smutty *form* of the speech distinguishes it from βλασφημία) and Barth and Blanke, *Colossians*, 408.

[11] *Pol.* 1336b4 (αἰσχρολογία).

[12] *Eth. nic.* 1128a23 (αἰσχρολογία).

The word was still being used centuries later in the ways Aristotle used it.[13] Epictetus warned about using "foul language" when trying to raise a laugh[14] and when he described leaving behind the smutty talk of the pre-philosophical life.[15] And just as Aristotle could use the word for the language of certain cults in the fourth century, so in the first century B.C., Diodorus Siculus[16] used the cognate verb and the noun in describing the foul language used in the rites of Demeter; and Plutarch[17] and Julius Pollux[18] would later use αἰσχρολογία when describing similar rites. In these cases the language was sometimes lewd (recall the "suggestions for adultery" at the Haloa) and abusive (jeering the other participants).

As we saw earlier, Plato forbade the guardians of his ideal state from imitating men who revile each other and "speak foul words."[19] Here the context seems to be one of foul abuse, but the context is not exactly clear; possibly "speaking foul words" means simply using obscenities, and it was mentioned alongside "abuse" because Plato was addressing a spectrum of speech vices. Several other texts use αἰσχρολογία in contexts that clearly imply abuse. Polybius uses αἰσχρολογία for "foul abuse" presented orally or in writing. The content of Timaeus's attacks on Demochares is all too clear, even in Polybius's more modest paraphrase. [20] And Polybius complains about the way that Gaius Sulpicius Gallus asked for accusations against King Eumenes, and describes what

---

[13] Siems, "Aischrologia," 26.

[14] Epictetus, *Ench.* 33.16 (αἰσχρολογία).

[15] *Diatr.* 4.3.2 (αἰσχρολογία); 4.4.46 (τὸ αἰσχρολόγον).

[16] *Bibl.* 5.4.7.

[17] Plutarch, *Mor.* 417C (αἰσχρολογίαι πρὸς ἱεροῖς); *Mor.* 361B (αἰσχρολογία).

[18] *Onomastica,* 4.105.

[19] *Resp.* 395e, using the participle, αἰσχρολογοῦντας: "Nor yet, as it seems, bad men who are cowards and who do the opposite of the things we just now spoke of, reviling and lampooning one another [κακηγοροῦντάς τε καὶ κωμῳδοῦντας ἀλλήλους], speaking foul words [αἰσχρολογοῦντας] in their cups or when sober and in other ways sinning against themselves and others in word and deed after the fashion of such men" (Shorey, LCL).

[20] Demochares had played the whore with the upper parts of his body (ἡταιρηκέναι μὲν τοῖς ἄνω μέρεσι τοῦ σώματος). In case that was too vague, Timaeus said that he had thereby rendered himself unworthy to blow the holy fire, and had exceeded the descriptions of the sexual manuals.
Polybius also labels Theopompus's description of Philip and his court αἰσχρολογία: "As for the shameful accusations he brings against Philip's friends, I don't think he could give a defense, but would grant that he had gone far beyond what was proper" (πρὸς δὲ τὴν κατὰ τῶν φίλων αἰσχρολογίαν οὐκ ἂν οἶμαι δυνηθῆναι λόγον αὐτὸν ἀποδοῦναι, συγχωρῆσαι δὲ διότι πολύ τι παρέπεσε τοῦ καθήκοντος [*Hist.* 8.11.8]). But in this case Polybius has himself quoted Theopompus's descriptions of these debaucheries (8.9);

was then presented as αἰσχρολογία καὶ λοιδορία (*Hist.* 31.6.4), which suggests that the nature of the accusation was sordid. It does not tell us what terms were used, though the fact that these accusations were made in the presence of a magistrate probably means that they gave an account of lewd activities but not in lewd terms. In any event, the fact that Gallus was willing to listen to "every kind of foul and abusive language" is presented as part of his depravity (*Hist.* 31.6.4).

Although this survey of the word αἰσχρολογία is restricted to occurrences prior to or roughly contemporaneous with Colossians, it is hard not to mention the colorful example of a papyrus from A.D. 359 which complains that someone "came and spoke a lot of foul language to my face" (καὶ ἐπελθὼν πολλὰς ἐ[σ]χρολογίας εἰς πρόσωπόν μου ἐξειπών).[21]

Often it is not clear whether fighting words or simply lewd or offensive words are meant. Xenophon says that the Lacedaemonians focused conversation on noble deeds and, because of the presence of elders with the youth at public meals, avoided foul language.[22] Since it occurs in close connection with αἰσχρουργία, which usually has a sexual connotation, it presumably means that they refrained from sexual jokes and stories.[23] Pseudo-Plutarch urges that children be kept from foul language since, according to Democritus, a word is the shadow of a deed;[24] but he does not further specify the sort of language he has in mind, the context in which they might encounter it, or the deeds that might follow from these words. When Dorotheus the astrologer lists being a speaker of foul language as a characteristic of someone

---

although Polybius thinks it obvious that they are "shamefully and inappropriately" (αἰσχρῶς καὶ ἀπρεπῶς) composed (8.10.2), no "obscene" words are used.

[21] BGU III 909 lines 11–12; cited by Wikenhauser, "Zum Wörterbuch," 271 and in BGAD.

[22] Xenophon, *Lac.* 5.4–7: "Now what opportunity did these public messes give a man to ruin himself or his estate by gluttony or wine-bibbing? Note that in other states the company usually consists of men of the same age, where modesty is apt to be conspicuous by its absence from the board [μεθ' ὧνπερ καὶ ἐλαχίστη αἰδὼς παραγίγνεται]. But Lycurgus introduced mixed companies at Sparta, so that the experience of the elders might contribute largely to the education of the juniors. In point of fact, by the custom of the country the conversation at the public meals turns on the great deeds wrought in the state, and so there is little room for insolence or drunken uproar, for unseemly conduct or indecent talk [αἰσχρουργίαν καὶ αἰσχρολογίαν]" (Marchant, LCL).

[23] For offense at the thought of an old man actually talking about sex with young men present, cf. Plutarch, *Mor.* 653B–C.

[24] Pseudo-Plutarch, *De Liberis educandis* (*Mor.* 9F).

born under the sign of Ares, it appears in a string of adjectives (e.g. hairy, tall, curly-haired, low-born, jokesters).²⁵

Words formed analogously to αἰσχρολογ-, such as αἰσχροεπής/ αἰσχροεπεῖν,²⁶ and αἰσχρομυθεῖν²⁷ are less common, but show a similar range of meaning the few times they occur. When an author mentions τὸ αἰσχροεπές of Archilochus, it presumably refers to his use of obscene words in attacking his victims.²⁸ It is used once by Hippocrates simply for putting something down.²⁹ αἰσχρορρημεῖν and its cognates are more common. In one instance the verb very clearly refers to using foul terms (Stobaeus 4.2.24, quoting Charondas).³⁰ In the *Testament of Judah*, one result of alcohol's shame-reducing properties is that the drinker will "become foul-mouthed."³¹ Chrysippus said that the entrance of disorderly revelers who "speak foul words" (τοὺς ἐπεισκωμάζοντας καὶ αἰσχρορρημονοῦντας) could break up a symposium.³²

²⁵ ὁ μὲν γὰρ Κριὸς δασεῖς, εὐμήκεις δηλοῖ τοὺς κλέπτας, τῷ προσώπῳ νεύοντας κάτω, οὐλότριχας, δειλούς, παιγνιώδεις, αἰσχρολόγους (*Carmen astrologicum* 142 line 27). This passage is quoted by Hephaestion of Theses (ca. A.D. 415) in his *Apotelesmatica*. Hephaestion also uses the word in similar descriptions.
²⁶ For the synonymity of αἰσχρολογεῖν and αἰσχροεπεῖν, see Phrynichus, *Praeparatio sophistica* (*Epitome*, 46.1). Athenaeus (*Deipn.* 571a–b) quotes a line that connects αἰσχροεπεῖν to gauche rusticity: "You are so gauche and uncouth speaking foul language [αἰσχροεπῶν]; you keep your tongue on the left side of your mouth" (ὡς σκαιὸς εἶ κἄγροικος αἰσχροεπῶν· ἔα, ἐπ' ἀριστέρ' ἐν τῷ στόματι τὴν γλῶσσαν φορεῖς).
²⁷ Hippocrates, *Epid.* 3.17.11; 4.15 (quoted above, p. 14n66).
²⁸ Claudius Aelianus, *apud* Suda s.v. Archilochus: Ἀρχίλοχον γοῦν, ποιητὴν γενναῖον τἆλλα, εἴ τις αὐτοῦ τὸ αἰσχροεπὲς καὶ τὸ κακόρρημον ἀφέλοι καὶ οἱονεὶ κηλῖδα ἀπορρύψειεν ("Archilochus was a noble poet in other respects if one were to take away his foul mouth and slanderous speech and wash them away like a stain") (Gerber, *Greek Iambic Poetry*, 39).
²⁹ Hippocrates, *De arte* 1.1: "There are some who have made an art of speaking badly of the arts" (εἰσί τινες οἳ τέχνην πεποίηνται τὸ τὰς τέκνας αἰσχροεπεῖν).
³⁰ Stobaeus, *Ecl.* 4.2.24: "Let nobody speak shamefully lest he drag his thoughts to shameful deeds or fill his soul with shamelessness and pollutions. For we call things that are seemly and pleasant with their proper names, those given by custom; but we avoid openly naming those things toward which we are inimical because of the shamefulness of it. Let it be shameful even to say that which is shameful" (αἰσχρορρημονείτω δὲ μηδείς, ὅπως ἂν μὴ παρελκύῃ τὴν διάνοιαν ἔργοις αἰσχροῖς μηδὲ ἀναπιμπλῇ τὴν ψυχὴν ἀναιδείας καὶ μιασμάτων. τὰ μὲν γὰρ εὐσχήμονα καὶ φίλα τοῖς οἰκείοις ὀνόμασι καὶ κειμένοις ὑπὸ τοῦ νόμου προσαγορεύομεν, πρὸς ἃ δ' ἂν ἐχθρῶς ἔχωμεν, ἐξιστάμεθα καὶ τῆς προσηγορίας διὰ τὸ αἰσχρόν. ἔστω δὲ καὶ αἰσχρὸν εἰπεῖν τὸ αἰσχρόν).
³¹ *T. Jud.* 14.8: "If he exceeds this boundary, the spirit of error invades his mind and makes the drunkard become foul-mouthed and lawless; yet rather than be ashamed, he boasts in his dishonorable action and considers it to be fine" (ἐὰν δὲ παρέλθῃ τὸν ὅρον τοῦτον, ἐμβάλλει εἰς τὸν νοῦν καὶ ποιεῖ τὸ πνεῦμα τῆς πλάνης· καὶ ποιεῖ τὸν μέθυσον αἰσχρορρημονεῖν καὶ παρανομεῖν καὶ μὴ αἰσχύνεσθαι, ἀλλὰ καὶ ἐγκαυχᾶσθαι τῇ ἀτιμίᾳ, νομίζοντα εἶναι καλόν).
³² *SVF* 3.768.

Turning back to the command in Colossians with this range of meanings in mind, the context in Col 3:8 strongly suggests that αἰσχρολογία refers to abusive language. The word comes after a list of terms dealing with anger, and follows immediately on "slander" (βλασφημία). Unlike its English cognate, βλασφημία refers to the charges made against men[33] *or* gods; it means not "blasphemy" but "defamation" or "slander." "Slander" was a natural outgrowth of anger;[34] the word could be used of the abuse that the Cynics doled out.[35] Taken as a whole, Col 3:8 is forbidding anger and the sort of angry, vehement attack on others that so often involved nasty language. Colossians is not addressing foul language from the perspective of Aristotle. The vices listed in Col 3:8 have nothing to do with using prohibited words in playful conversations. They have nothing to do with what sort of drama to watch, what poetry to enjoy, or what jokes to tell. The vices have to do with anger and the words one uses when angry. This is not to deny the fact that what makes something αἰσχρολογία and not simply λοιδορία was that something shameful—in terms of vocabulary or content—was said. It is one thing to call someone "rat"[36] or "scum of the earth"[37] or "whitewashed wall";[38] it is another to say that he is "wide-arsed" or that he suffered a dislocated jaw while fellating his

---

[33] LSJ, s.v. βλασφημία 2: "defamation, slander." So O. Hofius, *EDNT*, 1.220; cf. Mark 7:22; Eph 4:31; 1 Tim 6:4. Secular and Christian writers alike use this word for charges against humans or against gods. When Suetonius wrote a book on terms of abuse, he titled it Περὶ βλασφημιῶν.

[34] For βλασφημία and ὀργή together, cf. Plutarch, *Mor.* 468B.

[35] E.g., Plutarch, *Mor.* 468A (Metrocles chastizes Stilpo for Stilpo's daughter's loose life; the chastizement [ὀνειδίζειν] is βλασφημία). Troy Martin (*By Philosophy and Empty Deceit: Colossians as Response to a Cynic Critique* [JSNTSup 118; Sheffield: Sheffield Academic Press, 1996]) could have used Col 3:8 to strengthen his thesis that Colossians addresses Cynic philosophy, for certainly no group in the ancient world was more notorious for "foul-mouthed abuse" (taking *blasphemia* and *aischrologia* together) than the Cynics.

[36] E.g. Petronius, *Sat.* 58 (one of Trimalchio's freedmen, Hermeros, to Giton for laughing so loudly). For many examples of (mostly non-obscene) Latin terms of abuse, see Ilona Opelt's *Die lateinischen Schimpfwörter und verwandte sprachliche Erscheinungen: Eine Typologie* (Heidelberg: C. Winter, 1965) and eadem, *Vom Spott der Römer* (Munich: E. Heimeran, 1969).

[37] So a Cynic addresses others at dinner with ὦ καθάρματα (Lucian, *Symp.* 16); and later one person calls another κάθαρμα, and one of the others then ἀντελοιδορεῖτο, "responded with abuse in kind" (*Symp.* 40). Trimalchio's wife calls him "low scum" (*Sat.* 74).

[38] As Paul calls the high priest in Acts 23.3; the remark is identified as λοιδορία in the next verse (τὸν ἀρχιερέα τοῦ θεοῦ λοιδορεῖς;).

well-endowed slave.[39] Either type of abuse could be called λοιδορία, but only the latter αἰσχρολογία, for αἰσχρολογία "denotes the form in which the injurious βλασφημία finds expression."[40] αἰσχρολογία might extend to "spreading malicious gossip behind a person's back,"[41] but only if that gossip was sordid.

So Colossians is picking out an obscene sort of speech, and no doubt the obscenity is part of what Colossians objected to. But in Colossians we do not have an exposition of what was wrong with obscenity *per se*. For Aristotle αἰσχρολογία was inconsistent with a free citizen's character. It was slavish, clownish, and unrefined to use certain words, regardless of whether the speaker was angry or not. Epictetus worried about how listening to or using obscene language would cost one respect. As we have seen, this is a widely attested sentiment.[42] But Colossians says nothing about what one will listen to. What was one to do when the mimes were performed in the street? When friends shared lewd jokes? And Colossians does not lay out the limits of humorous language. Could a Christian use primary obscenities? What about *double entendres*? Could someone engage in an explicit discussion of sex if one avoided obscenities? What was it about foul words that made them so bad? Did some words have a dangerous power, or were they just vulgar? When we ask these questions, we see that Colossians was not approaching the problem of foul language from this angle at all. The point needs to be emphasized because Colossians's brief mention of αἰσχρολογία can be contrasted with Ephesians's more elaborate objection to inappropriate language of a humorous nature.

It is also clear from the context of Col 3:8—"anger, wrath, malice, slander, αἰσχρολογία"—that Colossians is not drawing on the connection between foul language and sexual activity that we saw in *Did.* 3.3. This is noteworthy given that *Did.* 3.3 and 5.1 would seem to represent the uses of αἰσχρολογία nearest to Colossians in terms of date and cultural milieu. As we saw, according to *Did.* 3.3, the outcome of being

---

[39] Lucian, *Pseud.* 27. On the range of language that can be used in abuse, cf. Bianca-Jeanette Schröder, *DNP* 11.175 (s.v. "Schimfwörter").

[40] T. K. Abbott, *The Epistles to the Ephesians and to the Colossians* (ICC; New York: Charles Scribner's Sons, 1902), 283; Gnilka, *Kolosserbrief*, 185.

[41] Eduard Schweizer, *Letter to the Colossians* (trans. Andrew Chester; Minneapolis: Fortress, 1982), 193.

[42] Cf. Lucian, *Salt.* 1–3, where Crato criticizes Lycinus for taking in "bawdy songs"; the entertainment is base and effeminate, and the fact that Lycinus enjoys it suggests that he does not belong among the "serious-minded" (τῶν σπουδαίων).

a foul-mouthed person and a "lifter of the eyes" is adultery.[43] This connection is picked up in later Christian authors, as well. Clement of Alexandria and John Chrysostom worried about the way lewd speech (their understanding of αἰσχρολογία) would lead to sex, Chrysostom calling it "the chariot of fornication."[44] But in Colossians there is no indication that the danger in foul words is that they lead to sexual misconduct. αἰσχρολογία is named as part of a separate list of sins from the sexual (and possibly sexual) sins of Col 3:5.

So why might Colossians oppose an angry, slanderous use of foul language? Philosophical treatises on how to control anger recognized angry words as both a symptom and a source of the malady they sought to cure. Where Colossians simply forbids slander and foul language alongside anger, Plutarch argued that holding the tongue in check was one of the therapies for anger.[45] Sometimes opening one's mouth can act as a release valve for powerful emotions, Plutarch concedes. For those experiencing love or sorrow, singing a serenade or wailing a lament might afford them some relief; but speaking when angry tends only to exacerbate the problem (*Mor.* 455C). In so arguing, Plutarch was addressing the popular assumption that by giving free rein to some abusive words an angry person could "get it all out." The impotent Encolpius berated his limp organ and then, momentarily ashamed to find himself involved in such a discussion, finally asks what harm he had done if he "relieved his grief" with some abuse.[46]

But in addition to fueling rage, Plutarch (and others) thought angry words reflected badly on the people who spoke them.[47] Plutarch argues that, whereas a rough sea is said to cleanse itself by spewing forth

---

[43] τέκνον μου, μὴ γίνου...αἰσχρολόγος μηδὲ ὑψηλόφθαλμος· ἐκ γὰρ τούτων ἀπάντων μοιχεῖαι γεννῶνται.

[44] Chrysostom, *Hom. Eph.* (PG 62:118): ἀλλ' ὥσπερ ἐκεῖ [i.e. Eph 4:31] τὴν κραυγὴν περιεῖλεν, ὄχημα οὖσαν τῆς ὀργῆς, οὕτω νῦν [Eph 5:3] τὴν αἰσχρολογίαν καὶ εὐτραπελίαν ὄχημα οὖσαν τῆς πορνείας. It is striking that Chrysostom links αἰσχρολογία to Ephesians, where the word is not actually used. He obviously felt that the thrust of Colossians 3, where αἰσχρολογία was used, was against angry words, not lewd words.

[45] *Mor.* 455A-E; 456E; *et passim.* Chrysostom would later make the same observation in his sermons on abuvise language (e.g. *Hom. Eph.* 16).

[46] "quid autem ego" inquam "mali feci, si dolorem meum naturali convicio exoneravi?" (*Sat.* 132).

[47] Cf. Cicero, *Fin.* 1.27 (Rackham, LCL): "I always feel that insult and abuse, or ill-tempered wrangling and bitter, obstinate controversy are beneath the dignity of philosophy" (*maledicta, contumeliae, tum iracundae contentiones concertationesque in disputando pertinaces indignae* [*iracundiae,* mss.] *philosophia mihi videri solent*).

seaweed, an enraged person who shouts out "intemperate, bitter, and vulgar words" defiles the soul and earns disrepute (*Mor.* 456C–D). When people are angry their tongues turn "rough and dirty" (τραχεῖα καὶ ῥυπαρά) and they say inappropriate words (λόγους ἀτόπους [*Mor.* 456D]). Those who make such outbursts are perceived to be "hostile, slanderous, and malicious" (ἐχθροὶ καὶ κακολόγοι καὶ κακοήθεις). Philo says that an ancient once refused a match of reviling (λοιδορία) because in such affairs the victor is worse than the vanquished (Philo, *De Ag.* 110). Even the vulgar Trimalchio knew that in a battle of words, "the one who gives in always comes off best" (*Sat.* 59). When near contemporaries such as these held such opinions, it is no surprise that Colossians saw slander and foul language as behavior inappropriate for the "new person" created in God's image (3:10–11).

Strife and commotion and foul abuse were perceived as uncivilized at best,[48] beastly[49] and sub-human at worst. Philo explicitly contrasts the order and decorum of the Therapeutae with the way most Greeks "bellow and rave like wild dogs."[50] Apuleius compares the rowdy abuse of a band of robbers to the drunken brawl between the Lapiths and the Centaurs.[51] Dio Chrysostom also uses the image of the Lapiths when contrasting the conduct of the wise with fools, for the wise will not behave inappropriately (ἀπρεπῶς) but with seemliness and courtesy. The foolish, on the other hand, "behave disgustingly and without restraint [ἀπηνῶς καὶ ἀκολάστως], giving vent to anger or to laughter with shouts and disorder,... as we are told was the case at the party once held by the Centaurs" (*Alex.* 53 [Crosby, LCL]). One of the titles for Lucian's portrayal of a drunken banquet is "The Lapiths." Lucian describes a wedding feast at which philosophers belonging to the various schools of thought get drunk and trade insults and blows. In the uproar they exchange the standard accusations of sexual misconduct.[52] The narrator says that every philosopher was at fault: some did shameful things,

---

[48] Cf. the goatherd and shepherd of Theocritus's *Idylls*, exhibiting their crass rusticity with obscene insults (5.41–44, 116–19).

[49] Cf. Plato, *Leg.* 935A: "He makes a wild beast of himself through his rancorous life."

[50] *Contempl.* 41–47.

[51] "They played raucously, sang deafeningly, and joked abusively [*conviciis iocantur*], and in every other respect behaved just like those half-beasts, the Lapiths and Centaurs" (Apuleius, *Metam.* 4.8 [Hanson, LCL]).

[52] One says to another that after getting caught in adultery with a student's wife, τὰ αἴσχιστα ἔπαθες, "you suffered the most shameful things." The Stoics mock the Epicureans as hedonists, but are told that they themselves both do and *endure* the most

others *said* things that were "more shameful still."[53] The upshot of the whole affair, from the narrator's perspective, is that an allegiance to philosophy does not yield moral betterment (*Symp.* 34). It was actually the non-philosophers (ἰδιῶται) who behaved with decorum (κοσμίως [*Symp.* 35]); and in fact, the philosophers' bad conduct simply confirmed the popular perception that too much book learning addles men's wits (*Symp.* 34). There was nothing admirable in the philosophers hurling such accusations. It was not a venerable, philosophic boldness; it was shameful—and comical to those who heard about it.

In addition to giving us a sense of what it would have meant for a group with pretensions of leading a higher life to vent nasty accusations, Lucian's story also points to the symposium as one of the occasions where such things were especially likely to happen.[54] But Lucian's *Symposium* is doubly interesting because it gives us not one but two moments in the night when foul language occurred; considering them both helps bring Col 3:8 into sharper focus.

Before any of this uproar had happened at the symposium, Lucian says that there was a lull between dishes. To keep the guests entertained, the host ordered a clown (γελωτοποιός) to "do or say something funny, that the guests might be even more relaxed."[55] The clown then regaled them with some ribald verses (recited in an Egyptian accent) and by teasing the guests. Although the content of these particular verses is not mentioned, from various discussions about the decency of dinner entertainment, it is clear that they were often indecent (recall Quintilian's complaint that "every dinner party resounds with obscene songs [*omne convivium obscenis canticis strepit*]").[56]

Here we have two occasions in the course of the same gathering when language that could be labeled αἰσχρολογία was present: some

---

shameful things for the sake of pleasure (αὐτοὶ τὰ αἴσχιστα ἡδονῆς ἕνεκα ποιεῖτε καὶ πάσχετε [*Symp.* 37]). In this instance, a sexual sense for πάσχω seems all but certain.

[53] οἱ μὲν ἐποίουν αἰσχρά, οἱ δ' ἔλεγον αἰσχίω (*Symp.* 34).

[54] Cf. Petronius, *Sat.* 74. The *Testament of Judah* (14.8) and Sirach (23:12–15; 31:12–32:13) also worried about wine or the symposium as a place were foul language might be used.

[55] εἰπεῖν τι ἢ πρᾶξαι γελοῖον, ὡς ἔτι μᾶλλον οἱ συμπόται διαχυθεῖεν (*Symp.* 18).

[56] *Inst.* 1.2.8. On cinaedic poetry, often recited at symposia, cf. Athenaeus, *Deipn.* 14.620e–621a. Plutarch devotes an essay to "What Kinds of Entertainment are Most Appropriate at Dinner" (Τίσι μάλιστα χρηστέον ἀκροάμασι παρὰ δεῖπνον [*Mor.* 711A–713F]), and Varro had said that "not everything should be read at a dinner party" (*apud* Aulus Gellius, *Noct. att.* 13.11.5). For jokesters at banquets, cf. Josephus, *A.J.* 12.212; Philo, *Contempl.* 58.

light entertainment and the shameful accusations exchanged in rage. We find the same two moments in Petronius's *Cena Trimalchionis*: Atellan singers perform at one point, and aggressive disputes burst out at another. (We could also add the language of Trimalchio's off-handed comments at dinner, such as his swearing while playing a game, his boasting of "banging" [*debattuere*] his mistress [*Sat.* 69], and his concern that nobody "shit" on his memorial [*Sat.* 71].) For heuristic purposes, we can ask which of these situations Colossians was addressing: Whether or not to say gross things in the passion of anger, or how to react to (and whether to use) off-color language in light-hearted conversation and entertainment? It is clearly the former that best fits the context in Colossians. Colossians is addressing angry outbursts of foul-mouthed slander.

Other authors, such as Plato and Philo, connect βλασφημία and saying something αἰσχρόν, since they assumed that when angry people attacked each other they might "utter something shameful." Plato says that when people "abuse one another slanderously" (κακῶς ἀλλήλους βλασφημοῦντες) they employ shameful words (δι' αἰσχρῶν ὀνομάτων [*Leg.* 934ff.]). Philo speaks of slander (βλασφημίαι) in the context of "uttering something shameful" (φθέγγεσθαί τι τῶν αἰσχρῶν [*Dec.* 93]; cf. *Spec. Leg.* 3.174, where an enraged woman might say one of the "prohibited" words). The *Testament of Judah* warns that wine might lead to foul language (14.8), and then reiterates the advice not to touch wine "in order that you might not sin with words of *insolence*, of *fighting*, of *calumny*" and die before one's time.[57] The connection of foul words and fighting is, indeed, quite widespread.[58]

So Colossians was not forbidding foul language because it might lead to something worse; such language was simply inappropriate for the Christian's new, heavenly life. One passage from Epictetus provides a particularly close parallel to the thought that putting away (ἀποτίθημι) angry, foul talk (τὸ αἰσχρολόγον) was a mark of moral progress. Epictetus says that his students can rejoice "if you have put away [ἀποτέθεισαι]

---

[57] ἵνα μὴ ἁμάρτητε ἐν λόγοις ὕβρεως καὶ μάχῃ καὶ συκοφαντίας καὶ παραβάσεως ἐντολῶν θεοῦ, καὶ ἀπολεῖσθε οὐκ ἐν καιρῷ ὑμῶν (*T. Jud.* 16.3).

[58] Anton Vögtle suggested that Paul was perhaps facing the "special weaknesses of the Asiatic character" when he listed πικρία, κραυγή, and βλασφημία in Col 3:8 (*Die Tugend- und Lasterkataloge im Neuen Testament* [Münster: Aschendorff, 1936], 34), but it seems that these vices may have afflicted other ethnic groups as well.

or lessened maliciousness and reviling, or rashness, or foul language [τὸ αἰσχρολόγον], or thoughtlessness, or slovenliness."[59]

James Dunn[60] and Eduard Lohse[61] suggest that James 3:1–12 gives an exposition of the sin addressed here in Col 3:8. James is indeed concerned with the speech of anger and fighting (1:19; 3:9; 4:11), but James addresses actual cursing (i.e. imprecations) rather than obscene abuse. Colossians does place the vice in the context of an eschatological tension, between the old life and the new (3:7, 9–10), between the earthly and the heavenly (3:1–2, 5), between a secret existence "in Christ" and the world (3:1–4, 9–11).[62] But in Colossians, speech is listed alongside its *emotional* sources—anger, wrath, and malice. The bad behavior described in Colossians 3:1–9 is a thing of the earth (Col 3:2, 5), not of Hell. The rhetoric of defilement is not employed.[63] Nothing in Colossians suggests the tongue is an unconquerable adversary, or that controlling it is the key to gaining mastery over the whole body. Furthermore, James is troubled by more than just fighting words. James is also bothered by the way the tongue "boasts great things" (James 3:5; cf. 4:13–17). Most importantly, Colossians envisions a broader range of positive roles for the tongue. James wanted silence (James 1:19). "Blessing God" was the tongue's proper function, but even reference to that activity just reminds James of the horrible fact that the same tongue that blesses also curses (James 3:9–12). Where James expresses reservations about teaching (James 3:1–2), Colossians commends it without qualification (Col 3:16). Finally, it is very difficult to imagine James encouraging his readers to make their conversation charming and pleasant so as to engage more effectively their unbelieving interlocutors. This is precisely what Colossians does when it commends "speech seasoned with salt" (Col 4:6).

---

[59] εἰ τὸ κακόηθες καὶ λοίδορον ἀποτέθεισαι, μεμείωκας, εἰ τὸ προπετές, εἰ τὸ αἰσχρολόγον, εἰ τὸ εἰκαῖον, εἰ τὸ ἐπισεσυρμένον (Epictetus, *Diatr.* 4.4.46).

[60] *The Epistle to the Colossians* (NIGTC; Grand Rapids: Eerdmans, 1996), 219.

[61] *Colossians*, 140–41n42.

[62] On the eschatological and apocalyptic aspects of these ethics, see Kamlah, *Form*, 32–33.

[63] *Contra* Margaret Y. MacDonald, *Colossians and Ephesians* (Sacra Pagina; Collegeville, Minn.: Liturgical Press, 2000), 148–49.

I.A. *Colossians 4:6: "Season Your Speech with Salt"*

Toward the end of the epistle comes a request for prayers, so that Paul and his companions might proclaim the mystery of Christ boldly (Col 4:2–4). This entreaty continues with an exhortation that addresses how the Colossians themselves should speak with non-believers: "Conduct yourselves wisely toward outsiders, making the most of the time. Let your speech always be gracious, seasoned with salt, so that you may know how you ought to answer every one" (Col 4:5–6, RSV).[64] It has not always been recognized that Colossians is here commending *witty, charming, ingratiating* speech. The word "gracious" is apt in so far as it has the sense of "charming" or "winsome." But "gracious" tends to mean "courteous" or "kind," and that misses the mark, for in the context of "words," χάρις connotes not so much "kindness" and "benevolence" as something aesthetic, like "attractiveness" or "charm."[65] Because χάρις is used here to describe speech, it need not conjure up the theological concept of "grace," as it it often has for commentators determined to find a more "religious" sense.[66] And in fact, χάρις was not only a standard word for the "attractiveness" or "charm" of words ("grace" in the aesthetic sense),[67] but it is also used for the winsomeness of

---

[64] ἐν σοφίᾳ περιπατεῖτε πρὸς τοὺς ἔξω τὸν καιρὸν ἐξαγοραζόμενοι. ὁ λόγος ὑμῶν πάντοτε ἐν χάριτι, ἅλατι ἠρτυμένος, εἰδέναι πῶς δεῖ ὑμᾶς ἑνὶ ἑκάστῳ ἀποκρίνεσθαι.

[65] The word has a different sense in Col 3:16, where χάρις is used in the context of praising God with song (ὁ λόγος τοῦ Χριστοῦ ἐνοικείτω ἐν ὑμῖν πλουσίως, ἐν πάσῃ σοφίᾳ διδάσκοντες καὶ νουθετοῦντες ἑαυτούς, ψαλμοῖς ὕμνοις ᾠδαῖς πνευματικαῖς ἐν [τῇ] χάριτι ᾄδοντες ἐν ταῖς καρδίαις ὑμῶν τῷ θεῷ). "Singing ἐν τῇ χάριτι" probably does not mean singing "with charm" in an aesthetic sense, although the view has its defenders. Theophylact said divine songs should have a πνευματική χάρις just as secular songs have their own χάρις; and there is biblical precedent for χάρις in the aesthetic sense of "charm" or "grace" (Psa 45:2 [LXX 44:3]: ἐξεχύθη χάρις ἐν χείλεσί σου; Eccl 10:12: λόγοι στόματος σοφοῦ χάρις [in each case for חן]). But a more likely sense for Col 3:16 would be singing "with thankfulness" (RSV; Abbott, *Ephesians and Colossians*, 291; BGAD, s.v. χάρις, 5), as indicated by the context (cf. 3:15, εὐχάριστοι; 3:17, εὐχαριστοῦντες).

[66] E.g. Ernst Lohmeyer, *Die Briefe an die Philipper, an die Kolosser und an Philemon* [KEK 9; 12th ed.; Göttingen: Vandenhoeck & Ruprecht, 1961], 163; Gnilka, *Kolosserbrief*, 231; Erich Haupt, *Die Gefangenschaftsbriefe* (KEK 8–9; 7th ed.; Göttingen: Vandenhoeck & Ruprecht, 1902), 166; Barth and Blanke, *Colossians*, 456.

[67] BGAD, s.v. χάρις, 1; LSJ, s.v. χάρις, I.1. Cf. Plutarch, *Moralia* 514F: "But if a remark is neither useful to the speaker nor of serious importance to the hearers, and if pleasure or charm [χάρις] is not in it, why it it made?" Uses in pagan Greek are ubiquitous, but such usage can be found in Jewish and Christian literature as well. Cf. Sirach 20:13: "The wise man makes himself beloved with words, but fools' pleasantries (χάριτες) are wasted" (my trans.); here the parallelism of "words" and χάριτες suggests *verbal* charms are in view.

wit.[68] And the reference to speech "seasoned with salt" (ἅλατι ἠρτυμένος) suggests that a humorous sort of "charm" is precisely what is being commended here, for *salt* was frequently used for piquant wit;[69] the metaphor drew on salt's flavor enhancing, rather than its preserving, properties.[70] Murray Harris's paraphrase perfectly captures the sense of the sentence as a whole: "Let your conversation always be graciously winsome and seasoned with the salt of wit and pungency."[71]

In Greek and Latin *salt* was such a common metaphor for "wit"[72] that there is no reason to interpret Col 4:6 in light of Jesus' words about salt that has lost its saltiness (Mark 9:49–50; Matt 5:13; Luke 14:34–35).[73] These passages are themselves rather obscure,[74] and more importantly,

---

[68] Lucian can speak of ἡ κωμικὴ χάρις, the "charm" of comic *wit* (Lucian, *Musc. laud.* 11). Cf. Plutarch, *Mor.* 1065D–E, on the Stoics' idea that the "funny lines" (ἐπιγράμματα γελοῖα) in Comedy—even if they are themselves φαῦλα—give "a certain charm [χάριν τινά]" to the piece as a whole. Even Chrysostom knew that wittiness might be taken as χάρις. "It seems to have a certain *charm*, yet there is nothing more *unpleasant* than this.... Now there is nothing more shameless than the jokester; so in fact his mouth is not full of charm [χάριτος], but of pain" (*Hom. Eph.* [PG 62:120]).

[69] So Ewald and Dibelius note that the addition of the words "seasoned with salt" confirms that χάρις must mean "Anmut" in Col 4:6 (Paul Ewald, *Die Briefe des Paulus an die Epheser, Kolosser und Philemon.* [2d ed.; Leipzig: Deichert, 1910], 437; Martin Dibelius, *An die Kolosser, Epheser, An Philemon* [revised by H. Greeven; 3d ed.; HNT 12; Tübingen: Mohr, 1953], 50).

[70] BGAD, s.v. ἅλας (b): "Of speech that is winsome or witty"; Muddiman, *Ephesians*, 232: "At Col. 4.6 speech towards outsiders that is gracious and 'seasoned with salt' (the regular Greek metaphor for 'wit') is positively commended." On the connection between "salt" and "charm," note that Plutarch says that some actually call "salt" "charms" (χάριτας) because it makes food enjoyable (*Mor.* 685A).

[71] Murray J. Harris, *Colossians and Philemon* (EGGNT; Grand Rapids: Eerdmans, 1991), 198; cf. the NJB: "Always talk pleasantly and with a flavor of wit."

[72] So Dibelius suggests that Paul is passing on a secular saying (*Kolosser*, 51). He says that εἰδέναι through the end of verse 6 "ist der verchristlichende Zusatz, der sagt, warum auch der Christ sich solcher hellenischen Regel fügen solle" (*Kolosser*, 51).

[73] E.g. Barth and Blanke, who reject the suggestion that Colossians is favoring "ingratiating" speech: "The image employed here could be that of salt in its function of preventing decay or rot. Then, analogously again to the thought in v 3, the 'secret' would be understood as the salt that makes the speech of the Colossians an *imperishable* word (of God)" (*Colossians*, 457). Lohse belives—rightly, in my view—that Col. 4:6 is talking about salt as the spice of wit, but he treats this as similar to the uses of "salt" in the gospels (Eduard Lohse, *Colossians and Philemon* [trans. William R. Poehlmann and Robert J. Karris; Hermeneia; Philadelphia: Fortress, 1971]). It seems to me that whatever Jesus was telling the disciples, it was not a lesson about having an attractive conversational style.

[74] Unlike Matthew (ὑμεῖς ἐστε τὸ ἅλας τῆς γῆς) and Mark (ἔχετε ἐν ἑαυτοῖς ἅλα καὶ εἰρηνεύετε ἐν ἀλλήλοις), Luke never says anything explicit about the *disciples* being salty; yet given its context in Luke, it might still somehow relate to the nature of discipleship (so Joseph A. Fitzmyer, S.J., *The Gospel According to Luke* [2 vols.; AB 28–28A; New York: Doubleday, 1981–85], 1067–70). Mark might be urging "sharing salt" in the sense of

they are not addressing salty *speech*. Rather, language "seasoned with salt" means language with the spice of humor. When Plutarch contrasted the humor in Menander and Aristophanes, he described their respective "salts";[75] and Cicero called Attic wit *sales Attici*.[76] Cicero advises orators to make use of wit (*sal*) and humor (*facetiae*).[77] Catullus and Martial use "salt" as a reference to salacious wit and frankness about sexual matters,[78] perhaps because actual salt was believed to be a spur to sex.[79]

The "salt" of wit was to keep speech from becoming boring and to keep listeners listening. Quintilian says "salty" speech denotes "a sort of simple seasoning of speech, perceived by an unconscious judgement—by the palate as it were—which stimulates and saves a speech from becoming tedious."[80] Timon complained that the Academics' speech was ἀνάλιστος, "insipid."[81]

What a "salty" wit gave to speech was, in short, "charm." When Epictetus said that the Cynic must know how to make witty, biting ripostes, he said that they needed χάρις and ὀξύτης, charm and sharpness of

---

eating together (Morna Hooker, *The Gospel According to Mark* [BNTC 2; London: A & C Black, 1991], 233) but what that has to do with the prediction that "everything will be salted with fire" is hardly obvious. Mark has clearly brought together several (obscure) expressions because of the catchwords "fire" and "salt." The only thing all three gospels agree on is that salt is worthless if it is not salty. Since salt is an extremely flexible symbol—Davies and Allison list ten different uses (*Matthew*, 1:472–73)—it is hard to know what is being commended. Davies and Allison conclude that "you are the salt of the earth" is a very general reference to goodness in more or less the same way as "you are the *light* of the world" (Matt 5:14).

[75] Plutarch (*Mor.* 854C) says that "Menander's comedies contain an abundance of salty wit [ἁλῶν]," and that Aristophanes's "wit is bitter and rough [ἅλες πικροὶ καὶ τραχεῖς]." Socrates said that humor, like "salt," should be used sparingly (τῷ γελοίῳ καθάπερ ἁλὶ πεφεισμένως δεῖ χρῆσθαι [Stobaeus, *Ecl.* 3.34.18]).

[76] *Fam.* 9.15.2. Cf. Martial 3.20.9 (*Attico sales*).

[77] *Or. Brut.* 99; cf. *De or.* 1.34: *facetiarum quidam lepos quo, tanquam sale, perspergatur omnis oratio.*

[78] Catullus 16.7–11; Martial, *Epig.* 8.3.

[79] Plutarch explains why ships carrying a lot of salt breed so many rats. It is not, as some assert, because the females conceive without intercourse by merely licking the salt, but rather because "the saltiness imparts a sting to the sexual members and serves to stimulate copulation. For this reason, perhaps, womanly beauty is called 'salty' and 'piquant' when it is not passive nor unyielding, but has charm [χάριτι] and provocativeness" (Plutarch, *Mor.* 685D–E).

[80] *salsum igitur erit, quod non erit insulsum, velut quoddam simplex orationis condimentum, quod sentitur latente iudicio velut palato, excitatque et a taedio defendit orationem* (Quintilian, *Inst.* 6.3.19 [Russell, LCL]; cf. *Inst.* 6.3.18).

[81] D.L. 4.67; cited by BGAD, s.v. ἅλας 2.

wit.[82] Ancient authors describing charmingly witty speech sometimes even use χάρις with, of all words, εὐτραπελία, the very "wittiness" that Eph 5:4 forbids! Dionysius of Halicarnassus reports that many people used the word χάρις for εὐτραπελία;[83] and not infrequently the words occur together, a sort of Greek equivalent of the Latin *lepos et facetiae*.[84] Josephus, for instance, in portraying the winsome *savoir faire* of Joseph son of Tobias, says that King Ptolemy was pleased by the young man's "charm and ready wit" (ἡσθεὶς δ' ἐπὶ τῇ χάριτι καὶ τῇ εὐτραπελίᾳ τοῦ νεανίσκου [*A.J.* 12.173]). Philo uses χάρις and εὐτραπελία together in a similar way, saying that the Emperor Gaius's courtiers laughed at one of his comments in order "to make the remark seem *witty and charming* [ὑπὲρ τοῦ τὸ λεχθὲν δοκεῖν σὺν εὐτραπελίᾳ καὶ χάριτι εἰρῆσθαι]" (Philo, *Legat.* 361). Plutarch also uses χάρις and εὐτραπελία together in a similar way.[85]

The advice to use charming, salty speech in Col 4:6 makes excellent sense when understood as advice about the aesthetics of the speech. Although the words ἅλας and ἀρτύω are used together only here and in patristic authors dependent on this passage, we have seen that the metaphors of "salt" and "grace" for speech are not rare;[86] and a reference to salty wit provides a much more meaningful interpretation of Col 4:6 than references to divine grace. If the commendation of "charming, piquant speech" seems a bit dilettantish for the ethos of

---

[82] Epictetus, *Diatr.* 3.22.90: "Furthermore, the Cynic ought to possess great natural charm and readiness of wit—otherwise he becomes mere snivel, and nothing else—so as to be able to meet readily and aptly whatever befalls" (Oldfather, LCL). Epictetus's examples of this χάρις and ὀξύτης include the *chreia* in which Diogenes is asked if it is true that he does not believe in the gods. Diogenes replies, "And how can that be? You I regard as hated by the gods!" (*Diatr.* 3.22.91).

[83] Some people said that "Demosthenes's style lacks wit, which many call 'charm'" (ὅτι...ἡ Δημοσθένους λέξις λείπεται εὐτραπελίας, ἣν οἱ πολλοὶ καλοῦσι χάριν [*De Demosthenis dictione* 54]).

[84] Krostenko, *Language of Social Performance*, 99n32.

[85] Plutarch, *Mor.* 629F: "surely it was right for Gobryas to admire the urbanity [τὴν εὐτραπελίαν] and understanding of men whose very jokes offered pleasure and gratification [χάριν] to those who were the butts?" (πῶς οὐκ ἄξιον ἦν ἄγασθαι τὴν εὐτραπελίαν ἐκείνων καὶ τὴν σύνεσιν, ὧν καὶ τὰ σκώμματα τοῖς σκωπτομένοις ἡδονὴν καὶ χάριν παρεῖχεν [Clement and Hoffleit, LCL]); cf. *Mor.* 52E. Cf. Plato, *Resp.* 563a: "the old, accommodating themselves to the young, are full of *pleasantry and graciousness* [εὐτραπελίας τε καὶ χαριεντισμοῦ]" [Shorey, LCL]); Thucydides speaks of the Athenians showing themselves self-sufficient "with the utmost grace and versatility" (μετὰ χαρίτων μάλιστ' ἂν εὐτραπέλως [2.41.1]).

[86] Dio Chrysostom says, "For just as no meat without *salt* will be gratifying to the taste, so no branch of literature, as it seems to me, could possibly be pleasing to the ear if it lacked the Socratic *grace* [χάριτος Σωκρατικῆς]" (*Dic. exercit.* 13 [Cohoon, LCL]).

Colossians,[87] we need only note that "salt" and "charm" need not be ends in themselves. Quintilian says that the benefit of "salty" speech is that it arouses a "thirst for listening" (*Inst.* 6.3.19).[88] That sentiment suits the context in Colossians admirably.

Colossians's brief comment urges the addressees that their conversation ought not be unpleasant. Being unpleasant conversationalists would do nothing to help advance the gospel; "redeeming the time" meant being the sort of people with whom others would want to talk. While silence was widely praised, it was also necessary to speak during times of relaxation if one was not to be a bore. Aristotle said that the person who could not make or enjoy a joke was useless for conversation.[89] Varro said that a dinner needed cheerful conversation; there was no point inviting the silent.[90] Others concurred. Cicero said that some loose talk was "appropriate for dinner" (*Off.* 1.144), and Plutarch noted that the man who keeps silent while drinking with friends "is disagreeable and irksome to the company" (*Mor.* 456E); knowing how to joke charmingly and tastefully was, he said, a mark of refinement and culture.[91] In the *Satyricon*, Trimalchio complains to a dinner companion, "You used to be better company at a party. You're keeping very quiet nowadays: you don't say a word" (*Sat.* 61). In Plautus's *Miles Gloriosus*, an old man boasts about his good conversation skills, noting both his restraint but also his timely wit: "I'm the perfect party guest—*I'm quick with very clever quips*. And I never interrupt another person when he's talking. I refrain from rudeness, I'm restrained with guests and never rowdy. *I remember to contribute my share of conversation*."[92] Such values surface in

---

[87] An objection often raised. Haupt is emphatic: "Das wäre wahrlich das Letzte gewesen, was P. den Christen zur Pflicht gemacht hätte" (*Gefangenschaftsbriefe*, 165); cf. Lohmeyer, *Die Briefe an die Philipper, an die Kolosser und an Philemon*, 163; Dibelius, *Kolosser*, 50.

[88] Plutarch compares the use of pleasant conversation to salt, since both give savor to something else. He says people speak because they need something, for the benefit of their hearers, or simply because "they seek to ingratiate themselves with each other by seasoning with the salt of conversation the pastime or business in which they happen to be engaged" (ἢ χάριν τινὰ παρασκευάζοντες ἀλλήλοις ὥσπερ ἁλσὶ τοῖς λόγοις ἐφηδύνουσι τὴν διατριβὴν καὶ τὴν πρᾶξιν ἐν ᾗ τυγχάνουσιν ὄντες); if there is no χάρις to these words, they are pointless (*Mor.* 514F).

[89] *Eth. nic.* 1128b1–4.

[90] *Apud* Aulus Gellius, *Noct. att.* 13.11.4–5.

[91] οἱ δὲ τὸν καιρὸν εἰδότες καὶ φυλάττοντες αὐτῷ τῷ Πλάτωνι μαρτυροῦσιν, ὅτι τοῦ πεπαιδευμένου καλῶς ἔργον ἐστὶ τὸ παίζειν ἐμμελῶς καὶ κεχαρισμένως (*Mor.* 634F).

[92] *Mil. glor.* 642–45 (translation by Erich Segal in Slavitt and Bovie, eds., *Plautus: The Comedies*, 115–16).

Jewish works as well. We saw above that Josephus recognized the social value of Joseph's wit; and Sirach advised people to contribute their share of the conversation at a banquet (Sirach 32). It is thus not out of place to find Colossians advocating pleasant speech as part of making oneself friendly and attractive to others, so as to open opportunities for spreading the gospel.[93]

Over a century ago J. B. Lightfoot recognized that Colossians was endorsing wit with this reference to "salty speech." He saw immediately that this would appear to contradict Ephesians's prohibition of εὐτραπελία, since the conventional "notion of 'salt'...was wit, and generally the kind of wit which degenerated into the εὐτραπελία denounced by St Paul in Ephes. v.4."[94] But if Ephesians was not written by the author of Colossians, we can retain Lightfoot's insight about "salty speech," and ask why Ephesians was unable to endorse the sentiment.

II. Ephesians

In the second half of the Epistle to the Ephesians, using language reminiscent of Colossians, the author urges the addressees to "lead a life worthy of the calling to which you have been called" (4:1 RSV; cf. Col 1:10). One of the ways Ephesians depicts the worthy life is by contrasting it starkly with the blackness of the outside world. Prior to and outside of a Christian existence is the realm of sin, wrath, lust, and death; it is a godless realm controlled by malevolent forces. A

---

[93] So generally: O'Brien, *Colossians*, 242; Dunn, *Colossians*, 266–67; Jean-Noël Aletti, S.J., *Saint Paul Épitre aux Colossiens* (Ebib n.s. 20; Paris: Gabalda, 1993), 261–62; James P. Sweeney, "Guidelines on Christian Witness in Colossians 4:5–6," *BSac* 159 (2002): 459–60. It is interesting to note that some patristic sources understood the phrase as comending a winsome speech that had a positive impact on the hearers. Athanasius says that Antony, despite his lifestyle, was not "wild," but was rather "charming" (χαρίεις), his speech "seasoned with the divine salt," so that everyone who came to him was cheered (*Vit. Ant.* [PG 26:945]). Olympiodorus cites Col 4:6 as evidence that the wise person's speech should not be "austere" (αὐστηρός) but rather "charming" (χαρίεις) (*Comm. Eccl.* [PG 93:600–601]).

[94] *Colossians*, 231. Ceslas Spicq also notes the tension between Eph 5:4 and Col 4:6, but, arguing in the opposite direction from Lightfoot, Spicq used the commendation of wit in Col 4:6 to mitigate the severity of Eph 5:4. In Eph 5:4 Paul meant only to "debar God's children from this habitual lack of brotherly love and decency," not to forbid wit, for "God knows he [Paul] had a sense of humor, and he had told the Colossians that their language should be 'seasoned with salt' (Col 4:6)" (*TLNT* 2:146).

worthy life requires "putting off the old person" (4:22), and "living no longer as the gentiles do" (4:17). Under the rubric of "putting off" the old person and putting on the new,[95] the author addresses lying (4:25), anger (4:26), and theft (4:28). He also commands: "Let no *rotten talk* [λόγος σαπρός] come out of your mouths" (4:29). As with the other admonitions in this section of Ephesians, these instructions are related to the goal of building up the community. Lying is to be replaced by truth because "we are members one of another"; the thief must work "so that he may be able to give to those in need"; and instead of "rotten speech," there should be only such talk as is "helpful for building others up according to their needs, that it may benefit those who listen" (4:30 NIV). There is also a spiritual dimension to this advice: anger must not be allowed to give "an opportunity to the devil" (4:27),[96] and evil speech must not "vex the Holy Spirit" (4:30).

Following an interjection about imitating God and Christ (5:1–2), the author continues to warn against inappropriate ways of speaking (5:3–14):

> But fornication and all impurity or covetousness must *not even be named among you*, as is fitting among holy people. (4) And let there be no *ugliness*, nor *stupid talk*, nor *facetiousness*, which are not fitting, but rather thanksgiving. (5) For you may be sure of this, that no fornicator or impure person, or one who is covetous (that is, an idolater), has any inheritance in the kingdom of Christ and of God. (6) Let no one deceive you with empty words, for it is because of these things that the wrath of God comes upon the sons of disobedience. (7) Therefore do not associate with them, (8) for once you were darkness, but now you are light in the Lord; walk as children of light (9) (for the fruit of light is found in all goodness, righteousness, and truth), (10) and try to learn what is pleasing to the Lord. (11) Take no part in the unfruitful works of darkness, but instead expose them. (12) For it is shameful *even to speak* of the things that they do in secret; (13) but when anything is exposed by the light it becomes visible, (14) for anything that becomes visible is light. Therefore it says, "Awake, O sleeper, and arise from the dead, and Christ will shine upon you." (My translation)

---

[95] Eph 4:25; cf. Col 3:8–10.

[96] For the connection of anger and falsehood with the devil, cf. *T. Dan* 5.1–2: ἀπόστητε δὲ ἀπὸ θυμοῦ καὶ μισήσατε τὸ ψεῦδος ἵνα κύριος κατοικήσῃ ἐν ὑμῖν καὶ φύγῃ ἀφ᾽ ὑμῶν ὁ Βελίαρ. ἀλήθειαν φθέγγεσθε ἕκαστος πρὸς τὸν πλησίον αὐτοῦ.

At several points the logic of the passage is confusing.[97] If "let them not be named among you" (v. 3) means "do not even talk about them," then both verses 3 and 4 have sins of the tongue in view, and v. 4 expands on and explicates v. 3: "Do not let such sins be named; in fact (so that you know what this means), let there be no obscenity, stupid talk, or facetious wit." But if vv. 3 and 4 both treat speech, then v. 5 appears to be a *non sequitur*, since it does not warn against *saying* "obscene, stupid, and facetious" things about πορνεία, ἀκαθαρσία, and πλεονεξία, but instead tells the readers that those who commit such sins—the πόρνος, the ἀκάθαρτος, and the πλεονέκτης—have no place in the kingdom. We might have expected 5:4 to be followed by some argument against these three forms of bad *speech*—something like, "for such speech is evil," or, "for this sort of talk lowers you in the eyes of outsiders," or, "for such speech is an affront to God's holiness." Instead there seems to be a missing term, as the passage jumps from "no bad *speech*" to the warning about three types of bad *people* having no inheritance in the kingdom. Is the missing term here the idea that speech *leads* to such "fornication, uncleanness and greed," as in *Did.* 3.3?[98] Is the idea that the speech is itself *tantamount* to such activities—with some sort of quasi magical notion about the power of words?[99] Is the idea that it is

---

[97] So Brooke Foss Westcott (commenting specifically on 5:12–13): "The course of the argument is certainly obscure" (*Saint Paul's Epistle to the Ephesians* [London: Macmillan, 1906], 79).

[98] Several commentators suggest that this is the link: "Presumably, the assumption behind this prohibition is that thinking and talking about sexual sins creates an atmosphere in which they are tolerated and which can indirectly even promote their practice" (Andrew T. Lincoln, *Ephesians* [WBC 42; Dallas: Word Books, 1990], 322; so 324, 333–34). Cf. MacDonald: "the implication is that talking about such acts is tantamount to *encouraging* them" (*Colossians and Ephesians*, 311, emphasis added); Rudolf Schnackenburg, *Ephesians* (trans. Helen Heron; Edinburgh: T. & T. Clark, 1991), 218; Barth, *Ephesians 4–6* (AB 34B; Garden City: Doubleday, 1974), 561; Vögtle says, "Pl hebt hier speziell auf die Keuschheit gefährdende Zungensünden ab, albernes (μωρολογία) und zweideutiges (εὐτραπελία) Gerede, während λόγος σαπρός 4,29 (= eine in ihrem sittlichen Gehalt 'faule' Rede) geradezu ausschließlich liebloses Reden zu meinen scheint…so sollen die Christen, um von den heidnischen Hauptsünden (Unkeuschheit) gänzlich abzurücken, in ihren Reden das αἰσχρόν der andern in gar keiner Weise beachten" (*Tugend- und Lasterkataloge*, 34n69).

[99] So Barth: "To mention foul things by name (*onomazo*, cf. 1:21; 3:15) is as much as to make them present, to initiate their operation, and to accept their control. Evil talk and bad language resemble a magical incantation" (*Ephesians*, 561). Commenting on Eph 5:12 MacDonald says, "The notion that speaking about such acts is tantamount to *participating* in them is also found in 5:3, as is the implicit relationship between pollution that occurs through the mouth and sexual immorality" (*Colossians and Ephesians*, 315, emphasis added).

inappropriate to *talk lightly* about such matters *since* the stakes are so high (i.e., "Stop talking this way: people face a terrifying divine punishment for the sins you tell dirty jokes about!")?

Similarly surprising is the way that the addressees are told on the one hand to "rebuke" (to use the most common sense of ἐλέγχετε) the fruitless deeds of darkness (5:11), but then are reminded in the next verse that it is "shameful *even to say* what is done by them in secret" (5:12). How is one to rebuke what one cannot name? Should ἐλέγχετε be understood as "expose" or "convict" or "bring to light" rather than "reprove"?

Larry Kreitzer has written the only article that tries to get at the historical reality that prompted Ephesians's prohibition of foul language.[100] Early in his study Kreitzer poses an either/or question about these strictures: "Are these remarks simply part of [the author's] general advice-giving…, or might they indicate something more specific, more concrete, about the situation at hand?" (54–55). Most readers of Ephesians would probably pick the former, since Ephesians's advice is notorious for its *lack* of specificity (unlike Paul's authentic letters, where concrete situations are clearly addressed). But the answer Kreitzer requires is the latter one: he argues that the "shameful language" of Eph 5:4 was the very foul language women spoke to each other during festivals in honor of Demeter/Cybele.[101] Kreitzer's article gives a very helpful description of the role of foul language at these ceremonies, but in the end it is difficult to imagine that the author of Ephesians, if he thought that Christian women were worshipping Demeter at an annual, three-day festival involving phalli, sacrificed piglets, and ritual obscenity, would choose to address the matter merely by urging the church to avoid "ugliness, foolish language, and wittiness."[102] In the end, Kreitzer is honest about the uncertainty of his own proposal (his last sentence appeals to the fact that "stranger interpretations of Eph. 5.4 and 5.12 have been offered before" [76–77]). He cannot make a persuasive case that the prohibition of foul speech is anything other

---

[100] "'Crude Language' and 'Shameful Things Done in Secret' (Ephesians 5.4, 12): Allusions to the Cult of Demeter/Cybele in Hierapolis?" *JSNT* 71 (1998): 51–77.

[101] Kreitzer thinks that Colossians's mention of αἰσχρολογία might also be "a result of Paul once again encountering the cult of Demeter" ("'Crude Language,'" 71).

[102] To say nothing of the fact that none of Ephesians's three terms in 5:4 is used in the numerous ancient descriptions of the language at such festivals.

than "general advice-giving." We turn now to trying to understand it as such.

II.A. *Exegesis of Ephesians 5:3–14*

To understand the flow of the whole passage in Ephesians 5 we need to understand better the meaning of several of its terms and phrases. It is not entirely clear how much of the passage is actually addressing speech. In v. 4, for instance, "foolish talk" and "wittiness" (μωρολογία and εὐτραπελία) clearly refer to speech.[103] But commentators have occasionally proposed that αἰσχρότης meant "filthy conduct," in which case it would not refer to a sin of the tongue.[104] Furthermore, many see μηδὲ ὀνομαζέσθω ἐν ὑμῖν in v. 3 as an idiomatic way of saying "there must not be *even a hint*" of such vices (NIV). On this reading, "let them not even be named among you" is not advice about how to *talk*, but is simply a way of saying that these sins themselves should be far removed. This interpretation has the advantage of improving the fit between the imperative in v. 3 and the warning in v. 5 that people who practice such sins will not inherit the kingdom.

Figuring out which individual elements of Eph 5:3–12 address speech is made more difficult by the fact that there is no clear indication of the *context* for the problematic speech. Were people joking with friends? Were they going to religious festivals where lewd speech played a role? Enjoying the mimes? Spreading lurid gossip? Reading and writing graffiti? Also, in Ephesians there is no description of what exactly counts as objectionable speech. Is it the use of specific words, or merely broaching certain topics, or treating certain topics with an inappropriate levity? Aristotle and Plutarch contrasted the humor of Old and Middle Comedy, Epictetus named specific pornographic writers, and the Emperor Julian listed specific authors and genres to make clear what bad language they had in mind. Similarly Cicero and Quintilian listed specific words or referred to the humor of the mimes. By contrast, Ephesians offers no example of the sort of "wit" that was "not appropriate." Ephesians also has no warning against *listening*

---

[103] While εὐτραπελία did not have to refer to speech, it usually did refer to a *verbal* flexibility; and certainly here, linked with "foolish talk" and contrasted with "thanksgiving," it refers to something verbal.

[104] Or at least not to a sin of speech. LSJ, s.v. αἰσχρότης 2, notes that the scholiast on Aristophanes's *Frogs* used it as a euphemism for *fellatio*.

to obscene speech,[105] and no suggestions for how to react when lewd speech is used (contrast Epictetus and later Clement of Alexandria). Finally, the passage in Ephesians does not explain *why* "ugliness, foolish talk, and facetiousness" are wrong. It simply declares such talk to be shameful (5:12) and not *fitting* for holy people (5:3, 4).

We should now consider in more detail several specific questions, such as the sense of ὀνομαζέσθω (5:3), ἐλέγχω (5:11), and "shameful even to mention" (5:12); and the meaning of αἰσχρότης, μωρολογία, and εὐτραπελία.

II.A.1. *"Let them not even be named among you" (Eph 5:3)*
It is not clear that we are to take μηδὲ ὀνομαζέσθω ἐν ὑμῖν in the sense of "let them not even be *mentioned.*" It could also mean "let it not be said that such things *occur* among you."[106] In defense of this latter interpretation, commentators appeal to the phrase ὅλως ἀκούεται ἐν ὑμῖν πορνεία in 1 Cor 5:1, where, unless this *porneia* was very loud indeed,[107] the phrase obviously means "it is actually heard *that there is* sexual immorality among you." Such expressions are not uncommon. In addressing what jobs Christians could hold, Tertullian said, "There should not even be *talk* about astrologers!" (*de astrologis ne loquendum quidem est* [*Idol.* 9]). Clearly he did not mean that it was offensive to *talk* about astrologers; rather, he sought a forceful expression to convey

---

[105] Unless perhaps ὀνομαζέσθω ἐν ὑμῖν should be understood to prohibit *letting* such things be named, whether by insiders or outsiders: "let it not be named in your presence" with the sense "stop their mouths before they say such things."

[106] Robert G. Bratcher and Eugene A. Nida, *A Translator's Handbook on Paul's Letter to the Ephesians* (London: United Bible Societies, 1982), 125–26; Gnilka, *Kolosserbrief*, 247; Schnackenburg, *Ephesians*, 223; Dahl, *Studies*, 423 (though not commenting on this point *per se*); Dibelius, *Kolosser*, 88–89; Heinrich Schlier, *Der Brief an die Epheser* (7th ed.; Düsseldorf: Patmos, 1971), 233.This is also apparently the way the phrase was interpreted by Origen and by Chrysostom (μὴ εἴπῃς ἀστεῖα μηδ᾽ αἰσχρά, μηδὲ πράξῃς, καὶ κατασβέσεις τὴν φλόγα. μηδὲ ὀνομαζέσθω, φησίν, ἐν ὑμῖν· τουτέστι, μηδαμοῦ μηδὲ φαινέσθω. τοῦτο καὶ Κορινθίοις γράφων ἔλεγεν· ὅλως ἀκούεται ἐν ὑμῖν πορνεία [*Hom. Eph.* (PG 62:118)]). Several patristic interpreters construe the vices of Eph 5:4 with the verb ὀνομαζέσθω. In this case, the verb must mean "let there *be no hint* of stupid talk…" since there is nothing objectionable in *naming* "stupid talk" (a point made by Schlier, *Epheser*, 233). But it seems better to construe the vices of 5:4 as grammatically independent from ὀνομαζέσθω (which is connected only with "fornication, impurity, and covetousness"); in 5:4, "let there not be" should be supplied for the subsequent three vices (so Joachim Gnilka, *Der Epheserbrief* [HTK 10.2; 2d ed.; Freiburg: Herder, 1977], 247; Schnackenburger, *Ephesians*, 223).

[107] Cf. *b. Ket.* 72b.

that he should not even have to discuss the *possibility* of Christians in that line of work.

But there are difficulties with taking Eph 5:3 in this way. For one thing, as Abbott noted, ὀνομάζεσθαι means something different than ἀκούεσθαι. Whereas ἀκούεσθαι is used in the sense "it is reported" elsewhere in the NT (Matt 28:14; Mark 2:1), "naming" generally means either giving a name (i.e. to a child), or actually pronouncing a name or a word.[108] This pattern of usage suggests that "naming" picks out a verbal activity. Furthermore, commentators have pointed to the emphatic μηδέ ("not even") as evidence that ὀνομαζέσθω did not mean "mention as committed" but rather "do *not even* mention."[109]

Even more important than the usage of ὀνομάζεσθαι is the fact that Eph 5:4 clearly addresses inappropriate speech, and Eph 5:12 says unambiguously that it is shameful "even to mention" what the outsiders do in secret. The author of Ephesians clearly objected to talk about evil deeds; and 5:4 is introduced with καί,[110] as though it continues the thought of v. 3. Hence most commentators agree that v. 3 is addressing how the Ephesians are to speak:[111] they are not to talk about sexual vices at all.

---

[108] BGAD, s.v. ὀνομάζω 1, 2 (BGAD includes Eph 5:3 under this latter meaning).

[109] Abbott claims μηδέ is "decisive" evidence (*Ephesians and Colossians*, 149); his judgment was followed by, e.g., Barth, *Ephesians*, 561. This argument does not seem as conclusive as many have thought. While it may be slightly more natural on lexical grounds to take ὀνομαζέσθω to mean literally "naming" these sexual vices, it could apparently also be understood in the sense "do not even let them be named as having occurred," for some late NT manuscripts added ὀνομάζεται to 1 Cor 5.1 (ἥτις οὐδὲ ἐν τοῖς ἔθνεσιν ὀνομάζεται). This reading even has the verb alongside the equivalent negative particle (οὐδέ). The earliest manuscript with this addition is the seventh-century P⁶⁸ (Gordon Fee, *The First Epistle to the Corinthians* [NICNT; Grand Rapids: Eerdmans, 1987], 198).

[110] Many mss. have ἤ (A D* F G Ψ 81 104 1241ˢ pc latt sa), which, as Best notes, "is difficult to fit into the context" (*Ephesians*, 478).

[111] Clement of Alexandria, *Strom.* 3.28.5–6; *Paed.* 2.98; cf. *Paed.* 2.50; Chrysostom, *Hom. Eph.* 17; Theophylact, *Eph.* (PG 124:1104): "Let them not be named among you.... For words are the path to deeds; so if you are holy, let also your tongue be holy"; Abbott, *Ephesians and Colossians*, 148–49; Schnackenburg, *Ephesians*, 218; Lincoln, *Ephesians*, 322; MacDonald, *Colossians and Ephesians*, 311; Pheme Perkins, *Ephesians* (ANTC; Nashville: Abingdon, 1997), 115 (concerning 5:3–4 together, Perkins says, "Christians are not to even speak of such vices"); F. F. Bruce, *Ephesians* (London: Pickering & Inglis, 1961), 102 ("it should not even be mentioned"; "unfitting for their minds to dwell upon or their tongues to name"); Haupt, *Gefangenschaftsbriefe*, 190 ("sie nicht einmal Gegenstand der Rede bilden dürfen"); E. Gaugler, *Der Epheserbrief* (Zürich: EVZ Verlag, 1966), 199; Franz Mußner, *Der Brief an die Epheser* (ÖTK 10; Gütersloh: Gütersloher Verlagshaus Gerd Mohn, 1982), 143 ("Laster, die unter Christen nicht einmal beim Namen genannt werden sollen"); Best tends in this direction ("None of these three sins should be even

Of course, this interpretation can make sense only if πορνεία, ἀκαθαρσία, and πλεονεξία are the sorts of vices someone might be hesi-
tant to speak about. The vast majority of the "bad language" we have
encountered so far was about sexual topics. The word πορνεία could
be used for a wide variety of "unsanctioned sexual intercourse,"[112] so
it obviously qualifies. It might not be as clear, however, that anyone
could speak in an offensive manner about "impurity" (ἀκαθαρσία) or
"covetousness" (πλεονεξία), were it not for the fact that both of these
terms could be used by Jewish and Christian authors to refer to sexual
vices.[113] In addition, Ephesians has already used the terms "impurity"
and "covetousness" to describe the gentiles' debauchery (Eph 4:19:
ἑαυτοὺς παρέδωκαν τῇ ἀσελγείᾳ εἰς ἐργασίαν ἀκαθαρσίας πάσης ἐν
πλεονεξίᾳ). So we know for certain that Eph 5:12 says it is shameful even
to mention what the gentiles do in secret, and that Eph 4:19 describes
what they do in secret with ἀκαθαρσία and πλεονεξία. It therefore
makes sense to understand 5:3 as forbidding "naming" their "unclean"
and "covetous" activities. Various ancient interpreters agreed that even
ἀκαθαρσία and πλεονεξία were of a sexual nature. Origen said that
porneia was the scriptural term for sex with a prostitute; "uncleanness"

---

mentioned," *Ephesians*, 476–77); Harold W. Hoehner, *Ephesians: An Exegetical Commentary*
(Grand Rapids: Baker Academic, 2002), 653; Muddiman, *Ephesians*, 232 ("It is not so
much the commission of these sins which is prohibited as the very mention of them;
those who actually commit them are beyond the pale altogether...").

[112] BGAD. Whether or not it means "fornication" is not critical here, as one could
certainly make indecent comments about the whole range of activities that πορνεία
might cover (including incest). (For debate about the meaning of the word, cf. F. Hauck
and S. Schulz, "πορνή, κ.τ.λ.," *TDNT* 6:579–95; Bruce Malina, "Does *Porneia* Mean
Fornication?" *NT* 14 [1972]: 10–17; J. Jensen, "Does *Porneia* Mean Fornication? A
Critique of Bruce Malina," *NT* 20 [1978]: 161–84.)

[113] ἀκαθαρσία is used with πορνεία several times in the NT (2 Cor 12:21; Gal 5:19;
1 Thess 4:3, 7; Col 3:5). Dibelius says of ἀκαθαρσία in Col 3:5, "wegen der Nach-
barschaft von πορνεία wohl im sexuellen Sinn" (*Kolosser*, 89). πλεονεξία is also found in
connection with sexual immorality in *T. Levi* 14.5–6 (cf. *T. Jud.* 18.2), as is πλεονεκτεῖν
in 1 Thess 4:6 (cf. also Mark 7:21). ἀκαθαρσία and πλεονεξία occur together at Eph
4.19. For taking πλεονεξία in a sexual sense, cf. Perkins, *Ephesians*, 115; Abbott, *Ephesians and Colossians*, 148; Lincoln, *Ephesians*, 322 ("Because of the context, πλεονεξία,
'covetousness,' should also be taken as the sort of unrestrained sexual greed whereby
a person assumes that others exist for his or her own gratification."). For arguments
against understanding πλεονεξία in sexual terms, cf. Brian S. Rosner, *Greed as Idolatry:
The Origin and Meaning of a Pauline Metaphor* (Grand Rapids: Eerdmans, 2007) 103–29;
nonetheless, Rosner would not necessarily disagree with the present line of thought
about Ephesians and the potential for indecent speech, for he notes, "In the list of
vices in 5:3–5 sexual sins dominate, a stress that is carried on with the referenes to
'deeds of darkness' and 'what is done in secret' in 5:11–12" (57).

was a catchall term for other sexual activities; and "covetousness" most likely referred to adultery, since that is what the cognate term meant in 1 Thess 4:6.[114] Basil and Chrysostom felt that with the general term "uncleanness," Paul was taking his own advice, and passing over actions that were not appropriate "even to mention."[115]

II.A.2. Ἐλέγχετε (Eph 5:11)

At this point we should consider vv. 11–13, where the readers are urged strenuously to live out their new status as "sons of light" (5:8) by rejecting the behavior that deserves God's wrath: " Take no part in the unfruitful works of darkness, but instead ἐλέγχετε [reprove/expose] them. For it is shameful *even to speak* of the things that they do in secret. But when anything is ἐλεγχόμενα [rebuked/exposed] by the light it becomes visible, for anything that becomes visible is light."

It is difficult to know how one should understand ἐλέγχειν. The word was used often "in the philosophical cure of souls"[116] for the attempt to persuade people that their approach to life was wrong— that they needed to change their ways.[117] It is used similarly in Jewish and Christian texts for the need to reprove an errant member of the community, frequently under the influence of Lev 19:17: "You shall not hate your kinsfolk in your heart. Reprove your kinsman [הוכח תוכיח את עמיתך; ἐλεγμῷ ἐλέγξεις τὸν πλησίον σου][118] but incur no guilt because of him" (JPS). [119]

But despite the fact that ἐλέγχειν often means "reprove" or "rebuke," such a meaning in Eph 5:11 would sit rather awkwardly with the

---

[114] Origen, *Com. Eph.* in Eph 5:3–4.

[115] Basil, *Ep.* 160.3 ("by the word 'uncleanness' the Apostle Paul includes the unmentionable acts of males and of females"); Chrysostom, *Hom. Col.* (PG 62:352): παρῆκε τὰ πράγματα, ἃ οὐδὲ εἰπεῖν καλόν, καὶ διὰ τῆς ἀκαθαρσίας ἅπαντα ἐνέφηνε.

[116] Friedrich Büchsel, "ἐλέγχω, κ.τ.λ.," *TDNT* 2:475.

[117] Troels Engberg-Pedersen defines the root idea for all uses of ἐλέγχειν as "confronting somebody or something with the aim of showing him or it to be, in some determinate respect, at fault" ("Ephesians 5,12–13: ἐλέγχειν and Conversion in the New Testament," *ZNW* 80 [1989]: 97). The lexicons offer a rather wide array of meanings. LSJ (s.v. ἐλέγχω II) includes: 1. cross-examine, question; 2. test, bring to the proof; 3. prove, bring convincing proof; 4. refute, confute; 5. get the better of; 6. expose (τινὰ ληροῦντα); 7. decide.

[118] Most of the occurrences of ἐλέγχειν in the LXX translate יכח.

[119] Sir 19:12–16; 1QS 5.24; CD 6.21–7.3; 9.2–8; Matt 18:15–17; cf. *T. Gad* 6.3–7. On the history of Leviticus 19:17, see James L. Kugel, "On Hidden Hatred and Open Reproach: Early Exegesis of Leviticus 19:17," *HTR* 80 (1987): 43–61. Naturally, "reprove" or "correct" was also a common meaning of the verb in Jewish and Christian texts that were not specifically dealing with Lev 19:17 (e.g. Luke 3:19; *Did.* 15.3).

reason given in the next verse. It is hard to understand what the author would have meant by "rebuke these deeds, *for* [γάρ] it is shameful even to mention them." As Abbott noted, "If the conjunction had been 'although' and not 'for,' it would be intelligible."[120] Besides, Ephesians seems to want believers to have as little contact with the "sons of disobedience" as possible (5:7).[121] Would Ephesians really urge believers to engage with the sons of darkness and to rebuke what they were not even to name?[122]

The command in Ephesians makes more sense when it is recognized that ἐλέγχειν can also designate a non-verbal activity such as "exposing" (RSV; NASB).[123] Many modern commentators have agreed that, in light of v. 12, Ephesians must refer to "exposure,"[124] with the understanding that the Ephesians's *behavior* would make the sinfulness of pagan conduct evident. The Euthalian Apparatus (probably fourth century), in fact, summarizes this section of Ephesians with the heading "Exposing evil with deeds, not with words [ἔργοις τὴν κακίαν

---

[120] Abbott, *Ephesians and Colossians*, 154. Hans Hübner, who interprets ἐλέγχειν as something verbal, recognizes that v. 12 might appear to be "ein gewisser Widerspruch zu 11b" (*An Philemon, An die Kolosser, An die Epheser* [HNT 12; Tübingen: Mohr, 1997], 233). He concludes v. 12 must mean not conversing in such a way that one approves bad behavior. Schlier sees v. 12 as concessive (*Epheser*, 239); Haupt discusses the problem in more detail than most (*Gefangenschaftsbriefe*, 198–201).

[121] Cf. the way 1QS *forbids* rebuking "the men of the pit" (1QS IX, 16).

[122] If Ephesians does have some verbal activity in mind, I suspect it has nothing to do with urging pagans to be converted (*pace* K. G. Kuhn) or wayward Christians to reform (*pace* Best). Since the object of ἐλέγχετε is "deeds," I suspect the verb could refer to a recounting of people's sins. This "rebuke by light" could even have been a sort of jargon for ritual recounting of sins, such that it was safe to "rebuke by light" even those vices it was not decent to "talk about." The passage from 1QS that contrasts foul speech with thanksgiving contains also the following: "My tongue shall enumerate always God's righteousness *and the unfaithfulness of men to the point of their complete sinfulness*" (X, 23–24). This is not rebuking or evangelizing; it is *enumerating* (תספר) the outsiders' evil deeds.

[123] BGAD gives this meaning for Eph 5:11, 13, noting that "the darkness-light theme suggests exposure, with implication of censure" (s.v. ἐλέγχω 1).

[124] J. O. F. Murray, *Epistle of Paul the Apostle to the Ephesians* (Cambridge: Cambridge University Press, 1914), 88; Lincoln, *Ephesians*, 330; Abbott, *Ephesians and Colossians*, 154–55; Perkins, *Ephesians*, 118 (though she suggests this exposure is achieved by means of words [119]); Schnackenburg, *Ephesians*, 226; Schlier, *Epheser*, 239 (including also a sense of examination and conviction); Barth, *Ephesians*, 570–72, opts for "disproving," but emphasizes that it is something non-verbal ("by your conduct"); Hübner acknowledges the ambiguity of ἐλέγχειν, but argues that here the sense is "die Bösen in ihrem bösen Tun überführen" (*Philemon*, 233); Muddiman, *Ephesians*, 239 (allowing for other possibilities).

ἐλέγχοντας, μὴ λόγοις]."[125] Understanding ἐλέγχειν to mean "expose" is especially appropriate when things, rather than persons, are the object of the verb,[126] as is the case here.[127] That "exposure" is the right sense receives some further confirmation by the fact that vv. 13–14 speak of "becoming manifest" and "light": "And everything exposed by the light becomes manifest, for everything that is manifest is light" (τὰ δὲ πάντα ἐλεγχόμενα ὑπὸ τοῦ φωτὸς φανεροῦται, πᾶν γὰρ τὸ φανερούμενον φῶς ἐστιν). John 3:20–21 furnishes a striking parallel, using the same words for "expose," "light," and "manifest." John says that the doer of bad deeds does not come to the light ἵνα μὴ ἐλεγχθῇ τὰ ἔργα αὐτοῦ, "so his deeds may not be exposed" (John 3:20). This is contrasted with the doer of truth, who comes to the light that his deeds may be made manifest (John 3:21).[128]

While the passage from John clarifies the sense of ἐλέγχειν, it cannot illuminate what Ephesians means by "everything that is exposed by light becomes manifest, for everything manifest is light."[129] Nevertheless, the overall thrust of these verses is clear enough. If the quotation in 5:14 comes from a baptismal hymn,[130] then the addressees themselves went from being darkness to light (5:8) when "Christ shone upon" them (5:14). The author argues that they must not join the sons of disobedience (5:7) or participate in their dark, fruitless deeds (5:11), which are so perverse as to be unnamable (5:12). But although the

---

[125] Cited from Dahl, *Studies*, 272.

[126] So Büchsel, *TDNT* 2:474n8; Abbott, *Ephesians and Colossians*, 154 (who notes that when Artemidorus speaks of dreams which indicate a revealing of secrets, he uses τὰ κρυπτὰ ἐλέγχεσθαι).

[127] The "fruitless deeds of darkness" (5:11) are the same as "what is done by them in secret" (5:12); it is these *deeds*, not the people doing them, which are "exposed" (note the neuter in v. 13: τὰ δὲ πάντα ἐλεγχόμενα). In 5:11, where there is no explicit object after ἐλέγχετε, the nearest antecedent is "fruitless deeds of darkness" (μὴ συνκοινωνεῖτε τοῖς ἔργοις τοῖς ἀκάρποις τοῦ σκότους, μᾶλλον δὲ καὶ ἐλέγχετε). Not since 5:7 have the *doers* of such deeds been mentioned (μὴ οὖν γίνεσθε συνμέτοχοι αὐτῶν).

[128] Cf. the similar language in 1 Cor 14:24–25: εἰσέλθῃ δέ τις ἄπιστος ἢ ἰδιώτης, ἐλέγχεται ὑπὸ πάντων, ἀνακρίνεται ὑπὸ πάντων, τὰ κρυπτὰ τῆς καρδίας αὐτοῦ φανερὰ γίνεται. Here ἐλέγχειν seems to have the meaning of "convict," as it can elsewhere in the NT and in Philo (who can also compare ἔλεγχος to "a bolt of light" [*Deus Immut.* 135]).

[129] Virtually every commentator acknowledges that the argument here is perplexing. Hübner's analysis is particularly detailed (*Philemon*, 233–36). I tend to agree with MacDonald that "it is perhaps best not to press this highly metaphoral [*sic*] language too hard for precise meaning" (*Colossians and Ephesians*, 316).

[130] So, e.g., Lincoln, *Ephesians*, 331; Best, *Ephesians*, 497–98; Barth, *Ephesians*, 547–75; Schnackenburg, *Ephesians*, 229; Dibelius-Greeven, 90–91; Schlier, *Epheser*, 240–41.

believers cannot join the world, they can have an effect on it. Just as *they* were transformed, so can they, by their conduct and presence as "sons of light," make the world's hidden deeds manifest and thus see them transformed into Christ's light, thereby fulfilling the process by which Christ "fills all things" and becomes "all in all" (1:23).

II.A.3. *"Shameful Even to Mention" (Eph 5:12)*
The phrase "it is shameful even to mention" (αἰσχρόν ἐστιν καὶ λέγειν) is in part simply rhetorical, meant here to emphasize the enormity of the pagans' sins. Such expressions were quite common, especially when accusing others of base sexual misconduct.[131] That it is rhetorical can be seen in how often people professed a reluctance to describe some misdeeds and then proceeded to do so anyway.[132] In a perfect illustration of such a move, Epiphanius actually quotes this very passage from Ephesians, only to dismiss it:

> When these wretches have joined with each other and—the truth is I am ashamed to relate the shameful things that take place among these people, for according to the holy Apostle, the things done among them are "shameful even to say"—nevertheless I will not be ashamed to describe what they are not ashamed to do, so that I may in every way stir up repulsion in those who hear what shameful acts are undertaken in their midst. (*Panarion* 26.4.4–5)

But even if people did not always find it particularly shameful to describe that which was "shameful even to say," this sort of expression nevertheless pointed to the very real sense that some things could not be decently discussed.[133] And from this general sensibility came the actual

---

[131] Aeschines, *Against Ctesiphon* (3.162): καὶ τὸ πρᾶγμα οὐδαμῶς εὔσχημον ἐμοὶ λέγειν; Philo, *Opif.* 80 (passions and cravings which it is not right even to mention [ἃς οὐδ᾽ εἰπεῖν θέμις]); *Plant.* 68; *Contempl.* 8; Dio Chrysostom, *Pol.* 12 (καὶ πολλὰ ἕτερα ποιῶν ἃ αἰσχύνομαι καθ᾽ ἕκαστον λέγειν); Tatian, *Oration* 23; Clement, *Paed.* 3.35.3 (of gold and silver utensils for purposes he is ashamed even to mention); Eusebius, *Hist. eccl.* 5.1.11.

[132] Cf. Lucian, *Ind.* 16 (οὐδ᾽ εἰπεῖν καλόν), with the rest of the text (e.g. ὦ κατάπυγον, *Ind.* 23). Similarly in *The Mistaken Critic* Lucian professes shame about what he must describe (αἰσχρὸν ἴσως ἐμοί [20]; αἰσχύνομαι διηγεῖσθαι [27]). Cf. also Suetonius, *Tib.* 44: "Some aspects of his criminal obscenity are almost too vile to discuss, much less believe" (Rolfe, LCL); Suetonius, of course, musters the courage to describe Tiberius's perversions in considerable detail.

[133] Demosthenes (*Ep.* 4.12 [DeWitt, LCL]), speaking about Theramenes, illustrates how these sorts of expressions could have a rhetorical force (emphasize just how bad some deeds were), while at the same time drawing attention to one's own laudable unwillingness to describe unseemly things in too much detail: "For many terrible and

moral advice to avoid discussing certain topics with plain language. From such diverse individuals as Democtritus,[134] Isocrates,[135] the author of the *Rhetorica ad Alexandrum*,[136] Charondas,[137] and Aelius Aristides,[138] we find the warning that what was shameful to do was shameful also to mention. According to Herodotus, the Persians had forbidden even naming those things they ought not do.[139] Ephesians 5:12 certainly has a rhetorical function of emphasizing just how depraved the "things done in secret" are. But coming after the explicit instructions about speech in 5:4, this phrase serves to remind the readers that it would be shameful even to discuss the pagans' worst behavior.[140]

II.A.4. αἰσχρότης

Having stated that sexual debaucheries were not even to be named by Christians, Ephesians proceeds to explain just what sort of talk it finds inappropriate for the saints. But before "foolish" and "witty" talk are mentioned, Ephesians uses the word αἰσχρότης, generally understood to be "obscenity" of deeds or words. Yet when one considers the few uses of the word αἰσχρότης outside of Ephesians 5:4, one is surprised that the word was set alongside two sins of the tongue; and Origen

---

shameful things, which a man would shrink from telling and would guard against mentioning in writing and, as I think, would be disgusted to hear of, each one of you, reminded by these words, knows to attach to this man, so that nothing indecent has been uttered by me and this man upon sight is a reminder to all of his own vices" (ἃ γὰρ εἰπεῖν ἄν τις ὀκνήσαι καὶ γράψαι φυλάξαιτ᾽ ἄν, οἶμαι δὲ κἂν ἀκούσαντα δυσχερᾶναι, ταῦτ᾽ ἀπὸ τούτων μνησθεὶς οἶδεν ἕκαστος ὑμῶν πολλὰ καὶ δεινὰ καὶ αἰσχρὰ τούτῳ προσόντα, ὥστ᾽ ἐμοί τε μηδὲν ἀναιδὲς εἰρῆσθαι, καὶ τοῦτον ὑπόμνημα τῶν ἑαυτοῦ κακῶν ὀφθέντα πᾶσιν εἶναι).

[134] "Even the talk of base deeds should be avoided" (φαύλων ἔργων καὶ τοὺς λόγους παραιτητέον) (Herman Diels, *Die Fragmente der Vorsokratiker* (6th ed.; Berlin: Weidmannsche, 1951), 2:184 [fragment B190]).

[135] "Whatever is shameful to do you must not consider it honourable even to mention" (ἃ ποιεῖν αἰσχρόν, ταῦτα νόμιζε μηδὲ λέγειν εἶναι καλόν [*Demon.* 15]).

[136] Pseudo-Aristotle, *Rhetorica ad Alexandrum* 1441b21: "Guard against describing even his shameful actions with shameful names " (φυλάττου δὲ καὶ τὰς αἰσχρὰς πράξεις μὴ αἰσχροῖς ὀνόμασι λέγειν).

[137] "Let it even be considered shameful to say that which is shameful" (*apud* Stobaeus, *Ecl.* 4.2.24).

[138] Aelius Aristides says that children are taught that what is shameful to do is not good even to mention (ὡς ἃ ποιεῖν αἰσχρόν, οὐδὲ λέγειν καλόν [*Or.* 29.13]).

[139] Herodotus, *Hist.* 1.138.

[140] Clement of Alexandria, for example, took the whole passage from Eph 5:4 to 5:12 to be instruction on purity of speech (*Strom.* 3.28.6). For the idea, cf. Ignatius, *Smyrn.* 7.2.

felt that it must be some sort of sexual sin.[141] The basic meaning of the word is "ugliness" or "deformity." Plato uses αἰσχρότης of a soul full of disproportion and "ugliness" or "deformity."[142] The Aristotelian *Divisiones* say that "disorder in the body is called *ugliness*."[143] Philodemus uses the word in a discussion of poetry (the *unattractiveness* of sounds).[144] Artemidorus, in a long list of opposites (e.g., "joy and sorrow"; "birth and death"), names αἰσχρότης as the opposite of κάλλος, i.e. "ugliness" as the opposite of beauty.[145] It is also used by Athenaeus of the *ugliness* of physical appearance (τὴν αἰσχρότητα τοῦ εἴδους [*Deipn.* 14.617A]). One would be surprised to learn from these uses that αἰσχρότης "is a general word indicating various forms of obscene action or speech,"[146] or that it "can be a synonym of *aischrologia*."[147] Judging from the way other authors used the word, it would have sounded to its first readers like "ugliness," with no more connection to bad behavior *or* bad language than the word "ugliness" does in English.

Commentators frequently understand αἰσχρότης as a synonym of αἰσχρολογία because they take αἰσχρότης in Eph 5:4 to be the analogue of the word αἰσχρολογία in Col 3:8.[148] But the vices that lead up to αἰσχρολογία in Col 3:8 are listed at Eph 4:31, not Eph 5:3–4.

---

[141] When commenting on Eph 5:5, Origen says that Paul only excludes the fornicator, the unclean person and the greedy person from the kingdom, since judgment would appear too harsh if people who used foolish talk and wittiness were also excluded. But Origen does not list αἰσχρότης with "foolish talk" and "wittiness" as if it were one more human frailty that it would be excessively harsh to condemn. To the contrary, he says that it comes as something of a surprise that Paul did not add that the "shameful" (αἰσχρός) person would be excluded from the kingdom. Thus Origen viewed αἰσχρότης as more like the (sexual) sins of v. 3 than the speaking sins of v. 4. In trying to account for why no judgment is pronounced on αἰσχρότης, Origen suggests that it might refer to some inner sin of passion that *leads* to fornication and uncleanness. Paul Ewald also understood αἰσχρότης to go more closely with what precedes than with what follows (*Epheser, Kolosser und Philemon*, 217–18).

[142] *Gorg.* 525a5.

[143] *Divisiones* 55.2: ἡ δὲ ἐν τῷ σώματι ἀταξία αἰσχρότης καλεῖται.

[144] Philodemus, *On Poems*, Fragment 84 line 12 (R. Janko, *Philodemus: On Poems, Book 1: Introduction, Translation and Commentary* [Oxford: Oxford University Press, 2000], 280).

[145] *Onirocriticon* 4.2.40.

[146] So Best, who also says "αἰσχρότης strictly refers to shameful behaviour" (*Ephesians*, 478); similarly Hoehner, *Ephesians*, 655.

[147] Barth, *Ephesians*, 561; so many commentaries. Nägeli claimed the word was restricted to Attic literature, and that it might therefore appear learned (*Wortschatz*, 14, 85). But the word occurs so rarely (only three times prior to Ephesians) that it is difficult to draw any conclusions about its register.

[148] So BGAD ("abstr. for concr. = αἰσχρολογία"); Karl Georg Kuhn, "Der Epheserbrief im Lichte der Qumrantexte," *NTS* 7 (1960–61): 339; Baker, *Speech-Ethics*, 171n121;

Eph 4:31	Col 3:8	Eph 4:29
πᾶσα πικρία (no parallel)	νυνὶ δὲ ἀπόθεσθε καὶ ὑμεῖς τὰ πάντα,	
θυμός	ὀργήν	
ὀργή	θυμόν	
κραυγή (= αἰσχρολογία?)	κακίαν	
βλασφημία ἀρθήτω ἀφ' ὑμῶν	βλασφημίαν	
σὺν πάσῃ κακίᾳ	αἰσχρολογίαν ἐκ τοῦ στόματος ὑμῶν	λόγος σαπρὸς ἐκ τοῦ στόματος ὑμῶν μὴ ἐκπορευέσθω

Figure 4.1: Ephesians 4:31, Colossians 3:8, and Ephesians 4:29

The only vice mentioned in Col 3:8 that is not mentioned in Eph 4:31 is αἰσχρολογία. And since only "bitterness" (πικρία) and "shouting" (κραυγή) in the Ephesians list lack a corresponding vice in Col 3:8, it is quite possible that Ephesians is representing αἰσχρολογία with κραυγή[149]—and perhaps also with λόγος σαπρός in Eph 4:29, where "let no rotten speech come *out of your mouth*" picks up the wording of Col 3:8 ("foul language *out of your mouth*").[150] The way Ephesians has rearranged and expanded Colossians will be discussed further below. The important point for the sense of αἰσχρότης is that it does *not* appear simply to be a parallel to Colossians's use of αἰσχρολογία: first, because αἰσχρότης was not a Greek word that normally *meant* αἰσχρολογία, and second, because Ephesians was not working its way through the vices of Col 3:8 when it mentions αἰσχρότης.

Rudolf Bultmann, "αἰσχύνω, κ.τ.λ.," *TDNT* 1:191; Vögtle, *Tugend- und Lasterkataloge*, 223n110; MacDonald, *Colossians and Ephesians*, 312; Lincoln, *Ephesians*, 319, 323; Bruce, *Ephesians*, 103 ("probably"); Kreitzer, "'Crude Language,'" 54.

[149] This is noted by Gnilka, *Kolosserbrief*, 185n37, and Hübner, *Philemon*, 221. That Ephesians seems to represent αἰσχρολογία with κραυγή indicates that Ephesians also perceived that Colossians had angry, abusive speech in view.

[150] Some manuscripts (F G it vg^mss co; Ambst) add μὴ ἐκπορευέσθω after αἰσχρολογία at Col 3:8, suggesting that they associated αἰσχρολογία with the λόγος σαπρός of Eph 4:29, as did many patristic commentators.

Despite Origen's understanding of the word, αἰσχρότης should be understood in connection with μωρολογία and εὐτραπελία.[151] αἰχρότης is associated so closely with the following two vices[152] that it must describe something "ugly" about *speech*.[153] And although it is not the case that αἰσχρότης *means* "foul language" in the way that αἰσχρολογία means "foul language," nevertheless when the author says, "you should not even name certain (sexual) sins, and let there be no ugliness and stupid talk or facetious wit," the word *ugliness* does designate some related behavior. In conjunction with "stupid talk" and "facetious wit," it picks out an aspect of what is objectionable in the speech the author wants to prohibit.

Abbott and Best have rightly wondered why, if the author of Ephesians meant to refer here to obscene speech, he did not use αἰσχρολογία, a word which is far more common, which refers to foul speech, and which he must have known from Colossians. I believe that the author of Ephesians sought to emphasize the quality of *ugliness* as one of the objectionable aspects of humorous talk. The effect is not to prohibit something less than Colossians's αἰσχρολογία, but rather to say more about foul language. Ephesians has, after all, expanded Colossians's one mention of foul language. It says no rotten language is to leave the mouth (4:29); there is to be no slander or shouting (4:31); sexual vices are not to be discussed at all (5:3, 12). Ephesians then drives home what

---

[151] Clement of Alexandria uses the word αἰσχρότης only twice (*Paed.* 2.50.1; *Strom.* 3.28.6), both times quoting Eph 5:4. In neither case does he say anything that illuminates how he understood it, but when discussing Eph 5:4, Clement treats the trio of sins as referring to obscene speech, so αἰσχρότης does not seem to have stuck out for him the way it did for Origen. Clement himself prefers to use the more familiar term αἰσχρολογία rather than any of the terms in Eph 5:4.

[152] The καί being understood explicatively (Haupt, *Gefangenschaftsbriefe*, 190n1; Schlier, *Epheser*, 234). Some manuscripts follow αἰσχρότης with the particle ἤ (א* A D* F G P 0278 81 104 326 365 1175 1241ˢ 1739 2464 *pc* latt syʰ sa boᵐˢˢ; Irˡᵃᵗ) instead of καί, thereby bringing it into even closer connection with the speech sins μωρολογία and εὐτραπελία. Best notes that the reading ἤ would set all three vices "on a level" (*Ephesians*, 478); and Gnilka, who prefers this reading, sees μωρολογία and εὐτραπελία as two species of the general category αἰσχρότης, meant to clarify it (*Epheserbrief*, 246–47). Several manuscripts read ἤ for all three connecting particles in 5:4, thereby connecting αἰσχρότης both to what precedes and to what follows (A D* F G 81 104 1241ˢ latt sa Irˡᵃᵗ).

[153] So Dibelius: "αἰσχρότης ist parallel mit den folgenden Ausdrücken wohl hauptsächlich auf die Rede zu beziehen" (*Kolosser*, 89); Lincoln, *Ephesians*, 323; Michel Bouttier, *L'Épitre de Saint Paul aux Éphésiens* (CNT 9b; Geneva: Labor et Fides, 1991), 221 ("obscénité, insanité, frivolité"—which would make a fine motto for a francophone fraternity). So Chrysostom, *Hom. Eph.* (PG 62:119), Theophylact, *Eph.* (PG 124:1104), and Oecumenius, *Eph.* (PG 118:1236) treat it as a speech vice.

is meant by "not even naming" by forbidding "ugliness, stupid talk, and facetiousness." Every student of Ephesians knows that this author was not reluctant to use several words where one might have sufficed. I suspect that in 5:4 αἰσχρότης, μωρολογία, and εὐτραπελία all refer to the same types of speech—as if to say, "no ugly, stupid, facetious talk."[154] The word αἰσχρότης picks out one of the qualities that the author finds repulsive in foul speech: such speech is ugly and deformed.

It is interesting to note in this regard that Iamblichus thought the foul language in religious rites symbolized and helped to acquaint people with (and turn them away from) the "ugliness" of matter.[155] Furthermore, Ephesians's use of "ugliness" for obscene language has an analogue of sorts in Latin. Quintilian and Augustine used *deformitas* for "foul language,"[156] despite the fact that in normal Latin usage *deformitas* meant "ugliness" or "deformity," just as αἰσχρότης did in Greek.[157]

II.A.5. μωρολογία

The meaning of μωρολογία is less mysterious than αἰσχρότης, thanks in part to a transparent etymology. Aristotle said that "large and outstanding ears" were a sign of "foolish talk and chatter" (μωρολογίας καὶ ἀδολεσχίας [*Hist. an.* 492b2–3]). Plutarch said it was precisely the drunken twaddle and foolish talk (μωρολογία) that makes drinking drunkenness.[158] Josephus uses μωρολογία to describe the "*nonsense* and

---

[154] Cf. Barth, *Ephesians*, 2:561. Some medieval interpretations of Eph 5:4 did draw interesting distinctions between these forms of sinful speech (*turpitudo, stultiloquium,* and *scurrilitas*). See the survey by Casagrande and Vecchio, *Les Péchés de la langue*, 281–89.

[155] Iamblichus, *De Mysteriis* 1.11: "And as for the 'obscene utterances' [τὰς δ' αἰσχρορρημοσύνας], my view is that they have the role of expressing the absence of beauty which is characteristic of matter and the previous ugliness of those things that are going to be brought to order, which, since they suffer from a lack of ordering, yearn for it in the same degree as they spurn the unseemliness that was previously their lot. So then, once again, one is prompted to seek after the causes of *form* and *beauty* when one learns the nature of *ugliness* from the utterance of obscenities [ἀπὸ τῆς τῶν αἰσχρῶν ῥήσεως τὸ αἰσχρὸν καταμανθάνοντα]; one rejects the practice of obscenities, while by means of uttering them one makes clear one's knowledge of them, and thus turns one's impulses in the opposite direction" (trans. Clarke, Dillon, and Hershbell, modified).

[156] Quintilian, *Inst.* 8.3.48; cf. 6.1.36; 8.3.49; Augustine, *De Dialectica* 7. Cf. *OLD* s.v. *deformitas* 4, "A lack of good taste (esp. in speech, writing), inelegance, impropriety." Cicero twice uses the word to refer to ugliness in speech, but not to obscenity (*De Orat.* 1.156; *Orat. Brut.* 56).

[157] Cf. also Cicero's use of *turpitudo* and *turpis* (as roughly synonymous with *obscenitas* and *obscenus*) in *Fam.* 9.22.

[158] "And the philosophers even in their very definition of drunkenness say that it is intoxicated and foolish talking [τὴν μέθην λέγουσιν εἶναι λήρησιν πάροινον]; thus drinking is not blamed if silence attends the drinking, but it is foolish talk which converts

lies" of Apion's stories about the Jews;[159] Sextus Empiricus uses it of the pointless "nonsense" of the grammarians (*Math.* 1.174). The word μωρολογία in Eph 5:4 may have a parallel in the Hebrew נבלות as it occurs in 1QS X, 21.[160]

II.A.6. εὐτραπελία

The "vice" that has attracted the most attention among interpreters of the New Testament is εὐτραπελία. Since Aristotle used εὐτραπελία to designate the golden mean in humorous badinage,[161] commentators have been led to wonder if Ephesians was ruling out not only grosser forms of speech but even a pleasant wit. Under the influence of Eph 5:4, Christian writers used εὐτραπελία and εὐτράπελος negatively.[162] But literature prior to or uninfluenced by Ephesians consistently treats the word in a positive sense.

Aristotle was not the only ancient author to speak of εὐτραπελία as a good thing, though nobody else had his precise taxonomy with εὐτραπελία as the mean between βωμολοχία and ἀγροικία.[163] In general εὐτραπελία was viewed as winsome; as was noted above, it is not infrequently joined with χάρις, "charm." A letter is more pleasant to read, a rebuke more easily absorbed, a cheeky remark more likely to be tolerated when εὐτραπελία was present, that is, if it was witty, quick, and clever.

It should be noted that εὐτραπελία can have a broader application than "wit": it is a cleverness, quickness, adaptability, or adroitness which can be applied to realms other than speech.[164] Several authors

---

the influence of wine into drunkenness [ἡ μωρολογία μέθην ποιεῖ τὴν οἴνωσιν]" (*Mor.* 504B [Helmbold, LCL]).

[159] *C. Ap.* 2.115: τῆς μωρολογίας ἅμα καὶ τῶν ψευσμάτων κατάγομον.

[160] See the discussion of that passage below, pp. 197–98.

[161] *Eth. eud.* 1234a4, 12, 15; *Eth. nic.* 1108a24; *Magna moralia* 1193a11–12; *Rhet.* 1389b11.

[162] So, for instance, Basil of Caesarea, who links εὐτράπελος with αἰσχρολόγος, whereas for Aristotle these represented a mean and an extreme. Basil (*Hom. Ps.* [PG 29:476]) grumbles about those who call the witty person "charming" and the foul-mouthed "urbane" (χαρίεντα μὲν τὸν εὐτράπελον λέγοντες, τὸν δὲ αἰσχρολόγον πολιτικόν). Thomas Aquinas was an exception to this trend. When he addressed "Whether There Can Be a Virtue About Games?" (2.2 Q. 168 Art. 2 *sed contra*), he quoted Aristotle as evidence that relaxation is good for the mind, and he described εὐτραπελία as a virtue.

[163] εὐτραπελία δ' ἐστὶ μεσότης βωμολοχίας καὶ ἀγροικίας, ἔστιν δὲ περὶ τὰ σκώμματα (*Magna moralia* 1193a11–12).

[164] Van der Horst, "Wittiness," 173.

refer to the etymology—"easily turning."[165] The adjective and adverb can describe versatility not only in speech,[166] but also in life[167] or politics[168]—or even in wrestling.[169] The adjectival form of the word seems to have been more liable to a negative sense—a "flexibility" verging on "fickleness." Pindar may have used εὐτράπελος negatively, though in both cases where he might have used the word the text is uncertain;[170] Aristophanes[171] and Isocrates[172] used the adjective in a somewhat negative sense.[173]

In an article that has persuaded many subsequent commentators on Ephesians 5, P. W. van der Horst seized on these negative instances

---

[165] Aristotle, *Eth. nic.* 1128a10; *Etym. Magn.* s.v., παρὰ τὸ εὖ τρέπεσθαι τὸν λόγον εἴρηται; cf. John Chrysostom, *Hom. Eph.* (PG 62:119): εὐτράπελος λέγεται ὁ ποικίλος, ὁ παντοδαπός, ὁ ἄστατος, ὁ εὔκολος, ὁ πάντα γινόμενος...Ταχέως τρέπεται ὁ τοιοῦτος καὶ μεθίσταται.

[166] Plutarch can at times still speak of εὐτραπελία *at* joking and conversation, thus specifying what sort of "adroitness" he had in mind (e.g. *Antony* 43.3: ἡ περὶ τὰς παιδιὰς καὶ τὰς ὁμιλίας εὐτραπελία; *Cicero* 5.6: ἡ δὲ περὶ τὰ σκώμματα καὶ τὴν παιδιὰν ταύτην εὐτραπελία).

[167] Thucydides 2.41.1: Athenians could show themselves sufficient for various tasks "with charm and versatility" (μετὰ χαρίτων μάλιστ᾽ ἂν εὐτραπέλως). Plutarch (*Mor.* 52E) says Alcibiades "joked, raised horses, and lived with urbanity and charm" (σκώπτων καὶ ἱπποτροφῶν καὶ μετ᾽ εὐτραπελίας ζῶν καὶ χάριτος).

[168] Aelian, *Varia Historia* 5.13.

[169] Plutarch, *Mor.* 274D: εὐτράπελοι καὶ παλαιστρῖται καλοί.

[170] At *Pyth.* 1.92 some manuscripts have κέρδεσιν εὐτραπέλοις, "cunning gains," others κέρδεσιν ἐντραπέλοις, "shameful gains." Similarly, εὐτράπελον has been conjectured for ἐντράπελον at *Pyth.* 4.104–5 (οὔτε ἔργον οὔτ᾽ ἔπος ἐντράπελον κείνοισιν εἰπών). Bruno Snell (*Pindari Carmina cum Fragmentis* [Leipzig: Teubner, 1953]) and Alexander Turyn (*Pindari Carmina cum Fragmentis* [Oxford: Basil Blackwell, 1952]) do not print εὐτράπ- for either passage.

[171] *Vesp.* 467–70: "[You] debar us from our country's established legal rights, without making any excuse or dextrous argument [λόγον εὐτράπελον], but autocratically?" (Henderson, LCL).

[172] Speaking of the decline in morals, Isocrates lamented that those who were "witty and good at joking" (τοὺς εὐτραπέλους δὲ καὶ τοὺς σκώπτειν δυναμένους) were in his day considered to be of good disposition, but in the past had been regarded as unfortunate (δυστυχεῖς) (*Areop.* 49).

[173] The word εὐτράπελος is used for the "wags" in some jokes from the *Philogelos* (e.g. 140–53; 262–64), but the humor and language in these jokes is no more risqué than the others. As racy as they get is *Philogelos* 151b = 260, a joke about an eye-doctor anointing a pretty young woman, where the comment of the "wag" plays on the ambiguity of κόρη ("girl"/"pupil"). But the words of the εὐτράπελος were often entirely wholesome, as in *Philogelos* 55, where a "funny student" (σχολαστικὸς εὐτράπελος), who had sold his books because he was broke, wrote to his father: "Congratulate me, Dad, for my books are really nourishing me!" For Aesop as a foul-mouthed "wag," cf. W *Vita Aesopi* 32: just after Aesop says to his owner's wife that she looks like she is "eager to fuck" (G *Vita*: κινητιᾶν; W *Vita*: βινητιῶσα), she says that this rotten (σαπρός, cf. Eph 4:29) slave is both talkative and a wise-guy (εὐτράπελος), and she wants to be reconciled.

in an effort to demonstrate that εὐτραπελία was a *"vox media*, having negative overtones nearly as often as positive ones."[174] This is a remarkable conclusion to draw from the evidence assembled. Aside from the handful of cases mentioned above, εὐτραπελία is almost always used positively,[175] as the following survey will demonstrate.[176]

Aristotle uses both the noun and adjective positively. Van der Horst cites Aristotle's comment that people call buffoons *"eutrapeloi"* (καὶ οἱ βωμολόχοι εὐτράπελοι προσαγορεύονται [*Eth. nic.* 1128a14–15]) as evidence that Aristotle "is aware of negative connotations as well" (174). But simply because Aristotle disagreed with others about who deserved to be called "witty" does not mean that he thought the term "witty" had negative connotations. (To say, "Nowadays anyone who can read is called 'smart,'" would not suggest that there was something negative about the word "smart.")[177]

When Plutarch complained about the fact that Chrysippus listed εὐτραπελία among the virtues (*Mor.* 441B), it was not because Plutarch thought there was something unvirtuous about εὐτραπελία; rather he was objecting to the way Chrysippus multiplied the number of virtues. Certainly Plutarch did not think εὐτραπελία was a bad thing, for he consistently uses the word positively. Antony was popular with the soldiers, he says, because of his "wit in jokes and conversations."[178] A rebuke made μετ᾽ εὐτραπελίας is one that a good man should receive cheerfully and without offence.[179] εὐτραπελία can be used negatively only in the sense that someone can take a good thing too far. Plutarch says of Cicero, "His adroitness [εὐτραπελία] with jests and fun was thought indeed to be a pleasant characteristic of a pleader; but he carried it to excess and so annoyed many and got the reputation of being

---

[174] P. W. van der Horst, "Is Wittiness Unchristian? A Note on εὐτραπελία in Eph. v. 4," in *Miscellanea Neotestamentica* (ed. T. Baarda, A. F. J. Klijn, and W. C. van Unnik; NovTSup 48; Leiden: Brill, 1978), 2:173.

[175] Cf. BGAD, s.v. εὐτραπελία: "mostly in a good sense."

[176] Spicq, who used van der Horst's article, recognized this positive pattern: "From this collection of texts—there are hardly any others before the Christian era—we can see that *eutrapelia* took on a more and more favorable sense, apparently the opposite of its Pauline meaning…" (Spicq, "εὐτραπελία," *TLNT* 2:146). But Spicq goes on to mitigate this conclusion with some of van der Horst's arguments about "the primitive pejorative sense of the word" (ibid.).

[177] Cicero (*Fam.* 7.32.2) complains that the dregs of the city find that which is tasteless to be charming (*venustus*). This does not mean *venustus* had a negative sense; it means that Cicero disagreed with the dregs' judgment.

[178] *Antony*, 43.3.

[179] *Mor.* 46D; cf. *Mor.* 629F.

malicious."[180] The point here is that Cicero's *wit* was good and others found it suitable for his craft; it was by overdoing it that he offended others.[181] On the whole, Plutarch—who was quick to complain about words when he deemed them too numerous, bitter, vulgar, or lewd— consistently used εὐτραπελία in a good sense.[182]

Plato says that older people use εὐτραπελία to ingratiate themselves to the young.[183] A Hippocratic text suggests doctors should use εὐτραπελία so as not to be unpleasantly dour with their patients.[184] Isocrates lists εὐτραπελία as part of an orator's education.[185] Polybius lists it as a positive attribute of Cleomenes of Sparta's private life (as distinct from his bad side as tyrant).[186] Polybius also uses it of a witticism that relaxed a court,[187] and as one aspect of savvy person's social skills.[188] Cicero used it of a friend's "graceful badinage," the quality that made his letter a pleasure to read.[189] Dionysius of Halicarnassus knows only a good sense for the word.[190] Diodurus Siculus describes Dionysius tolerating a bold statement because it was enjoyable witty.[191] We have already discussed

---

[180] ἡ δὲ περὶ τὰ σκώμματα καὶ τὴν παιδιὰν ταύτην εὐτραπελία δικανικὸν μὲν ἐδόκει καὶ γλαφυρόν, χρώμενος δ᾽ αὐτῇ κατακόρως πολλοὺς ἐλύπει καὶ κακοηθείας ἐλάμβανε δόξαν (*Cic.* 5.4 [Perrin, LCL]).

[181] Similarly, it is no strike against the goodness of εὐτραπελία that Diodorus Siculus mentions it in relation to drinking: "Through the jesting at the drinking bouts [διὰ τὴν ἐν τοῖς πότοις εὐτραπελίαν] he [Agathocles] discovered which of those who were flushed with wine were hostile to his tyranny" (*Bibl.* 20.63.6 [Greer, LCL]). Had Diodorus said, "while they were relaxed and enjoying themselves they betrayed their thoughts on the tyranny," it would not be evidence that "relaxation" or "enjoyment" were ambiguous words.

[182] *Agis et Cleomenes* 33.4.8; at *Mor.* 1066A it represents one type of joke; it is not equivalent to γέλως or βωμολοχία.

[183] *Resp.* 563a8.

[184] *Dec.* 7: "The physician must have at his command a certain ready wit [τινὰ εὐτραπελίην παρακειμένην], as dourness [τὸ αὐστηρόν] is repulsive both to the healthy and to the sick" (Jones, LCL).

[185] *Antid.* 296: "And, in addition to these advantages, they consider that the catholicity and moderation of our [the Athenians'] speech, as well as our flexibility of mind (τὴν ἄλλην εὐτραπελίαν) and love of letters, contribute in no small degree to the education of the orator."

[186] "...as a private individual most urbane and philanthropic" (εὐτραπελώτατος δὲ πάλιν ἰδιώτης καὶ φιλανθρωπότατος [*Hist.* 9.23.3]).

[187] *Hist.* 12.16.14.

[188] *Hist.* 23.5.7.

[189] *Fam.* 7.32.1.

[190] *De Demosthenis dictione* 54.54.

[191] "Now at the time Dionysius, smiling at the ready wit of the words [τὴν εὐτραπελίαν τῶν λόγων], tolerated the freedom of speech, since the joke took the edge off the censure" (*Bibl.* 15.6.4 [Oldfather, LCL]).

the positive uses in Philo[192] and Josephus.[193] We can only conclude that εὐτραπελία described a clever wit that was consistently recognized as an admirable talent, and that endeared one to others. Although several centuries removed, John Chrysostom's sermons about εὐτραπελία reveal that he suspects his listeners will find it a bit much to come down so hard on mere "wittiness."[194]

The question, then, is why would anybody would want to forbid *that*? Why did Ephesians object to εὐτραπελία as "inappropriate"? There are Mishnaic prohibitions against jesting and levity, activities that, like being "witty," might seem innocuous enough. Rabbi Akiba said, "Jesting and levity [שחוק וקלות] accustom a man to lewdness [לערוה]" (*m. Abot* 3.13).[195] The idea that levity led to sexual misdeeds would account very nicely for the connection between Eph 5:3–4 and 5:5. But Ephesians

---

[192] *Legat.* 361, cited above, p. 171. It is true that Philo is dismayed by the emperor's joke and disgusted at his attendants' flattery. But the force of σὺν εὐτραπελίᾳ καὶ χάριτι has to be positive, for nobody flatters an emperor by acting like he has said something "buffoonish" or "in bad taste." The attendants were suggesting that there was something *charming* and *witty* in the emperor's words. That Philo disagrees with their assessment of the humor is irrelevant to the sense of the words σὺν εὐτραπελίᾳ καὶ χάριτι.

[193] In addition to *A.J.* 12.170–73, discussed above (p. 171), cf. *A.J.* 12.214, where Hyrcanus gives a reply at dinner that impresses King Ptolemy as "clever," and the king orders all to applaud to show approval of the "wit" (εὐτραπελία).

Because van der Horst sees something negative in these cases—namely a willingness to make jokes at the expense of others—we must emphasize that Josephus's entire portrayal of Joseph is positive. Because of Joseph's impeccable manners, those who knew him "greatly admired his liberality and the dignity of his character" (τὸ γὰρ ἐλευθέριον αὐτοῦ καὶ τὸ σεμνὸν τοῦ ἤθους λίαν ἠγάπησεν [*A.J.* 12.166]). Athenion describes Joseph to Ptolemy as an ἀγαθός and φιλότιμος νεανίσκος (*A.J.* 12.171). Thus Josephus portrays a young man as ἀγαθός and φιλότιμος, possessing τὸ ἐλευθέριον and τὸ σεμνὸν τοῦ ἤθους—in short, someone who is dignified (not craven or prone to flattery) and who understands and executes duties such as hospitality. In painting this picture, Josephus includes among Joseph's attractive qualities the fact that he won over the king with his χάρις and εὐτραπελία.

[194] *Hom. Eph.* 17 is full of examples. Chrysostom expects his listeners will "think it nothing" to joke and say urbane things (PG 62:118); he admits he must prove the gravity of the sin lest he appear to be going on about something entirely trivial (PG 62:120).

Clement of Alexandria can omit εὐτραπελία even when quoting Eph 5:4 (*Strom.* 3.28.6). Was it perhaps more comfortable for him to imagine the Apostle condemning "ugly" and "foolish" talk than "wittiness"? This probably makes too much of the omission, for Clement includes the word when quoting Eph 5:4 at *Paed.* 2.50.1; cf. *Paed.* 2.53.3.

[195] Cf. *m. Abot* 6:6: "Greater is [learning in] the Law than priesthood or kingship; for kingship is acquired by thirty excellences and the priesthood by twenty-four; but [learning in] the Law by forty-eight. And these are they: by study, by the hearing of the ear, *by the ordering of the lips*, by the understanding of the heart, … *by moderation in* … conversation, and *jesting.*"

does *not* say "for such talk leads to sex." Once again we can contrast Eph 5:3–5 with *Did.* 3.3, where the connection (if not the mechanism) between foul language and adultery is made explicit. It is precisely the absence of such an explanation that makes Ephesians all the more striking. Instead of learning what εὐτραπελία *leads to*, we are told that it is itself (along with αἰσχρότης and μωρολογία) "inappropriate" (ἃ οὐκ ἀνῆκεν). Yet we have seen that *eutrapelia* was not normally inappropriate. We have no evidence of anyone else rejecting *eutrapelia* outright, the way they rejected "buffoonery" (βωμολοχία) or foul language (αἰσχρολογία). Many groups or individuals seeking a philosophical, virtuous life disapproved of tawdry, lewd, or vulgar talk. But forbidding εὐτραπελία at the end of the first century would have sounded as strange and severe as forbidding "wittiness" today.[196] The opposite of being "witty" was being "austere"[197] or inhumane[198]—or being the sort of "rustic" who lacked the culture to make or enjoy jokes.[199]

To be fair to Ephesians, the word εὐτραπελία is not here used on its own; it is used with two other terms that had more pejorative connotations: "ugliness" and "stupid talk." That fact might suggest that Ephesians objects not to the best in wit but to "ugly, stupid wit" (this is why I have translated εὐτραπελία in Eph 5:4 with "facetiousness," which has a slightly more negative tone). Nonetheless, it would have been just as easy to object to "ugly, stupid *buffoonery*," or to contrast "ugly wit" with "charming, good-natured wit," thereby avoiding the implication that wit itself might be "inappropriate."[200] Is Ephesians trying to encourage the creation of serious *personae*—trying to out-do the Catos and the Pythagorases of the world? Perhaps Ephesians aspires for a community so serious that it will not tolerate any form of drollery

---

[196] Bouttier, *Éphésiens*, 221.

[197] Philo, *Plant.* 167. So the Hippocratic corpus (*Dec.* 7, noted above), and Aristotle, who says that the austere (αὐστηροί) enjoy their *opposites*, the εὐτράπελοι (*Eth. eud.* 1240a2–3).

[198] Cicero said that the Celts lacked *lepos* (charm, wit) and *humanitas* (humanity) (*Prov. cons.* 29, noted by Krostenko, *Language of Social Performance*, 5).

[199] John Burnett suggests Aristotle's use of the term ἄγροικος picked out the boors who were stock characters in comedy, "people who steer clear of pleasures even in moderate and necessary indulgences" (John Burnett, *The Ethics of Aristotle* [London: Methuen & Co., 1900], 198).

[200] Philo thinks twaddle (ληρεῖν) is inappropriate, but he commends *proper humor*. God and Moses were in favor of some joking (and some drinking) as entirely fitting for the wise man (*Plant.* 167–70).

at all.[201] Philo admired the Therapeutae, Josephus praised the Essenes, and many people lauded the Pythagoreans for their severe control of the tongue (and Cicero actually gives Pythagoras as his example of how a person could achieve greatness even without a quick wit [*Off.* 1.108]). But where other texts cite abstaining from drollery as the characteristic of "severe" people, Ephesians excludes wit "for the holy." And instead of describing what sort of attractive humor should take the place of ugly jokes, Ephesians presents *thanksgiving* (εὐχαριστία) as the alternative. Just how unusual this contrast is can be seen in Origen's effort to interpret the verse. Origen thought that in Eph 5:4 εὐχαριστία must be a sort of semitic equivalent for εὐχαριτία, "graciousness."[202]

Although foreign to Greek and Roman discussions of inappropriate language, this very contrast between ugly talk and thanksgiving is also found in the Rule of the Community. I believe that a closer examination of that text can provide a helpful model for the moral logic at work in Ephesians's treatment of speech.

II.B. *Speech Rules in 1QS*

Scholars comparing Ephesians and the texts from Qumran[203] have noted a wide variety of similarities. The Rule of the Community (1QS), in particular, shares not only a dualistic outlook ("sons of light" and "sons

---

[201] Perkins says of εὐτραπελία, "This [i.e. *sensu malo*] use of the word may reflect a cultural sense that the proper bearing of a wise person requires seriousness in speech" (*Ephesians*, 115).

[202] Origen concludes from 5:4, "Therefore one must not be stupid and facetious, but agreeable and charming" (μωρόλογον μὲν οὖν καὶ εὐτράπελον οὐ δεῖ εἶναι, εὐχάριτον δὲ καὶ χαρίεντα). This is almost certainly not what Ephesians meant (*pace* Odo Casel, "Εὐχαριστία-εὐχαριτία," *BZ* 18 [1929]: 84–85), but it indicates what an educated Greek might expect to see contrasted with "ugliness, stupid talk, and facetiousness." Origen also expresses his perplexity at finding εὐχαριστία contrasted with foolish and vulgar speech in his commentary on Romans: "Why does he take 'thanksgiving' as a substitute for 'foolish speech' and 'vulgar speech' which are 'not proper'...? It seemed to me, therefore, that 'thanksgiving' had been taken as a substitute for 'graciousness' as it were, not at all excluding, among the proper forms of speech, that which is gracious or refined and cheerful in conversations, but foolish and vulgar speech as buffoonery" (translation by Ronald E. Heine, *The Commentaries of Origen and Jerome on St Paul's Epistle to the Ephesians* [Oxford: Oxford University Press, 2002], 211n12).

[203] Franz Mußner, "Contributions made by Qumran to the Understanding of the Epistle to the Ephesians," in *Paul and Qumran* (ed. Jerome Murphy-O'Connor; Chicago: The Pilgrim Press, 1968), 159–78; K. G. Kuhn, "The Epistle to the Ephesians in the Light of the Qumran Texts" in *Paul and Qumran* (ed. Jerome Murphy O'Connor, O. P.; Chicago: Priory Press, 1968), 115–31 (Reprint of Kuhn, "Der Epheserbrief im Lichte der Qumrantexte," *NTS* 7 [1960–61]: 334–46); Nils Alstrup Dahl, *Studies*, 107–44.

of darkness"), but even bears a certain resemblance in its prose style.[204] The similarities include comments about speech that bear striking resemblance to Eph 5:3–4.[205] One passage from 1QS contrasts lewd and detestable speech with thanksgiving in a way similar to Eph 5:4:

> Neither shall be heard from my mouth lewdness [ולוא ישמע בפי נבלות] and iniquitous deceit, nor craftiness and lies be found on my lips. But the fruit of holiness (shall be) on my tongue, and abominations [שקוצים] shall not be found on it. With thanksgiving hymns I will open my mouth, and my tongue shall enumerate always God's righteousness and the unfaithfulness of men to the point of their complete sinfulness. (1QS X, 21–23)[206]

Not only does the contrast between bad speech and "thanksgiving" resemble that of Eph 5:4, but שקוצים, like the Greek αἰσχρότης, is not a term normally associated with speech at all.[207] Many have seen μωρολογία as parallel to נבלות, "foolishness."[208] It is also possible, however, that נבלות had connotations of *lewdness*.[209] נבלות means immodesty or shamelessness; it is used in Hosea 2:12 of the harlot's lewdness (or perhaps her vagina).[210] As we saw above (pp. 116–17), several rabbinic passages use נבלות for lewd or obscene discussions of sex. The noun נבלות[211] and the piel of נבל with פה meant to speak obscenely.[212] If נבלות פה was used this way in later Hebrew, it is quite possible that already in 1QS the prayer that נבלות never be heard from one's פה is a prayer about avoiding lewd, obscene speech.

---

[204] For examples, see Kuhn, "Ephesians in the Light of the Qumran Texts," 116–18; Dahl, *Studies*, 111–12.

[205] Most of the recent commentaries cite 1QS 10.21–23 as a parallel to Eph 5:3–4. Less persuasive is Kuhn's idea that Eph 5:3–5 is related to the "three nets of Belial" (CD 4.15–17) ("Ephesians in the Light of the Qumran Texts," 121).

[206] Trans. James H. Charlesworth, *Rule of the Community and Related Documents* (vol. 1 of *The Dead Sea Scrolls*; ed. James H. Charlesworth; Tübingen: Mohr, 1993).

[207] In the Bible it is used often of idols (Deut 29:16; 1 Kings 11:5; 2 Kings 23:13, 24); of the pagan altar in the temple (Dan 11:31; 12:11); of Israel when idolatrous (Hos 9:10); once it is used of "filth" (Nah 3:6).

[208] Kuhn, "Epheserbrief im Lichte der Qumrantexte," 339; Wibbing, *Tugend- und Lasterkataloge*, 94; Gnilka, *Epheserbrief*, 247.

[209] Florentino García Martínez renders it here with "vulgarity" (*The Dead Sea Scrolls Translated* [trans. Wilfred G. E. Watson; 2d ed.; Leiden: Brill, 1994]). It is also rendered "foolishness" (Michael Wise, Martin Abegg, Jr., and Edward Cook, eds., *The Dead Sea Scrolls: A New Translation* [San Francisco: HarperSanFrancisco, 1996]).

[210] *HALOT* s.v.

[211] Cf. *Leviticus Rabbah* 5.3: דברי נבלות.

[212] As it does in Modern Hebrew. Reuben Alcalay, *The Complete Hebrew-English Dictionary* (Ramat-Gan: Massada Publishing Co., 1981): "to talk obscenely, to swear like a trooper."

1QS also prohibits silly or light talk. A punishment of three months is decreed for the person who "utters in his mouth a foolish word [ידבר בפיהו דבר נבל]" (1QS VII, 9).[213] This statement is followed by several rules that seem to have in common a concern with courtesy and decorum (and perhaps an avoidance of inauspicious actions). Forbidden are: talking in the middle of the words of one's fellow; going to sleep; leaving; walking around naked; spitting; exposing one's "hand" and wearing clothes which allow nakedness to be seen; giggling inanely; and gesticulating with one's left hand. Kuhn suggests that the commands against a foolish word (1QS VII, 9) and "giggling inanely" (ישחק בסכלות, 1QS VII, 14) can account for Ephesians's curiously negative stance toward εὐτραπελία.[214] But even if one accepted his claim that Ephesians is in some sense based on a common tradition,[215] we will have merely pushed the need for explanation back one more step. Why was 1QS opposed to vulgar, disgusting talk and silly laughter?

Rather than appealing to a common source for 1QS and Ephesians, we might also ask what patterns of piety, what assumptions about God, and what uses of scripture they have in common. Both Ephesians and several texts from Qumran imagine God to be present in the community on analogy with the way the Bible presents God as present in the temple. Could that common assumption account for some of the behavior that these various texts find unacceptable? Baruch Bokser has shown that in the literature from Qumran and in some early rabbinic literature, the idea that God was present in the community or in a special liturgical moment (e.g. prayer or reading scripture) led to the application of biblical rules for God's presence.[216] This may offer a fruitful model for understanding Ephesians as well. It was the holiness of the community that made certain speech inappropriate (5:3–4); this holiness derives in part from the fact that the believers have been brought into the presence of God, a sacred space in which no unseemly thing could be brought—or uttered.

---

[213] נבל means "futile," "worthless," "godless" (*HALOT* s.v.). Although it is cognate with נבלות, it is not used specifically of lewdness or obscenity.

[214] Kuhn, "Ephesians in the Light of the Qumran Texts," 122.

[215] Kuhn suggests more direct dependence, insisting that the similarities can "hardly be explained except on the basis of a continuity of tradition" ("Ephesians in the Light of the Qumran Texts," 120).

[216] Bokser, "Approaching Sacred Space," *HTR* 78 (1985): 279–99.

II.C. *Profaning a Sanctum*

The Bible depicts God both as omnipresent (Psa 139:8), but also as dwelling in specific places such as the tabernacle, the temple, or the war camp.[217] These spaces where God was especially present required special behavior. Moses was told to take off his shoes before approaching the burning bush (Exod 3:5); the priests wore a special undergarment so that their nakedness would not show when they ascended to the altar (Exod 20:23 [26 English]; 28:42–43); and all of Israel had to avoid impurities before approaching the tabernacle. Numbers 5:2–3 applies rules of the tabernacle to the whole camp, since it claims that God dwells in the camp.[218] Deuteronomy 23:9–14 (10–15 Hebrew) states that God's presence in the war camp was incompatible with anything indecent such as nocturnal emission or defecation:

> When you are encamped against your enemies you shall guard against any impropriety [מכל דבר רע]. If there is among you any man who is not clean by reason of what chances to him by night, then he shall go outside the camp, he shall not come within the camp; but when evening comes on, he shall bathe himself in water, and when the sun is down, he may come within the camp. You shall have a place outside the camp and you shall go out to it; and you shall have a stick with your weapons; and when you sit down outside, you shall dig a hole with it, and turn back and cover up your excrement. *Because the LORD your God walks in the midst of your camp*, to save you and to give up your enemies before you, therefore your camp must be holy, that he may not see anything *indecent* [ערות דבר] among you, and *turn away from you*. (Deut 23:9–14 RSV)

Because God is present in the camp, Deuteronomy says, there must be nothing unseemly or unbecoming.[219]

What we find in the Dead Sea Scrolls (including 1QS), in Josephus's description of the Essenes, and in some rabbinic literature is that this "injunction to avoid what is unseemly" was extended when the place of

---

[217] These views were apparently not felt to be mutually exclusive. Even as Solomon dedicated a temple to God, he acknowledged that "even heaven and the highest heaven cannot contain you, much less this house that I have built!" (1 Kings 8:27).

[218] "Command the Israelites to put out of the camp everyone who is leprous, or has a discharge, and everyone who is unclean through contact with a corpse; you shall put out both male and female, putting them outside the camp; they must not defile their camp, where I dwell among them" (Num 5:2–3).

[219] The bull's dung was also taken outside the camp (Exod 29:14). Somewhat different is Num 35:34, which is concerned with *moral* impurity rather than with things that are ritually impure or simply unseemly (for the distinction, cf. Jonathan Klawans, *Impurity and Sin in Ancient Judaism* [Oxford: Oxford University Press, 2000]).

God's presence was redefined.[220] In several of the texts from Qumran, the idea that community was the locus of God's presence led them to apply the biblical laws about the tabernacle or the war camp to their whole community. In the Temple Scroll, for instance, the biblical restrictions for the camp (Deut 23), the purificatory rituals of Exod 19:10–15 (in preparation for the revelation at Sinai), and the purity regulations of Lev 13 are all applied to the whole "city of the sanctuary" (עיר המקדש).[221] Similarly, in the War Scroll the idea of an eschatological battle in which God and his angels would be in the warriors' midst made the rules of Deut 23:10–15 relevant. The War Scroll speaks of the need "to keep ourselves from any immodest nakedness [כול ערות דבר רע]" because "you, great and terrible God, will be in our midst" (1QM X, 1).[222] Here the War Scroll's phrase כול ערות דבר רע points toward the rules of Deut 23, combining the דבר רע of Deut 23:10 with the ערות דבר of Deut 23:15. 1QM VII, 4–7 combines these words in the same way, relating the need for decency this time to the presence of the angels among the community.[223]

Josephus's account of the Essenes suggests that they applied the rule of the war camp to their communal life. Josephus says that the Essenes were given shovels so that they could bury their excrement; on the Sabbath they avoided defecation altogether (*B.J.* 2.147–49). This reflects an application of Deut 23:10–15 to their communal life, with the most holy day of the week requiring an even more stringent avoidance of the profane. The rabbis applied these biblical rules to moments when "an individual acts so as to elicit the sacred."[224] An example of such

---

[220] Bokser, "Approaching Sacred Space," 281.

[221] So Lawrence H. Schiffman, *The Eschatological Community of the Dead Sea Scrolls: A Study of the Rule of the Congregation* (SBLMS 38; Atlanta: Scholars Press, 1989), 40–42. Cf. 11QT³ XLV, 7–18, which excludes a person with nocturnal emissions (Deut 23:11). 11QT³ XLVI, 13–16 says that the outhouses must be out of view of the Temple city; lepers are also excluded. Cf. Bokser, "Approaching," 282–83.

[222] This and all further translations of the scrolls are taken from Martínez, *The Dead Sea Scrolls Translated*.

[223] "And no lame, blind, paralysed person nor any man who has an indelible blemish on his flesh, nor any man suffering from uncleanness in his flesh, none of these will go out to war with them. All these shall be volunteers for war, perfect in spirit and in body, and ready for the day of vengeance. And every man who has not cleansed himself of his 'spring' on the day of battle will not go down with them, *for the holy angels are together with their armies*. And there will be a space between all their camps and 'the place of the hand' of about two thousand cubits. *And no immodest nakedness* [וכול ערות דבר רע] will be seen in the surroundings of all their camps" (1QM VII, 4–7).

[224] Bokser, "Approaching," 287.

an act was reciting the Shema', which was not to be done too close to stinking water or urine and excrement.[225]

Other texts that did not specifically apply the rules of Deuteronomy or Leviticus still argue that if God dwelt among the people, heightened purity was required.[226] For instance 2 Cor 6:14–7:1, a passage that bears many similarities to the literature from Qumran,[227] uses the image of God dwelling in the people's midst to urge separation and purity: "'Therefore come out from them, and be separate from them, says the Lord, and *touch nothing unclean....*' Since we have these promises, beloved, let us *cleanse ourselves from every defilement of body and of spirit*, making holiness perfect in the fear of God" (2 Cor 6:17–7:1).

II.D. *Not Fitting for Holy Ones*

Ephesians also claims that the space in which the believers exist has been made holy by God's presence. (And apropos of the martial imagery of Deut 23:9–14 and 1QM, we should not forget that Ephesians says that the church is engaged in a spiritual, eschatological war [Eph 6:10–17]). Corporately the community represents "God's household" and "temple," and God dwells in them in the Spirit (2:19–22).[228] Furthermore, the believer is said to have been "seated with Christ in the

---

[225] Bokser discusses *m. Ber.* 3; 9:5; *t. Ber.* 2.12–21; *t. Meg.* 12.18; *Sifre Deut.* 258 ("Approaching," 292–95); see also Bokser's *Post Mishnaic Judaism in Transition: Samuel on Berakhot and the Beginnings of Gemara* (BJS 17; Chico, Calif.: Scholars Press, 1980): 22–24. Bokser's thesis finds further confirmation when one considers Christian texts roughly contemporaneous with these rabbinic texts. The *Didascalia apostolorum*, for instance, addresses Christians who were unwilling to come to prayer or to hear scripture read during menstruation or after sexual relations.

[226] Much has been written on the image of the temple and dwelling of God. For treatment of many of the texts, as well as references to secondary literature, see Christoph Gregor Müller, *Gottes Pflanzung, Gottes Bau, Gottes Tempel* (Frankfurt am Main: Josef Knecht, 1995).

[227] On this passage, cf. J. A. Fitzmyer, S.J., "Qumran and the Interpolated Paragraph in 2 Cor 6:14–7:1," *CBQ* 23 (1961): 271–80; J. Gnilka, "2 Cor 6.14–7:1 in the Light of the Qumran Texts and the Testaments of the Twelve Patriarchs," in *Paul and Qumran*, 48–68; H. D. Betz, "2 Cor 6:14–7:1: An Anti-Pauline Fragment?" *JBL* 92 (1973): 88–108.

[228] "So then you are no longer strangers and sojourners, but you are fellow citizens with the saints and members of the household of God, built upon the foundation of the apostles and prophets, Christ Jesus himself being the cornerstone, in whom the whole structure is joined together and grows into a holy temple in the Lord [εἰς ναὸν ἅγιον ἐν κυρίῳ]; in whom you also are built into it for a dwelling place [κατοικητήριον] of God in the Spirit" (Eph 2:19–22 RSV).

heavenly places" (2:6).[229] In both images, the individual believer and the community exist in God's sacred presence. Ephesians even uses cultic terms for holiness to express the purpose of God's election and cleansing of the church. God chose believers "to be *holy* and *blameless*" (1:4),[230] and Christ will "present the church to himself in splendor, without a spot or wrinkle or thing of the kind—yes, so that she may be *holy* and *without blemish*" (5:27).[231] These terms (used also in Col 1:22) were used in the LXX for the sacrificial animals and the priests.[232] For Ephesians, God's presence is central to the good news the letter is so interested in celebrating. It is God's presence in the Spirit that provides the gentile believers their access to God (2:18) and their oneness with the commonwealth of Israel (2:12, 18). The believers' holiness and God's presence were related, both because a holy God could only dwell among holy people, and because the people were sanctified by God's presence.

In Eph 5:3–4 the author says that the Ephesians are not to discuss and make jokes about[233] the gentiles' sexual vices because such talk is not "fitting"[234] for *holy* people. The word ἁγίοις lacks the definite article, thus stressing the *quality* of holiness (rather than simply naming a group, "the saints").[235] When Aristotle, Plutarch, and Cicero discuss "fittingness" (τὸ πρέπον or *decorum*), they say that poets must make utter-

---

[229] συνεκάθισεν ἐν τοῖς ἐπουρανίοις ἐν Χριστῷ Ἰησοῦ.

[230] καθὼς ἐξελέξατο ἡμᾶς ἐν αὐτῷ πρὸ καταβολῆς κόσμου εἶναι ἡμᾶς ἁγίους καὶ ἀμώμους.

[231] μὴ ἔχουσαν σπίλον ἢ ῥυτίδα ἤ τι τῶν τοιούτων, ἀλλ᾽ ἵνα ᾖ ἁγία καὶ ἄμωμος.

[232] Num 6:14; 19:2; cf. Philo, *Sacr.* 51; of Christ *qua* sacrifice, 1 Pet 1:19. Dahl notes: "It may be compared with the notion of ritual purification, when the purpose of Christ's activity is seen as intended to make the church 'holy and unblemished', like a sacrifice or like a priest when he stands before the altar" (*Studies*, 421).

[233] The words μωρολογία and εὐτραπελία are not used to designate the sort of abusive language people use when fighting, so we can be fairly confident that joking, rather than fighting, is in view.

[234] καθὼς πρέπει ἁγίοις (5:3). Surely in 5:4 the phrase "which are not fitting" (ἃ οὐκ ἀνῆκεν) also implies "not fitting *for the holy*," since it would be impossible to say *simpliciter* that εὐτραπελία was "inappropriate" (Heinrich Schlier, "ἀνήκει," *TDNT* 1:360: "This unsuitability may concur with the judgment of the world [Col 3:18] or it may contradict it [Eph. 5:4: εὐτραπελία, for example, is accepted by the world]"). On the tense of ἀνῆκεν, cf. Ernest de Witt Burton, *Syntax of the Moods and Tenses in New Testament Greek* [3d ed.; Edinburgh: T. & T. Clark, 1898] §32; Harris, *Colossians and Philemon*, 178–79; BDF §358.

[235] So Schnackenburg, *Ephesians*, 218; Lincoln, *Ephesians*, 322; Best, *Ephesians*, 477. Perkins suggests 5:3 "might be trading on the semantic ambiguity of the term 'saints.'... This dual meaning provides the logical force behind the phrase. Such vices would not belong to speech among the angels" (*Ephesians*, 115).

ances fit the characters who speak them.[236] Nasty words might never be attractive, but they are *fitting* for a bad man.[237] It is significant that Ephesians says καθὼς πρέπει ἁγίοις and not καθὼς πρέπει σέμνοις or ἀγαθοῖς. Others said foul speech was inappropriate for a good man,[238] for a king,[239] for a serious person,[240] for an orator,[241] for an upright citizen,[242] or for a well-ruled city.[243] Yet for Ephesians, it is the *holiness* of the congregation that makes foul and frivolous talk unacceptable. Ephesians objects to loose talk as inappropriate and unfitting because Christians are holy; they are holy in part because they are in God's holy presence.

The objection could be raised at this point that most of the texts that have been cited about decency in the presence of God were concerned with *actual* nudity, physical imperfections, and excrement, not with *words* about such things. But the rabbinic concern with removing the profane from God's presence extends beyond physically repulsive items to profane or obscene speech. The Mishnah says that "a man should not behave himself unseemly [יקל]"[244] while opposite the Eastern Gate [of the Temple] since it faces toward the Holy of Holies" (*m. Ber.* 9.5). More striking is the fact that Leviticus Rabbah interprets the "unseemly thing" (עֶרְוַת דָּבָר) of Deut 23:15 as "unseemly talk" (עֶרְוַת דָּבָר), which R. Samuel bar Nahman (A.D. *ca.* 260) said meant "lascivious talk" (נִבְל הַפֶּה).[245] At a literary level, this midrash is made

---

[236] Cf. Aristotle, *Rhet.* 1404b12–18.

[237] Cf. Plutarch, *Mor.* 18D: οἰκεῖα δὲ καὶ πρέποντα τοῖς αἰσχροῖς τὰ αἰσχρά. One of Plutarch's complaints about Aristophanes was that the characters' words were not *fitted* to their characters (*Mor.* 853D).

[238] Epictetus *Diatr.* 4.9.8 speaks of someone who used to utter words "worthy of a good man" (λόγους ἐλάλεις πρέποντας ἀνδρὶ ἀγαθῷ).

[239] Dio Chrysostom (*2 Regn.* 3) has Alexander tell his father that he refuses any poetry other than Homer since not all poetry is "fitting for a king" (δοκεῖ μοι, ὦ πάτερ, οὐ πᾶσα ποίησις βασιλεῖ πρέπειν).

[240] Quintilian (*Inst.* 6.3.25) refers to a jest "which was not appropriate for an orator or any *serious* man" (*quod neque oratori neque ulli viro gravi conveniat*).

[241] Quintilian, *Inst.* 6.3.46; 6.3.29.

[242] Aristotle; Quintilian, *Inst.* 6.3.83 (Russell, LCL): "On the other hand, foul or brutal language, however funny, is unworthy of a decent citizen" (*illud vero, etiamsi ridiculum est, indignum tamen est homine liberali, quod aut turpiter aut impotenter dicitur*).

[243] Plato says it is not fitting (οὐ πρέπον) for there to be any bitter or nasty speech in a well-ruled city (*Leg.* 935E).

[244] Or should not "act silly" (Tzvee Zahavy and Alan J. Avery-Peck in Jacob Neusner, *The Mishnah: A New Translation* [New Haven: Yale University Press, 1988]).

[245] *Leviticus Rabbah* 24.7 (trans. by J. Israelstam and Judah J. Slotki, *Midrash Rabbah: Leviticus* [London: Soncino Press, 1939]).

possible by the fact that one can get "thing" or "speaking" out of the consonants דבר. But the paronomasia was only relevant because of the sense that obscene or lascivious talk was inappropriate for God's presence.[246] A similar sentiment is found elsewhere in rabbinic texts, though not always as expressly about obscene language.[247]

Ephesians did not cite Deuteronomy 23 the way several of the texts from Qumran did. But one did not need the Bible to arrive at the conclusion that foul language was not appropriate for holy persons[248] or gods.[249] Epictetus emphasized God's omnipresence when he urged more moral and decorous behavior:

> You are a fragment of God; you have within you a part of Him...whenever you mix in society, whenever you take physical exercise, whenever you converse, do you not know that you are nourishing God, exercising God?...It is within yourself that you bear Him, and do not perceive that you are defiling Him with impure thoughts and filthy actions. Yet in the

---

[246] Note that 1 Enoch 62.3 says that "no nonsensical talk shall be uttered in his presence" (Isaac, OTP; cf. also 49.4; 67.9). Similarly, in the *Ascension of Isaiah*, an angel explains that in the third heaven there was no mention of human life: "Nothing of the vanity of that world is named here" (7.24–26).

[247] Less specific than the Leviticus Rabbah passage, the Babylonian Talmud says: "The Divine Presence rests [upon man] neither through gloom, nor through sloth, nor through frivolity [שחוק], nor through levity [קלות ראש], nor through talk (שיחה), nor through idle chatter, but only at a word of joy over a fulfilled command" (*b. Shabbat* 30b; Similarly *b. Berak.* 1a).

Josephus says of the Essenes: "Before the sun is up they utter nothing profane" (οὐδὲν φθέγγονται τῶν βεβήλων [*B.J.* 2.128]). He adds that "no clamour [κραυγή] or disturbance [θόρυβος] ever pollutes [μιαίνει] their dwelling" (*B.J.* 2.132–33).

John Chrysostom also emphasized Lev 26:12 in relation to speech: "For he says, 'I will dwell in them, and walk in them.' For when the mind has become righteous, and has put off its sins, it becomes God's dwelling. But when God indwells, nothing human remains. Thus the mind becomes godly, uttering everything from this new source, as a house with God dwelling in it. Therefore the one who speaks obscenely does not have this godly mind, nor does the one who delights in wit and laughter" (*Hom. 2 Cor.* [PG 61:401]).

[248] Cf. Seneca, *Contr.* 1.2.7: *coram sacerdote obscenis homines abstinent.* In another example of the impulse to speak properly before holy figures, Iamblichus reports that when some men who were sailing with Pythagoras recognized his divine nature, they used more reverent words with him and with one another (σεμνοτέροις ἤπερ εἰώθεσαν ὀνόμασί τε καὶ πράγμασιν ἐχρήσαντο πρός τε ἀλλήλους καὶ πρὸς αὐτόν [*VP* 16]).

[249] On saying nothing shameful before gods, cf. Aelius Aristides, *Or.* 29.8. Lucian invokes the god "Reproof" to help him attack his opponent, but pleads that the god not say too much since it is not fitting for a god to describe something abominable (*Pseud.* 4). On the obscene language at cults, we have already mentioned Xenocrates's sense that such talk could not be for the pleasure of proper gods (*apud* Plutarch, *Mor.* 361B, 417C; cf. Augustine, *Civ.* 2.4). On the idea that human words—even prayers, let alone obscenity—could defile gods, cf. Augustine, *Civ.* 9.16.

presence of even an image of God you would not dare to do anything of the things you are now doing. But when God Himself is present within you, seeing and hearing everything, are you not ashamed to be thinking and doing such things as these, O Insensible of your own nature, and object of God's wrath! (*Diatr.* 2.8.11–14 [Oldfather LCL])

My argument, then, is that Ephesians exhibits a sense that the believers are holy and dwell in God's holy presence. This sense led other Jewish groups to avoid profane objects, often because they applied the biblical passages about God's presence to their own group. Keeping the profane separate from the sacred was of paramount importance because God's presence might depart. Some later Jewish texts extend the warnings in Deut 23.9–14 to lewd speech. And even when Deut 23 was not in view, light behavior was deemed inappropriate for God's presence (*m. Ber.* 9.5; Epictetus, *Diatr.* 2.8.11–14). For Ephesians, believers were not simply opposite the Eastern Gate of the Temple; they *were* the temple in which God dwelt by the Spirit (2:21–22). The widely felt impulse to avoid foul language in the presence of the holy was now applied to all places and times: the Ephesians were seated in heaven, they were always in sacred space. Thus for the author of Ephesians there is no need to explain what foul language might *lead* to. It is simply out of place. It is not fitting for holy ones. He and his readers might have agreed with *Did.* 3.3 and *m. Abot* 3:14 that lewd talk could result in illicit sex. He and his readers probably knew, along with Sirach 23:12–15 and a host of pagan Greek and Roman moralists, that such talk might lower them in the eyes of others. But Ephesians does not give these reasons any more than Leviticus explains why a priest with a physical defect cannot enter the sanctuary: such deformity was deemed not to be fitting for God's holiness. The very language Ephesians uses for inappropriate speech coheres well with this picture: some speech *is* "deformity" (αἰσχρότης); some language is "rotten" and "putrid" (λόγος σαπρός), and could grieve the Holy Spirit (4:29–30).[250] Foul language and even light language were inconsistent with the believers' holiness, and were inappropriate in God's holy presence. Excluding εὐτραπελία was not

---

[250] On sin, defilement, and the departure of the divine presence, cf. Klawans, *Impurity*, 118–35; 154–55. It is interesting to contrast Aristotle's concern with causing pain to the butt of a joke (μὴ λυπεῖν τὸν σκωπτόμενον; τῷ μὴ λυπεῖν τὸν ἀκούοντα [*Eth. nic.* 1128a]) with Ephesians's concern not to *grieve* the holy spirit (μὴ λυπεῖτε τὸ πνεῦμα τὸ ἅγιον τοῦ θεοῦ).

motivated by a desire to fit in. It might have been motivated by a desire to keep the profane out.

III. Speech and Christian Identities

It should now be apparent that Colossians and Ephesians envision speech functioning differently in the lives of Christians. Naturally, they also have much in common. For both epistles, speech is a necessary part of the Christian calling, because the message must be spread and the community must be built up. For Proverbs or Sirach, the mouth can win approval if used well and can get a person into a good deal of trouble if used wrongly. The best policy is to keep it shut a good deal of the time. Interestingly, neither Ephesians nor Colossians puts such a premium on silence. The mouth can express thanks to God and can upbuild the community. There are false teachings in the world (Col 2:8; Eph 4:14; 5:6), so believers, with "Christ's word dwelling in them," must "teach and admonish one another" with wisdom and with song (Col 3:16; Eph 5:19). And in addition to keeping the community on track doctrinally, "the mystery of the gospel" must be proclaimed (Eph 6:19; Col 4:3). Hence speech is sanctified as one apparatus in God's redemption of the world.

But although both Colossians and Ephesians refer to Paul's bold proclamation of the "mystery," they have rather different things to say about how other Christians should speak with outsiders. Toward the end of both epistles "Paul" requests prayer on his behalf, that God might open a door so that he may spread the message boldly (Fig. 4.2). But if one continues reading past the end of these requests for prayer, we can see rather different outlooks in these two books. In Colossians the prayer for Paul's bold speech is followed by advice about how the addressees should conduct themselves with outsiders: "Walk wisely toward outsiders, buying up the time. Let your conversation always be winsome and seasoned with the salt of wit" (Col 4:5–6, Harris). Colossians then says that Paul has sent Tychicus with information and encouragement (4:7–8). Ephesians, on the other hand, goes directly from the prayer for Paul to the sending of Tychicus (6:21–22). Ephesians has *nothing* parallel to Col 4:6, and although several elements from Col 4:5 ("walking," "wisdom," and "redeeming the time") appear in Eph 5:16–17, they have been reworked in such a way as to emphasize the depravity of the world. Colossians's advice about conduct toward outsiders is gone:

Colossians	Ephesians
(4:2) τῇ προσευχῇ προσκαρτερεῖτε, γρηγοροῦντες ἐν αὐτῇ ἐν εὐχαριστίᾳ	(6:18) διὰ πάσης προσευχῆς καὶ δεήσεως προσευχόμενοι ἐν παντὶ καιρῷ ἐν πνεύματι, καὶ εἰς αὐτὸ ἀγρυπνοῦντες ἐν πάσῃ προσκαρτερήσει καὶ δεήσει περὶ πάντων τῶν ἁγίων
(4:3) προσευχόμενοι ἅμα καὶ περὶ ἡμῶν, ἵνα ὁ θεὸς ἀνοίξῃ ἡμῖν θύραν τοῦ λόγου λαλῆσαι τὸ μυστήριον τοῦ Χριστοῦ,	(6:19) καὶ ὑπὲρ ἐμοῦ, ἵνα μοι δοθῇ λόγος ἐν ἀνοίξει τοῦ στόματός μου, ἐν παρρησίᾳ γνωρίσαι τὸ μυστήριον τοῦ εὐαγγελίου,
δι᾽ ὃ καὶ δέδεμαι,	(6:20) ὑπὲρ οὗ πρεσβεύω ἐν ἁλύσει,
(4:4) ἵνα φανερώσω αὐτὸ ὡς δεῖ με λαλῆσαι.	ἵνα ἐν αὐτῷ παρρησιάσωμαι ὡς δεῖ με λαλῆσαι
(4:5) ἐν σοφίᾳ περιπατεῖτε πρὸς τοὺς ἔξω τὸν καιρὸν ἐξαγοραζόμενοι.	5:15–16: βλέπετε οὖν ἀκριβῶς πῶς περιπατεῖτε μὴ ὡς ἄσοφοι ἀλλ᾽ ὡς σοφοί, ἐξαγοραζόμενοι τὸν καιρόν, ὅτι αἱ ἡμέραι πονηραί εἰσιν.
(4:6) ὁ λόγος ὑμῶν πάντοτε ἐν χάριτι, ἅλατι ἠρτυμένος, εἰδέναι πῶς δεῖ ὑμᾶς ἑνὶ ἑκάστῳ ἀποκρίνεσθαι.	
(4:7) τὰ κατ᾽ ἐμὲ	(6:21) ἵνα δὲ εἰδῆτε καὶ ὑμεῖς τὰ κατ᾽ ἐμέ, τί πράσσω,
πάντα γνωρίσει ὑμῖν Τύχικος ὁ ἀγαπητὸς ἀδελφὸς καὶ πιστὸς διάκονος καὶ σύνδουλος ἐν κυρίῳ,	πάντα γνωρίσει ὑμῖν Τύχικος ὁ ἀγαπητὸς ἀδελφὸς καὶ πιστὸς διάκονος ἐν κυρίῳ,
(4:8) ὃν ἔπεμψα πρὸς ὑμᾶς εἰς αὐτὸ τοῦτο, ἵνα γνῶτε τὰ περὶ ἡμῶν καὶ παρεκαλέσῃ τὰς καρδίας ὑμῶν.	(6:22) ὃν ἔπεμψα πρὸς ὑμᾶς εἰς αὐτὸ τοῦτο, ἵνα γνῶτε τὰ περὶ ἡμῶν καὶ παρακαλέσῃ τὰς καρδίας ὑμῶν.

Figure 4.2: Colossians 4:2–8 and Ephesians 6:18–22; 5:15–16

In Colossians, the advice to "redeem the time" with outsiders is fleshed out in terms of using winsome speech. In Ephesians, the references to "outsiders" and "winsome speech" are missing, and the tone is transformed into something more menacing: "Be careful then how you live...because the days are evil" (5:15–16). In fact, Ephesians might even be interpreting Colossians's "let your word always be winsome" (ὁ λόγος ὑμῶν πάντοτε ἐν χάριτι) in a way more congenial to its own inward focus on the edification of the community when it contrasts "rotten language" with language that is "good" and can "give *grace* to the hearers" (δῷ χάριν τοῖς ἀκούουσιν, 4:29).

When James Dunn describes Colossians's vision for engaging outsiders, his words allude to the fact that contemporary churches still struggle to get beyond their own jargon so as to speak effectively with non-members: "The final exhortation explicitly envisages a church in communication with those around it, not cut off in a 'holy huddle' speaking only 'the language of Zion' to insiders (contrast Eph. 4:29), but engaged in regular conversation with others, and in such a way as to allow plenty of opportunity to bear testimony to their faith."[251] Similarly, MacDonald proposes that the group in Colossians resembles Bryan Wilson's "conversionist" sect, a sect that desires to remain distinct but also worries about a mission to the world.[252]

In looking at how Ephesians has used Colossians, we see that it is not only more reserved about contact with outsiders, but also that it is more concerned with foul speech. Colossians does not expand on αἰσχρολογία at all: the word occurs in a list of five vices and the topic is not revisited. Ephesians has considerably more to say on the topic. First, when it uses the material from Col 3:8, it does not use Colossians's word αἰσχρολογία, but has instead "shouting" (κραυγή [Eph 4:31]). Here Ephesians treats the destructive speech used in anger, with "shouting" and "slander"[253] following on "bitterness," "anger," and "wrath."

---

[251] Dunn, *Colossians*, 266. Dunn goes on: "such advice envisages a group of Christians in a sufficiently positive relation with the surrounding community for such conversations to be natural, a group not fearful or threatened, but open to and in positive relationship with its neighbors (even as 'outsiders,' 4:5).... Here, evidently, was a church not on the defensive against powerful forces organized against it, but expected to hold its own in the social setting of marketplace, baths, and meal table and to win attention by the attractiveness of its life and speech" (*Colossians*, 267).

[252] "The compromising of sectarian values is an ever-present danger to groups that remain open to recruiting new members and continually in dialogue with the values of the outside world. This is in contrast with more 'introversionist' sects that often physically separate themselves from the rest of society in the hope of guaranteeing isolation from an evil world" (*Colossians and Ephesians*, 174, making reference to Bryan Wilson, *Patterns of Sectarianism* [London: Heinemann, 1967]: 36–41).

[253] For the conjunction of βλασφημία and κραυγή, cf. Lucian, *Eunuch*. 2, describing the laughable scene of philosophers heaping "cartloads of charges" (βλασφημιῶν) at the top of their lungs (κεκραγότες).

But Ephesians also draws on the wording of Col 3:8 (αἰσχρολογίαν ἐκ τοῦ στόματος ὑμῶν) when it forbids letting "any rotten language from your mouths" (λόγος σαπρὸς ἐκ τοῦ στόματος ὑμῶν [Eph 4:29]). This "rotten language"[254] refers not simply to "foul" speech in the sense of obscene speech, but to a broader category of unedifying, destructive speech; this is made clear by the contrast with "good" speech that edifies and imparts grace (ἀλλὰ εἴ τις ἀγαθὸς πρὸς οἰκοδομὴν τῆς χρείας, ἵνα δῷ χάριν τοῖς ἀκούουσιν).[255] Nevertheless, "foul" language was certainly one species of destructive speech, and given the way the phrase in Eph 4:29 echoes Col 3:8, it is not surprising that this "rotten language" has often been understood to include obscene abuse.[256]

Having drawn on the language of Col 3:8 in Eph 4:29–31, Ephesians then returns to the topic of foul language by changing the material of Col 3:5 into a warning about *speaking* of sexual sins: these must not even be named (5:3), and there must be no ugly, stupid humor about them (5:4). This is one of Ephesians's most striking redactions of Colossians, since in Col 3:5 there is no reference to speaking.[257] Then again at 5:12 Ephesians forbids the mere mention of what outsiders do.

At the outset of the chapter I noted that the flow of the argument in Eph 5:3–14 was difficult to follow—especially the connection between vv. 3–4 and v. 5. Considering how Ephesians has used Col 3:5 might help account for how these verses fit together. After Ephesians lists sins from Col 3:5 and addresses them as things not to talk about (Eph 5:3),

---

[254] The basic sense of σαπρός is "decayed" or "rotten," but it is used figuratively with the sense of "bad," "evil," "unwholesome" (for example of the word used with this moral sense, cf. BGAD, s.v. σαπρός, 2). σαπρός is not regularly used of "speech," but Epictetus refers to bad doctrines as σαπρὰ δόγματα (*Diatr.* 3.22.61; cf. 3.16.7: τὰ σαπρὰ ταῦτα...λαλοῦσιν); cf. also Marcus Aurelius, *Med.*, 11.15. The metaphor of rotting is applied to words with terms other than σαπρός, and these combinations can refer to "obscene" words. Dio Chrysostom complains about the mischievous craze for "spoiled" or "corrupt words" (λόγων διεφθορότων [2 *Regn.* 55]); Lucian speaks of a bad man who enjoys hearing διεφθορότων ᾀσμάτων (*Nigr.* 15).

[255] So Dibelius. The opposite of "obscene" speech would have been something more narrow such as σεμνός or κόσμιος.

[256] MacDonald calls it a "synonym of *aischrologia*" (*Colossians and Ephesians*, 308); Muddiman suggests "it presumably has the same sexual connotations as 'repulsive talk' (*aischrologia*) at Col. 3.8" (*Ephesians*, 228).

[257] Dibelius felt the references to speech in Eph 5:4 were so abrupt that they pointed to a pre-existing vice list: "Daß dann mit Zungensünden fortgefahren wird, obwohl von diesen schon 4:29f. die Rede war, beweist aufs neue, daß der Autor diese Mahnungen bereits fixiert übernahm und höchstens kombinierte" (*Kolosser*, 89). Vögtle rejected this suggestion and proposed that sins of the tongue might have been suggested by the word ὀνομαζέσθω (*Tugend- und Lasterkataloge*, 34n69).

Col 3:5–6 ["put to death what is earthly in you:"]	Eph 5:3 ["do not mention"]	Eph 5:5–6	Cf. Eph 4:19 [on outsiders]
πορνείαν	πορνεία	πᾶς πόρνος	
ἀκαθαρσίαν	ἀκαθαρσία πᾶσα	ἀκάθαρτος	εἰς ἐργασίαν ἀκαθαρσίας πάσης
πάθος, ἐπιθυμίαν κακήν			
καὶ τὴν πλεονεξίαν	πλεονεξία	πλεονέκτης	ἐν πλεονεξίᾳ
ἥτις ἐστὶν εἰδωλολατρία		ὅ ἐστιν εἰδωλολάτρης	
6. δι' ἃ ἔρχεται ἡ ὀργὴ τοῦ θεοῦ [ἐπὶ τοὺς υἱοὺς τῆς ἀπειθείας]		6. διὰ ταῦτα γὰρ ἔρχεται ἡ ὀργὴ τοῦ θεοῦ ἐπὶ τοὺς υἱοὺς τῆς ἀπειθείας	

Figure 4.3: Colossians 3:5–6, Ephesians 5:3; 5:5–6; 4:19

it explicates what it means by "let them not be named" in v. 4 with the phrase "and let there be no ugliness, or stupid talk, or facetiousness." But the author of Ephesians then returns to Colossians's equation of "covetousness" and "idolatry," as well as Colossians's warning about God's wrath (Col 3:5–6). So Ephesians restates Col 3:5, not in terms of vices but of the people who *practice* such vices. Ephesians's use of Colossians for two purposes—first to address what not to say, then to warn of God's wrath—helps account for the uneasy fit between Eph 5:3–4 and Eph 5:5–6.

One of Ephesians's chief themes is the need for unity among believers (e.g. 2:14–16, 18; 4:3–6, 13, 16).[258] Toward this end it employs the images of "body" and "building" to reinforce the believers' interconnectedness (2:20–22; 4:12–16, 25). The tongue contributes to God's work of building up and unifying this group: there must no longer be

---

[258] Dahl, *Studies*, 418.

falsehood, outbursts of anger, or "rotten language." Instead speech should be used for the edification of the hearers (4:29; 5:19). Shameful and foolish language is to be replaced by "thanksgiving" (5:4, 20),[259] as befits holy people. Note that in all of this the use of the tongue focuses on the group, not outsiders. Even the proclamation of the gospel (6:15) is framed not in terms of compassion for the lost but in terms of the spiritual *armor* that will enable believers to withstand the evil spiritual onslaught (6:10–17).

Another way Ephesians rhetorically evokes the unity of the group is by depicting it as vastly and irremediably different from the dark world outside. The outsiders not only behave differently (4:17–19; 5:7–8, 11), but they are in the grip of an evil force, "the ruler of the power of the air, the spirit that is now at work among those who are disobedient" (2:2). The Ephesians once found themselves in this dark and godless realm (2:1–3, 5, 11–19; 4:17–19; 5:8), but are now "sealed" in God's spirit (1:13–14; cf. 1:17; 2:18; 4:4, 30; 6:17),[260] "fellow citizens with the holy ones" (2:19).[261] Much of the Epistle to the Ephesians is spent recounting the blessings they have received, congratulating Christians on what God has done for them in Christ.[262]

But it is quite likely that the recipients of this letter were socially integrated in the life of their city.[263] The gap between the "sons of light" and the "sons of darkness" was greater metaphysically than it was socially. So in addition to reminding the addressees of the difference

---

[259] John Chrysostom often mentioned the eucharist when fulminating against foul speech (e.g. *Exp. Psalm.* [PG 55:433]: "Consider that this is the part with which we speak with God, with which we offer up praise. *This is the part with which we receive the terrible sacrifice.* The faithful know of what I speak!"). It is interesting that Ephesians, even when contrasting bad speech with εὐχαριστία, never used this rhetoric.

[260] God's "spirit" is more prominent in Ephesians than in Colossians (Col 1:8, 9; 2:5; 3:16).

[261] Note all the συν- words: συμπολῖται (2:19), συναρμολογουμένη (2:21), συνοικοδομεῖσθε (2:22), συγκληρονόμα, σύσσωμα, συμμέτοχα (3:6). This repetition of συν- blessings makes the negative command in Eph 5:7 all the more forceful: μὴ οὖν γίνεσθε συμμέτοχοι αὐτῶν.

[262] Dahl, *Studies*, 471–72. So Hugo Odeberg said of the cosmic language in Ephesians: "the terms in question, probably, do not form part of a definite system but are freely used to impress upon the Church the far-reaching and momentous importance of its spiritual situation" (*The View of the Universe in the Epistle to the Ephesians* [Lund: Gleerup, 1934], 20).

[263] As Margaret MacDonald notes, "we do not find the clearly articulated, visible and physical measures to encourage segregation in Ephesians that we find in the QL" ("The Politics of Identity in Ephesians," *JSNT* 26 [2004]: 423).

and urging them to remind themselves, Ephesians tells them to desist joking about the evil practices of the pagans.[264]

For those Christians who took the message to heart, their purified speech might not actually have been much different from the clean speech of the strictest of philosophers. A disciple of Epictetus who agreed to eschew *any* casual conversation (*Ench.* 33.2), who agreed to forgo both laughter (*Ench.* 33.4) and trying to raise a laugh (*Ench.* 33.15), who avoided shouting at spectacles (*Ench.* 33.10) and lapses into foul language (*Ench.* 33.16)—this person's speech would have achieved all the purity that Ephesians wanted from Christians. Yet Christians' speech patterns would have reminded them of their uniquely holy, spirit-led life, even as similar speech would have reminded the disciples of Epictetus that they were *philosophers*, not laymen.[265] As Fredrik Barth pointed out, so far as forming identity is concerned, those aspects of behavior that "the actors themselves regard as significant" are equal in importance to "'objective' differences."[266]

Margaret MacDonald notes that in the absence of some of the physical separation of the covenanters at Qumran, Ephesians looks to erect practical barriers against the spiritual powers of the outside world, and "virtue is the armor that will protect them against all menacing forces (6:10–20)."[267] I would add that a strict discipline of the tongue provides another "practical barrier," another means of separating believers from the outside world with whom they must continue to brush shoulders. Noting the communal nature of many Christian ethical practices, Wayne Meeks has observed that such practices

> are means of reminding individuals even when alone that they are not merely devotees of the Christians' God, they are members of Christ's body, the people of God. That was how the Christian movement differed most visibly from the other cults that fit more easily into the normal expectations of "religion" in the Roman world. The Christians' practices were

---

[264] Wayne Meeks has illustrated that "The repetition of distinctive practices drums into us the sense of who we are, because this is what *we* do. Often the practice is so constructed as to remind us that what we do is different from what *they* do" (Wayne A. Meeks, *The Origins of Christian Morality* [New Haven: Yale University Press, 1993], 109–10).

[265] John M. G. Barclay makes a similar point about the ethics of Colossians ("Ordinary but Different: Colossians and Hidden Moral Identity," *Australian Biblical Review* 49 [2001]: 45).

[266] Fredrik Barth, *Ethnic Groups and Boundaries* (Boston: Little, Brown and Company, 1969), 11, 14.

[267] MacDonald, *Colossians and Ephesians*, 21.

not confined to sacred occasions and sacred locations—shrines, sacrifices, processions—but were integral to the formation of communities with a distinctive self-awareness.[268]

What better than the mouth—always with a person, and something that ancients were always watching—to inculcate a sense of the omni-presence of God and the constant connection to the holy body of Christ?

---

[268] Meeks, *Morality*, 110.

CHAPTER FIVE

CLEMENT OF ALEXANDRIA ON FOUL LANGUAGE

Clement of Alexandria[1] wrote more about foul language than any Christian before him—more, in fact, than anyone before John Chrysostom. Like Christians before and after him, Clement opposes foul language, grounding his ethic in a dozen biblical references and a variety of moral arguments. The well-read[2] Alexandrian is the first Christian to reveal an awareness of the claim made by some philosophers that there was nothing wrong with "obscene" words. In fact—and this is what makes Clement so interesting—Clement is not only aware of this position, but at one point actually presents it as *his own view*, and claims to have shown that "in a deeper sense" there is nothing obscene in the terms for sexual organs or their functions.[3] Yet Clement makes this bold statement at the *end* of his treatment of αἰσχρολογία, after he has forbidden foul language, railed against its multifarious dangers, and cited with admiration the way the Apostle Paul "lashed out" against it in his Epistle to the Ephesians.

I. The Divine Paedagogue and Christian Manners

The bulk of Clement's discussion of foul language is found in the *Paedagogue*, and a few words about the nature of that work will help to situate his comments. At the outset of the *Paedagogue* Clement says that when the divine Word calls people to salvation and addresses their habits and customs, he acts as a προτρεπτικὸς λόγος.[4] The same Word

---

[1] For ancient comments on Clement's life, cf. Eusebius *Hist. eccl.* 5.11; 6.11.6; 6.14.8; 6.19.6; Jerome *Vir. ill.* 38; for birth in Athens or Alexandria, Epiphanius, *Pan.* 32.6; on his conversion, *Paed.* 1.1.1, 2.8.62; Eusebius, *Dem. ev.* 2.2.64. For a modern account of his life, see John Ferguson, *Clement of Alexandria* (New York: Twayne Publishers, 1974).

[2] For positive evaluations of the breadth of Clement's learning (i.e. that he was not simply posing as intellectual), cf. Robert P. Casey, "Clement of Alexandria and the Beginnings of Christian Platonism," *HTR* 18 (1925): 47, and Henry Chadwick, *Early Christian Thought and the Classical Tradition* (Oxford: Clarendon, 1966), 35–36.

[3] *Paed.* 2.52.2.

[4] Hence Προτρεπτικὸς πρὸς Ἕλληνας, usually taken to be Clement's first work (so Patrick, *Clement of Alexandria*, 11).

216 CHAPTER FIVE

who first persuades then "heals and counsels" and offers a cure for the passions, and in this capacity is called παιδαγωγός. In another work, Clement says that the Word will act as "teacher" (ὁ διδασκαλικός).[5] As the Paedagogue, the Word addresses deeds and is πρακτικός, giving advice that should heal the passions. Only after the soul has been cured of passion will it be healthy enough to receive the knowledge revealed by the Teacher.[6] Clement apparently never wrote this third piece of the proposed trilogy,[7] but his comments clarify the role he imagined for the second work, the *Paedagogue*. It was to lay down the rules that would prepare Christians for a deeper instruction.

That the *Paedogogus* is πρακτικός no one can doubt. Even to the casual reader of the *Paedagogue* it is immediately apparent that the profundities of the Christian faith are not herein disclosed. The would-be gnostic longing for learned lectures on the contemplation of God finds little in *these* pages to satisfy her hunger. No, here the divine Word speaks not as teacher but as tutor (practically as nanny), concerned with actions of the most mundane kind. His advice pertains to how to eat and drink, how to set the table, how to behave at banquets, how to laugh and how to dress, how to walk, how and when to have sex. No detail is too small to merit attention. Clearing the throat and wiping the nose? The divine Paedagogue has advice. Which designs are appropriate for a signet ring? See Book 3. The Paedagogue even offers instructions on the best way to belch discreetly. Extended parts of the work read like an etiquette guide for aristocratic Christians,[8] an Emily Post guided by the Holy Ghost.[9]

---

[5] Clement concludes his introduction: "Therefore, the all-loving Word...makes effective use of an order well adapted to our development; at first, He persuades [προτρέπων], then He educates [παιδαγωγῶν], and after all this He teaches [ἐκδιδάσκων]" (*Paed.* 1.3.1).

[6] *Strom.* 1.9.1; cf. Harry O. Maier, "Clement of Alexandria and the Care of the Self," *JAAR* 62 (1994): 729.

[7] The *Stromateis* is probably not this third work (Max Pohlenz, "Klemens von Alexandreia und sein hellenisches Christentum," *Nachrichten von der Akademie der Wissenschaften in Göttingen.* Philologisch-Historische Klasse 3 [1943]: 45–46; John Ferguson, *Stromateis 1–3* [FC; Washington, D.C.: Catholic University of America Press, 1991], 11–12; *contra* Casey, "Clement," 45–46).

[8] Cf. Blake Leyerle, "Clement of Alexandria on the Importance of Table Etiquette," *JECS* 3 (1995): 123–41. Henri-Irénée Marrou notes, "Tous ces conseils s'inspirent moins de l'idéal chrétien que d'une morale esthétique, aristocratique" (Henri-Irénée Marrou et al., *Clément d'Alexandrie: Le Pédagogue* [3 vols.; Paris: Cerf, 1960–70], 2:121n7).

[9] Apparently Post is less interested in foul language than was Clement. The 16th Edition of *Emily Post's Etiquette* has only one comment about obscene speech in almost

Clement wanted to raise Christians to the same societal level as the educated Greek, and as Max Pohlenz said, the Stoics provided good models for his task.[10] Not only the aristocrat Panaetius but even the former slave Epictetus had worried about good manners.[11] Clement wrote at a time when Stoic ethics were at their most popular and exercised an enormous influence on all culture and thought,[12] a time when Christians lacked anything comparable to Cicero's *De Officiis* or Panaetius's Περὶ τοῦ καθήκοντος. Clement seems to have turned to such works in his attempt to give Christians a thorough treatment of the practical duties enjoined by *logos*.[13] In *De Officiis*, for example, Cicero covers such topics as dress (1.130), gait (1.131), the use of obscene words (1.103, 104, 127), conversation skills (1.132), and proper pronunciation (1.133)—all topics taken up by Clement in the *Paedagogue*. And parts of Books 2 and 3 of the *Paedagogue* bear striking resemblance to the teachings of Musonius Rufus.[14]

The specific precepts issued by the Paedagogue are grounded by appeals to scripture (ἡ γραφή), to physical principles,[15] and to what is "fitting" (τὸ πρέπον). A man should shave his head both to show himself "severe" (a concern with appearance), but also to prevent the hair on his

---

a thousand pages of advice: "Avoid it" (Peggy Post, *Emily Post's Etiquette* [HarperCollins: New York, 1997], 116).

[10] Pohlenz, "Klemens," 57.

[11] Ibid.

[12] H.-I. Marrou, *Le Pédagogue*, 1:51.

[13] Pohlenz comments, "Die praktische Ethik trägt Klemens im Paidagogos nach dem Schema der Pflichtenlehre vor, das die Stoa der Kaiserzeit festgelegt hatte" ("Klemens," 56). Cf. *Paed.* 1.101–2, where Clement uses the term καθῆκον and relates it to Christian terms and concepts. Marrou notes, "on reconnaît le programme du Pédagogue: c'est en effet le domaine des devoirs concrets, καθήκοντα, que Clément présentera en détail au cours de ses livre II et III" (*Le Pédagogue*, 1:13).

[14] Paul Wendland thought that Clement had simply taken over large parts of a lost treatise of Musonius Rufus ("Quaestiones Mussoniae," Ph.D. diss., Berlin, 1886). On Clement and Musonius, cf. C. P. Parker, "Musonius in Clement," *Harvard Studies in Classical Philology* 12 [1901]: 191–200; D. J. M. Bradley, "The Transformation of the Stoic Ethic in Clement of Alexandria," *Augustinianum* 14 [1974]: 59; Lutz, "Musonius Rufus," 20n83.

[15] So wine is bad for young people because it combines a hot liquid with a hot age, and the ensuing "fire" swells the sexual organs and hastens their development (*Paed.* 2.20.3–4); Clement allows the elderly to drink a bit more wine "to stimulate new warmth for the growing chill of old age" (*Paed.* 2.22). Clement recommends vegetarianism since the fumes from meat are "dense" and "darken the soul" (*Paed.* 2.11.1; cf. Musonius Rufus 18A). Many more examples could be given where Clement offers physiological grounds for his advice.

head from absorbing moistures into the brain.[16] Proper exercise will give women a natural beauty, and will also prevent the retention of excess foods which would gather around the genitals and produce lusts.[17]

Quite often the dominant concern is how Christians will appear in the eyes of others. In all one's movements at table, for instance, thought is to be given to "decency" or "seemliness."[18] Resting the chin on the hands or crossing one's legs at a banquet is ignoble (ἀγεννές);[19] constant shifting is a sign of lightness of character (κουφότητος σύμβολον).[20] It would be a "shameful spectacle" for a man to shave his chin.[21] For women, the danger in drinking lies not only in drunkenness but in the unseemly (ἀσχημόνως) distending of the lips, in the indecorous (οὐ κοσμίως) tipping back of the head, and in "belching like men—or rather like slaves!"[22] Despite all the discomfort of a hangover and the scriptural prohibitions of drunkenness, the really unnerving thought about drinking too much is that Christians would become such a ridiculous spectacle before others.[23] Clement invokes the Lord's presence to undergird the need for decent comportment: "We must always behave with good manners [κοσμίως], realizing that the Lord is present" (Paed. 2.33.5). Imatatio Christi takes on new implications when one knows, as Clement does, that when Jesus drank wine, he did not gulp it down but consumed it in a way that was well-bred and civilized (ἀστείως and κοσμίως [Paed. 2.32.2]).

It is in this sort of discussion that Clement tackles an ethics/etiquette of the tongue. And although he ultimately claims that there is no obscenity in words, he first advises strongly against using or even tolerating lewd speech. It is to the dangers of foul language that we now turn.

---

[16] Paed. 3.62.1.

[17] Paed. 3.64.2–66.1.

[18] εὐσχημοσύνη (Paed. 2.31.1). In a single paragraph on not gulping beverages, the vocabulary includes: τὸ κόσμιον, κοσμίως, ἀπρεπὲς τὸ θέαμα, and αἰσχρόν (Paed. 2.31.1–3).

[19] Paed. 2.54.3.

[20] Paed. 2.55.1.

[21] Paed. 3.60.3; cf. Musonius Rufus, Frag. 21.

[22] Paed. 2.33.1; cf. Philo, Contempl. 45.

[23] θέαμα ἄλλοις <καὶ> γέλως γενώμεθα (Paed. 2.26.2).

II. On Foul Language

On the topic of foul language, Clement announces his position at once and in no uncertain terms: "We must avoid foul language altogether, and we should shut up those who use it with a sharp look, or by turning our face away, or by the so-called turning up of the nose—and often also with a harsh word!"[24] When Clement supports this with the logion of Jesus, "What comes out of the mouth defiles" (*Paed.* 2.49.1; Matt 15:18), his concern with status is evident, for he uses κοινόω to emphasize "vulgarity" rather than "defilement":[25] *aischrologia*, Clement says, "makes common" (κοινοῖ), that is, it shows a person to be "*vulgar* [κοινός],[26] heathen, uneducated and dissolute, and lacking self-respect, manners, or self-control."[27]

The ears must be blocked against foul language lest "the melody of fornication penetrate to the destruction of the soul."[28] Aware of such a danger, the divine Paedagogue has conferred "chaste words" to serve as ear-caps (τοὺς σώφρονας περιτίθησι λόγους καθάπερ ἀντωτίδας), to protect against hearing anything indecent.[29]

Clement applies several New Testament warnings about words to obscene speech. So he cites Ephesians 4:29 ("let no rotten language come forth from your mouth") as an instance where Paul "lashes out at αἰσχρολογία."[30] Clement adds Eph 5:4 ("let there be no obscenity,

---

[24] αἰσχρολογίας δὲ παντελῶς αὐτοῖς τε ἡμῖν ἀεκτέον καὶ τοὺς χρωμένους αὐτῇ ἐπιστομιστέον καὶ ὄψει δριμυτέρᾳ καὶ προσώπου ἀποστροφῇ καὶ τῷ ἀπομυκτηρισμῷ καλουμένῳ, πολλάκις δὲ καὶ λόγῳ τραχυτέρῳ (*Paed.* 2.49.1). Ἀπομυκτηρισμός was not used before Clement; it is used again when this passage is quoted by John of Damascus in his chapter Περὶ αἰσχρολογίας (PG 96:1256). *PGL* (s.v.) offers "turning up of the nose, derision"; Simon Wood "what is called a grunt of disgust" (*Christ the Educator* [New York: Fathers of the Church, 1954]); and Claude Mondésert "ce qu'on appelle un air moqueur" (in Marrou et al., *Le Pédagogue*).

[25] *Contra PGL, s.v.* κοινός 3 (citing this passage from the *Paedagogue*). Cf. John Ferguson, *Clement of Alexandria*, 83.

[26] So Wood ("uncouth") and Mondésert ("vulgaire").

[27] *Paed.* 2.49.1: τὰ ἐξιόντα, φησίν, ἐκ τοῦ στόματος κοινοῖ τὸν ἄνθρωπον, κοινὸν καὶ ἐθνικὸν καὶ ἀπαίδευτον καὶ ἀσελῆ δείκνυσιν αὐτόν, οὐχὶ δὲ ἴδιον καὶ κόσμιον καὶ σώφρονα. (This is an unusual use of ἴδιος; *PGL* tentatively suggests "self-respecting.")

[28] *Paed.* 2.49.2: ἐξικνεῖσθαι εἰς θραῦσιν τῆς ψυχῆς τὸ κροῦμα τῆς πορνείας.

[29] *Paed.* 2.49.2. The idea of ear-guards (an athletic image) resembles a suggestion of Xenocrates, where ear-guards were to serve a similar purpose (*apud* Plutarch, *Mor.* 38B).

[30] Ephesians does not actually use the word αἰσχρολογία. But patristic sources often join or conflate Col 3:8, which does use the word, with Eph 4:29, since both passages have the identical phrase ἐκ τοῦ στόματος ὑμῶν. Clement only explicitly quotes Col 3:8 at *Strom.* 3.43.5, where the mention of αἰσχρολογία is incidental to his argument.

foolish talk, or facetiousness") to Eph 4:29, which he then links to Matt
5:22 by means of the root μωρ-: "If he who merely calls his brother
a fool [μωρόν] is liable to judgment, what will we declare about the
one engaging in 'foolish talk'?"[31] Having now referred to the Gospel
of Matthew, Clement also cites Matt 12:36–37: "And about this it is
written, 'Whoever speaks an idle word, he will give an account to the
Lord in the day of judgment,' and again, 'from your word you will be
justified,' he says, 'and from your word you will be condemned.'"[32]

For Clement, lewd discussions of sexual topics reveal and expose
what should be covered; not talking about such matters is of a piece
with not seeing them. "In every way we must avoid hearing, speaking,
or seeing shameful things" (*Paed.* 2.51.1). After forbidding shameful
words, he adds that Christians are to avoid revealing any of the body's
limbs, or seeing the genitals (τῶν ἀπορρητοτέρων μερῶν). The metaphor
of covering is developed in a reference to Genesis 9:21–23: just as a
modest son could not look at the nakedness of his father, so "it is no
less urgent that we keep ourselves pure in the utterance of speech, with
respect to which the ears of those who believe in Christ must be holy. It
seems to me that this is why the Paedagogue has forbidden us to utter
anything that is unseemly, keeping us far from licentiousness."[33]

Clement here treats the avoidance of foul words as a sort of hedge
around the Torah. Just as the Paedagogue, "expert at cutting out the
roots of sins," safeguarded the command "You shall not commit adultery" by adding the more restrictive "You shall not lust" (*Paed.* 2.51.2),
so also "the Paedagogue forbade the fearless use of certain terms,
thereby cutting away the fearless contact with immorality"; for "to be
undisciplined with words accustoms one to be indiscreet in acts. But
practicing modesty in speech is resistance to sensuality."[34] For Clement
"sensuality" (λαγνεία)—which is vulgar, common, impure, and preoccupied with copulation—will lead to other lusts until a lack of restraint

---

[31] *Paed.* 2.50.2: τί περὶ τοῦ μωρολογοῦντος ἀποφανούμεθα.
[32] Matt 12:36–37; *Paed.* 2.50.2.
[33] καθαρευτέον δὲ οὐδὲν ἧττον κἂν ταῖς προφοραῖς τῶν φωνῶν, αἷς ἄβατα εἶναι χρὴ
τὰ ὦτα τῶν ἐν Χριστῷ πεπιστευκότων. ταύτῃ μοι δοκεῖ ὁ παιδαγωγὸς μηδὲ φθέγξασθαί
τι τῶν τῆς ἀσχημοσύνης ἐφιέναι ἡμῖν, πόρρωθεν διαβάλλων πρὸς τὴν ἀκολασίαν
(*Paed.* 2.51.2).
[34] ὁμοίως οὖν κἀνταῦθα ὁ παιδαγωγὸς [πρὸς] τὴν ἀδεᾶ τῶν ὀνομάτων [ὡς] χρῆσιν
διαβέβληκεν, τὴν ἀδεᾶ τῆς ἀκολασίας ἐπιμιξίαν ἐκκόπτων. Τὸ γὰρ ἐν τοῖς ὀνόμασιν
ἀτακτεῖν μελέτην ἐμποιεῖ τοῦ καὶ εἰς τὰ ἔργα ἀκοσμεῖν, τὸ δὲ περὶ τὴν φωνὴν σωφρονεῖν
ἀσκεῖν ἐστι λαγνείας καρτερεῖν (*Paed.* 2.52.1).

destroys the ἦθος (*Paed.* 2.93.2–3). Thus the avoidance of foul words plays a key role in the battle against desire.

Clement's discussion of foul language bears several similarities to prior philosophers, perhaps most notably Aristotle and Epictetus. Both Clement and Aristotle describe joking as a relaxation,[35] and both urge that this be done in good taste (ἐμμελῶς),[36] since it is indicative of *character*.[37] For both, the difference between decent and indecent is the difference between slave and free, educated and uneducated.[38] And both men connect hearing lewd things with seeing lewd things, either of which poses a threat—especially for the young.[39]

Epictetus proposed some of the same responses to foul language that Clement recommends, including reproof, a disapproving facial expression, and blushing:

> And it is also dangerous to proceed into foul language [αἰσχρολογίαν]. When, therefore, such speech is used, if the situation is appropriate, rebuke [ἐπίπληξον] the person who has gone so far; but if it is not appropriate, make it clear that you dislike such speech by remaining silent, blushing [ἐρυθριᾶσαι], and frowning [σκυθρωπάσαι]. (*Ench.* 33.16)

Very similarly, Clement urged that people not smile but rather "blush" and "frown" when something "shameful" has been said.[40] Unlike

---

[35] On jests in relaxation, cf. also Cicero, *Off.* 1.104. Clement seems to know several of Aristotle's comments about humor, including one that is not attested in Aristotle's surviving works (*Paed.* 3.84.1, where Clement states that "Aristotle does not permit men ever to laugh with slaves").

[36] Plutarch also uses this word frequently in discussing appropriate wittiness in conversation: "'For no small portion of the art of conversation,' you said, 'is the knowledge and observance of good taste in question-posing and fun-making'" (οὐ γάρ τι μικρόν, ἔφης, τῆς ὁμιλητικῆς μόριον ἡ περὶ τὰς ἐρωτήσεις καὶ τὰς παιδιὰς τοῦ ἐμμελοῦς ἐπιστήμη καὶ τήρησις [*Mor.* 629F]); "Furthermore, those who jokingly apply abusive words to anything praiseworthy, if they do so with tact [ἂν ἐμμελῶς ποιῶσιν], give more pleasure than even men straightforward in their praise" (*Mor.* 632D); "The man who would make tactful [ἐμμελῶς] use of joking..." (*Mor.* 633A [Clement and Hoffleit, LCL]).

[37] Aristotle: τοῦ γὰρ ἤθους αἱ τοιαῦται δοκοῦσι κινήσεις εἶναι (*Eth. nic.* 1128a11). Clement: ἀπὸ διανοίας καὶ ἤθους (*Paed.* 2.45.1, about laughable words).

[38] Aristotle: ἡ τοῦ ἐλευθερίου παιδιὰ διαφέρει τῆς τοῦ ἀνδραποδώδους, καὶ πεπαιδευμένου καὶ ἀπαιδεύτου (*Eth. nic.* 1128a20–21); Clement: ἀνελεύθερον ὄψιν τε καὶ ἀκοὴν (*Paed.* 2.41.3); ἀπαίδευτον (*Paed.* 2.49.1). Cf. Sirach 23:13.

[39] Aristotle, *Pol.* 1336a41–b8.

[40] καὶ εἰ μὲν ἐπ' αἰσχροῖς εἴη, ἐρυθριῶντας μᾶλλον ἢ μειδιῶντας φαίνεσθαι, μὴ συνήδεσθαι διὰ συμπάθειαν δοκῶμεν (*Paed.* 2.47.2). For frowning at foul language, cf. *Priapea* 1, 49; *Anth. Pal.* 12.2; Martial 1.4.12, 11.16.9.

Epictetus (and later Julian), Clement never mentions *reading* lewd writings.[41]

Excursus: Clement and the Didache

It is perhaps surprising, given how many texts Clement brings together on the topic of foul language, that he nowhere quotes *Did.* 3.3, since this verse makes precisely the point Clement wishes to make, namely, that foul language *leads* to sexual activity. Elsewhere Clement appears to quote the *Didache*—quoting, in fact, from this very section—when he cites *Did.* 3.5 as "scripture."[42] He also seems to know the tradition we find in *Did.* 2.2 and *Barn.* 19.4, in which "You shall not corrupt boys" is added to "You shall not commit adultery."[43] In these cases Clement may have known the Jewish source underlying *Did.* 3.1–6,[44] or an independent Two Ways tractate.[45] Other scholars have argued that Clement knew the *Didache* itself and accepted its authority.[46] We might cautiously add to this discussion of Clement's knowledge of the *Didache* that the absence of any reference to *Did.* 3.3 suggests that Clement *did not* know the version of *Did.* 3.1–6 we have in the Bryennios manuscript. This is only an argument from silence, but it is not difficult to imagine that Clement knew the saying in *Did.* 3.5 from another writing, one that lacked *Did.* 3.3. We have evidence for precisely such a form of the material in *Did.* 3.1–6, namely, the *Doctrina apostolorum*, which has *Did.* 3.1–2, 4–6 but not *Did.* 3.3. Clement could well have known only such a version of the material from *Did.* 3.1–6.

---

[41] Epictetus, *Diatr.* 4.9.6; Julian, *Ep.* 89b (300C).

[42] *Strom.* 1.100.4; cf. *Strom.* 3.26.5.

[43] *Strom.* 3.36.5 (οὐ μοιχεύσεις καὶ οὐ παιδοφθορήσεις); quoted also at *Protr.* 108.5; *Paed.* 2.89.1 (attributed to Moses); 3.89.1 (called part of the Decalogue).

[44] So James Muilenburg, "The Literary Relations of the Epistle of Barnabas and the Teaching of the Twelve Apostles" (Ph.D. diss., Yale University, 1929), 33–34, cited by Niederwimmer, *Didache*, 7n32.

[45] Niederwimmer, *Didache*, 7.

[46] Taylor, *Teaching of the Twelve Apostles*, 29–30. J. E. L. Oulton argues that Clement quoted the *Didache* itself and not one of its sources ("Clement of Alexandria and the Didache," *JTS* 41 [1940]: 177–79).

II.A. *A "Deeper Logos" about Foul Language*

Near the end of his section on αἰσχρολογία Clement says, "In more profound discussion [βαθυτέρῳ λόγῳ], we have shown that it is not the terms, or the sexual organs, or the marriage act, to which names not in common use describing intercourse are affixed, that we should consider obscene."[47] If Clement is referring to a written treatment of this topic,[48] then the work is lost.[49] Some have proposed that Clement is referring to *Strom.* 2.23 or *Strom.* 3, but this is unlikely. Although Clement does discuss marriage and sex in these sections of the *Stromateis*, he does not discuss the decency of names or the nature of obscenity, which is what this passage promises. Clement is here referring to a topic addressed by many moralists (i.e. obscene language), not simply to a general discussion of sexuality. If one were to guess which of Clement's known works contained such a discussion, his Περὶ καταλαλιᾶς ("On Slander") would make a more promising candidate.[50]

Clement claims that he has shown that "it is not the knee, or the thigh, or the names given to them, or even the use made of them, that is

---

[47] διειλήφαμεν δὲ βαθυτέρῳ λόγῳ ὡς ἄρα οὔτε ἐν τοῖς ὀνόμασιν οὐδὲ μὴν ἐν τοῖς συνουσιαστικοῖς μορίοις καὶ τῇ κατὰ γάμον συμπλοκῇ, καθ᾽ ὧν κεῖται τὰ ὀνόματα τὰ περὶ τὴν συνήθειαν οὐ τετριμμένα, ἡ τοῦ ὄντως αἰσχροῦ προσηγορία τάττεται (*Paed.* 2.52.2).

[48] So he is understood by several translators: "We have shown in a *more exhaustive treatise...*" (W. Wilson, *ANF*); "In a more profound *discussion*, we have shown that..." (Wood); so Otto Stählin: "Wir haben aber in gründlicherer Darstellung gezeigt...," on which he comments in a note, "Wir wissen nicht, in welcher Schrift dies geschah" (*Des Clemens von Alexandreia ausgewählte Schriften aus dem Griechischen übersetzt* [Munich: Josef Kösel & Friedrich Pustet, 1934], 2:61 and 2:61n5).

I have reservations about whether this is the correct way to translate διειλήφαμεν δὲ βαθυτέρῳ λόγῳ. Mondésert's translation ("Nous avons expliqué d'une façon plus approfondie") may be preferable to those that suggest λόγος refers to a written work. It is common for other Christian writers to use βαθύτερος λόγος to refer to the "deeper sense" (frequently the "deeper *and mystical* sense" of scripture). And while διαλαμβάνω *can* mean "to discuss," we would have expected Clement to have said διειλήφαμεν *ἐν* βαθυτέρῳ λόγῳ had he been referring to another writing or even another section of this writing. Note the way Origen, referring back to an earlier section of the *Contra Celsum*, says περὶ ὧν ἐν τοῖς ἀνωτέρω ἐπ᾽ ὀλίγον διειλήφαμεν, λέγοντες ὅτι κ.τ.λ. [Origen, *Cels.* 5.45]). Ultimately the difference might not amount to much. Even if these words are best translated "I have shown in a *deeper sense* that there is nothing obscene," Clement would still be referring to some other *writing* where this explanation is found, because he has shown no such thing here.

[49] Clement himself, as well as Eusebius and Jerome, mention other writings which do not survive. For a discussion of his corpus, cf. Patrick, *Clement of Alexandria*, 301–8; Ferguson, *Clement of Alexandria*, 179–91.

[50] Eusebius, *Hist. eccl.* 6.13. Suetonius's work by a similar title (Περὶ βλασφημιῶν) deals with various terms of abuse.

obscene. (In fact, a person's genitals [τὰ αἰδοῖα] deserve modest respect [αἰδοῦς], not shame [αἰσχύνης].) All that is shameful is their *unlawful* activity; this deserves shame [αἴσχους], reproach and punishment. In fact, only evil and things done in accordance with evil are actually shameful."[51] Correspondingly, Clement will not define foul language as specific words for body parts or activities, but rather as talk about what is really evil. Clement says, "In keeping with these claims" about the innocence of words and body parts, "foul language could be defined as making discourse about wicked activities—that is, talking about adultery or pederasty or the like" (τούτοις δὲ ἀναλόγως αἰσχρολογία εἰκότως ἂν καλοῖτο ἡ περὶ τῶν τῆς κακίας ἔργων λογοποιία· οἷον τὸ περὶ μοιχείας διαλέγεσθαι ἢ παιδεραστίας καὶ τὰ παραπλήσια [*Paed.* 2.52.3]). On the one hand, this is an extremely broad definition and would include even all those forms of invective, humor, and amorous tales that allude to such sexual activities without using obscenities. If in Clement's eyes, even Homer "teaches adultery,"[52] then an enormous amount of less wholesome storytelling must also be excluded. But what is striking is that Clement is *redefining* the common term αἰσχρολογία so that it better accords with his claim that words and body parts (and their lawful functions) are not in themselves problematic (thus he prefaces his definition with τούτοις δὲ ἀναλόγως, "analogously with these claims"). This leaves open the question, at least theoretically, whether it would be acceptable to speak of amoral things with "obscene" terms. Could one speak of the *lawful* use of πέος and κύσθος using those words? Clement gives as his examples two rather innocent body parts (γόνυ and κνήμη), no doubt because he has no desire to shock or offend his readers.

Clement's claim that there is nothing inherently shameful in words or their referents is unparalleled among early Christians, and surfaces only rarely in any Greek or Latin literature. Despite how little Clement says, his comments bear a certain resemblance to the argument that Cicero ascribes to Zeno and the Stoics. As a first step in this argument, the Stoics stated that "if there is anything shocking in obscenity, it

---

[51] οὐδὲ γὰρ γόνυ καὶ κνήμη τὰ μέλη ταῦτα οὐδὲ μὴν τὰ ἐπ᾽ αὐτοῖς ὀνόματα καὶ ἡ δι᾽ αὐτῶν ἐνέργεια αἰσχρά ἐστιν—μέλη δὲ καὶ τὰ αἰδοῖα τοῦ ἀνθρώπου, αἰδοῦς, οὐκ αἰσχύνης κατηξιωμένα. αἰσχρὸν δὲ ἡ παράνομος αὐτῶν ἐνέργεια... · μόνον γὰρ τῷ ὄντι αἰσχρὸν ἡ κακία καὶ τὰ κατὰ ταύτην ἐνεργούμενα (*Paed.* 2.52.2).

[52] Clement quotes Homer's account of Ares and Aphrodite and interjects: "Homer, stop the song; it is not noble; it teaches adultery. And we must avoid adultery even with our ears" (*Prot.* 59.1–2).

lies either in the matter or in the word; there is no third possibility."[53] Clement twice makes this same *nomen/res* distinction, saying that there is nothing shameful in the words or the things.[54] As we have already discussed, Cicero himself argued, *contra* these Stoics, that when propriety is observed, "neither the parts nor the functions are called by their real names," and in so arguing he again mentions the same three topics addressed by Clement: body parts, their use, and their names.[55] In a sense, Clement theologizes Zeno's case for using "real" names by appealing to God's work in creation: "Now it is not shameful for us to name the generative organs for the aid of those listening, when *God* is not ashamed to have made them."[56]

Clement says so little about why he believes that words are not indecent that it is impossible to say with certainty where he got the idea; but it is not unreasonable to conjecture that he was influenced by the Stoics. Clement was familiar with a wide range of Hellenistic philosophy, and his writings show the influence of the Platonic, Aristotelian, and Stoic systems.[57] His own teacher and predecessor in Alexandria, Pantaenus, was a converted Stoic,[58] and as noted above, Clement appears to have known the sorts of Stoic writings the *Paedagogue* so closely resembles. In addition to the Stoic imprint on so many of Clement's ethics,[59]

---

[53] *Si quod sit in obscenitate flagitium, id aut in re esse aut in verbo; nihil esse tertium* (*Fam.* 9.22.1).

[54] οὔτε ἐν τοῖς ὀνόμασιν οὐδὲ μὴν ἐν τοῖς συνουσιαστικοῖς μορίοις… οὐδὲ… τὰ μέλη ταῦτα οὐδὲ μὴν τὰ ἐπ᾽ αὐτοῖς ὀνόματα (*Paed.* 2.52.2).

[55] *eas neque partes neque earum usus suis nominibus appellant* (*Off.* 1.127). Admittedly, distinguishing *nomen* and *res* is familiar from a wide variety of contexts.

[56] οὐκ αἰσχρὸν δὲ ἡμῖν ἐπ᾽ ὠφελείᾳ τῶν ἀκουόντων τὰ κυητικὰ ὀνομάζειν ὄργανα, ὧν οὐκ ἐπῃσχύνθη τὴν δημιουργίαν ὁ θεός (*Paed.* 2.92.3). Following common usage, Clement calls them the "unmentionable" parts (cf. *Paed.* 2.51.1: τῶν ἀπορρητοτέρων μερῶν; *Paed.* 3.20.2: τὰ ἀπόρρητα; cf. 3.21; *Protrep.* 2.23.1: μόρια ἄρρητα; cf. also *Protrep.* 2.22.4). In general, Clement uses standard euphemisms for the sexual parts and activities, although we might note the derisive use of ὀχεύω at *Strom.* 3.47.3 (instructions for people who would unrestrainedly eat and screw).

[57] Many scholars have tried to pick the predominant system (Maier, "Clement of Alexandria," 719). Henry Chadwick describes Clement's eclecticism as "the common blend of Platonist metaphysics and Stoic ethics together with Aristotelian logic and terminology" (*Early Christian Thought*, 40–41).

[58] Eusebius, *Hist. eccl.* 5.10; 6.6.1.

[59] Even Clement's distinction between αἰδώς and αἰσχύνη (the genitals deserve "modesty" not "shame") might offer another small clue that he knows a specifically Stoic argument about foul language, since the Stoics designated αἰδώς the rational version of the irrational passion αἰσχύνη. For the Stoics distinction, see Plutarch, *Mor.* 449A; 529D. For a similar distinction (in this case between φόβος and εὐλάβεια), cf. *Strom.* 2.32.3–4 with *SVF* 3.175, 431; Cicero, *Tusc.* 4.6.13; Plutarch, *Mor.* 1037F.

Clement was also familiar with Stoic linguistics. He cites Cleanthes on λεκτά,[60] uses a Stoic example for distinguishing a sound from a word,[61] and addresses Chrysippus's paradox that what one says passes through one's mouth.[62]

But however like the Stoics Clement may sound when he talks about the innocence of words and their referents, he is at the same time quite staunchly opposed to *aischrologia*. Why would a man who finds nothing shameful in words recommend "saving ear-guards" (*Paed.* 2.52.3)? Why worry that freedom of speech might lead to αἰσχρολογία if there is nothing αἰσχρόν in λόγοι? Why advise Christians to blush and frown when shameful things are said? Why not rather, like the Cynics and Stoics, show the world how truly λογικοί Christians were by *not* blushing at utterances that shocked others? Why not urge Christians to use the "real" names for body parts and activities?

Clement's opposition to foul language is easier to account for than his claim that there is nothing inherently wrong with it. Since Clement had before him in "scripture" two Pauline epistles that condemned foul language, it is little surprise that Clement would also oppose it, even if he knew and recognized the validity of the argument that names and topics are not inherently obscene. But obviously a simple appeal to Clement's biblicism does not tell the whole story;[63] it is not as though Clement found himself pressing up against an immovable object which forced his course. Had Clement harbored a deep appre-

---

On Clement and Stoic teachings more generally, cf. J. Stelzenberger, *Die Beziehungen der frühchristlichen Sittenlehre zur Ethik der Stoa* (Munich: Max Hueber, 1933); M. Spanneut, *Le Stoïcisme et les Pères de l'Église, de Clément de Rome à Clément d'Alexandrie* (rev. ed.; Paris: Éditions du Seuil, 1969). In some instances, it is true, Clement may have gotten his Stoic wording from Philo rather than from Stoic sources themselves (Marrou, *Le Pédagogue*, 1:51n2; cf. also Salvatore R. C. Lilla, *Clement of Alexandria: A Study in Christian Platonism and Gnosticism* [Oxford: Oxford University Press, 1971]: 112–13), but he makes multiple explicit references to both Zeno and Cleanthes.

[60] *Strom.* 8.26.4; cf. D.L. 7.63.

[61] Cf. *Strom.* 8.3.1 ("Blityri is a mere sound, signifying nothing") with D.L. 7.57.

[62] *Strom.* 8.25.4–5; cf. D.L. 7.187 (Chrysippus poses the paradox: "If you say something, it passes through your lips: now you say wagon, consequently a wagon passes through your lips.")

[63] It is true that Clement could *write* as though scripture was the ultimate authority. When addressing the philosophers who criticize "fear," he concludes that they *must* be wrong because the Law enjoins fear (*Strom.* 2.32). Similarly, despite all of his concerns about sex, Clement finally concedes that it cannot be entirely bad, since the scripture commands "Be fruitful and multiply" (*Paed.* 2.95.1). But I think Marrou underestimates how pliable scripture can be when he says "L'ascétisme de Clément trouve sa limite dans la Révélation" (*Le Pédagogue*, 2:182n5).

ciation for four-letter words, the biblical texts could have been ignored[64] or reinterpreted. (No biblical texts kept Clement from declaring that Christ had been "entirely impassible" [*Strom.* 6.71.2].) But Clement did *not* like foul language.[65] To the contrary, he shared the wide-spread sense that foul language had absolutely no place in the high-minded pursuits of a godly and philosophical life. Between the biblical texts and the general antipathy to lewd talk we find among moralists of all stripes, it is not difficult to understand why Clement says all he does *against* foul language.

But this leaves unanswered the question why Clement would have written in favor of a perspective that would seem to undermine the moral precepts he was recommending. What rhetorical effect could he have hoped to achieve by mentioning the non-obscenity of words in the very chapter that denounces them?

I believe Clement's comments actually fit quite well with his larger program of showing Christianity to be the true philosophy, the life according to *logos*. Like Philo before him (from whom he drew), Clement endeavored to harmonize the scriptures with what he regarded as best in philosophy. He rejected that Christian view which claimed philosophy was superfluous or introduced by the devil (*Strom.* 6.66.1); on the contrary, he says, it is both necessary and is in some manner a work of divine providence (*Strom.* 1.18). Clement uses the ambiguity

---

[64] The famously foul-mouthed Martin Luther wrote verse-by-verse commentaries on both Ephesians and Colossians without saying a word about their strictures against bad language.

[65] Clement was, however, no prude when it came to writing about sex. Although never using offensive terms, he is frank and explicit, and seems to have believed his own claim that there was nothing shameful in discussing the sexual organs. When he follows the *Epistle of Barnabas* in interpreting the Mosaic command not to eat hare or hyena as a rejection of pederasty and sensuality (*Barn.* 10.6–7 from Lev 11:6 [there is no command in the Pentateuch about the hyena]), he enters into an elaborate description of the mounting and copulating of rabbits (who grow an extra anus for every year of their lives), and of the hyena's peculiar sexual organs (which is quite explicit because he wants to take issue with the claim that the hyena changes sex each year). The mistake, Clement says, resulted from the hyena's unusual anatomy: nature fitted this animal with a bit of flesh under its tail and in front of its anus, which looks like a vagina (*Paed.* 2.85.3). This opening does not go anywhere, it simply receives the ineffectual sexual act. The details matter to Clement because he wants to claim that "nature has not granted even that most sensual of animals to get pregnant through the passage of evacuation" (*Paed.* 2.87.1).

Clement's nineteenth-century translators—who admired his chapter on foul language ("This is a very precious chapter" [*ANF*, 2.250n5])—found themselves unable to commit any of these anatomical discussions to English ("For obvious reasons, we have given the greater part of this chapter in the Latin version" [2.259n3]).

of the word λόγος ("the Word," or "reason," or "word," etc.) when he defines the Christian life in philosophical terms.[66] "Faith" is simply obedience to reason (λόγος), and therefore "faith" gives rise to "duty" (καθῆκον) in a rational way (*Paed.* 1.101.1). "Sin" is whatever contradicts right reason.[67] The life of the Christian is a system of "logical deeds enjoined by reason" (*Paed.* 1.102.4), and hence the Christian life is a pure philosophy,[68] wisdom given by God.[69]

But if Clement wants to describe Christianity as a philosophy, he is also obligated to respond to the sorts of charges that the various philosophical schools made against each other. Cicero, it will be recalled, complained that the Cynics and Stoics "*censure* and *ridicule* us [Academics] for holding that the mere mention of some actions that are not immoral is shameful."[70] Put simply, I propose that Clement did not want to expose his "philosophy" to such ridicule. Besides the criticism of the Stoics, it is at least possible that some other Christian groups argued in favor of foul language, and it could have been their potential objections, as well, that prompted Clement's disclaimer. Clement once accuses "Prodicus's school" of confusing "immoderation and obscene language" with "freedom."[71] Little is known about Prodicus,[72] and therefore it can remain nothing more than a guess that his group advocated foul language (and mocked those unenlight-

---

[66] Pohlenz, "Klemens," 43.

[67] πᾶν τὸ παρὰ τὸν λόγον τὸν ὀρθὸν τοῦτο ἁμάρτημά ἐστιν (*Paed.* 1.101.1); cf. *SVF* 3:500.

[68] Greek philosophy is, he says, "a stepping-stone to the philosophy in accordance with Christ" (ὑποβάθραν οὖσαν τῆς κατὰ Χριστὸν φιλοσοφίας [*Strom.* 6.67.1]).

[69] *Strom.* 1.90.1. Clement speaks frequently of the ideal Christian as a philosopher (*Strom.* 2.46.1; 2.126.1; 6.108.1; etc.).

[70] Cicero, *Off.* 1.128.

[71] *Strom.* 3.30.3: πῶς δὲ ἐλεύθερον ἡ ἀκρασία καὶ ἡ αἰσχρολογία.

[72] Prodicus is mentioned twice by Tertullian, both times in conjunction with Valentinus: once as introducing multiplicity of gods (*Adv. Prax.* 3); another time as denying the need for confession and martyrdom (*Scorpiace* 15). He is mentioned four times by Clement. Clement says that Prodicus, like Marcion, was not content with "ecclesiastical gnosis" (*Strom.* 7.103.6); the followers of Prodicus's sect (αἵρεσις) deny the need for prayer, a point on which he says they prided themselves (*Strom.* 7.41.1–2); they also claimed to possess secret books of Zoroaster (*Strom.* 1.69.6). They falsely take the name "gnostics" and claim to be by nature children of the first god (*Strom.* 3.30.1). Clement says that they consider themselves "princes superior to all humankind" and to use this high birth to "do what they want." Clement charges that what they want is, in fact, pleasure (καταχρώμενοι δὲ τῇ εὐγενείᾳ καὶ τῇ ἐλευθερίᾳ ζῶσιν ὡς βούλονται βούλονται δὲ φιληδόνως). Their claim to be regal (βασίλειοι παῖδες) and therefore free from rules (βασιλεῖ δέ, φασί, νόμος ἄγραφος), is consonant with the Cynic idea that all things are legitimate for the philosopher king (cf. Downing, *Cynics, Paul, and*

ened Christians who eschewed it). But be it from educated pagans or from a free-speaking group of Christians, it is likely that Clement had heard the charge that concern over mere words was irrational. With his philosophical aspirations, Clement was sensitive to this charge and wanted to respond, but had to do so without abandoning his own moral intuition and the biblical prohibitions. Thus he condemns lewd talk, but, to forestall the charge that this was linguistically naive, he makes a point of saying that he knows perfectly well that obscenity inheres neither in words nor their referents.[73]

Clement's comments about the non-obscenity of words also allow him to distinguish Christian motives from the sorts of superstitious or irrational motives philosophers so often criticized in the masses. Clement repeatedly contrasts gentile superstition to *true* Christian beliefs, attempting to show that Christians are concerned with what is *truly* evil or *truly* pure, while the heathen are preoccupied with irrational externals. So, for instance, Clement picks up the philosophical lampoon of external purity and then concludes, "For in reality, purity is nothing other than avoiding sins."[74] He contrasts Christian vegetarianism with that of the Pythagoreans, since the Christian avoids meat with good reason (λόγῳ τινὶ εὐλόγῳ χρῆται), unlike Pythagoras and his followers with their silly dreams about the transmigration of the soul (*Strom.* 7.32.8).

When one recognizes how pervasively Clement uses this rhetoric, one can see how reluctant he would have been to leave himself open to the charge that he irrationally regarded certain words and body parts as

---

the Pauline Churches, 103). Perhaps their αἰσχρολογία was also of a piece with a Cynic outlook that denied that the world's rules applied to them.

Prodicus is not mentioned by the main heresiologists (Irenaeus, Hippolytus, Epiphanius); after Clement he is next mentioned in Theodoret, who "had no more real knowledge of Prodicus than what he learned from Clement whom he quotes" (George Salmon, "Prodicus," in *A Dictionary of Christian Biography* [ed. William Smith and Henry Wace; 4 vols.; London: John Murray, 1877], 4:490). Theodoret does connect Prodicus to the nudist Adamites, but it is not clear this is based on any real knowledge (Ferguson, *Stromateis 1–3*, 274n100).

[73] Aside from being prompted by criticism, Clement may also have been impelled to reflect deeply about the nature of foul language from his desire to *understand* commands, not simply to obey them blindly (*Strom.* 6.108.3). Walther Völker notes that for Clement, the gnostic must understand what he does (*Der Wahre Gnostiker Nach Clemens Alexandrinus* [Berlin: Hinrichs, 1952], 447–453).

[74] τῷ γὰρ ὄντι ἡ ἁγνεία οὐκ ἄλλη τίς ἐστιν πλὴν ἡ τῶν ἁμαρτημάτων ἀποχή (*Strom.* 7.27.4). Similarly at *Strom.* 7.26.2 Clement mocks heathen superstition about the nature of holiness (employing Greek philosophical critiques) and contrasts the Christian view that "God—the *true* God [ὁ τῷ ὄντι θεός]—knows that only the character of the righteous man is holy."

taboo. By mentioning and briefly describing his awareness that words
are not obscene, Clement can agree that the Stoics (or whoever) are
right so far as linguistics are concerned (thereby avoiding the charge of
irrationality). Then, by claiming that there are altogether *different* reasons
for avoiding foul language, he can also uphold the biblical imperatives
and remain in line with a widely felt sentiment.

For Clement the *real* problem with shameful words is that they will
lead to shameful deeds,[75] and some deeds *are* evil.[76] Thus it is clear why
Clement defines αἰσχρολογία as he does. Since only evil is shameful
(αἰσχρόν), it makes sense to call αἰσχρολογία the making of stories
(λογοποιία) about evil—that is, talking about adultery or pederasty
and the like (*Paed.* 2.52.3, cited above 224). God really does (τῷ ὄντι)
approve of seemliness in speech because "foul language is the road to
shamelessness, and shameful *behavior* results from both."[77] In some ways
Clement's view of words is analogous to his view of nudity: the naked
body is not in itself offensive *to God*, yet there is a tremendous danger
that the smallest patch of uncovered flesh will stimulate lust in others,
and for *that* reason it must be strenuously avoided.[78]

How exactly will words lead to deeds? Just as the sight of naked
flesh enters into the body through the eyes and excites lust, so lewd
words work through the ears.[79] The young must avoid banquets lest
"the unusual things they hear and inappropriate things they see" stir
up their thoughts and work together with the instability of their age to
make them victims of lust (*Paed.* 2.53.5). The theater is a place where
"erotic desires" are kindled through the eyes and the shameless talk of
the comedians enters the ears and then, like a virus, reproduces itself

---

[75] διὰ τῶν ὀνομάτων αὐτῶν ἐπὶ τὰ αἰσχρὰ τῶν ἔργων ἐθίζων (*Paed.* 2.45.4). As we
have seen, this was a familiar concern.

[76] So the law teaches Christians to avoid the *real* evils (τὰ τῷ ὄντι κακά)—adultery,
shameless behavior, pederasty, ignorance, injustice, spiritual sickness, death (*Strom.*
2.34.2).

[77] θεοφιλὲς γὰρ τῷ ὄντι ἀπὸ τῆς γλώττης ἐπὶ τὰ ἔργα τὸ κόσμιον διαχειραγωγεῖν,
ὁδὸς δὲ ἐπ᾽ ἀναισχυντίαν ἡ αἰσχρολογία, καὶ τέλος ἀμφοῖν ἡ αἰσχρουργία (*Strom.*
2.145.2).

[78] Cf. *Paed.* 3.31–33 on seeing naked bodies at the baths.

[79] Cf. "listening to or gazing upon indecent things" (*Paed.* 2.49.2); "neither listen
to nor look at nor talk about obscene things" (*Paed.* 2.51.1). Contrast Plutarch, *Mor.*
681B–C, who describes the powerful "melting" effect of seeing an attractive person,
and concludes: "neither by touch nor by hearing do they suffer so deep a wound as
by seeing and being seen."

later (*Paed.* 3.77.1–2).[80] To see or hear depictions of sex is almost to have committed the act.[81] In the *Protrepticus*, Clement says to the pagans— with their public depictions of naked girls, drunken Satyrs, swollen members (*Protr.* 61.1), and their private paintings of the positions of Philaenis (*Protr.* 61.2)—"Your ears have played the harlot; your eyes have fornicated; what is strangest, your looks have commited adultery before you even embrace."[82] Even looking at or hearing about such things is wrong.[83]

Using foul language, or listening to it without visible evidence of disapproval, also gives others the impression that sexual advances might be welcomed. So Clement warns that if women tolerate lewd talk from their slaves, they will reveal themselves to be eager for sex: "I do not think it appropriate for the female servants who walk along to the left of the woman or follow after them to speak or act indecently [αἰσχρολογεῖν ἢ αἰσχροεργεῖν]; on the contrary, they should be mod- est [σωφρονίζεσθαι] in the presence of their mistresses" (*Paed.* 3.73.1). The servant's ἀκολασία reflects on the mistress, and if the mistress fails to register indignation, she suggests that she herself is inclined in the same direction (*Paed.* 3.73.3). If a servant's naughty talk reflects badly, the language of a dissolute crowd of actors is that much worse. When Clement expresses his disgust with women who keep the company of the wrong sorts of men, he draws attention not only to the men's indecent words but even to their lust-inducing sounds:

> These women delight in the company of androgyns, and throngs of bab- bling *kinaidoi* come in, defiled in body, defiled in language, manly only when it comes to delivering their dissolute services, servants of adultery, giggling and whispering and shamelessly snorting through their noses the sounds of debauched sex to provoke immorality; striving to please with wanton word and gestures, summoning everyone to laughter, the precursor of fornication. (*Paed.* 3.29.2–3)[84]

---

[80] Lounging around taverns and barber shops presents a similar risk to eyes and ears (*Paed.* 3.75.1).

[81] See Simon Goldhill, "The Erotic Experience of Looking," 381–84.

[82] ἡταίρηκεν ὑμῖν τὰ ὦτα, πεπορνεύκασιν οἱ ὀφθαλμοὶ καὶ τὸ καινότατον πρὸ τῆς συμπλοκῆς αἱ ὄψεις ὑμῖν μεμοιχεύκασιν (*Protr.* 61.3).

[83] *Protr.* 61.3: τούτων οὐ μόνον τῆς χρήσεως, πρὸς δὲ καὶ τῆς ὄψεως καὶ τῆς ἀκοῆς αὐτῆς ἀμνηστίαν καταγγέλλομεν.

[84] ἇι δὲ ἀνδρογύνων συνουσίαις ἥδονται, παρεισρέουσι δὲ ἔνδον κιναίδων ὄχλοι ἀθυρόγλωσσοι, μιαροὶ μὲν τὰ σώματα, μιαροὶ δὲ τὰ φθέγματα, εἰς ὑπουργίας ἀκολάστους ἠνδρωμένοι, μοιχείας διάκονοι, κικλίζοντες καὶ ψιθυρίζοντες καὶ τὸ πορνικὸν ἀνέδην

A woman's display of annoyance at lewd talk is of a piece with her keeping her limbs covered (*Paed.* 2.114.1)—it lets the world know that she is not interested in sex.[85] For the same reason Clement wants young men's appearance and gestures to "give no hope to the dissolute."[86] This is why men must have "no traces of softness" visible in the face, body, movements, or posture.[87] And although one should not be gloomy (*Paed.* 2.47.1), even the smile must be subject to discipline—and, as mentioned already, one ought to blush rather than smile at indecencies (*Paed.* 2.47.2). In his treatment of laughter,[88] Clement sees dangers to dignity—the risk that a lack of seriousness will be revealed to the watching world. Furthermore, he associates laughter with seduction or the appearance thereof.[89] One of the chief virtues of a serious expression is that it will repel tempters.[90] Words flow from the temperament and character (ἀπὸ διανοίας καὶ ἤθους); funny words indicate a laughable character.[91] In the unending effort to show the world a manly face, a drunken giggle is a fatal misstep. Wine leads to laughter and dance, turning an already "androgynous" character altogether "soft" (εἰς μαλακίαν ἐκτρέπων τὸ ἀνδρόγυνον ἦθος [*Paed.* 2.48.1–2]). Clement says that "we must observe that bold language turns unbecoming speech into foul language."[92]

Both of these concerns—words' lust-inspiring impact on the soul and the need to maintain a chaste mien—help explain why foul language is especially dangerous for women and the young.[93] Just as the elderly are not threatened by the heat of wine, their bodies being cool, so they are less susceptible to words' power to kindle their imagination. The young are already working against the instability of their age;[94] their systems

---

εἰς ἀσέλγειαν διὰ ῥινῶν ἐπιψοφοῦντες κιναίδισμα, ἀκολάστοις ῥήμασι καὶ σχήμασι τέρπειν πειρώμενοι καὶ εἰς γέλωτα ἐκκαλούμενοι πορνείας πρόδρομον.

[85] Cf. *Strom.* 2.146.1 on a wife's avoiding excessive beautification and avoiding going out, so that she can be above accusation.

[86] *Paed.* 3.74.3 (citing Zeno for how they should appear.).

[87] *Paed.* 3.69; 3.73.5; 3.74.1.

[88] *Paed.* 2.45–48, immediately preceding the discussion of foul language.

[89] "Especially among boys and women, laughter leads to accusations" (μάλιστα γὰρ μειρακίοις καὶ γυναιξὶν ὄλισθος εἰς διαβολὰς ὁ γέλως ἐστίν [*Paed.* 2.47.3]).

[90] *Paed.* 2.48.1.

[91] *Paed.* 2.45.1.

[92] καὶ σκοπεῖν δεῖ πῶς ἐντεῦθεν ἡ παρρησία τὴν ἀκοσμίαν εἰς αἰσχρολογίαν αὔξει (*Paed.* 2.48.2).

[93] *Paed.* 2.57.1 permits some joking for those who are older, but only for educational purposes.

[94] τὸ ἄστατον τῆς ἡλικίας (*Paed.* 2.53.5).

cannot handle words about sex or glimpses of body parts. Likewise
Clement imagines women and younger people as the primary objects of
sexual desire. So to discourage potential seducers, it is paramount that
these groups make an exhibition of their disapproval of dirty talk.

III. Comparing Clement

We have seen that Clement developed his morality of the tongue in
a way he thought would protect Christians both from passions *and*
from the charge of naïveté. His program, if followed, was to ward off
suitors by its chaste and serious air, and ward off intellectual attack
because it was rationally grounded. We can see how different Clement's concerns are from those of the text he so admired, the Epistle
to the Ephesians.

In Ephesians, as in the Mishnah and the literature from Qumran, the
idea that the community had been sanctified like the temple invoked the
Mosaic rule that there be "nothing indecent" in God's presence lest he
"turn away." The idea that the holy community dwells in sacred space
(Eph 2:6; 2:20–22) means that dirty language brings indecency into the
divine presence and profanes the members who were to be sanctified
like priests (Eph 1:4; 5:27). Two centuries after Clement, John Chrysostom expressed a similar fear: using foul language was tantamount,
he claimed, to dumping dung in the doorway of the temple; the Holy
Spirit would depart because of the stench.

Clement has no such worries about words' power to desecrate or drive
away the divine presence. We might assume that this has more to do
with his view of God than with his view of obscene speech. After all,
Clement claimed that God was incorporeal, existing neither in space
nor time, always retreating from those seeking him since the Creator
could never be fully reached by the creation.[95] How could such a God
be defiled by *anything*? But Clement could occasionally speak of God's
indwelling presence[96]—and he could speak of God's departing from
a Christian because of things that were genuinely sinful. For instance,
the Word and the Spirit depart in cases of πορνεία, for, as Clement

---

[95] *Strom.* 2.5.3–4.
[96] Cf., for example, his use of Lev 26:12 (*Strom.* 3.73).

explains, "What is holy shrinks from being defiled."[97] Furthermore, Clement can occasionally connect God's omnipresence to speech ethics, as when he claims that the gnostic will not swear, knowing that God is everywhere.[98] So despite talk of God's distance from creation, Clement at times uses the biblical images of God's dwelling in the community and departing because of sin. Thus the fact that Clement did *not* speak of obscene speech offending or defiling the deity seems to confirm that Clement, despite all of his fears about what bad language might say about or do to people, genuinely meant what he said when he claimed that, so far as God was concerned, there was nothing wrong with "obscene" words.

Whereas Ephesians, seeking to inculcate a sense of sanctity, of the separation of the "holy ones" from the "sons of disobedience," wants the voices of believers to join with those of the angels (the other "holy ones") in singing God's praise (Eph 5:19), Clement seeks to inculcate a sense of dignity and chastity. His angelic life is the life of a high-minded philosopher, whose every move, gesture, and word express nobility and self-mastery.

---

[97] διὸ καὶ πάντως ὁ πορνεύων ἀπέθανεν θεῷ, καὶ καταλέλειπται ὑπὸ τοῦ λόγου, καθάπερ ὑπὸ τοῦ πνεύματος [ὁ] νεκρός. Βδελύττεται γὰρ τὸ ἅγιον μολύνεσθαι, ὥσπερ οὖν εἰκός (*Paed.* 2.100.1).

[98] *Strom.* 7.51.7–8. Clement is confusing on the topic of oaths. He says alternately that the gnostic prefers a simple "yes" and "no" to swearing (cf. Matt 5:37; James 5:12), then that he swears truly but not often, and then that he will not swear even when asked for his oath (*Strom.* 7.50–51).

CONCLUSIONS

Foul language had no small place in the ancient world. It wounded the victims of iambic poetry; it burst off the comic stage; it was whispered and shouted in religious rites; it was scrawled crudely on walls and written cleverly in poems. The pressure to avoid obscene words at the wrong times could be intense, as countless ancient apologies and circumlocutions attest. From Plato to the Emperor Julian there was a sense that foul speech was lowly and slavish, contrary to moral earnestness. This despite the fact that people of even the highest echelons of society were known to use foul language in their poetry and over their wine.

The Cynics violated normal mores of polite speech as part of their assault on unnatural convention. Their witty, abusive, and often off-color jabs were renowned from the time of Diogenes to the end of late antiquity. A dog not only defecates in public, he also howls and barks. The Stoics considered foul language from a more theoretical perspective, and concluded that avoiding particular words was absurd. That their opinion on the matter was one of the doctrines that demarcated them from other philosophical schools is attested by Cicero, who says there was a "great battle" between the Stoa and the Academy on this topic. But beginning with Panaetius, more and more Stoics argued that decorous speech was actually what "nature" decreed. Towering Stoic figures such as Cato or Musonius Rufus carefully avoided indecent speech. In Epictetus we have a Stoic whose discipline of the tongue has gone to the other extreme. Not only must a philosopher be polite, but to the greatest degree possible he must avoid *all* talk about mundane affairs. In Epictetus's regimen the tongue instills in the philosopher a profound sense of the distinction between him and the "laymen," of whose vulgar conversation he must beware. I argued that Ephesians also urges distinctive patterns of speech that, in a similar way, would remind Christians that they were a people set apart from the "sons of disobedience."

But the concerns that so many Greek and Roman moralists had about foul language are notably absent from the Hebrew scriptures, from Jesus' sayings, and from Paul's authentic letters. Sirach, the *Didache*, and Colossians make brief mentions of foul language. Ephesians is more expansive than Colossians, and Clement of Alexandria has quite a lot to say about this topic. While I have tried to show that the way these texts talk about foul language reveals interesting things about their social locations and how they understood their relationship to the world, it would certainly be a mistake to suggest that foul language constituted one of the burning ethical questions faced by early Christianity. In fact, in the Christian literature written between the end of the first century (Ephesians) and the end of the second (Clement of Alexandria), there are very few comments on the topic. The *Shepherd of Hermas* mentions incidentally a man saying a lascivious word to a woman (Herm. *Vis.* 1.1.7). The *Testament of Judah* warns that drunkenness results in a shameless display of foul language (14.8; 16.3). It is possible that this was composed by Christians; at the very least, it was being read and copied by them. But on the whole, the Christian writings of the second century have little to say on this topic. They mention the same types of speech as Jewish wisdom literature, urging people to limit their words (*1 Clem.* 21.7; 30.4; Herm. *Mand.* 5.2.6; Ignatius, *Eph.* 15.1; cf. *Barn.* 19.8) and warning against slander (*1 Clem.* 30.1, 3; 35.5, 8; Ignatius, *Eph.* 10.2; *Barn.* 20.2; Herm. *Mand.* 2.2, 3; 8.3), grumbling (*Barn.* 19.11), and abuse (*Diognetus* 5.15). Avoiding destructive and disreputable forms of speech was a way to promote peace within the churches and a good reputation with those outside. Speech was not something that was meant to set Christians apart, and foul speech did not call for special comment.

It is highly likely that all of these authors did, in fact, object to foul speech, which was widely regarded by most moralists as a far grosser vice than merely being talkative. But the second-century Christians evidently felt no need to deal with foul language directly. There was so clearly a sense of propriety about the matter that it did not often need to be addressed. We get a sense for how a Christian author could take his readers' moral intuition about foul speech for granted in Tertullian's writings. Tertullian does not cite the specific commands of Eph 5:3–4 or Col 3:8, and he never writes a chapter "On Foul Language." But when explaining why Christians must not attend the *Atellanae*, he asks rhetorically: "If we ought to abominate all that is immodest, on what ground is it right to hear what we must not speak [*cur liceat audire quod loqui non licet*]?" (*Spect.* 17 [*ANF* 3:87]). Tertullian can take for granted that his readers will agree with him that there are things they must not utter; from this he can argue that there are also things that they should not hear.

It is at least possible to imagine how Christians could have arrived at a different conclusion about foul language, rejecting the common mores in the way the Stoics did, rather than endorsing the world's sense of propriety. They could have advocated foul language and used it as one of the hallmarks of their "freedom in Christ." Christian baptism claimed to return the baptized to humanity's earliest condition (cf. Gal 3:28; Col 3:9–11). What if Christians had asked themselves what speech was like in the Garden of Eden?[1] Is not the thought of Edenic euphemism absurd? How could Adam and Eve have used veiled words when even their naked bodies caused no shame (Gen 2:25)? The Cynics, who strove to live out the golden age of Chronus, used the ribald speech of the festival of Chronus (the Saturnalia), where the normal rules of decorum were set aside. We could at least imagine a group of Christians behaving similarly. If humans were meant to be free from shame (Genesis 2); if God had once inspired a prophet to talk about the genitalia of horses (Ezek 23:20); if "for the pure, all things are pure" (Tit 1:15), then perhaps Christians should call things by their "real" names, thereby showing that they transcended the senseless cultural conventions of "the present evil age" (Gal 1:4).

But there do not appear to have been any such Christians. Clement of Alexandria accused the followers of Prodicus of using foul language, and Theodoret connected them to the nudist Adamites. Could this have been a group of Christians that reinstituted the life of Eden with naked bodies and naked words? Christendom would one day have its Cynic-style "fools for Christ";[2] it would one day have Martin Luther, who regularly told the devil to lick his ass and eat his shit.[3] But in the writings that survive from the first two centuries, the closest Christians

---

[1] A question that was contemplated in antiquity (e.g. Jubilees 3.28; 12.26), as it has been more recently (Umberto Eco devotes an essay to the "Possibility of Generating Aesthetic Messages in an Edenic Language" in *The Role of the Reader: Explorations in the Semiotics of Texts* [Bloomington: Indiana University Press, 1979]: 90–104). On the place of foul language in paradise regained, cf. Bakhtin, *Rabelais*, 16. Augustine himself claimed that, were it not for the Fall, there would have been nothing obscene in using the "proper" terms for sexual organs (*Civ.* 14.23).

[2] See Derek Krueger, *Symeon the Holy Fool: Leontius's Life and the Late Antique City* (Berkeley: University of California Press, 1996).

[3] For a rich analysis of Luther's scatological language, see Carlos M. N. Eire, "'Bite This, Satan!' The Devil in Luther's *Table Talk*," in *Piety and Family in Early Modern Europe: Essays in Honour of Steven Ozment* (ed. Marc R. Forster and Benjamin J. Kaplan; Burlington, VT: Ashgate, 2005): 70–93; for a more apologetic approach, cf. Heiko A. Oberman, *Luther: Man Between God and the Devil* (trans. Eileen Walliser-Schwarzbart; New Haven: Yale University Press, 1989), 106–9.

came to using foul language is the rare piece of graphic invective, such as Papias's description of Judas's demise—and even this uses a euphemistic term for Judas's swollen and pussy genitals.[4]

The first Christian to address foul language in a theoretical, systematic way was Clement of Alexandria. Only in Clement do we find an awareness of the philosophical arguments that there was no such thing as foul language, a view that, quite remarkably, he affirmed. And yet Clement also wrote more about what foul language said about people and did to them than any Christian before him. Clement worried about how foul language might degrade Christians socially or threaten their sexual purity. Christians' speech, like their dress, gait, and bearing, should project an image of dignity and self-mastery.

I suggested in chapter 4 that Ephesians's prohibition of wittiness would have sounded severe, since humor was so integral a part of pleasant conversation. Colossians's advocacy of charming speech would seem to have been a more likely way to win friends and influence people. It is not clear which ethos prevailed among Christians of the second century. In Minucius Felix's *Octavius*, the pagan disputant Caecilius thinks the Christians a gloomy lot, "ungraced by manners or culture" (12.7), who make a mockery of God by suggesting that he "pries with scrupulous care into the morals and actions of all men, *even down to their words* and hidden thoughts" (10.5).[5] Is this a reaction to austere Christians who frowned at every joke? Perhaps Minucius Felix wanted to correct just this sort of dour impression when, in the graceful and leisurely opening chapters of his dialogue, he depicts his characters walking peacefully along the shore, "whiling away the time with pleasant stories"—stories, he takes care to add, "which were from Octavius" (3.4). Here the Christian Octavius exemplifies the advice of Col 4:6.

I hope this study will provoke questions about the use of foul language that were not previously asked. Given the limitations of our data, some of the most intriguing questions must remain unanswered—at least for the first two centuries of Christianity. (John Chrysostom's frequent tirades against foul language give a much fuller picture of

---

[4] "His genitals [τὸ αἰδοῖον] became more disgusting and larger than anyone's; simply by relieving himself, to his wanton shame, he emitted pus and worms that flowed through his entire body" (Papias, *Exposition of the Sayings of the Lord*, *apud* Apollinarus of Laodicea [Ehrman, LCL]).

[5] Trans. G. W. Clarke, *The* Octavius *of Marcus Minucius Felix* (Ancient Christian Writers 39; New York: Newman Press, 1974).

how Christians were speaking at the end of the fourth century.) We do not know, for instance, what Christian slaves or freedmen did when their masters had written lewd poems and ordered them to attend and cheer at the readings.[6] Or worse—demanded that the slaves or freedmen *perform* the public reading.[7] Did Christians refuse when they were asked to shout abuse against a patron's enemies? Clement comes the closest to answering these sorts of practical questions, but he addresses only the upper-class Christians—the ones who had control over their own mouths. The way slaves speak is mentioned only when Clement advises slave *owners* to keep slaves strictly under control. Perhaps it is noteworthy, then, that Colossians and Ephesians—though they could give advice that was specific to a believer's station in life—declare foul language inappropriate for all Christians. That both slave and free had a new and holy existence "in Christ" meant that foul language was now as inappropriate for the slaves as it was for their masters.

---

[6] Cf. Pliny, *Ep.* 6.21.2–4. On the unique moral predicament of Christian slaves, cf. Jennifer A. Glancy, *Slavery in Early Christianity* (New York: Oxford University Press, 2002).

[7] Cf. Pliny, 9.34; Fantham, *Roman Literary Culture*, 220.

WORKS CITED

A. Texts, Translations, and Reference Works

Aeschines. *The Speeches of Aeschines*. Translated by Charles Darwin Adams. Loeb Classical Library. Cambridge: Harvard University Press, 1968.

Alcalay, Reuben. *The Complete Hebrew-English Dictionary*. Ramat-Gan: Massada Publishing Co., 1981.

The Ante-Nicene Fathers. Edited by Alexander Roberts and James Donaldson. 1885–1887. 10 vols. Repr. Peabody, Mass.: Hendrickson, 1994.

Apollodorus. *The Library*. Translated by James George Frazer. 2 vols. Loeb Classical Library. Cambridge: Harvard University Press, 1921.

Apollonius of Rhodes. *Argonautica*. Translated by R. C. Seaton. Loeb Classical Library. Cambridge: Harvard University Press, 1955.

The Apostolic Fathers. Translated by Kirsopp Lake. 2 vols. Loeb Classical Library. Cambridge: Harvard University Press, 1912–13.

——. Translated by Bart D. Ehrman. 2 vols. Loeb Classical Library. Cambridge: Harvard University Press, 2003.

Apuleius. *Metamorphoses*. Translated by J. Arthur Hanson. 2 vols. Loeb Classical Library. Cambridge: Harvard University Press, 1989.

Aristophanes. Translated by Jeffrey Henderson. 4 vols. Loeb Classical Library. Cambridge: Harvard University Press, 1998–2002.

Aristotle. Translated by Harold P. Cooke et al. 23 vols. Loeb Classical Library. Cambridge: Harvard University Press, 1926–1995.

Astbury, Raymond, ed. *Saturarum Menippearum Fragmenta*. Leipzig: Teubner, 1985.

Athenaeus. *The Deipnosophists*. Translated by Charles Burton Gulick. 7 vols. Loeb Classical Library. Cambridge: Harvard University Press, 1930.

Augustine. *The City of God*. Translated by Henry Bettenson. London: Penguin Books, 1972.

Aulus Gellius. *The Attic Nights*. Translated by John C. Rolfe. 3 vols. Loeb Classical Library. Cambridge: Harvard University Press, 1927.

Balz, Horst and Gerhard Schneider, eds. *Exegetical Dictionary of the New Testament*. 3 vols. Grand Rapids: Eerdmans, 1990–93.

Bechtel, Friedrich. *Die historischen Personennamen des Griechischen bis zur Kaiserzeit*. Halle: Niemeyer, 1917.

Bethe, E., ed. *Pollucis onomasticon*. 2 vols. Leipzig: Teubner, 1900–31.

Bidez, J., G. Rochefort, and Ch. Lacombrade, eds. *L'Empereur Julien: Oeuvre completes*. 4 vols. Budé. Paris, 1924–64.

Blass, F. and A. Debrunner. *A Greek Grammar of the New Testament and Other Early Christian Literature*. Translated and revised by Robert W. Funk. Chicago: University of Chicago, 1961.

Brown, F., S. R. Driver, and C. A. Briggs. *Hebrew and English Lexicon of the Old Testament*. Oxford: Clarendon Press, 1907.

Brown, Malcolm Kenneth. *The Narratives of Konon*. Munich: K. G. Saur, 2002.

Buettner-Wobst, Theodorus, ed. *Polybii historiae*. 4 vols. Leipzig: Teubner, 1889–1905.

Burton, Ernest de Witt. *Syntax of the Moods and Tenses in New Testament Greek*. 3d ed. Edinburgh: T. & T. Clark, 1898.

Celsus. *On Medicine*. Translated by W. G. Spencer. 3 vols. Loeb Classical Library. Cambridge: Harvard University Press, 1935–1938.

Chantraine, Pierre. *Dictionnaire étymologique de la langue grecque, histoire des mots*. Paris: Édi-tions Klincksieck, 1968.

Charles, R. H., ed. *Apocrypha and Pseudepigrapha of the Old Testament*. 2 vols. Oxford: Clarendon, 1913.

Charlesworth, James H. *Rule of the Community and Related Documents*. Vol. 1 of *The Dead Sea Scrolls*. Edited by James H. Charlesworth. Tübingen: Mohr, 1993.

———, ed. *The Old Testament Pseudepigrapha*. 2 vols. New York: Doubleday, 1983–85.

Cicero. Translated by Walter C. A. Ker, et al. 28 vols. Cambridge: Harvard University Press, 1923–28.

———. *Letters to Friends*. Translated by D. R. Shackleton Bailey. 3 vols. Loeb Classical Library. Cambridge: Harvard University Press, 2001.

Clarke, Emma C., John M. Dillon, and Jackson P. Hershbell. *Iamblichus*: De mysteriis. Writings from the Greco-Roman World 4. Leiden: Brill, 2004.

Clarke, G. W. *The Octavius of Marcus Minucius Felix*. Ancient Christian Writers 39; New York: Newman Press, 1974.

Cunningham, I. C. *Herodae: Mimiambi*. Leipzig: Teubner, 1987.

———. *Herodas: Mimiambi*. Oxford: Clarendon, 1971.

Danby, H. D. D. *The Mishnah. Translated from the Hebrew with Introduction and Brief Explana-tory Notes*. Oxford: Oxford University Press, 1933.

Daniel, Robert W., and Franco Maltomini, eds. *Supplementum Magicum*. 2 vols. Abhand-lungen der rheinisch-westfälischen Akademie der Wissenschaften. Sonderreihe: Papyrologica Coloniensia 16.1 and 16.2. Opladen: Westdeutscher Verlag, 1992.

De Jonge, M., H. W. Hollander, and Th. Korteweg, eds. *The Testaments of the Twelve Patriarchs: A Critical Edition of the Greek Text*. Pseudepigrapha Veteris Testamenti Graece 1.2; Leiden: Brill, 1978.

Demosthenes. Translated by J. H. Vince et al. 7 vols. Loeb Classical Library. Cambridge: Harvard University Press, 1930–49.

Diels, Hermann. *Die Fragmente der Vorsokratiker*. 6th ed. 3 vols. Berlin: Weidmannsche, 1951.

Dillon, John and Jackson Hershbell. *Iamblichus: On the Pythagorean Way of Life*. Atlanta: Scholars Press, 1991.

Dio Chrysostom. Translated by J. W. Cohoon and H. Lamar Crosby. 5 vols. Loeb Classical Library. Cambridge: Harvard University Press, 1971.

Diodorus Siculus. Translated by C. H. Oldfather et al. 12 vols. Loeb Classical Library. Cambridge: Harvard University Press, 1933–1967.

Diogenes Laertius. *Lives of Eminent Philosophers*. Translated by R. D. Hicks. 2 vols. Loeb Classical Library. Cambridge: Harvard University Press, 1972.

Dorandi, Tiziano. "Filodemo. Gli Stoici (PHerc. 155 E339)." *Cronache Ercolanesi* 12 (1982): 91–133.

Edelstein, L. and I. G. Kidd, eds. *Posidonius*. Volume 1. *The Fragments*. Cambridge: Cambridge University Press, 1972.

Elliger, K. and W. Rudolf, eds. *Biblia Hebraica Stuttgartensia*. Stuttgart: Deutsche Bibel-gesellschaft, 1984.

Epictetus. *The Discourses as Reported by Arrian, the Manual, and Fragments*. Translated by W. A. Oldfather. 2 vols. Loeb Classical Library. Cambridge: Harvard University Press, 1925.

Epstein, Isidore, ed. *The Babylonian Talmud*. 18 vols. London: Soncino Press, 1961.

Fraser, P. M. and E. Matthews, eds. *A Lexicon of Greek Personal Names*. Volume 1. *The Aegean Islands, Cyprus, Cyrenaica*. Oxford: Clarendon, 1987.

Freedman, David N., ed. *The Anchor Bible Dictionary*. 6 vols. New York: Doubleday, 1992.

García Martínez, Florentino. *The Dead Sea Scrolls Translated*. Translated by Wilfred G. E. Watson. 2d ed. Leiden: Brill, 1994.

Gerber, Douglas E. *Greek Iambic Poetry*. Loeb Classical Library. Cambridge: Harvard University Press, 1999.

Glare, P. G. W., ed. *Oxford Latin Dictionary*. Oxford: Oxford University Press, 1982.

Greek Anthology. Translated by W. R. Paton. 5 vols. Cambridge: Harvard University Press, 1916–18.

Gregg, J. A. F. "The Commentary of Origen upon the Epistle to the Ephesians," *Journal of Theological Studies* 3 (1902): 233–44, 398–420, 554–76.

Heine, Ronald E. *The Commentaries of Origen and Jerome on St Paul's Epistle to the Ephesians*. Oxford: Oxford University Press, 2002.

Hippocrates. Translated by W. H. S. Jones et al. 8 vols. Loeb Classical Library. Cambridge: Harvard University Press, 1923–1995.

Horace. *Satires, Epistles and Ars Poetica*. Translated by H. Rushton Fairclough. Loeb Classical Library. London: Heinemann, 1966.

Irwin, Terence. *Aristotle: Nichomachean Ethics*. Indianapolis: Hackett Publishing Company, 1985.

Israelstam, J. and Judah J. Slotki. *Midrash Rabbah: Leviticus*. London: Soncino Press, 1939.

Isocrates. Translated by George Norlin and Larue van Hook. 3 vols. Loeb Classical Library. Cambridge: Harvard University Press, 1928–1945.

Janko, R. *Philodemus*: On Poems, *Book 1: Introduction, Translation and Commentary*. Oxford: Oxford University Press, 2000.

Josephus. Translated by H. St. J. Thackeray et al. 10 vols. Loeb Classical Library. Cambridge: Harvard University Press, 1926–1965.

Julian. Translated by Wilmer Cave Wright. 3 vols. Loeb Classical Library. London: Heinemann, 1954.

Juvenal and Persius. Edited and translated by Susanna Morton Braund. Loeb Classical Library. Cambridge: Harvard University Press, 2004.

Kittel, Gerhard and Gerhard Friedrich. *Theological Dictionary of the New Testament*. 10 vols. Translated by G. W. Bromiley. Grand Rapids: Eerdmans, 1964–76.

Koerte, Alfred, ed. *Menandri Quae Supersunt*. Revised by Andreas Thierfelder. 2 vols. Leipzig: Teubner, 1952–1953.

Lampe, G. W. H. *A Patristic Greek Lexicon*. Oxford: Clarendon Press, 1961.

Latte, Kurt, ed. *Hesychii Alexandrini lexicon (A–O)*. 2 vols. Copenhagen: Munksgaard, 1953.

Liddell, Henry George, Robert Scott and Henry Stuart Jones. *A Greek-English Lexicon*. 9th ed. Oxford: Clarendon, 1996.

Lindsay, Wallace M. ed. *Sexti Pompei Festi De verborum significatu quae supersunt: Cum Pauli Epitome*. Stuttgart: Teubner, 1997.

Lucian. Translated by A. M. Harmon et al. 8 vols. Loeb Classical Library. Cambridge: Harvard University Press, 1913–1967.

Lutz, Cora. "Musonius Rufus: 'The Roman Socrates.'" *Yale Classical Studies* 10 (1947): 3–147.

Lysias. Translated by W. R. M. Lamb. Loeb Classical Library. Cambridge: Harvard University Press, 1976

Majercik, Ruth. *The Chaldean Oracles: Text, Translation, and Commentary*. Studies in Greek and Roman Religion 5. Leiden: Brill, 1989.

Malherbe, Abraham J., ed. *The Cynic Epistles: A Study Edition*. SBLSBS 12. Missoula, Mont.: Scholars Press, 1977.

Marcovich, M., ed. *Clementis Alexandrini* Paedagogus. Supplements to *Vigiliae Christianae*. Texts and Studies of Early Christian Life and Language 61. Leiden: Brill, 2002.

———. *Clementis Alexandrini* Protrepticus. Supplements to *Vigiliae Christianae*. Texts and Studies of Early Christian Life and Language 34. Leiden: Brill, 1995.

Marcus Aurelius Antoninus. *The Communings with Himself*. Translated by C. R. Haines. Loeb Classical Library. Cambridge: Harvard University Press, 1961.

Marrou, Henri-Irénée, et al. *Clément d'Alexandrie: Le Pédagogue.* 3 vols. Paris: Cerf, 1960–70.

Martial. *Epigrams.* Translated by D. R. Shackleton Bailey. 3 vols. Loeb Classical Library. Cambridge: Harvard University Press, 1993.

Metzger, Bruce M. *A Textual Commentary on the Greek New Testament.* Rev. ed. London: United Bible Societies, 1975.

Metzger, Bruce M., and Michael D. Coogan, eds. *The Oxford Companion to the Bible.* New York: Oxford University Press, 1993.

Metzger, Marcel. *Les Constitutions apostoliques.* 3 vols. Paris: Cerf, 1985–87.

Moulton, J. H., and G. Milligan. *The Vocabulary of the Greek Testament.* Reprint. Peabody, Mass.: Hendrickson, 1997.

Mutschmann, H., ed. *Divisiones quae vulgo dicuntur Aristoteleae.* Leipzig: Teubner, 1906.

Nestle, Erwin and Kurt Aland. *Novum Testamentum Graece.* 27th ed. Stuttgart: Deutsche Bibelgesellschaft, 1993.

Neusner, Jacob. *The Mishnah: A New Translation.* New Haven: Yale University Press, 1988.

Ovid. *Fasti.* Translated by J. G. Frazer. Loeb Classical Library. Cambridge: Harvard University Press, 1931.

———. *The Art of Love, and Other Poems.* Translated by J. H. Mozley. Loeb Classical Library. Cambridge: Harvard, 1947.

Pack, Roger A., ed. *Artemidori Daldiani Onirocriticon libri* v. Leipzig: Teubner, 1963.

Page, D. L. *Greek Literary Papyri.* 2 vols. Loeb Classical Library. Cambridge: Harvard University Press, 1942.

Papyri Graecae Magicae: Die Griechischen Zauberpapyri. Edited by Karl Preisendanz. 2 vols. Stuttgart: Teubner, 1974 (1928).

Parker, W. H. *Priapea: Poems for a Phallic God.* London: Croom Helm, 1988.

Patillon, Michel, ed. *Aelius Théon: Progymnasmata.* Paris: Les belles lettres, 1997.

Parsons, P. J. ed. *The Oxyrhynchus Papyri* XLII. The Egypt Exploration Socitety: London, 1974.

Patrologia latina. Edited by J.-P. Migne. 217 vols. Paris, 1844–1864.

Patrologia graeca. Edited by J.-P. Migne. 162 vols. Paris, 1857–1886.

Pausanias. *Description of Greece.* Translated by W. H. S. Jones. 4 vols. Loeb Classical Library. Cambridge: Harvard University Press, 1918–1935.

Perry, Ben Edwin. *Aesopica.* Volume 1. *Greek and Latin Texts.* Urbana: University of Illinois Press, 1952.

Philo. Translated by F. H. Colson et al. 12 vols. Loeb Classical Library. Cambridge: Harvard University Press, 1929–53.

Pingree, David, ed. *Dorothei Sidonii Carmen astrologicum.* Leipzig: Teubner, 1976.

Plato. Translated by W. R. M. Lamb et al. 12 vols. Loeb Classical Library. Cambridge: Harvard University Press, 1921–62.

Pliny. *Letters.* Translated by Betty Radice. 2 vols. Loeb Classical Library. Cambridge: Harvard University Press, 1969.

———. *Natural History.* Translated by H. Rackham et al. 10 vols. Loeb Classical Library. Cambridge: Harvard University Press, 1938–62.

Plutarch. *Moralia.* Translated by Frank Cole Babbitt et al. 16 vols. Loeb Classical Library. Cambridge: Harvard University Press. 1927–2004.

———. *Lives.* Translated by Bernadotte Perrin. 11 vols. Loeb Classical Library. Cambridge: Harvard University Press, 1914–26.

Quintilian. *The Orator's Education.* 5 vols. Translated by Donald A. Russell. Loeb Classical Library. Cambridge: Harvard University Press, 2001.

Rahlfs, Alfred, ed. *Septuaginta: Id est Vetus Testamentum graece iuxta LXX interpretes.* Stuttgart: Deutsche Bibelgesellschaft, 1979.

Richardson, N. J. *The Homeric Hymn to Demeter.* Oxford: Clarendon, 1974.

Ritter, Joachim, ed. *Historisches Wörterbuch der Philosophie.* 8 vols. Basel: Schwabe, 1971.

Rordorf, Willy and André Tuilier. *La Doctrine des douze apôtres*. Paris: Cerf, 1978.
Roth, Martha T. *Law Collections from Mesopotamia and Asia Minor*. Atlanta: Scholars Press, 1995.
Rusten, Jeffrey, I. C. Cunningham, and A. D. Knox, eds. *Characters/Theophrastus. Mimes/ Herodas. Cercidas and the Choliambic Poets*. Loeb Classical Library. Cambridge: Harvard University Press, 1993.
Segal, Erich. *Four Comedies: Plautus*. Oxford: Oxford University Press, 1996.
Segal, Moshe S. *Sefer Ben Sira Hashalem* (Hebrew). Jerusalem: Mosad Byalik, 1958.
Seneca. Translated by John W. Basore, et al. 10 vols. Loeb Classical Library. Cambridge: Harvard University Press, 1928–2004.
Sextus Empiricus. Translated by R. G. Bury. 4 vols. Loeb Classical Library; Cambridge: Harvard University Press, 1933–49.
Sider, David. *The Epigrams of Philodemus*. New York: Oxford University Press, 1997.
Slavitt, David R. and Palmer Bovie, eds. *Plautus: The Comedies*. 4 vols. Complete Roman Drama in Translation; Baltimore: Johns Hopkins, 1995.
Smith, J. Payne. *A Compendious Syriac Dictionary*. Oxford: Oxford University Press, 1903.
Smith, Martin S., ed. *Petronii Arbitri: Cena Trimalchionis*. Oxford: Clarendon, 1975.
Snell, Bruno, ed. *Pindari Carmina cum Fragmentis*. Leipzig: Teubner, 1953.
Sokoloff, Michael. *Dictionary of Jewish Palestinian Aramaic of the Byzantine Period*. Ramat-Gan: Bar Ilan University Press, 1990.
Spicq, Ceslas. *Lexique théologique du Nouveau Testament*. Fribourg: Cerf, 1991.
———. *Theological Lexicon of the New Testament*. 3 vols. Translated and edited by James D. Ernest. Peabody, Massachusetts: Hendrickson, 1994.
Stählen, Otto. *Des Clemens von Alexandreia ausgewählte Schriften aus dem Griechischen übersetzt*. 5 vols. Munich: Josef Kösel & Friedrich Pustet, 1934.
Stern, Menahem. *Greek and Latin Authors on Jews and Judaism*. 3 vols. Jerusalem: The Israel Academy of Sciences and Humanities, 1980.
Strabo. Translated by Horace Leonard Jones. 8 vols. Loeb Classical Library. Cambridge: Harvard University Press, 1917–32.
Strack, Hermann L., and Paul Billerbeck. *Kommentar zum Neuen Testament aus Talmud und Midrasch*. 6 vols. Munich: C. H. Beck, 1922–1961.
Suetonius. Translated by John C. Rolfe. 2 vols. Loeb Classical Library; Cambridge: Harvard University Press, 1997.
Suggs, M. Jack, Katharine Doob Sakenfeld, and James R. Mueller, eds. *Oxford Study Bible*. New York: Oxford University Press, 1992.
Sullivan, J. P. *Petronius: The Satyricon; Seneca: The Apocolocyntosis of the Divine Claudius*. London: Penguin Books, 1998.
Tacitus. *The Histories and The Annals*. Translated by C. H. Moore and J. Jackson. 4 vols. Loeb Classical Library. Cambridge: Harvard University Press, 1937.
Taillardat, Jean. *Suétone: ΠΕΡΙ ΒΛΑΣΦΗΜΙΩΝ. ΠΕΡΙ ΠΑΙΔΙΩΝ*. Paris: Les belles lettres, 1967.
Tatum, James. *Plautus: The Darker Comedies*. Baltimore: Johns Hopkins University Press, 1983.
Turyn, Alexander. *Pindari Carmina cum Fragmentis*. Oxford: Basil Blackwell, 1952.
Valerius Maximus. *Memorable Doings and Sayings*. Translated by D. R. Shackleton Bailey. 2 vols. Loeb Classical Library. Cambridge: Harvard University Press, 2000.
Van Straaten, Modestus, ed. *Panaetii Rhodii Fragmenta*. Leiden: Brill, 1952.
Vööbus, Arthur. *The Didascalia apostolorum in Syriac*. 4 vols. *Corpus scriptorum christianorum orientalium* 401, 402, 407, 408; Louvain: Secrétariat du CorpusSCO, 1979.
Warmington, E. H. *Remains of Old Latin*. 4 vols. Loeb Classical Library. Cambridge: Harvard University Press, 1967.
Wellmann, M., ed. *Pedanii Dioscorides Anazarbei de materia medica libri quinque*. 3 vols. Berlin: Weidmann, 1907–1914.

West, Martin L. *Homeric Hymns, Homeric Apocrypha, Lives of Homer.* Loeb Classical Library. Cambridge: Harvard University Press, 2003.

Wise, Michael, Martin Abegg, Jr., and Edward Cook, eds. *The Dead Sea Scrolls: A New Translation.* San Francisco: HarperSanFrancisco, 1996.

Xenophon. Translated by Carleton L. Brownson et al. 7 vols. Loeb Classical Library. Cambridge: Harvard University Press, 1918–1971.

B. SECONDARY LITERATURE

Abbott, T. K. *The Epistles to the Ephesians and to the Colossians.* International Critical Commentary. New York: Charles Scribner's Sons, 1902.

Abt, Adam. *Die Apologie des Apuleius von Madaura und die antike Zauberei: Beitrage zur Erläuterung der Schrift De magia.* Giessen: A. Topelmann, 1908.

Adams, J. N. *The Latin Sexual Vocabulary.* Baltimore: Johns Hopkins University Press, 1982.

Aletti, Jean-Noël, S. J. *Saint Paul Épitre aux Colossiens.* Études bibliques 20. Paris: Gabalda, 1993.

Alexander, William H. "The *Culpa* of Ovid." *Classical Journal* 53 (1957–58): 319–25.

Allan, Keith and Kate Burridge. *Euphemism and Dysphemism. Language Used as Shield and Weapon.* New York: Oxford University Press, 1991.

Alter, Robert. *The David Story.* New York: Norton, 1999.

Astbury, Raymond. "Petronius, P. Oxy. 3010, and Menippean Satire." *Classical Philology* 72 (1977): 22–31.

Audet, Jean-Paul. *La Didachè: Instructions des apôtres.* Paris: J. Gabalda, 1958.

Bain, D. M. "Two further observations on BINEIN." *Liverpool Classical Monthly* 6.2 (February 1981): 43–44.

——. "Six Greek Verbs of Sexual Congress." *Classical Quarterly* 41 (1991): 51–77.

Baker, William R. *Personal Speech-Ethics in the Epistle of James.* Wissenschaftliche Untersuchungen zum Neuen Testament 68. Tübingen: Mohr, 1995.

Bakhtin, Mikhail. *Rabelais and His World.* Translated by Helene Iswolsky. Cambridge: M.I.T. Press, 1968.

Baldwin, B. "Philaenis: The *Doyenne* of Ancient Sexology." *Corolla Londoniensis* 6 (1990): 1–7.

Balme, Maurice. *Menander: The Plays and the Fragments.* Oxford: Oxford University Press, 2001.

Barclay, John M. G. "Ordinary but Different: Colossians and Hidden Moral Identity." *Australian Biblical Review* 49 (2001): 34–52.

Barnard, L. W. "Hadrian and Judaism." *Journal of Roman History* 5 (1969): 285–98.

Barr, William. *Juvenal: The Satires.* Oxford: Clarendon, 1991.

Barth, Fredrik. *Ethnic Groups and Boundaries.* Boston: Little, Brown and Company, 1969.

Barth, Markus. *Ephesians.* 2 vols. The Anchor Bible 34–34A. Garden City: Doubleday, 1974.

Barth, Markus and Helmut Blanke. *Colossians.* Translated by Astrid B. Beck. The Anchor Bible 34B. New York: Doubleday, 1994.

Batey, Richard A. "Jesus and the Theatre." *New Testament Studies* 30 (1984): 563–74.

——. *Jesus and the Forgotten City: New Light on Sepphoris and the Urban World of Jesus.* Grand Rapids: Baker, 1991.

Beare, W. "Quintilian VI.iii.47 and the *Fabula Atellana.*" *Classical Review* 51 (1937): 213–15.

Berger, Adolf. "Encyclopedic Dictionary of Roman Law." *Transaction of the American Philological Society* 42 (1953): 333–808.

Best, Ernest. *A Critical and Exegetical Commentary on Ephesians.* International Critical Commentary. Edinburgh: T. & T. Clark, 1998.

Betz, Hans Dieter. "2 Cor 6:14–7:1: An Anti-Pauline Fragment?" *Journal of Biblical Literature* 92 (1973): 88–108.

——. *The Sermon on the Mount: A Commentary on the Sermon on the Mount, including the Sermon on the Plain (Matthew 5:3–7:27 and Luke 6:20–49)*. Hermeneia. Minneapolis: Fortress, 1995.

Bevere, Allan R. *Sharing the Inheritance: Identity and the Moral Life in Colossians*. Journal for the Study of the New Testament Supplement Series 226. Sheffield: Sheffield Academic Press, 2003.

Billerbeck, M. *Vom Kynismus: Epiktet*. Leiden: Brill, 1978.

——. *Der Kyniker Demetrius*. Leiden: Brill, 1979.

——. "The Ideal Cynic from Epictetus to Julian." Pages 205–21 in *The Cynics: The Cynic Movement in Antiquity and Its Legacy*. Edited by R. Bracht Branham and Marie-Odile Goulet-Cazé. Berkeley: University of California Press, 1996.

Birley, Anthony. *Marcus Aurelius: A Biography*. New Haven: Yale University Press, 1987.

Blenkinsopp, Joseph. *Wisdom and Law in the Old Testament: The Ordering of Life in Israel and Early Judaism*. Oxford Bible Series. Oxford: Oxford University Press, 1995.

Blunt, A. W. F. *The Epistle of Paul to the Galatians*. Oxford: Clarendon, 1947.

Bokser, Baruch. "Approaching Sacred Space." *Harvard Theological Review* 78 (1985): 279–99.

——. *Post Mishnaic Judaism in Transition: Samuel on Berakhot and the Beginnings of Gemara*. Brown Judaic Studies 17. Chico, Calif.: Scholars Press, 1980.

Bonhöffer, Adolf Friedrich. *The Ethics of the Stoic Epictetus*. Translated by William O. Stephens. New York: Peter Lang, 2006 [1894].

Bonnard, Pierre. *L'Épitre de Saint Paul aux Galates*. Commentaire du Nouveau Testament 9. Neuchâtel: Delachaux et Niestle, 1953.

Boswell, John. *Christianity, Social Tolerance, and Homosexuality: Gay People in Western Europe from the Beginning of the Christian Era to the Fourteenth Century*. Chicago: University of Chicago Press, 1981.

Bouttier, Michel. *L'Épître de saint Paul aux Éphésiens*. Commentaire du Nouveau Testament 9b. Geneva: Labor et Fides, 1991.

Bovon, François. *L'Évangile selon Saint Luc*. 3 vols. Commentaire du Nouveau Testament 3a. Geneva: Labor et Fides, 1991.

Box, G. H. and W. O. E. Oesterley. «Sirach.» Pages 268–517 in vol. 1 of *Apocrypha and Pseudepigrapha of the Old Testament*. Edited by R. H. Charles. 2 vols. Oxford: Clarendon, 1913.

Bradley, D. J. M. "The Transformation of the Stoic Ethic in Clement of Alexandria." *Augustinianum* 14 (1974): 41–66.

Bradley, Keith. "Law, Magic, and Culture in the *Apologia* of Apuleius." *Phoenix* 51 (1997): 203–23.

Bradshaw, Paul F., Maxwell E. Johnson, and L. Edward Phillips. *The Apostolic Tradition*. Hermeneia. Minneapolis: Fortress, 2002.

Bratcher, Robert G. and Eugene A. Nida. *A Translator's Handbook on Paul's Letter to the Ephesians*. London: United Bible Societies, 1982.

Braund, Susanna Morton. *Juvenal: Satires Book 1*. Cambridge: Cambridge University Press, 1996.

Bremmer, J. N. and N. M. Horsfall. *Roman Myth and Mythography*. Bulletin for the Institute of Classical Studies, Supplement 52. London: Institute of Classical Studies, 1987.

Bremmer, J. M. "Aristophanes on his own Poetry." Pages 125–72 in *Aristophane*. Edited by J. M. Bremer and E. W. Handley. Entretiens sur l'antiquité classique 38. Geneva: Foundation Hardt, 1993.

Bruce, F. F. *Ephesians*. London: Pickering & Inglis, 1961.

Brumfield, A. C. "Aporreta: Verbal and Ritual Obscenity in the Cults of Ancient Women." Pages 67–74 in *The Role of Religion in the Early Greek Polis: Proceedings of the Third International Seminar on Ancient Greek Cult, Organized by the Swedish Institute of Athens, 16–18 October 1992*. Edited by Robin Hägg. Acta Instituti Atheniensis Regni Sueciae, 80, 24. Stockholm: P. Åströms Förlag, 1996.

Brundage, James A. "Obscene and Lascivious: Behavioral Obscenity in Canon Law." Pages 246–59 in *Obscenity: Social Control and Artistic Creation in the European Middle Ages*. Edited by Jan M. Ziolkowski. Leiden: Brill, 1998.

Burkert, Walter. *Homo Necans*. Translated by Peter Bing. Berkeley: University of California Press, 1983.

———. *Greek Religion*. Translated by John Raffan. Cambridge: Harvard University Press, 1985.

Burnett, John. *The Ethics of Aristotle*. London: Methuen & Co., 1900.

Burton-Christie, Douglas. *The Word in the Desert. Scripture and the Quest for Holiness in Early Christian Monasticism*. New York: Oxford University Press, 1993.

Bussell, F. W. *Marcus Aurelius and the Later Stoics*. Edinburgh: T. & T. Clark, 1910.

Campenhausen, Hans von. "Ein Witz des Apostels Paulus und die Anfänge des christlichen Humors." Pages 189–93 in *Neutestamentliche Studien für Rudolf Bultmann*. Edited by Walther Eltester. Beihefte zur Zeitschrift für die neutestamentliche Wissenschaft 21. Berlin: A. Töpelmann, 1954.

Carey, Christopher. "The return of the radish, or, Just when you thought it was safe to go back into the kitchen." *Liverpool Classical Monthly* 18.4 (1993): 53–55.

Casagrande, Carla and Silvana Vecchio. *Les Péchés de la langue: Discipline et éthique de la parole dans la culture médiévale*. Translated by Philippe Baillet. Paris: Cerf, 1991.

Casel, Odo. "Εὐχαριστία-εὐχαριτία." *Biblische Zeitschrift* 18 (1929): 84–85.

Casey, Robert P. "Clement of Alexandria and the Beginnings of Christian Platonism." *Harvard Theological Review* 18 (1925): 39–101.

Chadwick, Henry. *Early Christian Thought and the Classical Tradition*. Oxford: Clarendon, 1966.

Collard, C. "βινεῖν and Aristophanes, Lysistrata 934." *Liverpool Classical Monthly* 4.10 (December 1979): 213–14.

Connolly, R. Hugh. "The Use of the Didache in the Didascalia." *Journal of Theological Studies* 24 (1923): 147–57.

———. *Didascalia Apostolorum: The Syriac Version Translated and Accompanied by the Verona Latin Fragments*. Oxford: Clarendon, 1929.

———. "The Didache in Relation to the Epistle of Barnabas." *Journal of Theological Studies* 33 (1932): 237–53.

Coseriu, Eugenio and Bimal K. Matilal. "Der φύσει-θέσει-Streit/Are words and things connected by nature or by convention?" Pages 880–900 in vol. 2 of *Sprachphilosophie: ein internationales Handbuch zeitgenössischer Forschung*. Edited by Marcelo Dascal et al. 2 vols. Berlin: Walter de Gruyter, 1996.

Crenshaw, James L. "Wisdom Literature." Pages 801–803 in *The Oxford Companion to the Bible*. Edited by Bruce M. Metzger and Michael D. Coogan. New York: Oxford University Press, 1993.

Crook, J. A. *Law and Life of Rome*. London: Thames and Hudson, 1967.

Crystal, David. *The Cambridge Encyclopedia of Language*. 2d ed. Cambridge: Cambridge University Press, 1997.

Csapo, Eric and William J. Slater. *The Context of Ancient Drama*. Ann Arbor: The University of Michigan Press, 1995.

Dahl, Nils Alstrup. *Studies in Ephesians: Introductory Questions, Text- and Edition-Critical Issues, Interpretation of Texts and Themes*. Edited by David Hellholm, Vemund Blomkvist, and Tord Fornberg. Wissenschaftliche Untersuchungen zum Neuen Testament 131. Tübingen: Mohr, 2000.

Danker, F. W., W. Bauer, W. F. Arndt, and F. W. Gingrich, eds. *Greek-English Lexicon of the New Testament and Other Early Christian Literature*. 3d ed. Chicago: University of Chicago Press, 2000.

Davies, W. D. and Dale Allison, Jr. *The Gospel According to Saint Matthew.* 3 vols. International Critical Commentary. Edinburgh: T. & T. Clark, 1988–97.

Desečar, A. J. "La Necedad en Sirac 23, 12–15." *Liber annuus Studii biblici franciscani* 20 (1970): 264–72.

Detienne, Marcel. *The Gardens of Adonis: Spices in Greek Mythology.* Translated by Janet Lloyd. Sussex: The Harvester Press, 1977.

———. "The Violence of Well-Born Ladies: Women in the Thesmophoria." Pages 129–47 in *The Cuisine of Sacrifice among the Greeks.* Edited by Marcel Detienne and J.-P. Vernant. Chicago: University of Chicago Press, 1989.

Dibelius, Martin. *An Die Thessalonicher I II; An die Philipper.* 3d ed. Tübingen: Mohr, 1937.

———. *An die Kolosser, Epheser, An Philemon.* 3d ed. Tübingen: Mohr, 1953.

Dillon, Matthew. *Girls and Women in Classical Greek Religion.* London: Routledge, 2002.

Dirlmeier, F. *Nikomachische Ethik.* Berlin: Akademie-Verlag, 1964.

Döring, Klaus. *Die Megariker.* Amsterdam: Verlag B. R. Grüner N.V., 1972.

Dover, K. J. "The Poetry of Archilochos." Pages 183–222 in *Archiloque.* Entretiens sur l'antiquité classique 10. Foundation Hardt: Geneva, 1964.

———. *Greek Popular Morality in the Time of Plato and Aristotle.* Oxford: Basil Blackwell, 1974.

———. *Greek Homosexuality.* Cambridge: Harvard University Press, 1978.

———. "Some Evaluative Terms in Aristophanes." Pages 85–97 in *The Language of Greek Comedy.* Edited by Andreas Willi. Oxford: Oxford University Press, 2002.

Downing, F. Gerald. "Words as Deeds and Deeds as Words." *Biblical Interpretation* 3 (1995): 129–43.

———. *Cynics, Paul and the Pauline Churches: Cynics and Christian Origins II.* London: Routledge, 1998.

Du Tois, Andrie. "Vilification in Early Christian Epistolography." *Biblica* 75 (1994): 403–12.

Duckworth, George E. *The Nature of Roman Comedy: A Study in Popular Entertainment.* Princeton: Princeton University Press, 1952.

Dudley, D. R. *A History of Cynicism from Diogenes to the Sixth Century A.D.* London: Methuen & Co., 1937.

Duesberg, Hilaire, O.S.B. and Paul Auvray. *L'Ecclésiastique.* Paris: Cerf, 1958.

Dunn, James. *Jesus, Paul, and the Law.* Louisville: Westminster/John Knox, 1990.

———. *The Epistle to the Colossians.* New International Greek Testament Commentary. Grand Rapids: Eerdmans, 1996.

Dyck, Andrew R. *A Commentary on Cicero, De Officiis.* Ann Arbor: University of Michigan Press, 1996.

Easterling, P. E. and E. J. Kenney, eds. *Cambridge History of Classical Literature.* Vol. 1. *Greek Literature.* Edited by P. E. Easterling and B. M. W. Knox. Vol. 2. *Latin Literature.* Edited by E. J. Kenney and W. V. Clausen. Cambridge: Cambridge University Press, 1982–85.

Easton, Burton Scott. "New Testament Ethical Lists." *Journal of Biblical Literature* 51 (1932): 1–12.

Eco, Umberto. *The Role of the Reader: Explorations in the Semiotics of Texts.* Bloomington: Indiana University Press, 1979.

Edwards, A. T. "Aristophanes' Comic Poetics: Τρύξ, Scatology, σκῶμμα." *Transactions of the American Philological Association* 121 (1991): 157–79.

———. "Historicizing the Popular Grotesque: Bakhtin's *Rabelais* and Attic Old Comedy." Pages 89–117 in *Theater and Society in the Classical World.* Edited by R. Scodel. Ann Arbor: University of Michigan Press, 1993.

Eire, Carlos M. N. "'Bite This, Satan!' The Devil in Luther's *Table Talk.*" Pages 70–93 in *Piety and Family in Early Modern Europe: Essays in Honour of Steven Ozment.* Edited by Marc R. Forster and Benjamin J. Kaplan. Burlington, VT: Ashgate, 2005.

Elliott, Robert C. *The Power of Satire: Magic, Ritual, Art*. Princeton: Princeton University Press, 1960.

Engberg-Pedersen, Troels. "Ephesians 5,12–13: ἐλέγχειν and Conversion in the New Testament." *Zeitschrift für die Neutestamentliche Wissenschaft und die Kunde der älteren Kirche* 80 (1989): 89–110.

Erskine, Andrew. *The Hellenistic Stoia: Political Thought and Action*. London: Duckworth, 1990.

Evans-Pritchard, E. "Some Collective Expessions of Obscenity in Africa." *Journal of the Royal Anthropological Institute of Great Britain and Ireland* 59 (1929): 311–31.

Ewald, Paul. *Die Briefe des Paulus an die Epheser, Kolosser und Philemon*. KNT 10. 2d ed. Leipzig: Deichert, 1910.

Exum, J. Cheryl. *Plotted, Shot and Painted: Cultural Representations of Biblical Women*. Sheffield: Sheffield Academic Press, 1996.

Fantham, Elaine. "The Missing Link in Roman Literary History." *Classical World* 82 (1988–89): 153–63.

———. *Roman Literary Culture: From Cicero to Apuleius*. Baltimore: Johns Hopkins University Press, 1996.

Fee, Gordon. *The First Epistle to the Corinthians*. NICNT. Grand Rapids: Eerdmans, 1987.

Ferguson, John. *Clement of Alexandria*. New York: Twayne Publishers, 1974.

———. *Stromateis 1–3*. Fathers of the Church. Washington, D.C.: Catholic University of America Press, 1991.

Fitzmyer, Joseph A., S.J. "Qumran and the Interpolated Paragraph in 2 Cor 6:14–7:1." *Catholic Biblical Quarterly* 23 (1961): 271–80.

———. *The Gospel According to Luke*. 2 vols. The Anchor Bible 28–28A. New York: Doubleday, 1981–85.

Fluck, Hanns. *Skurrile Riten in griechischen Kulten*. Endingen: Emil Wild, 1931.

Forssman, Bernhard. "ANNEMOTA in einer dorischen Gefäßinschrift." *Münchener Studien zur Sprachwissenschaft* 34 (1976): 39–46.

Fowler, W. Warde. *The Religious Experience of the Roman People*. London: MacMillan, 1911.

Fraenkel, Eduard. "Anzeige von Beckmann, *Zauberei und Recht in Roms Frühzeit*." *Gnomon* 1 (1925): 185–200.

———. "Two Poems of Catullus." *Journal of Roman Studies* 51 (1961): 46–53.

Frankemölle, Hubert. *Matthäus: Kommentar*. 2 vols. Düsseldorf: Patmos, 1994–1997.

Frazer, James George. *The Golden Bough*. 3d edition. Repr. London: Macmillan, 1966.

Frede, Michael. "Principles of Stoic Grammar." Pages 17–75 in *The Stoics*. Edited by John M. Rist. Berkeley: University of California Press, 1978.

Friedländer, Ludwig. *Roman Life and Manners Under the Early Empire*. Translated by Leonard A. Magnus. 4 vols. New York: Barnes & Noble, 1968.

Fritzsche, Otto Fridolin. *Die Weisheit Jesus-Sirach's*. Kurzgefasstes exegetisches Handbuch zu den Apokryphen des Alten Testamentes. 5th ed. Leipzig: S. Hirzel, 1859.

Funk, F. X. *Doctrina Duodecim Apostolorum: Canones Apostolorum Ecclesiastici ac Reliquae Doctrinae de Duabus Viis Expositiones Veteres*. Tübingen: Laupp, 1887.

Gaertringen, F. Hiller von. *Inschriften von Priene*. Berlin: Georg Reimer, 1906.

Garnsey, Peter. *Social Status and Legal Privilege in the Roman Empire*. Oxford: Clarendon, 1970.

Gerhard, Gustav. *Phoinix von Kolophon*. Leipzig: Teubner, 1909.

Gibson, Margaret Dunlop. *The Didascalia Apostolorum in English*. London: C. J. Clay and Sons, 1903.

Glancy, Jennifer A. *Slavery in Early Christianity*. New York: Oxford University Press, 2002.

Gnilka, Joachim. "2 Cor 6:14–7:1 in the Light of the Qumran Texts and the Testaments of the Twelve Patriarchs." Pages 48–68 in *Paul and Qumran*. Edited by Jerome Murphy O'Connor, O.P. Chicago: Priory Press, 1968.

———. *Der Epheserbrief.* Herders theologischer Kommentar zum Neuen Testament 10.2. Freiburg: Herder, 1977.

———. *Der Kolosserbrief.* Herders theologischer Kommentar zum Neuen Testament 10. Freiburg: Herder, 1980.

———. *Das Matthäusevangelium.* Herders theologischer Kommentar zum Neuen Testament 1.1; Freiburg: Herder, 1986.

Goldhill, Simon. *Foucault's Virginity: Ancient Erotic Fiction and the History of Sexuality.* Cambridge: Cambridge University Press, 1995.

———. "The Erotic Experience of Looking." Pages 374–99 in *The Sleep of Reason: Erotic Experience and Sexual Ethics in Ancient Greece and Rome.* Edited by Martha C. Nussbaum and Juha Sihvola. Chicago: University of Chicago Press, 2002.

Goodspeed, E. J. "The Didache, Barnabas and the Doctrina." *Anglican Theological Review* 27 (1945): 228–47.

Goulet-Cazé, Marie-Odile. *L'Ascèse Cynique.* Paris: J. Vrin, 1986.

———. *Les* Kynica *du stoïcisme.* Hermes Einzelschriften 89. Stuttgart: Franz Steiner Verlag, 2003.

Graves, Robert. *Lars Porsena; or, the Future of Swearing and Improper Language.* London: Martin Brian & O'Keefe Ltd., 1972 [1927].

Green, Peter. *Alexander to Actium: The Historical Evolution of the Hellenistic Age.* Berkeley: University of California Press, 1990.

———. *Classical Bearings: Interpreting Ancient History and Culture.* New York: Thames and Hudson, 1989.

Griffin, Miriam. "Cynicism and the Romans: Attraction and Repulsion." Pages 190–204 in *The Cynics: The Cynic Movement in Antiquity and Its Legacy.* Edited by R. Bracht Branham and Marie-Odile Goulet-Cazé. Berkeley: University of California Press, 1996.

Guelich, Robert A. "Mt 5,22: Its Meaning and Integrity." *Zeitschrift für die Neutestamentliche Wissenschaft und die Kunde der älteren Kirche* 64 (1973): 39–52.

———. *The Sermon on the Mount: A Foundation for Understanding.* Waco, Texas: Word Books, 1982.

Gundry, Robert H. *Matthew: A Commentary on His Handbook for a Mixed Church under Persecution.* 2d ed. Grand Rapids: Eerdmans, 1994.

Hahm, David. "Diogenes Laertus VII: On the Stoics." *ANRW* 36.6: 4076–4182. Part 2, Principat, 33.6. New York: de Gruyter, 1992.

Halliwell, S. "Ancient Interpretations of *onomasti komodein* in Aristophanes." *Classial Quarterly* 34 (1984): 83–88.

———. "Comic Satire and Freedom of Speech in Classical Athens." *Journal of Hellenic Studies* 111 (1991): 48–70.

———. "The Uses of Laughter in Greek Culture." *Classical Quarterly* 41 (1991): 279–96.

Hamp, V. *Das Buch Jesus Sirach.* Würzburg: Echter-Verlag, 1951.

Handley, E. W. *The Dyskolos of Menader.* Cambridge: Harvard University Press, 1965.

Hankinson, R. J. "Usage and Abusage: Galen on Language." Pages 166–87 in *Language.* Edited by Stephen Everson. Cambridge: Cambridge University Press, 1994.

Harré, Rom. "Obscenity and Blasphemy from the Linguistic Point of View." Pages 85–90 in *A Matter of Manners? The Limits of Broadcast Language.* Edited by Andrea Millwood Hargrave. London: John Libbey, 1991.

Harris, Murray J. *Colossians and Philemon.* Exegetical Guide to the Greek New Testament. Grand Rapids: Eerdmans, 1991.

Hartman, Louis F. "God, Names of." Columns 674–82 in volume 7 of *Encyclopaedia Judaica.* 16 vols. Jerusalem: Keter, 1972.

Haupt, Erich. *Die Gefangenschaftsbriefe.* Kritisch-exegetischer Kommentar über das Neue Testament (Meyer-Kommentar) 8–9. 7th ed. Göttingen: Vandenhoeck & Ruprecht, 1902.

Hawthorne, Gerald F. *Philippians.* Word Biblical Commentary 43. Waco, Texas: Word Books, 1983.

Henderson, Jeffrey. "The Cologne Epode and the Conventions of Early Greek Erotic Poetry." *Arethusa* 9 (1976): 159–79.

———. "Further thoughts on BINEIN." *Liverpool Classical Monthly* 5.10 (December 1980): 243.

———. "The *Demos* and Comic Competition." Pages 271–313 in *Nothing to do with Dionysos?* Edited by J. J. Winkler and F. I. Zeitlin. Princeton: Princeton University Press, 1990.

———. *The Maculate Muse: Obscene Language in Attic Comedy.* 2d ed. New York: Oxford University Press, 1991.

———. *Three Plays by Aristophanes.* New York: Routledge, 1996.

Hock, Ronald F. "Cynics and Rhetoric." Pages 755–73 in *Handbook of Classical Rhetoric in the Hellenistic Period 330 B.C.–A.D. 400.* Edited by Stanley E. Porter. Leiden: Brill, 1997.

Hock, Ronald F. and Edward N. O'Neil. *The Chreia in Ancient Rhetoric.* Volume 1. *The Progymnasmata.* SBL Texts and Translations 27. Atlanta: Scholars Press, 1986.

Hodge, Charles. *A Commentary on the Epistle to the Ephesians.* New York: Robert Carter and Brothers, 1858.

Hoehner, Harold W. *Ephesians: An Exegetical Commentary.* Grand Rapids: Baker Academic, 2002.

Hollander, H. W. and M. de Jonge. *The Testaments of the Twelve Patriarchs: A Commentary.* Studia in veteris testamenti pseudepigrapha 8. Leiden: Brill, 1985.

Hooker, Morna. *The Gospel According to Mark.* Black's New Testament Commentary 2. London: A & C Black, 1991.

Hooper, Richard W. *The Priapus Poems: Erotic Epigrams from Ancient Rome.* Urbana: University of Illinois Press, 1999.

Horsfall, Nicholas. *The Culture of the Roman Plebs.* London: Duckworth, 2003.

Hubbard, Thomas K., ed. *Homosexuality in Greece and Rome: A Sourcebook of Basic Documents.* Berkeley: University of California Press, 2003.

Hübner, Hans. *An Philemon, An die Kolosser, An die Epheser.* Handbuch zum Neuen Testament 12. Tübingen: Mohr, 1997.

Hughes, Geoffrey. *Swearing: A Social History of Foul Language, Oaths and Profanity in English.* 2d ed. London: Penguin, 1998.

Hunink, Vincent. *Pro se de magia: apologia.* 2 vols. Amsterdam: J.C. Gieben, 1997.

Ilan, Tal. *Jewish Women in Greco-Roman Palestine.* Tübingen: Mohr, 1995.

Jaeger, Werner. *Paideia: The Ideals of Greek Culture.* Translated by Gilbert Highet. 3 vols. New York: Oxford University Press, 1939.

Jensen, J. "Does *Porneia* Mean Fornication? A Critique of Bruce Malina." *Novum Testamentum* 20 (1978): 161–84.

Jocelyn, H. D. "A Greek Indecency and its Students: λαικάζειν." *Proceedings of the Cambridge Philological Society* n.s. 26 (1980): 12–66.

———. "Attic BINEIN and English F…" *Liverpool Classical Monthly* 5.3 (March 1980): 65–67.

———. "BINEIN yet again." *Liverpool Classical Monthly* 6.2 (February 1981): 45–46

———. "Concerning an American View of Latin Sexual Humor." *Echos du monde classique* 29 (1985): 1–30.

Johnson, Luke Timothy. "Taciturnity and True Religion." Pages 329–39 in *Greeks, Romans, and Christians: Essays in Honor of Abraham J. Malherbe.* Edited by David L. Balch, Everett Ferguson, and Wayne A. Meeks. Minneapolis: Fortress Press, 1990.

Jones, Alexander. "The Stoics and the Astronomical Sciences." Pages 328–44 in *The Cambridge Companion to the Stoics.* Edited by Brad Inwood. Cambridge: Cambridge University Press, 2003.

Jónsson, Jakob. *Humour and Irony in the New Testament.* Reykjavík: Bókaútgáfa Menningarsjóos, 1965. Repr. Leiden: Brill, 1985.

Kamlah, Ehrhard. *Die Form der katalogischen Paränese im Neuen Testament.* Wissenschaftliche Untersuchungen zum Neuen Testament 7. Tübingen: Mohr, 1964.

Kapparis, K. "Humiliating the Adulterer: The Law and the Practice in Classical Athens." *Revue internationale des droits de l'antiquité* 43 (1996): 63–77.

Kaser, Max. *Das römische Privatrecht.* Munich: C. H. Beck, 1955.

Kidd, I. G., trans. *Posidonius.* Volume 3. *The Translation of the Fragments.* Cambridge: Cambridge University Press, 1999.

———. *Posidonius.* Volume 2. *The Commentary.* 2 vols. Cambridge: Cambridge University Press, 1988.

Kiley, Mark. *Colossians as Pseudepigraphy.* The Biblical Seminar 4. Sheffield: JSOT Press, 1986.

Kindstrand, Jan Fredrik. *Bion of Borysthenes: A Collection of Fragments with Introduction and Commentary.* Studia Graeca Upsaliensia 11. Stockholm: Almqvist & Wiksell International, 1976.

Kirk, G. S. *Heraclitus: The Cosmic Fragments.* Cambridge: Cambridge University Press, 1962.

Klauser, Theodorus. *Doctrina Duodecim Apostolorum. Barnabae Epistula.* Bonn: Peter Hanstein, 1940.

Klawans, Jonathan. *Impurity and Sin in Ancient Judaism.* Oxford: Oxford University Press, 2000.

Kleijwegt, M. "*Iuuenes* and Roman Imperial Socieity." *Acta Classica* 37 (1994): 79–102.

Kloppenborg, John S. "The Transformation of Moral Exhortation in Didache 1–5." Pages 88–109 in *The Didache in Context: Essays on Its Text, History and Transmission.* Edited by Clayton N. Jefford. Leiden: Brill, 1995.

Köhler, K. "Zu Mt 5:22." *Zeitschrift für die Neutestamentliche Wissenschaft und die Kunde der älteren Kirche* 19 (1919): 91–95.

König, E. "Style of Scripture." Pages 156–69 in *Dictionary of the Bible.* Extra volume. Edited by James Hastings. New York: Charles Scribner's Sons, 1904.

Knabenbauer, Joseph, S. J. *Commentarius in Ecclesiasticum.* Cursus scripturae sacrae. Paris: P. Lethielleux, 1902.

Kraft, Robert A. *Barnabas and the Didache.* Vol. 3 of *The Apostolic Fathers.* Edited by Robert M. Grant. New York: Thomas Nelson & Sons, 1965.

Kreitzer, Larry. "'Crude Language' and 'Shameful Things Done in Secret' (Ephesians 5.4, 12): Allusions to the Cult of Demeter/Cybele in Hierapolis?" *Journal for the Study of the New Testament* 71 (1998): 51–77.

Krenkel, W. *Pompejanische Inschriften.* Heidelberg: L. Schneider, 1962.

———. "Masturbation in der Antike." *Wissenschaftliche Zeitschrift der Wilhelm-Pieck-Universität Rostock* 28 (1979): 159–78.

———. "Fellatio and Irrumatio." *Wissenschaftliche Zeitschrift der Wilhelm-Pieck-Universität Rostock* 29 (1980): 77–88.

———. "Tonguing." *Wissenschaftliche Zeitschrift der Wilhelm-Pieck-Universität Rostock* 30 (1981): 37–54.

Kroll, Wilhelm. *Studien zum Verständnis der römischen Literatur.* Stuttgart: J. B. Metzlerschen, 1924.

Krostenko, Brian A. *Cicero, Catullus, and the Language of Social Performance.* Chicago: The University of Chicago Press, 2001.

———. "*Arbitria Urbanitatis*: Language, Style, and Characterization in Catullus cc. 39 and 37." *Classical Antiquity* 20 (2001): 239–72.

Krueger, Derek. "The Bawdy and Society." Pages 222–39 in *The Cynics: The Cynic Movement in Antiquity and Its Legacy.* Edited by R. Bracht Branham and Marie-Odile Goulet-Cazé. Berkeley: University of California Press, 1996.

———. *Symeon the Holy Fool: Leontius's Life and the Late Antique City.* Berkeley: University of California Press, 1996.

Kugel, James L. "On Hidden Hatred and Open Reproach: Early Exegesis of Leviticus 19:17." *Harvard Theological Review* 80 (1987): 43–61.

Kuhn, Karl Georg. "The Epistle to the Ephesians in the Light of the Qumran Texts." Pages 115–31 in *Paul and Qumran*. Edited by Jerome Murphy O'Connor, O.P. Chicago: Priory Press, 1968. Repr. of "Der Epheserbrief im Lichte der Qumrantexte." *New Testament Studies* 7 (1960–61): 334–46.

LaBarre, Weston. "Obscenity: An Anthropological Appraisal." *Law and Contemporary Problems* 20 (1955): 533–43.

LaGrange, M.-J. *Saint Paul Épitre aux Galates*. Études bibliques. Paris: Librarire Lecoffre, 1950.

Lang, Mabel. *Graffiti in the Athenian Agora*. Excavations of the Athenian Agora Picture Books 14. Princeton: American School of Classical Studies at Athens, 1974.

———. *Graffiti and Dipinti*. Vol. 21 of *The Athenian Agora*. Princeton: The American School of Classical Studies at Athens, 1976.

Latte, Kurt. *Römische Religionsgeschichte*. Beck: Munich, 1967.

Layton, Bentley. "The Sources, Date, and Transmission of *Didache* 1.3b–2.1." *Harvard Theological Review* 61 (1968): 343–83.

———. *The Gnostic Scriptures*. New York: Doubleday, 1987.

Leithart, Peter J. "Nabal and His Wine." *Journal of Biblical Literature* 120 (2001): 525–27.

Leppä, Outi. *The Making of Colossians: A Study on the Formation and Purpose of a Deutero-Pauline Letter*. Publications of the Finnish Exegetical Society 86. Göttingen: Vandenhoeck & Ruprecht, 2003.

Lesky, Albin. *Geschichte der Griechischen Literatur*. 3d ed. Bern: Francke, 1971.

Lieberman, Saul. *Hellenism in Jewish Palestine*. New York: Jewish Theological Seminary of America, 1950.

Lightfoot, J. B. *Saint Paul's Epistle to the Galatians*. London: Macmillan, 1866.

———. *Saint Paul's Epistle to the Philippians*. 4th ed. London: Macmillan, 1913.

———. *Saint Paul's Epistles to the Colossians and to Philemon*. London: Macmillan, 1916.

Lilla, Salvatore R. C. *Clement of Alexandria: A Study in Christian Platonism and Gnosticism*. Oxford: Oxford University Press, 1971.

Lincoln, Andrew T. *Ephesians*. Word Biblical Commentary 42. Dallas: Word Books, 1990.

Lindemann, Andreas. *Der Erste Korintherbrief*. Handbuch zum Neuen Testament 9/1. Tübingen: Mohr, 2000.

Lohmeyer, Ernst. *Die Briefe an die Philipper, an die Kolosser und an Philemon*. Kritisch-exegetischer Kommentar über das Neue Testament (Meyer-Kommentar) 9.1. Göttingen: Vandenhoeck & Ruprecht, 1961.

Lohse, Eduard. *Colossians and Philemon*. Translated by William R. Poehlmann and Robert J. Karris. Hermeneia. Philadelphia: Fortress, 1971.

Long, A. A. *Hellenistic Philosophy: Stoics, Epicureans, Sceptics*. 2d ed. Berkeley: University of California Press, 1986.

———. *Stoic Studies*. Cambridge: Cambridge University Press, 1996.

Long, A. A. and D. N. Sedley. *The Hellenistic Philosophers*. 2 vols. Cambridge: Cambridge University Press, 1987.

MacDonald, Margaret Y. *Colossians and Ephesians*. Collegeville, Minnesota: The Liturgical Press, 2000.

———. "The Politics of Identity in Ephesians." *Journal for the Study of the New Testament* 26 (2004): 419–44.

McGinn, Thomas A. J. *The Economy of Prostitution in the Roman World: A Study of Social History and the Brothel*. Ann Arbor: University of Michigan Press, 2004.

Maier, Harry O. "Clement of Alexandria and the Care of the Self." *Journal of the American Academy of Religion* 62 (1994): 719–45.

Malherbe, Abraham J. *Paul and the Popular Philosophers*. Minneapolis: Fortress, 1989.

Malina, Bruce. "Does *Porneia* Mean Fornication?" *Novum Testamentum* 14 (1972): 10–17.

Mansfeld, Jap. "Diogenes Laertius on Stoic Philosophy." *Elenchos* 7 (1986): 297–382.

Marrou, Henri-Irénée. *A History of Education in Antiquity.* Translated by George Lamb. London: Sheed and Ward, 1956.

Martin, Troy. *By Philosophy and Empty Deceit: Colossians as Response to a Cynic Critique.* JSNTSup 118. Sheffield: Sheffield Academic Press, 1996.

Martyn, J. Louis. *Galatians.* The Anchor Bible. New York: Doubleday, 1997.

Masson, Olivier. "Nouvelles notes d'anthroponymie grecque." *Zeitschrift für Papyrologie und Epigraphik* 112 (1996): 143–50.

Maxwell-Stuart, P. G. "Strato and the Musa Puerilis." *Hermes* 100 (1972): 215–40.

McCarthy, Carmel. *The Tiqqune Sopherim.* Orbis Biblicus et Orientalis 36. Göttingen: Vandenhoeck and Ruprecht, 1981.

McClure, Laura. *Spoken Like a Woman: Speech and Gender in Athenian Drama.* Princeton: Princeton University Press, 1999.

McGinn, Thomas A. J. *The Economy of Prostitution in the Roman World: A Study of Social History and the Brothel.* Ann Arbor: University of Michigan Press, 2004.

McKane, William. "Functions of Language and Objectives of Discourse according to Proverbs, 10–30." Pages 166–85 in *La Sagesse de l'Ancien Testament.* Edited by Maruice Gilbert. Bibliotheca ephemeridum theologicarum lovaniensium 51. Leuven: Leuven University Press, 1990.

Meeks, Wayne A., ed. *The HarperCollins Study Bible.* San Francisco: HarperCollins, 1993.

———. *The Origins of Christian Morality.* New Haven: Yale University Press, 1993.

Merceron, Jacques E. "Obscenity and Hagiography in Three Anonymous *Sermons Joyeux* and in Jean Molinet's *Saint Billouart.*" Pages 332–44 in *Obscenity: Social Control and Artistic Creation in the European Middle Ages.* Edited by Jan M. Ziolkowski. Leiden: Brill, 1998.

Milgrom, Jacob. *Leviticus: A New Translation and Commentary.* 3 vols. The Anchor Bible 3–3B. Garden City: Doubleday, 1991–2001.

Milne, Marjorie J. and Dietrich von Bothmer. "ΚΑΤΑΠΥΓΩΝ, ΚΑΤΑΠΥΓΑΙΝΑ." *Hesperia* 22 (1953): 215–24.

Mitton, C. Leslie. *The Epistle to the Ephesians: Its Authorship, Origin and Purpose.* Oxford: Clarendon Press, 1951.

Moles, John. "The Cynics." Pages 415–34 in *The Cambridge History of Greek and Roman Political Thought.* Edited by Christopher Rowe and Malcolm Schofield. Cambridge: Cambridge University Press, 2000.

Mommsen, Theodor. *Römisches Strafrecht.* Berlin: Akademie-Verlag, 1899.

Montagu, Ashley. *The Anatomy of Swearing.* New York: Macmillan, 1967.

Moore, George Foot. *Judaism in the First Centuries of the Christian Era: The Age of the Tannaim.* 3 vols. Cambridge: Harvard University Press, 1927–30.

Morgan, Teresa. *Literate Education in the Hellenistic and Roman Worlds.* Cambridge: Cambridge University Press, 1998.

Moule, C. F. D. "Uncomfortable Words I. The Angry Word: Matthew 5.21f." *Expository Times* 81 (1969): 10–13.

Muddiman, John. *The Epistle to the Ephesians.* Black's New Testament Commentaries 10. London: Continuum, 2001.

Muilenburg, James. *The Literary Relations of the Epistle of Barnabas and the Teaching of the Twelve Apostles.* Ph.D. diss., Yale University, 1929.

Müller, Christoph Gregor. *Gottes Pflanzung, Gottes Bau, Gottes Tempel.* Frankfurt am Main: Josef Knecht, 1995.

Murray, J. O. F. *The Epistle of Paul the Apostle to the Ephesians.* Cambridge: Cambridge University Press, 1914.

Muscatine, Charles. "The Fabliaux, Courtly Culture, and the (Re)Invention of Vulgarity." Pages 281–92 in *Obscenity: Social Control and Artistic Creation in the European Middle Ages*. Edited by Jan M. Ziolkowski. Leiden: Brill, 1998.

Mussies, G. "The Use of Hebrew and Aramaic in the Greek New Testament." *New Testament Studies* 30 (1984): 416–32.

Mußner, Franz. "Contributions made by Qumran to the Understanding of the Epistle to the Ephesians." Pages 159–78 in *Paul and Qumran*. Edited by Jerome Murphy-O'Connor. Chicago: The Pilgrim Press, 1968.

——. *Der Brief an die Epheser*. ÖTK 10. Gütersloh: Gütersloher Verlagshaus Mohn, 1982.

——. *Der Galaterbrief*. Herders theologischer Kommentar zum Neuen Testament 9; Freiburg: Herder, 1988.

Nägeli, Theodor. *Der Wortschatz des Apostels Paulus*. Göttingen: Vandenhoeck & Ruprecht, 1905.

Newlands, Carole. "Transgressive Acts: Ovid's Treatment of the Ides of March." *Classical Philology* 91 (1996): 320–38.

Newman, W. L. *The Politics of Aristotle*. 4 vols. Oxford: Clarendon, 1887–1902.

Niederwimmer, Kurt. *The Didache*. Translated by Linda M. Maloney. Hermeneia. Minneapolis: Fortress, 1998.

Oberman, Heiko A. *Luther: Man Between God and the Devil*. Translated by Eileen Walliser-Schwarzbart. New Haven: Yale University Press, 1989.

O'Brien, Peter T. *Colossians and Philemon*. Word Biblical Commentary 44. Waco, Texas: Word Books, 1982.

Odeberg, Hugo. *The View of the Universe in the Epistle to the Ephesians*. Lund: Gleerup, 1934.

O'Higgins, Laurie. *Women and Humor in Classical Greece*. Cambridge: Cambridge University Press, 2003.

Okoye, John Ifeanyichukwu. *Speech in Ben Sira with special reference to 5,9–6,1*. European University Studies: Theology Series 23, 535; Frankfurt am Main: Peter Lang, 1995.

Olender, Maruice. "Aspects of Baubo: Ancient Texts and Contexts." Pages 83–113 in *Before Sexuality: The Construction of Erotic Experience in the Ancient Greek World*. Edited by David M. Halperin, John J. Winkler, and Froma I. Zeitlin. Princeton: Princeton university Press, 1990.

Opelt, Ilona. *Die lateinischen Schimpfwörter und verwandte sprachliche Erscheinungen. Eine Typologie*. Heidelberg: C. Winter, 1965.

——. *Vom Spott der Römer*. Munich: E. Heimeran, 1969.

Oulton, J. E. L. "Clement of Alexandria and the Didache." *Journal of Theological Studies* 41 (1940): 177–79.

Parker, C. P. "Musonius in Clement." *Harvard Studies in Classical Philology* 12 (1901): 191–200.

Paul, Shalom M. "Euphemistically 'Speaking' and a Covetous Eye." *Hebrew Annual Review* 14 (1994): 193–204.

Perkins, Pheme. *Ephesians*. Abingdon New Testament Commentaries. Nashville: Abingdon, 1997.

Pfeiffer, Rudolf. *History of Classical Scholarship*. Oxford: Clarendon Press, 1968.

Pickard-Cambridge, Sir Arthur. *The Dramatic Festivals of Athens*. 2d ed. Revised by John Gould and D. M. Lewis. Oxford: Clarendon Press, 1968.

Pilch, John J. and Bruce J. Malina, eds. *Biblical Social Values and Their Meaning*. Rev. ed. Peabody, Mass.: Hendrickson, 1998.

Pohlenz, Max. *Antikes Führertum: Cicero De Officiis und das Lebensideal des Panaitios*. Leipzig: Teubner, 1934.

——. "Klemens von Alexandreia und sein hellenisches Christentum." *Nachrichten von der Akademie der Wissenschaften in Göttingen. Philologisch-Historische Klasse* 3 (1943): 31–108.

Pope, Marvin H. "Bible, Euphemism and Dysphemism in the." Pages 720–25 in vol. 1 of *The Anchor Bible Dictionary*. Edited by David Noel Freedman. 6 vols. New York: Doubleday, 1992.

Popper, Karl R. *The Open Society and Its Enemies*. 2 vols. London: George Routledge & Sons, 1945.

Post, Peggy. *Emily Post's Etiquette*. HarperCollins: New York, 1997.

Quadlbauer, Franz. "Die Dichter der griechischen Komödie im literarischen Urteil der Antike." *Wiener Studien* 73 (1960): 40–82.

Rabinowitz, L. I. "Euphemism and Dysphmism." Columns 961–62 in vol. 6 of *Encyclopaedia Judaica*. 16 vols. Jerusalem: Keter, 1972.

Ramsay, W. M. *A Historical Commentary on St. Paul's Epistle to the Galatians*. New York: G. P. Putnam's Sons, 1900.

Rea, John. "ΕΠΙΤΟΙΧΟΓΡΑΦΟΣ." *Zeitschrift für Papyrologie und Epigraphik* 36 (1979): 309–10.

Reckford, Kenneth J. *Aristophanes' Old-and-New Comedy*. Chapel Hill: University of North Carolina, 1987.

Reed, Jonathan L. *Archaeology and the Galilean Jesus: A Re-Examination of the Evidence*. Harrisburg: Trinity Press International, 2000.

Reynolds, R. W. "The Adultery Mime." *Classical Quarterly* 40 (1946): 77–84.

Richlin, Amy. *The Garden of Priapus: Sexuality and Aggression in Roman Humor*. New Haven: Yale University Press, 1983.

———, ed. *Pornography and Representation in Greece and Rome*. New York: Oxford University Press, 1992.

Rinaldi, Giancarlo, ed. *Biblia Gentium*. Rome: Libreria Sacre Scritture, 1989.

Rist, J. M. *Epicurus: An Introduction*. Cambridge: Cambridge University Press, 1972.

Ritter, Fr. "Übertriebene Scheu der Römer vor gewissen Ausdrücken und Wortverbindungen." *Rheinisches Museum für Philologie* 3 (1835): 569–80.

Roon, A. van. *The Authenticity of Ephesians*. Leiden: Brill, 1974.

Rordorf, Willy. "Un chapitre d'éthique judéo-chrétienne: les Deux voies." *Recherches de science religieuse* 60 (1972): 109–28.

Rosen, Ralph M. *Old Comedy and the Iambographic Tradition*. American Classical Studies 19. Atlanta: Scholars Press, 1988.

Rösler, Wolfgang. "Über Aischrologie im archaischen und klassischen Griechenland." Pages 75–97 in *Karnevaleske Phänomene in antiken und nachantiken Kulturen und Literaturen*. Edited by Siegmar Döpp. Trier: Wissenschaftlicher Verlag, 1993.

Rosner, Brian S. *Greek as Idolatry: The Origin and Meaning of a Pauline Metaphor*. Grand Rapids: Eerdmans, 2007.

Rudd, Niall. *Themes in Roman Satire*. University of Oklahoma Press: Norman, 1986.

———. *Juvenal: The Satires*. Oxford: Clarendon, 1991.

Russell, D. A. *Ancient Literary Criticism*. Oxford: Clarendon Press, 1972.

Rutherford, R. B. *The Meditations of Marcus Aurelius: A Study*. Oxford: Clarendon, 1989.

Ryssell, V. *Die Sprüche Jesus', des Sohnes Sirach*. Pages 230–475 in vol. 1 of *Die Apokryphen und Pseudepigraphen des Alten Testaments*. Edited by E. Kautzsch. 2 vols. Tübingen: Mohr, 1900.

Sagarin, Edward. *The Anatomy of Dirty Words*. New York: L. Stuart, 1962.

Salmon, George. "Prodicus." Pages 490–91 in *A Dictionary of Christian Biography*. Edited by William Smith and Henry Wace. 4 vols. London: John Murray, 1877.

Sandbach, F. H. *The Stoics*. London: Chatto & Windus, 1975.

Sanders, Jack T. *Ben Sira and Demotic Wisdom*. Society of Biblical Literature Monograph Series 28. Chico, Calif.: Scholars Press, 1983.

Sandt, Hubertus Waltherus Maria van de. "Didache 3:1–6: A Transformation of an Existing Jewish Hortatory Pattern." *Journal for the Study of Judaism* 23 (1992): 21–41.

Schiffman, Lawrence H. *The Eschatological Community of the Dead Sea Scrolls: A Study of the Rule of the Congregation.* Society of Biblical Literature Monograph Series 38. Atlanta: Scholars Press, 1989.

Schilling, Othmar. *Das Buch Jesus Sirach.* Herders Bibelkommentar 7/2. Freiburg: Herder, 1956.

Schlier, Heinrich. *Der Brief an die Galater.* KEK 7. Göttingen: Vandenhoeck & Ruprecht, 1965.

———. *Der Brief an die Epheser.* 7th ed. Düsseldorf: Patmos, 1971.

Schorch, Stefan. *Euphemismen in der hebräischen Bibel.* Orientalia Biblica et Christiana 12. Wiesbaden: Harrassowitz, 2000.

Schnackenburg, Rudolf. *Ephesians.* Translated by Helen Heron. Edinburgh: T. & T. Clark, 1991.

Schofield, Malcolm. *The Stoic Idea of the City.* Cambridge: Cambridge University Press, 1991.

———. "Social and Political Thought." Pages 739–70 in *The Cambridge History of Hellenistic Philosophy.* Edited by Keimpe Algra et al. Cambridge: Cambridge University Press, 1999.

———. "Epicurean and Stoic Political Thought." Pages 435–56 in *The Cambridge History of Greek and Roman Political Thought.* Edited by Christopher Rowe and Malcolm Schofield. Cambridge: Cambridge University Press, 2000.

Schweizer, Eduard. *Letter to the Colossians.* Translated by Andrew Chester. Minneapolis: Fortress, 1982.

———. "Slaves of the Elements and Worshipers of Angels: Gal 4:3, 9 and Col 2:8, 18, 20." *Journal of Biblical Literature* 107 (1988): 455–68.

Scullard, Howard Hayes. *Festivals and Ceremonies of the Roman Republic.* London: Thames and Hudson, 1981.

Schütrumpf, Eckart. *Aristoteles: Werke.* Volume 9. *Politik*; Part 4. *Politik Buch VII/VIII.* Darmstadt: Wissenschaftliche Buchgesellschaft, 2005.

Shackleton Bailey, D. R. *Cicero: Epistulae Ad Familiares.* 2 vols. Cambridge Classical Texts and Commentaries 16–17. Cambridge: Cambridge University Press, 1977.

———. "Notes on Ovid's Poems from Exile." *Classical Quarterly* 32 (1982): 390–98.

Sherwin-White, A. N. *The Letters of Pliny: A Historical and Social Commentary.* Oxford: Clarendon, 1966.

Sherwood, Yvonne M. "Prophetic Scatology: Prophecy and the Art of Sensation." *Semeia* 82 (1998): 183–224.

Shields, Christopher. "Language, Ancient Philosophy of." Pages 356–61 in vol. 5 of *Routledge Encyclopedia of Philosophy.* Edited by Edward Craig. 10 vols. London: Routledge, 1998.

Siems, K. *Aischrologia.* "Das Sexuell-Hässliche im antiken Epigramm." Ph.D. diss., Göttingen, 1974.

Sikes, E. E. "Latin Literature of the Silver Age." Pages 708–42 in vol. 11 of *The Cambridge Ancient History.* Edited by S. A. Cook, F. E. Adcock, and M. P. Charlesworth. 12 vols. Cambridge: Cambridge University Press, 1936.

Skehan, Patrick W. and Alexander A. Di Lella. *The Wisdom of Ben Sira.* The Anchor Bible 39. New York: Doubleday, 1987.

Smend, Rudolf. *Die Weisheit des Jesus Sirach.* Berlin: Georg Reimer, 1906.

Smith, Morton. "Notes on Goodspeed's 'Problems of New Testament Translation.'" *Journal of Biblical Literature* 64 (1945): 501–14.

Solin, Heikki. "Ergüsse eines Lebemannes." *Glotta* 62 (1984): 167–74.

Sommerstein, Alan. "BINEIN." *Liverpool Classical Monthly* 5.2 (February 1980): 47.

———. "The Language of Athenian Women." Pages 61–85 in *Lo spettacolo delle voci.* Edited by Francesco de Martino and Alan Sommerstein. Bari: Levante, 1995.

Spanneut, M. *Le Stoïcisme et les Pères de l'Église, de Clément de Rome à Clément d'Alexandrie.* Rev. ed. Paris: Éditions du Seuil, 1969.

Standhartinger, Angela. *Studien zur Entstehungsgeschichte und Intention des Kolosserbriefs.* Novum Testamentum Supplements 94. Leiden: Brill, 1999.

———. "Colossians and the Pauline School." *New Testament Studies* 50 (2004): 572–93.

Stelzenberger, J. *Die Beziehungen der frühchristlichen Sittenlehre zur Ethik der Stoa.* Munich: Max Hueber, 1933.

Suggs, M. Jack. "The Christian Two Ways Tradition: Its Antiquity, Form and Function." Pages 60–74 in *Studies in New Testament and Early Christian Literature: Essays in Honor of Allen P. Wikgren.* Edited by David Edward Aune. NovTSup 33. Leiden: Brill, 1972.

Svartvik, Jesper. *Mark and Mission: Mk 7:1–23 in its Narrative and Historical Contexts.* Coniectanea Biblica New Testament Series 32. Stockholm: Almqvist & Wiksell International, 2000.

Sweeney, James P. "Guidelines on Christian Witness in Colossians 4:5–6." *Bibliotheca Sacra* 159 (2002): 449–61.

Tal, A. "Euphemisms in the Samaritan Targum of the Pentateuch." *Aramaic Studies* 1 (2003) 109–30.

Taylor, C. *The Teaching of the Twelve Apostles with Illustrations from the Talmud.* Cambridge: Deighton, Bell and Co., 1886.

Thiselton, Anthony C. *The First Epistle to the Corinthians: A Commentary on the Greek Text.* New International Greek Testament Commentary. Grand Rapids: Eerdmans, 2000

Thomson, Donald F. "The Joking Relationship and Organized Obscenity in North Queensland." *American Anthropologist* 37 (1935): 460–90.

Timroth, Wilhelm von. *Russian and Soviet Sociolinguistics and Taboo Varieties of the Russian Language (Argot, Jargon, Slang and "Mat").* Translated by Nortrud Gupta. Slavistische Beiträge 205. Munich: Otto Sagner, 1986.

Todd, S. C. *The Shape of Athenian Law.* Oxford: Clarendon Press, 1993.

Torrey, C. C. *The Four Gospels: A New Translation.* New York, Harper, 1933.

Trachtenberg, Joshua. *Jewish Magic and Superstition: A Study in Folk Religion.* Repr. Cleveland: Meridian Books, 1961.

Trask, R. L. *A Student's Dictionary of Language and Linguistics.* London: Arnold, 1997.

Tsantsanoglou, K. "The Memoirs of a Lady from Samos." *Zeitschrift für Papyrologie und Epigraphik* 12 (1973): 183–95.

Turner, Victor. *The Ritual Process: Structure and Anti-Structure.* Ithaca: Cornell University Press, 1969.

Ullendorff, Edward. "The Bawdy Bible." *Bulletin of the School of Oriental and African Studies* 42 (1979): 425–56.

Urrutia, Benjamin. "Rab-Shakeh's Verbal Aggression and Rabbinical Euphemism." *Maledicta* 5 (1981): 103–104.

Usener, Herman. "Italische Volksiustiz." *Rheinisches Museum für Philologie* 56 (1901): 1–28.

Van der Horst, P. W. "Is Wittiness Unchristian? A Note on εὐτραπελία in Eph. v 4." Pages 163–77 in vol. 2 of *Miscellanea Neotestamentica.* Edited by T. Baarda, A. F. J. Klijn, and W. C. van Unnik. NovTSup 48. Leiden: Brill, 1978.

Van de Sandt, Huub and David Flusser. *The Didache: Its Jewish Sources and Its Place in Early Judaism and Christianity.* Compendia Rerum Iudaicarum ad Novum Testamentum 3.5. Minneapolis: Fortress, 2002.

Versnel, H. S. *Inconsistencies in Greek and Roman Religion.* Vol. 2, *Transition and Reversal in Myth and Ritual.* Leiden: Brill, 1993.

Veyne, Paul. "La folklore à Rome et les droits de la conscience publique sur la conduite individuelle." *Latomus* 42 (1983): 3–30.

———. "The Roman Empire." Pages 6–233 in *A History of Private Life.* Volume 1. *From Pagan Rome to Byzantium.* Edited by Paul Veyne. Translated by Arthur Goldhammer. Cambridge: Harvard University Press, 1987.

Vincent, Marvin R. *The Epistles to the Philippians and to Philemon.* International Critical Commentary. New York: Charles Scribner's Sons, 1897.

Vögtle, Anton. *Die Tugend- und Lasterkataloge im Neuen Testament.* Münster: Aschendorff, 1936.

Völker, Walther. *Der Wahre Gnostiker Nach Clemens Alexandrinus.* Berlin: Hinrichs, 1952.

Weber, Thomas H. "Sirach." Pages 541–55 in *The Jerome Bible Commentary.* Englewood Cliffs, New Jersey: Prentice-Hall, 1968.

Weiss, Johannes. *Der Erste Korintherbrief.* Kritisch-exegetischer Kommentar über das Neue Testament (Meyer-Kommentar) 5; Göttingen: Vandenhoeck & Ruprecht, 1910.

Wendland, Paul. "Quaestiones Mussoniae." Ph.D. diss., Berlin, 1886.

Wendt, Wilhelm. "Ciceros Brief an Paetus IX 22." Ph.D. diss., Gießen, 1929.

West, M. L. *Studies in Greek Elegy and Iambus.* Untersuchungen zur antiken Literatur und Geschichte 14. Berlin: Watler de Gruyter, 1974.

Westcott, Brooke Foss. *Saint Paul's Epistle to the Ephesians.* London: Macmillan, 1906.

Whybray, R. N. *The Book of Proverbs: A Survey of Modern Study.* History of Biblical Interpreation Series; Leiden: Brill, 1995.

Wibbing, Siegfried. *Die Tugend- und Lasterkataloge im Neuen Testament.* Beihefte zur Zeitschrift für die neutestamentliche Wissenschaft 25. Berlin: Alfred Töpelmann, 1959.

Wikenhauser, Alfred. "Zum Wörterbuch des Neuen Testamentes." *Biblische Zeitschrift* 8 (1910): 271.

Wilkinson, L. P. *Classical Attitudes to Modern Issues.* London: William Kimber, 1978.

Willi, Andreas. "The Language of Greek Comedy: Introduction and Bibliographical Sketch." Pages 1–32 in *The Language of Greek Comedy.* Edited by Andreas Willi. Oxford: Oxford University Press, 2002.

Wilson, R. McL. *Colossians and Philemon.* International Critical Commentary. London: T. & T. Clark International, 2005.

Wines, Michael. "He Celebrates That Word, but He'd Stamp It Out." *New York Times,* 3 June 2002.

———. "Why Putin Boils Over: Chechnya Is His Personal War." *New York Times,* 12 November 2002.

Winkler, J. J. *The Constraints of Desire: The Anthropology of Sex and Gender in Ancient Greece.* New York: Routledge, 1990.

Wischmeyer, Oda. *Die Kultur des Buches Jesus Sirach.* Beihefte zur Zeitschrift für die neutestamentliche Wissenschaft 77. Berlin: de Gruyter, 1995.

Wiseman, T. P. "Satyrs in Rome? The Background to Horace's Ars Poetica." *Journal of Roman Studies* 78 (1988): 1–13.

Wohleb, Leo. *Die lateinische Übersetzung der Didache kritisch und sprachlich untersucht.* Paderborn: Schöningh, 1913.

Wood, Simon P. *Christ the Educator.* New York: Fathers of the Church, 1954.

Wright, Benjamin G. *No Small Difference: Sirach's Relationship to Its Hebrew Parent Text.* Society of Biblical Literature Septuagint and Cognate Studies Series 26. Atlanta: Scholars Press, 1989.

Zahn, Theodor. *Der Brief des Paulus an die Galater.* KNT 9. Leipzig: Deichert, 1905.

———. *Das Evangelium des Matthäus.* 4th ed. KNT 1. Leipzig: Deichert, 1922.

Zeitlin, Froma I. "Cultic Models of the Female: Rites of Dionysus and Demeter." *Arethusa* 15 (1982): 129–57.

Zeller, E. *Stoics, Epicureans, and Sceptics.* Translated by Oswald J. Reichel. Repr. New York: Russell & Russell, 1962.

Zimmerli, Walther. *Ezekiel.* Translated by Ronald E. Clements. 2 vols. Hermeneia. Philadelphia: Fortress, 1979.

Ziolkowski, Jan M., ed. "The Obscenities of Old Women: Vetularity and Vernacularity." Pages 73–89 in *Obscenity: Social Control and Artistic Creation in the European Middle Ages.* Edited by Jan M. Ziolkowski. Leiden: Brill, 1998.

INDEX OF PASSAGES CITED

B. Old Testament Pseudepigrapha

C. Dead Sea Scrolls

D. Rabbinic Material

E. Other Jewish Literature

F. New Testament

G. Early Christian Literature

H. GREEK AND LATIN AUTHORS